LIVERPOOL SECTARIANISM

Liverpool Sectarianism

The Rise and Demise

Keith Daniel Roberts

Liverpool University Press

First published 2017 by
Liverpool University Press
4 Cambridge Street
Liverpool
L69 7ZU

British Library Cataloguing-in-Publication data
A British Library CIP record is available

ISBN 978-1-78694-010-0 cased
ISBN 978-1-78138-317-9 limp

Typeset by Carnegie Book Production, Lancaster
Printed and bound by CPI Group (UK) Ltd, Croydon CR0 4YY

To Nan, for all you do and for everything you are:
the heart of our family, the matriarch, the don!

Contents

Figures and Table

Figures

Table

Acknowledgements

First and foremost, my thanks must go to Professor Jonathan Tonge, who has supervised both my undergraduate dissertation and my postgraduate doctoral thesis. His help and advice have been invaluable, and I am deeply indebted for both his professionalism and his munificence over the years. His assistance in helping me to attain funding, via the John Lennon Memorial Scholarship, is also much appreciated. My thanks are also extended to the John Lennon Memorial Trust for selecting me for receipt of the award.

To all those who have freely given their time in aid of this study, which has profited greatly from your input, I offer my gratitude: Bishop Tom Williams, Reverend John Williams MBE, Professor Philip Waller, Professor John Belchem, Right Honourable Andy Burnham MP, Joe Benton (MP, 1990–2015), Steve Rotheram MP, Dr John Pugh MP, Nadine Dorries MP, Peter Kilfoyle (MP, 1991–2010), Councillor Jimmy Mahon, Councillor Mike Murphy, Councillor Anna Rothery, Roy Hughes (Councillor, 1968–74), Howard Kendall (thanks also to James Allen, who put me in contact with Howard), Tony Birtill, Greg Quiery, Susanne Loughlin, Doris Bennett, Cliff Whittingham, Alf Mullins, Mike O'Brian, Brenda O'Brian, Helen Owen, Ian Henderson, Ian Woods, Jean Hill, Maria O'Reilly, Billy Smylie, Michelle Chambers, and Paul Stevenson Wade.

In addition, the following organisations, along with their noted representatives, have provided valued contributions: *The Loyal Orange Institution of England* – specifically, Billy Owens HDGM, Ron Bather HDGM, Dave Hughes, Keith Allcock, Tom Buckley, Reginald Chadwick, Lynn Hughes, Billy Tritton, and Yvonne Fearnehough [née Fogg]; *Cairde na hÉireann Liverpool* – Neil Dullin and Séafra Ó Cearbhail; *The Everton Heritage Society* – Paul Wharton and George Orr (thanks must also go to Reverend Canon Dr Ellen Loudon, who put me in touch with the aforementioned); Steve Higginson of the *James Larkin Society*; Billy Hayes, General Secretary of the *Communication Workers Union* (thanks also to Dorothy Lovett, for being so friendly and helpful when attaining contact with Billy); and finally Win Lawlor of *Irish Community Care Merseyside*.

Each of the aforementioned has helped construct a picture of events relating to the decline of sectarianism. The wealth of response, interpretation, and suggestion has been crucial to the study. Your comments have helped to challenge and/or reaffirm a variety of suggested hypotheses. Every rejoinder has provided much food for thought, and the study is enriched throughout thanks to your contributions.

Thanks also to the staff at Sydney Jones Library, Liverpool Central Library, Southport Library, and Crosby Library for their assistance. In particular, Jo Ashley, the University of Liverpool liaison for politics, went out of her way to help the author with a variety of enquiries, as have Margaret Andrews and Donna Martyn. My gratitude is extended to Pauline Furse, of the HMS Raleigh Learning Centre, for all of her help and advice in the latter period of this study.

Progress has also undoubtedly been aided by my PhD colleagues, who have enriched my experience as a postgraduate student. Dr Ben Williams and Dr Matt Atkinson, in particular, have kept me laughing despite the stress of a doctorate. Dr Sophie Whiting, Dr Samad Fatmi, Councillor James Roberts, and Dr Tony Williams have also kept a smile firmly etched on my face, as has Dr Kevin Hickson, with many of his dry, yet witty, interventions. I am grateful to all of my friends, whose amity has kept me sane during this process. Thanks are particularly owed to Shaun Smyth, who has on more than one occasion persuaded me that perseverance is the path to prosperity. Likewise, Natalie Murray has kept me on track through her ability to add colour no matter how grey the canvas.

My family: I quite simply could not have done this without you. Nobody could wish for better relatives; my parents, grandparents, siblings, aunties, uncles, cousins, and godchildren have provided stimulus throughout this work and my entire life. I will never be able to thank you enough for all you have done and for all you have given, deeds for which I will continually endeavour to recompense. You are everything. I love you all, with all my heart.

Finally, my thanks must go to the late Professor Frank Neal, whose work not only provided a platform for this study and others, but whose conference helped shed light on many of the subtle idiosyncrasies of nineteenth-century and early twentieth-century Liverpool. His contribution to the topic was paramount and his advice, friendship, generosity, passion, and determination are sorely missed.

Preface

The primary objective of this book is to identify why sectarianism has declined in Liverpool. In so doing, it is necessary to identify what sectarianism was in a Liverpool context, whilst also outlining its development. In relation to this, the part played by nineteenth-century Irish immigration, the Orange Order, and the Roman Catholic Church will be analysed. Although assessed, it is not the intention of this work to concentrate primarily on the sectarian violence that gripped the city, nor the complex relationship between sectarianism and politics in Liverpool: the latter having already been expertly covered by Waller (1981) and the former by Neal (1988). Nonetheless, in analysing the degeneration of denominational antagonism both the reduction in sectarian violence and the rapidity of its political disintegration will be considered.

For a period spanning two centuries the sectarian divide in Liverpool soured relations between its residents. Indeed, the city's political representatives were often elected on the basis of their ethno-religious pedigree. Politics continued to be influenced by religion until the mid-1970s. Weakening sectarianism, in the limited existing studies, is attributed largely to post-war slum clearance, but this book asserts that causality is much more complex. There are a range of factors that have contributed to the decline. As this book demonstrates, the downfall of sectarianism coincided with the creation of a collective identity; an identity based not on ethno-religious affiliations, but on a commonality, an acknowledgment that principles which united were more significant than factors which divided. Importantly, the success of the city's two football teams, Everton Football Club and Liverpool Football Club, gave the city a new focus based upon a healthy sporting rivalry rather than sectarian vehemence. A complex interplay of secularism and ecumenism, the economic misfortunes of Liverpool and their political impact in terms of class politics, the growth of a collective city identity and the omnipotence of (non-religiously derived) football affiliations combined to diminish Liverpool's once acute sectarian fault-line. This book examines how and why.

Religion has taken second place. It used to be the focus of everybody. Both sides would focus on religion and that was it. All that matters today is football, sex, and music.[1]

[1] Doris Bennett, 5 March 2013.

Introduction

In school I knew absolutely nothing about Liverpool's sectarian history. Yet, curiously, I knew I didn't like 'The Lodge', and I didn't know why. I remember them marching past our primary school, Lander Road, which was just off Linacre Road, Bootle, where the Orange Order still march today. The banging of the drums and bright colours attracted my mates, but the colour orange didn't attract me. My colour was blue. My earliest memory is looking up at the floodlights at Goodison Park and then looking down at the bright green pitch. It was a night game. The next thing the stadium erupted as Z Cars played and the Everton players, who would become my heroes, marched out. I have always been an Evertonian. It was chosen by my dad, with the blessing of my mum. What I am not is a Catholic. So why did I not like 'The Lodge'?

My mum's a Catholic and so is my nan and much of the family on her side. My dad was Church of England and apparently so was I and so were my siblings. This fact I was only really aware of because St Elizabeth's was the Catholic primary school, over the road from ours. We used to go the Linacre Mission, round the corner, which was Methodist. We all sang hymns in assembly and annually took part in or attended religious functions such as the Nativity. Sometimes the local reverend would come round to the school as well, but all of this was incidental to me. 'Lizzies' was not our rival, despite its close proximity, it was just another school. Somewhere down the line though, somebody must have told me that I was 'not Orange' or that 'the Orange didn't like Catholics'. I also remember being told, in school, about the *Protestant Party* that had existed in Liverpool, and that Liverpool had the highest proportion of Catholics in England.

It was not until I was in high school, when I was talking about football with my dad, that my interest began to grow. He explained to me about Scotland and the connection between Celtic Football Club and Rangers Football Club and religion. He also told me that, historically, Everton Football

Club was associated with Catholicism and Liverpool Football Club with Protestantism. This made little sense to me. Most of the Catholic members of my family were Liverpool fans. The more I learned about Everton and Liverpool, the more this connection seemed invalid. Nevertheless, a seed had been planted. When I got to college I started studying politics and took a particular interest in Ireland. By the time I got to university, I was hooked. They say, 'philosophy is best in pubs' and one fateful afternoon, during a slightly inebriated conversation with one of my professors, I was told that Liverpool was once considered the 'Belfast of England'. I wanted to know more. A few months later I attended a function at the Orange Provincial Club on Everton Brow. As half my family were Catholic, I initially had trepidation about entering. As it was, the Orange Institution would come to offer a lot of support when I was undertaking both my undergraduate dissertation and my postgraduate PhD thesis on sectarianism in Liverpool. This book is a product of that research.

A Shared Lineage of Green and Orange

The people of Liverpool and Ireland have a fair bit in common, as do Glaswegians. This is largely down to a colossal scale of Irish emigration in the mid-nineteenth century, of which Liverpool and Glasgow were primary recipients (Liverpool receiving a greater proportion than their Caledonian counterparts). In 1871, 15.56 per cent of Liverpool's total population had been born in Ireland; the highest proportion in the country. Its nearest mainland contender was Glasgow with 14.32 per cent. In contrast, London's Irish-born population was just 2.8 per cent of its total, while Manchester's (the second highest in England) was 8.59 per cent.[1] As such, it is understandable why Liverpool and Glasgow are sometimes depicted as somewhat Irish cities.

Irish heritage was not the only bi-product of Hibernian emigration. Most of the emigrants were Catholics in a Protestant society. As Ingram argues, 'anti-Catholicism was an integral part of British Protestant culture ... with its roots set well before the nineteenth century'.[2] Added to this was the sheer scale of Irish coming in, on account of the Famine. As Davis writes, 'the impression of being "swamped" was real enough in Liverpool'.[3] Irish

---

[1]   Figures cited by Fitzpatrick, 1989: 13.

[2]   Ingram, 1987: 295.

[3]   Davis, 1991: 3–4.

immigrants were depressing wages in both cities, and, while 'powerful employers' encouraged 'Orange and Green conflict to weaken the labour force' in the West of Scotland, 'religious hatred and sectarian violence found [a] most extreme and prolonged form in Liverpool',[4] caused, as Neal would argue, by 'the Irish Famine and the [subsequent] political manipulation of prejudices, fear, economic rivalry, and xenophobia'.[5] Nonetheless, both Liverpool and Glasgow 'avoided the permanent division and [literal] open warfare that scarred the city of Belfast'.[6]

Discord in the north of Ireland is centuries old, stemming, in many ways, from the 'colonisation' or 'plantation' of the north, by English and Scottish Protestants (particularly Scottish Presbyterians), in the seventeenth century; a reaction to Irish resistance against British rule in the sixteenth century. What developed were competing identities based around nationality and religion. Bitter sectarian violence took place in the nineteenth and early twentieth centuries (as it also did in Liverpool and Glasgow) over the issue of Home Rule for Ireland. Catholics by and large were Irish Nationalists or Republicans, whilst Protestants by and large were Unionists or Loyalists (loyal to the union between Great Britain and Ireland). These rival identities encompassed much of everyday life in the province, particularly in the capital city of Belfast. The quarrel extends to the title of the second largest city in Northern Ireland, which is referred to as Londonderry by Unionists, but known as Derry 'in Republican circles, to erase the hated imperial connection'.[7]

In 1921, following the Government of Ireland Act and the Anglo-Irish Treaty, Ireland was partitioned, as was the historic nine-county province of Ulster. Northern Ireland, a six-county state, was formed to ensure a Protestant/Unionist majority; a state which, for many, is synonymous with the word 'sectarian', as 'for over 50 years between 1921 and 1972, Northern Ireland existed in a sphere of self-orientated self-government',[8] largely sustaining and doing little to tackle 'a polarised population ... divided along ethno-religious lines ... by rival identities and loyalties'.[9] It is widely acknowledged that Roman Catholics were discriminated against

[4] Ibid., 4, 149.
[5] Neal, 1988: 239.
[6] Davis, 1991: 148.
[7] Gilmour, 1999: 11.
[8] Williams, 2010: 6.
[9] Ibid., 6–7.

in the semi-autonomous Northern Ireland. 'Direct Rule' from Britain was established in March 1972, dissolving Northern Ireland's traditionally Protestant-dominated (and sectarian-orientated) self-government. Stormont (the Northern Irish parliament) would not be officially reinstated until after the Good Friday Agreement, in 1998. This landmark multi-party pact is considered by many to have ended decades of sectarian civil war in Northern Ireland, often referred to as 'The Troubles'.

In 1969, in response to a series of bloody riots attendant to sectarian clashes at Irish Catholic civil rights rallies in the late 1960s, British military forces were brought in to restore order in Northern Ireland. In 1970, the Provisional IRA began operating a 'guerrilla war' in hope of attaining a 'united Ireland'. This coincided with the [re]establishment of the UVF, as well a number of other Loyalist and Republican groups. After 'Bloody Sunday', when British paratroopers shot and killed fourteen unarmed civilians, sectarian paramilitary activity grew out of control. The Provisional IRA launched a bombing campaign at home and in Britain, as Loyalist paramilitaries engaged in a 'dirty war', allegedly killing Republican targets as directed by members of the British military. Resultantly, 'over a period of thirty years, over 3,600 people were killed and thousands more injured'[10] during 'The Troubles' in Northern Ireland.

In July 1997, following the resumption of an IRA ceasefire, full-scale peace negotiations began in Belfast, comprising representatives from Ireland, Britain, the USA, and the majority of parties from Northern Ireland, including Sinn Féin (linked to the IRA). Although the Democratic Unionist Party (DUP) would not take part, due to Sinn Féin's involvement, a deal was agreed in April 1998, which was also mandated by people of Northern Ireland. Although smaller 'dissident' groups (most notably the Real IRA) maintained their armed campaigns, and while difficulties involving the implementation of the deal caused major stalls, due to the eventual enactment of certain compromises (such as the supervised disarmament of the Provisional IRA), the power-sharing agreement at Stormont became a reality in May 2007, as one-time enemies, Ian Paisley (leader of the Democratic Unionists) and Martin McGuinness (of Sinn Féin), were sworn in as leader and deputy leader of the Northern Ireland executive government.

Since the Good Friday agreement, relative peace has gradually arrived in Northern Ireland, but sectarianism remains and attempts to regulate

[10] BBC, 'Violence in the Troubles' (2013): www.bbc.co.uk/history/topics/troubles_violence.

sectarian controversies over the routes of Orange Order parades remain in place. Liverpool has a long history of such regulation of Orange versus Green. The regulation of marches in the Liverpool Corporation Act, 1912 was an important effort to reduce inter-communal antagonism, and the opportunities for riotous behaviour to occur, followed a public inquiry into sectarian riots in 1909. The inquiry took into account a broad spectrum of views. The result was legislation which was more preventative than punitive. As late as 1979, the Act was praised for its effectiveness by Conservative MP for Wirral, David Hunt:

> Particular processions are subject to closer control than others, including those held for the purpose of demonstrating against any form of religious faith or creed. Those byelaws are still in force and over the years they have established a practice and custom which the promoters of this Bill are anxious should continue ... The byelaws are effective to protect the marchers, as well as to secure the orderly behaviour of all concerned. There is no record of any prosecutions ever having been made under these byelaws ... this is a measure of their success.[11]

More recently, the Scottish Government has introduced measures to curb sectarian chants at football matches and on social media. The Offensive Behaviour at Football and Threatening Communications (Scotland) Act faced accusations of being 'railroaded' through, without proper consultation with those it would most affect.[12] Yet sectarianism is also a state of mind, not easily outlawed.

It is testament to its decline in Liverpool that sectarianism in Northern Ireland and Scotland has received much more contemporary analysis. At least implicitly, the experience and history of Liverpool and sectarianism is related to the histories of other British/Irish cities, notably Glasgow and Belfast. While each case is distinct, and as Smyth and Moore suggest, 'Sectarianism in Derry Londonderry ... is differentiated from sectarianism in Liverpool – or indeed Belfast – by the specificity of local conditions',[13] there are similarities, even if at the most basic level.

---

[11] County of Merseyside Bill, HC Deb. 13 March 1979, vol. 964 cols 345–408: http://hansard.millbanksystems.com/commons/1979/mar/13/county-of-merseyside-bill#S5CV0964P0_19790313_HOC_262.
[12] BBC, 'Labour Plan to Scrap Controversial Anti-Sectarian Law' (2014): www.bbc.co.uk/news/uk-scotland-scotland-politics-26664770.
[13] Smyth and Moore, 1996: 2: http://cain.ulst.ac.uk/issues/segregat/temple/confer1.htm.

Sectarianism in Belfast, Liverpool, and Glasgow has been based upon intra-Christian division, which in each case has been accompanied by a range of related other factors exacerbating inter-communal tensions. These include rival national identities (Irish versus British), political (Loyalist versus Republican), xenophobic (immigrant versus native), and even footballing (Celtic versus Rangers) rivalries. Each factor varies considerably depending upon local determinants. For example, the interchangeability of football and sectarianism is an element which is much more applicable in Scotland (specifically Glasgow) than (as will be argued) Liverpool, while it has been a factor in Northern Ireland, as Sugden and Bairner's *Sport, Sectarianism and Society in a Divided Ireland*[14] outlines. Moreover, the terms 'immigrant' and 'native' refer to different sects depending on locality. Historically, in relation to Liverpool sectarianism, most immigrants were Catholic and the 'natives' were Protestant; this situation is reversed in the perceptions of some Irish nationalists in the north of Ireland.

For reasons of space and focus, this book must necessarily concentrate on Liverpool's particularities. Nonetheless, it is important to acknowledge, at least in passing, the obvious parallels that can be drawn between Liverpool, Glasgow, Belfast, and, further afield and more historically, Toronto with the Orange Order and the Catholic Church (and its system of segregated education) at the heart of much of the controversy. Fraser's *The Irish Parading Tradition* comprises a series of articles on both 'Orange' and 'Green' marches in Northern Ireland and Scotland.[15] Notably, no chapter is devoted to Liverpool and there is very little comment on parades taking place in the city, despite its 'Orange' and 'Green' heritage. There have of course been exemplary studies of the Orange Order and sectarianism in England, notably those offered nationally by MacRaild[16] and in terms of a local case study (of Tyneside) by MacRaild and MacPherson,[17] while Sibbett's *Orangeism in Ireland and throughout the Empire* provided an official history of the organisation.[18]

Sectarianism in Ireland has more extensive documentation, reflecting its volume. Alan Ford, in *The Origins of Sectarianism in Early Modern Ireland*, comments that 'stories of sectarian cruelty provide a constant backdrop to

---

[14] Sugden and Bairner, 1993.
[15] Fraser, 2000.
[16] MacRaild, 2005.
[17] MacRaild and MacPherson, 2006: 137–60.
[18] Sibbett, 1915.

Irish history',[19] suggesting that sectarianism in Northern Ireland is 'not a product of recent events, such as partition, or 'The Troubles', rather it dates back to the early modern period, or even beyond to the Anglo-Norman invasion'.[20] Ford's account is the tip of the iceberg. A glut of other works on Irish and Northern Irish sectarianism is evident. Whilst publications on Northern Ireland sectarianism often suffer from a scholarly lack of precision in its definition, there is a plethora of work dealing with organisations labelled by critics as 'sectarian'.

One notable comparative work is Gareth Jenkins' 'Nationalism and Sectarian Violence in Liverpool and Belfast, 1880s–1920s', which argues that, 'in Liverpool, the dominant political culture was fundamentally parochial in character, feeding off local religious and ethnic rivalries. In Belfast, Ulster Unionism engaged in a national political debate critical to its very survival'.[21] Yet such comparative accounts are very rare and even some of the organisations associated with sectarianism, notably the Catholic Church and the Orange Order, were transnational. Jenkins also highlights the decline of sectarianism after 1920 in Liverpool, pointing to political dynamics, the effect of the war, and post-war slum clearance:[22] all factors analysed in this book. In contrast to Jenkins' research, the literature directly comparing sectarianism in Liverpool and Glasgow is limited to two articles by Joan Smith: 'Labour Tradition in Glasgow and Liverpool'[23] and 'Class, Skill and Sectarianism in Glasgow and Liverpool',[24] both of which are rare and important contributions to the topic, if relatively limited in scope. In addition, Sean Damer's review article, 'A Tale of Two Cities: Sectarianism in Glasgow and Liverpool'[25] draws on Frank Neal's excellent *Sectarian Violence* – a key point of historical reference for this book – and Tom Gallagher's *Glasgow: The Uneasy Peace*,[26] both authoritative works in their own field. Sectarianism of the Orange versus Green variety was common in Canada until petering out by the 1960s. Readers with a particular interest in the Orange Order and its role there, particularly in Toronto and

---

[19] Ford, 2012: 2.
[20] Ibid., 10.
[21] Jenkins, 2000: 177.
[22] Ibid., 172.
[23] Smith, 1984: 32–56.
[24] Smith, 1986: 158–215.
[25] Damer, 1989: 515–18.
[26] Gallagher, 1987.

across Ontario, are directed, as a starting point, to Houston and Smyth's magisterial work.[27]

It is important to note that the existence and extent of sectarianism in Scotland are contested, as is evident by Michael Rosie's work *The Sectarian Myth in Scotland*,[28] in which he argues that, 'Scotland is not a "sectarian" society [as] Scotland is an increasingly secular country where religion does not provide a significant marker of political and social cleavage'.[29] Such a proposition may rest upon the assumption that sectarianism and religion are synonymous: an assumption challenged by this study. This debate is particularly pertinent when it is considered that the Scottish Government has both acknowledged the existence of 'Scottish sectarianism' and even legislated against it[30] (perhaps without adequately defining exactly what it is they are legislating against, although an attempt has been made).[31] Additionally, *Sectarianism in Scotland*, by Steve Bruce, et al., which generally adopts a sceptical position on the matter, contends that, 'Scots are divided about the extent of sectarianism and that anecdotes can readily be found to support any position', while acknowledging that 'sectarianism is important enough to be studied seriously'.[32] Nonetheless, the Scottish Government and many others do believe sectarianism to exist in Scotland, and studies have been produced which suggest that 'football is the biggest factor fuelling sectarianism in Scotland',[33] while others believe that 'sectarianism runs far beyond our touchlines and terraces'.[34]

---

[27] Houston and Smyth, 1981.

[28] Rosie, 2004.

[29] Ibid., 144.

[30] In March 2012, The Offensive Behaviour at Football and Threatening Communications (Scotland) Act became law.

[31] Advisory Group on Tackling Sectarianism in Scotland, 'Independent Advice to Scottish Ministers and Report on Activity 9 August 2012–15 November 2013'. Edinburgh: The Scottish Government. (Their definition is highlighted in this study.)

[32] Bruce, Glendinning, Paterson, and Rosie, 2004: 2.

[33] *Herald Scotland*, 'Official Studies: It's Football which Fuels Scotland's Sectarianism, Not Parades' (2015). Available at: www.heraldscotland.com/news/home-news/football-biggest-contributor-to-scotlands-sectarianism-with-parade-fears-not-borne-ou.118874478?utm_source=headlines&utm_medium=email&utm_campaign=email%2Balert, citing the 'Scottish Social Attitude Survey, 2014': '88 per cent of respondents believed sectarianism to be a problem' with '55 per cent citing football as the main issue'.

[34] BBC, 'Labour Plan to Scrap Controversial Anti-Sectarian Law' (2014): www.bbc.co.uk/news/uk-scotland-scotland-politics-26664770.

Contributors to Devine's *Scotland's Shame?*[35] reflect the 'lack of consensus'[36] on the matter.

The lack of precision over what constitutes sectarianism and the near absence of detailed comparative studies, makes the task of analysing Liverpool's sectarianism that much harder. Nonetheless, difficulty of issue is not an excuse to avoid problem-tackling. As such, this work will attempt to define sectarianism and assess its outworking and eventual decline in a Liverpool context. In so doing, the book will remain cognisant that much of Liverpool's sectarianism was of a similar variety to that of Belfast and Glasgow, whilst also possessing distinctive features (lack of serious ethno-national armed clashes and absence of sporting outlet being two). That sectarianism remained in Belfast and Glasgow despite, for example, large programmes of slum clearance, might add to the desire to inquire further into the salience of such a factor in the removal of Liverpool's problems. Nonetheless, it is important to avoid glib or superficial conclusions prior to looking in detail at the Liverpool case, in the manner in which this book now proceeds.

Defining Sectarianism

Satisfactorily theorising or defining sectarianism is a task which has, thus far, not been adequately undertaken by political scientists or historians. It should be acknowledged that the task of measuring sectarianism (a multidimensional and a somewhat abstruse concept) is not easy. Similarly, the make-up of a 'sectarian' (that is, the characteristics which define an individual as such) is under-researched and ill-defined. This lack of theorisation of sectarianism has been acknowledged by McVeigh and by Gilligan, who note the 'neglect of the subject by academics'.[37] Likewise, Smyth and Moore have stated that 'existing literature ... yields little in the way of definitions of sectarianism, or explorations of its nature'.[38]

The most basic definitions of sectarianism often relate to the preference of, or valuing of, one particular section of the community over another.

---

[35] Devine, 2000.

[36] Ibid., 261.

[37] McVeigh, 1990: 119; C. Gilligan, 'Why has Sectarianism Been Undertheorised?', Political Studies Association of Ireland annual conference, Galway, 17–19 October 2014.

[38] Smyth and Moore, 1996: 2.

For instance, the *Oxford English Dictionary* defines the term 'sectarianism' as 'adherence or excessive attachment to a particular sect or party, esp. in religion; hence often, adherence or excessive attachment to, or undue favouring of, a particular "denomination"'.[39] Another description delineates 'sectarian' as an adjective 'denoting or concerning a sect or sects: i.e. the city's traditional sectarian divide', or '(of an action) carried out on the grounds of membership of a sect, denomination, or other group: i.e. sectarian killings'.[40] The *Cambridge Dictionary* supports this classification, yet it also describes a 'sectarian' in terms of the individual: '(a person) strongly supporting a particular religious group, especially in such a way as not to be willing to accept other beliefs'.[41] In addition, the *Merriam-Webster Dictionary* describes 'sectarian' as an adjective 'relating to religious or political sects and the differences between them'.[42] These definitions, however, are limited. They only paint part of a much more complex picture. What is required is a more holistic explanation.

In 2014, McVeigh wrote that 'despite the ubiquity of the term [sectarianism], it is [still] poorly conceptualised'.[43] Describing sectarianism in a Northern Irish context, he asserts:

> Sectarianism must be theorised as a structure. In what little analysis of sectarianism there is, sectarianism has been atomised. Thus, sectarianism becomes something that individual Protestants and Catholics do; consequently there is no analysis of structural sectarianism. But sectarianism in the Six Counties is not simply an aggregate of the deeds of unpleasant or deviant 'sectarians' – although these are an intrinsic part of sectarianism. Sectarianism structures every aspect of life in the Northern Ireland statelet ... it is more than a set of ideologies or a category of practices or an amalgam of individual actions;

---

[39] *Oxford English Dictionary*, q.v. 'sectarianism'.

[40] *Oxford Living Dictionaries*, q.v. 'sectarian'. Available at: http://oxforddictionaries.com/definition/sectarian#m_en_gb0748570.008.

[41] *Cambridge Dictionary*, q.v. 'sectarian'. Available at: http://dictionary.cambridge.org/dictionary/british/sectarian?q=sectarianism.

[42] *Merriam-Webster Dictionary*, q.v. 'sectarian'. Available at: http://merriam-webster.com/dictionary/sectarian.

[43] R. McVeigh, 'Sectarianism in Northern Ireland: Towards a Definition in Law'. Belfast: Equality Coalition, April 2014. Available at: www.niassembly.gov.uk/globalassets/documents/ofmdfm/inquiries/building-a-united-community/written-submissions/equality-coalition.pdf.

sectarianism is the modality in which life is lived by everybody in the Six Counties.[44]

While McVeigh's analysis is centred upon Northern Ireland, highlighting how violence served to construct and reproduce the difference between, and unequal status of, Northern Irish Protestants and Catholics, aspects of his perspective can be generalised. For example, sectarianism is not, and cannot be, simply an 'amalgam of individual actions'. A 'Sectarian' cannot exist in isolation – as a 'Sectarian' is, in fact, a product of their surroundings, their upbringing, their culture, their identity, and so forth. Sectarianism, it is argued, is a prerequisite to the 'Sectarian' (as in, the individual), as well as 'sectarian' actions.

McVeigh's submission, that 'sectarianism must be theorised as a structure', is important. 'Structural sectarianism' is about much more than just physical segregation of divided communities (whether 'engineered' or 'organic'). As McVeigh describes, it incorporates many aspects, including 'sectarian discrimination in employment and housing [and] blatant sectarian political gerrymandering'.[45] As will be outlined, 'structural sectarianism' was also exhibited in Liverpool, where there were alleged restrictions placed on Catholics and Protestants in terms of occupation in 'certain firms' or 'trades' (contentions discussed in later chapters). Furthermore, while political 'gerrymandering' was not apparent in Liverpool, the city's elected represent-atives reflected sectarian dividing lines. Although Liverpool (in contrast to Northern Ireland) never became a 'Protestant State for a Protestant People',[46] it was a city in which politics 'fed off local religious and ethnic rivalries'.[47]

Again in a Northern Irish context, Jarman offers a definition of sectar-ianism as 'prejudicial and discriminatory attitudes, behaviours and practices between members of the two majority communities in and about Northern Ireland, who may be defined as Catholic or Protestant; Irish or British; Nationalist or Unionist; Republican or Loyalist; or combinations thereof'.[48]

[44] McVeigh, 1990: 121–2.
[45] Ibid., 119.
[46] Paraphrasing two comments by Sir James Craig, both made in 1934: 'All I boast is a Protestant Parliament and a Protestant State' and 'That is my whole object in carrying on a Protestant Government for a Protestant people.' Full citations available at: http://cain.ulst. ac.uk/issues/discrimination/quotes.htm.
[47] Jenkins, 2010: 177.
[48] Jarman, 2012: 10.

Crucial to this study is that definition of sectarianism as prejudicial and discriminatory attitudes: they abounded in Liverpool in terms of Protestant versus Catholic rivalry, with religious labels acting as communal markers and 'justifications' for public displays of hostility to the opposite community. Intra-religion division (Liverpool's being intra-Christian) has formed part of the limited analysis of sectarianism. Nonetheless, religious sectarianism is not the only form of sectarianism, which may be multi-layered.

Moreover, sectarianism cannot be one sided, based upon a single set of prejudices and discrimination against another group. There needs to be at least two 'sides', usually in the same locality, both (though not necessarily equally) expressing prejudice and discriminating against the other. There needs to be both a 'thesis' and 'antithesis'. This prejudice can be more politically than religiously orientated, as Smyth and Moore's elevation of 'political' aspects of division in Northern Ireland stresses, although religious separation may make community identification easier and exacerbate division.[49]

Sugden and Bairner also offer a useful working definition:

> In its most general sense, the term sectarianism is used to describe attitudes, belief systems, symbols and practices through which one group of people sets itself apart from another within an otherwise shared culture ... the term is usually employed more specifically to describe divisions which are grounded in religious differences ... sectarianism can best be understood in two overlapping ways: first as a symbolic labelling process through which community divisions are defined and maintained, and second as an ideological justification for discrimination, community conflict and political violence.[50]

Sugden and Bairner's point, that 'one group of people sets itself apart from another within an otherwise shared culture', is important, and is related to Margalit's view that 'Sectarianism is the tendency to inflate a minor disagreement over beliefs or practices into the impossibility of living together'.[51] Sectarianism is an *intra-division* within a commonality. The unison (uniting factor) may be a political 'Wing' or a shared 'God' or even a fixed local geographic, such as a city or country. The key to sectarianism is a division *within: competition between two or more sections of a whole.*

---

[49] Smyth and Moore, 1996: 1, 4.
[50] Sugden and Bairner, 1993, cited ibid., 2.
[51] Margalit, 2008: 41.

The 'demand for theorising sectarianism'[52] was also directly addressed by Liechty and Clegg, who offer their own important perspective (a 'generic', 'working' definition):

> Sectarianism is a system of attitudes, actions, beliefs, and structures (at personal, communal, and institutional levels, which always involves religion, and typically involves a negative mixing of religion and politics) which arises as a distorted expression of positive human needs especially for belonging, identity, and the free expression of difference and is expressed in destructive patterns of relating [to] hardening the boundaries between groups; overlooking others; belittling, dehumanising, or demonising others; justifying or collaborating in the domination of others; [and/or] physically or verbally intimidating or attacking others.[53]

Additionally, a useful definition of a 'Sectarian' (as in a person) is also afforded: '"sectarian" is usually a negative judgment that people make about someone else's behaviour and rarely a label that they apply to themselves, their own sectarianism always being the hardest to see'.[54] This sentiment is also expressed by Smyth and Moore: 'The label "sectarian" is an interpretation based on subjective judgement, a perception which is usually projected onto others rather than owned as a quality possessed by oneself'.[55]

Although Liechty and Clegg's interpretations are in most respects pertinent, their suggestion that sectarianism 'always involves religion' is challenged by the author's own analysis. Likewise, Gilligan makes the point that 'the conflict [in Northern Ireland] (often described as "sectarian") is not really about religion':

> Religion is merely a marker of difference. The conflict is really about something else. The question, asking if you are Catholic or Protestant, is really asking which side you are on. The majority of the literature on the conflict takes that view; that the conflict is not about religion ... the majority of scholars have dismissed the significance of religion.[56]

[52] C. Gilligan, 'Why has Sectarianism Been Undertheorised?', Paper delivered at PSAI conference, Galway, 17–19 October 2014.

[53] Liechty and Clegg, 2001: 102–3.

[54] Ibid., 102.

[55] Smyth and Moore, 1996: 9.

[56] McVeigh, 'The Undertheorisation of Sectarianism', It is noted by Gilligan, as well as the author, that some academics do believe religion to be the focal point of the conflict (see, for example, Bruce, 1989: 308).

As will be discussed in the next section of this study, the author extends these sentiments to Liverpool, where sectarianism was, for many inhabitants in both communities, more about 'belonging' – religion was one dynamic amid a host of other factors.

Nonetheless, the equating of sectarianism and religion is often automatically assumed, admittedly sometimes due to local context. For example, the Scottish website nilbymouth.org, while acknowledging that 'the term can take on different meanings depending on how it is used', defines sectarianism as 'narrow-minded beliefs that lead to prejudice, discrimination, malice and ill-will towards members, or presumed members, of a religious denomination'.[57]

Although the Liverpool brand of sectarianism was a product of intra-Christian rivalry,[58] sectarianism, in a broader sense, does not have to be centred upon ecclesiastical divisions within Christendom. While both Scottish and Northern Irish sectarianism also relate to denominational rivalries in Christianity, sectarian disputes in other parts of the world involve tensions within, or between, entirely separate religious groups. Sectarian conflicts in many Muslim countries, for example (while sometimes encompassing other sects, such as Christians or Kurds), are primarily *intra-Islamic*.

Sectarianism involves subdivisions within a group. That group does not necessarily have to be theological. For instance, political sectarianism comprises subdivisions within a specific wing of the political spectrum: in-fighting between rival factions within the far-Left or within the far-Right (an example would be groups within the umbrella of Communism or Fascism, spending more time in-fighting than focusing on their 'natural enemy'). Thus, combatant factions within a political party or regime, who devote an excessive amount of time and energy denouncing each other, rather than their common adversaries, may be described as 'sectarian'. As Avishai Margalit indicates, 'this does not mean that [such] sectarians are necessarily religious', pointing to 'secular sects of the left, such as Trotskyite sects'.[59]

---

[57] nil by mouth.org, 'What is Sectarianism? A Definition'. Available at: http://nilbymouth. org/resources/what-is-sectarianism/ (accessed January 2017).

[58] In Liverpool, sectarianism most often took the form of disputes or clashes between 'Catholic' and 'Protestant' combatants.

[59] Margalit, 2008: 39.

In asserting that, 'It is not necessary to be religious in order to be sectarian – but it helps',[60] Margalit also states,

> Every sectarian war is a civil war, but not every civil war is a sectarian war. We call a war sectarian if and only if there is a religious dimension to the warring groups. This does not mean that a sectarian war is necessarily about religion. It means, however, that the sides of the conflict identify themselves by the use of religious labels.[61]

Such sentiments highlight the fact that sectarianism is often seen as a term for religious rivalry. Correctly, Smyth and Moore state the need to 'avoid seeing sectarianism as one dimensional or as the prerogative of any one discipline'.[62] Sectarianism is almost always multi-layered.

Another dynamic, further complicating matters, is the relationship between sectarianism and racism. As the British Government acknowledges, 'there is clearly some difficulty in formulating definitions which would effectively differentiate racial offences from sectarian offences',[63] yet it has maintained a distinction between the two types.[64] There also exists both 'a literature suggesting that sectarianism is – or is much the same as – racism and another literature that says it is different from racism'.[65] McVeigh argues that 'racism is a clearer and better descriptive for sectarianism in Northern Ireland than "institutional religious intolerance" [because] "perceived religious identity" or "community background" as it is understood in Northern Ireland reflects ethnicity rather than "faith"'.[66]

In 2011, the Director of the United Nations Council for Ethnic Minorities, Patrick Yu, expressed strong reservations about the 'sectarianism is racism' argument, contending it 'would be very unwise to conflate issues of sectarianism and racism ... [it would] draw the courts and others into disputes

---

[60] Ibid.

[61] Ibid., 43. (Margalit indicates conflicts between Protestants and Catholics in Northern Ireland, between Greek Cypriots and Turkish Cypriots, and between Shiites and Sunnis in Iraq as 'paradigmatic cases' of 'sectarian wars'.)

[62] Smyth and Moore, 1996: 1.

[63] 'Race Crime and Sectarian Crime Legislation in Northern Ireland: A Consultation Paper': Belfast Northern Ireland Office, November 2002.

[64] See ibid. and Northern Ireland Office, 'Race Crime and Sectarian Crime Legislation in Northern Ireland: A Summary Paper'. Belfast: Northern Ireland Office, November 2002.

[65] McVeigh, 2014: 2–3; Jarman, 2012; McVeigh and Rolston, 2007: 1–23 associate racism and sectarianism, whereas Brewer and Higgins, 1998 disassociate the concepts.

[66] McVeigh, 2014: 28–9.

about parading, Irish language and issues that are "majority" concerns in that they affect Protestants/ unionists and Catholics/nationalists, but not minority racial and religious groups found in Northern Ireland'.[67] In 2002, the UK Government's Northern Ireland Office produced the consultation paper, 'Race Crime and Sectarian Crime Legislation in Northern Ireland', in which 'cases of racially motivated attacks, [where] victims in by far the majority of cases belong to a relatively small group within the overall populations', were differentiated from 'sectarian offences, [where] there are victims in both the main groups, neither of which is particularly small'.[68] Moreover, in 2013, a report by the Advisory Group on Tackling Sectarianism in Scotland, stated:

> Sectarianism in Scotland has at times been closely associated with anti-Irish prejudice. However, the two are not identical. The religious dimension is distinctive in sectarianism. Anti-Irishness, in a cultural sense, is clearly a form of racism and should be named as such.[69]

The advisory group, chaired by Dr Duncan Morrow, offered the following, alternative, 'working definition' to the Scottish Government:

> Sectarianism in Scotland is a complex of perceptions, attitudes, beliefs, actions and structures, at personal and communal levels, which originate in religious difference and can involve a negative mixing of religion with politics, sporting allegiance and national identifications. It arises from a distorted expression of identity and belonging. It is expressed in destructive patterns of relating which segregate, exclude, discriminate against or are violent towards a specified religious other, with significant personal and social consequences.[70]

Whilst the description is limited to a particular facet of sectarianism (similar to other demarcations referring specifically to Northern Ireland), the report offered a rare (and helpful) example of an official attempt at a definition. Importantly, the report also clarified:

> Our definition does not presuppose that those who engage in sectarian behaviour are currently religious believers or have religious motivation; only that the original 'difference' had a religious element. In some

---

[67] Ibid.
[68] 'Race Crime and Sectarian Crime Legislation in Northern Ireland'.
[69] Advisory Group on Tackling Sectarianism in Scotland, 'Independent Advice', 18.
[70] Ibid.

circumstances that element may now be lost, leaving, perhaps, only 'them' and 'us' opposition.[71]

This is a pertinent recognition. Religion, whilst often synonymised with sectarianism, is not always at its core, even in situations where it may appear to be the case. It is important to understand that politics can play a huge role in sectarian conflicts, with tensions often exploited (or even generated) by 'elites who cynically manipulate sectarianism'.[72] It is clear that a variety of factors, such as religion, racism, politics, and tribalism, all play their part in sectarian situations and clearly it is 'difficult to disentangle these distinct [yet often overlapping] elements'.[73] Nonetheless, although there may be a range of dynamics at play and similar factors may be present in some cases, seldom, if ever, do two forms of sectarianism mimic each other to the extent that a definition of X can be applied appropriately to Y.

The word 'sectarianism' can be broken down into three distinct segments: 'sect', 'arian', and 'ism'. '- arian' (in the sense it is used in forming the words 'sectarianism', 'utilitarian', 'humanitarian', and so forth) is a *suffix*, 'used [itself] to form adjectives or corresponding nouns';[74] '-ism' is also utilised as a suffix, one which 'expresses the action or conduct of a class of persons'. Other examples of its use include 'heroism', 'patriotism', 'despotism', 'blackguardism', and 'barbarism'.[75]

By far the most important segment of 'sectarianism' is 'sect', defined as 'a body of persons who unite in holding certain views differing from those of others who are accounted to be of the same religion'. However, theology is not the only use of the term. A 'sect' is also described as 'a "section" of mankind', 'a school of opinion in politics, science, or the like', '[a] body of followers or adherents', and 'a class or kind (of persons)'.[76]

Notably, each of the aforementioned descriptions deem a 'sect' to be a part of a whole: phrases like a 'particular school of', 'a cutting from', 'a body of', 'a "section"', and 'a class or kind' indicate this. Thus, a 'sect', it is argued, is simply a subdivision of the word 'section'. The most fitting definition of

---

[71] Ibid.

[72] Project on Middle East Political Science, 'The Politics of Sectarianism', *POMEPS Studies*, 4 (13 November 2013). Available at: http://pomeps.org/2013/11/14/the-politics-of-sectarianism/.

[73] McVeigh, 2014: 3.

[74] *Oxford English Dictionary*, –arian, *suffix*.

[75] Ibid., –ism, *suffix*.

[76] Ibid., *Sect, n.*

'section' is 'a part separated or divided off from the remainder; one of the portions into which a thing is cut or divided' – 'a separable portion of any collection or aggregate of persons',[77] not necessarily a religious grouping.

So is 'sectarianism' when disaggregated from religion and racism still sectarianism? The answer, if we were to define the term simply (and inadequately) as *the preference of one segment of people[s] over another*, is yes. While sectarianism, more often than not (and certainly in Liverpool's case), comprises both (or either) a racial and religious dimension, neither religion nor race need be constituent parts of a sectarian situation. Yet, this definition (in isolation) is too broad. It leaves too much room for what *can* be described as 'sectarian'. For example, it does not sufficiently separate racism from sectarianism. Thus, if hatred of the Irish (with or without religious connotations) was 'sectarian', then there would be no distinction between sectarianism and predisposition. If detestation of a people (or peoples) simply because they originate in a different land or because of the colour of their skin or (returning to the theological argument) because they have a different interpretation of 'God's Will' means 'sectarian', then 'sectarianism' is little separated from prejudice.

Furthermore, the point must be made that if an individual is (or a group of individuals are) averse to another group of individuals who are not in the same vicinity (for example, Liverpool Protestants abhorring Irish Catholics, even if there were no Irish Catholics in Liverpool), then this ought not be classed as sectarianism, as there would be no competing 'sects' *within* the city. This latter point is crucial. An apt definition of sectarianism must reflect upon its localism.

Simply stating that sectarianism is *the preference of one segment of people[s] over another* does not suffice. The definition of sectarianism adopted by this study takes the perspective that, in fact, tribalism (while not the only factor) is a more important dynamic than either religion or race in producing attitudes which can be described as 'sectarian'. The existence of a local sect of people (united by some commonality) at odds with another local sect (or sects) of people (united by a rival commonality) is a prerequisite to sectarianism. Nonetheless, it has been considered that close-knit communities can see themselves as distinct (even superior) to another (or others) and may dislike the other[s] without ever acting upon it. It is acknowledged that such dormant rivalry can and does exist (probably within most hamlets, let alone cities or countries). Thus, other dynamics are required.

---

[77] Ibid., *Section, n.*

It is suggested that sectarianism has much more to do with identity than theology, racism, or tribalism. As Murshed argues,

> Identity is salient in defining antagonism in all forms of conflict since time immemorial. It indicates what people are willing to fight for ... It specially identifies which group(s) we have an affinity with. It can be multi-dimensional, extending from family, vocation, tribe, religion to nation. One of these identities can acquire relevance in the context of violence.[78]

Crucially, identity can encompass a plethora of individual factors (much like sectarianism itself): 'Nationalism; "my country" against another. For God, king and country is an age old refrain driving individuals into participation in conflict. Similarly, tribal, other ethnic (race, language) and religious differences define antagonists ... Patriotism, or identification with group causes, constitute an important intrinsic motivation'.[79] As such, because identity encompasses religion and racism, as well a multitude of other factors, it is a crucial and amalgamating aspect of sectarianism.

Furthermore, a sectarian situation only arises when there are two or more distinct sections of the community, who not only view themselves as divided, but also perceive each other in a negative way, and, decisively, they *act* upon their prejudices. This action, which can take a number of forms (from peaceful demonstration, to discrimination, to physical violence) gives sectional division tangibility. As such, while neither religion nor race is a requisite to sectarianism, action which divides and/ or maintains division is.

As McVeigh suggests, 'no act of defining is perfect – the very complexity of a phenomenon like sectarianism means that any definition begs refutation'.[80] Nonetheless, while the issue of definition (especially when considering such complex subject matter) is often contentious, this work delineates sectarianism, in its most basic form, as *the existence, within a locality, of two or more divided and actively competing communal identities, resulting is a strong sense of dualism which unremittingly transcends commonality, and is both culturally and physically manifest.*[81]

---

[78] Murshed, 2010: 1.

[79] Ibid., 2.

[80] McVeigh, 2014: 2.

[81] This definition is designed to demark 'sectarianism' at its most basic level. It is acknowledged that sectarianism takes many forms and is both complex and multifaceted. It is suggested that a much broader study is required fully to outline common parallels,

'Sectarianism' in a Liverpool Context

'Sectarianism' in a Liverpool context is multi-faceted. The root of much 'sectarian' animosity was economic competition between 'natives' and Irish migrants. Mass Irish immigration in the mid-nineteenth century also stretched very limited health and welfare resources, further fuelling anti-immigrant resentment.

Economic issues were, nonetheless, only one aspect of the resentments held. Religious antipathy towards the Catholic Irish was very strong. Protestant Orange lodges had been marching in the port since 1819 and sectarian clashes became common. Anti-Catholicism became perhaps the most prominent strand of a trio of resentments embracing economics, national identity, and religion. Whilst sectarian issues were Irish imports, sectarianism adopted distinctive features in Liverpool.

Liverpool sectarianism was arguably more tribal than religious or individualistic, although the construction of the 'tribe' is of course a sum of parts. Rather than individuals expressing a deep-seated abhorrence for the theology of their 'opposites', sectarianism in Liverpool developed more as a consequence of xenophobia and prejudice. Moreover, it is conceivable that a dogmatic identification with one's own community could more aptly denote the Liverpool 'sectarian', rather than an overarching repugnance for Protestant or Catholic neighbours. This is certainly not to say that the principles of religious faith did not have a significant role in Liverpool sectarianism, whipped up by fervent preachers and segregated, faith-based schooling. However, as in Scotland and Northern Ireland, faith is not always a 'live' issue for combatants. That is to say that 'Sectarians' 'may be "culturally" Catholic or Protestant but doctrinal difference may be either very weak or completely absent'.[82] As such, what often remains is the perception of 'them' and 'us' as opposites. Deep consideration of Protestant and Catholic theology was not necessary to belong to your respective sect.

Liverpool sectarianism meant different things at different periods of time for different people. In the mid-nineteenth century, it was arguably more racist in nature, by the early twentieth century there was genuinely

drawing upon a multitude of conflicts, to offer considered and appropriate 'qualifications' as to what ought and what ought not be described as 'sectarian' or as 'sectarianism'. It is hoped that the author's definition contributes to such research, which, regrettably, this book does not have sufficient enough space to engage with fully.

[82] Advisory Group on Tackling Sectarianism in Scotland, 'Independent Advice', 18.

more theological aversion, and by later in the twentieth century it was more about tribalism. At all times it was about identity. For the more religious, tension was centred upon theological issues; for local politicians, it was more political; for many working-class males, in particular, it was about competition for jobs, whilst for most it was about belonging, identity often a unifying factor. There were two core competitive identities: Irish Catholics and Lancastrian Protestants. In the nineteenth century, the local media were organs for anti-Irish rhetoric, giving racial prejudice an initial sense of 'legitimacy'. Anti-Irish 'media prejudice' faded greatly in the twentieth century, helping diminish stereotypical assertions surrounding the Liverpool Irish.

Liverpool sectarianism did not die off entirely, but became ritualistic and of little consequence: a largely historical footnote. Figure 1.1 maps the many aspects of Liverpool sectarianism: an illustration of some of the key components of Liverpool sectarianism. Liverpool sectarianism encompassed a wide range of elements: a complex, multi-dimensional phenomenon. Its components varied over time, but were overlain by a strong and particular sense of identity. Division between competing identities, comprising a range of different factors, was the key to Liverpool (and, as was previously argued, to all) sectarianism.

Orangeism was a key aspect of Liverpool sectarianism. It formed an important feature of 'Protestant' identity. In fact, Orangeism, for many, was the key component of their identity. It was also an aspect of Orangeism (the parading tradition) which was a protagonist of Liverpool sectarianism. In the early nineteenth century, Orange lodge parading in Liverpool prompted anger from the immigrant Irish, provoking street conflict. Yet, Orangeism would come to flourish in the port: culturally, physically, and politically. It was a key part of identity for many Protestants and it was the key contingent of the rival identity for many Catholics. The tradition of the twelfth of July celebrations became an important aspect of the longevity of Liverpool sectarianism.

'Protestants' and 'Catholics' became defining labels for the opposing sects, with justification. Even if only nominally religious, most combatants belonged to one denomination or the other. Many, often influenced by clergymen, had genuine aversion to their religious 'opposite'. Protestantism was the key contingent of Orangeism, with Catholicism the fundamental 'enemy'. A key uniting factor of Irish immigrants was their faith and the Catholic Church did much to help their 'flock'. Parochialism stemmed from this, as did structural segregation: both dynamics of sectarianism.

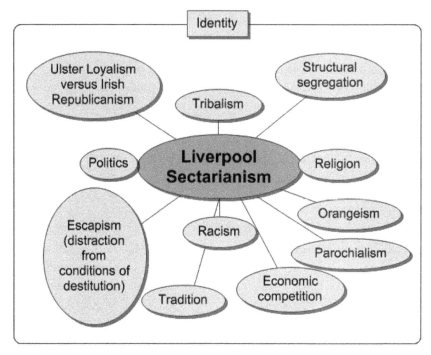

Figure 1.1   Manifestations of Liverpool Sectarianism

Catholic and Protestant parishes became very important. There were micro-identities within the main two identities, based on the local church, pub, and street. The local parish was very important and it built and sustained communities. This localism meant community and unity, which may have mattered far more than debates over transubstantiation. Conversely, segregation or 'ghettoisation' meant sustained division between Catholics and Protestants.

Catholics and Protestants were brought up in separate areas, and were (and in many cases, still are) educated separately. On weekends, they went to different churches. People seldom drank together, as they had 'their own' pubs. With physical division, tribalism flourished. There was a language of division: 'they're up there and we're down here' or 'we're up here and they're down there'. There was little dialogue between the people of different identities. With such strong localism (fed by parochialism and physical segregation), a 'them' and 'us' attitude developed. Amid conditions of abject poverty, people took solace in what little they did have: a strong sense of community. As such, there was a need to protect 'your' area. There was also an element of escapism in sectarianism. Life in Liverpool slums was monotonous. In contrast, confrontation at religious processions or Orange parades was exciting.

There were also political outlets to maintain sectarian division. Local political parties (particularly, but certainly not exclusively, the Conservatives) utilised sectarian tensions for personal gain. In the early twentieth century, the Irish War of Independence had support in Liverpool, as did the Ulster Covenant. Uniquely, in England, an Irish Nationalist MP represented part of the city. Today, Loyalist and Republican parades (of small size) are one of the few remaining visible aspects of Liverpool sectarianism, which, in terms of the dominant Protestant versus Catholic divide, has virtually expired.

Sectarianism in Liverpool: Scale and Origins

Over a period spanning two centuries, Liverpool was riven by deep-rooted ethno-religious tensions. These animosities first surfaced in 1819 when Protestant Orangemen and Irish Catholics were combatants in an 'Orange–Catholic' riot. Sectarianism was fuelled by a gargantuan scale of Irish immigration into Liverpool between 1845 and 1852. What developed was a cultural partition based around religious and national identities. During this period, denominational division between Protestants and Catholics, coupled with xenophobia expressed between 'native' Liverpudlians and immigrant Irish, caused significant conflict, as 'people were stigmatised for their religious beliefs within a city divided on sectarian lines'.[83]

Neal states that 'by the 1850s the working-class was split in Liverpool in a way that was unique in England'.[84] A decade later, the frequency of religious disputes was indicated by one contributor to the *Liverpool Mercury* who described as the 'follies and vices of this great town ... men causing dissention and every bad passion to arise, through foolish and useless religious differences'.[85]

Religious animosity was exacerbated by the actions and rhetoric of clergymen and politicians, whilst the Orange Order and the Roman Catholic Church acted as fixed badges of identity for their respective 'flocks'. After the

---

[83] Crowley, 2012: 22.
[84] Neal, 1988: 158.
[85] *Liverpool Mercury*, 11 May 1860.

Second World War, sectarianism began to decline in a piecemeal fashion, but it remained significant until at least the end of the 1960s. *Cilla*, an ITV television series, based on the early career of Cilla Black, made repeated reference to the social problems attributed to sectarianism in 1960s Liverpool.[86] As late as the 1990s, Channel 4's *Billy Boys* referred to Liverpool as 'England's last sectarian city'.[87] In 2008, Alexei Sayle, in a three-part series on the city, suggested that 'Liverpool is the only city in England where somebody can ask you if you are "Orange" and not be talking about your mobile phone network'.[88]

In the nineteenth century and early twentieth century, rioting was frequently juxtaposed with ostentatious religious celebrations in sectarian Liverpool. The main 'Green' and 'Orange' congregational days were St Patrick's Day and the twelfth of July respectively.[89] These days were often marred by sectarian violence. With a cited average 'Twelfth' turnout of '40–50,000 people by the 1870s',[90] and with Liverpool, by the 1890s, the largest Roman Catholic diocese in England (with over 400,000 people),[91] by the turn of the century, religion and sectarianism had become prominent features in the lives of many of the port's citizenry. Sectional hostilities continued (though increasingly in a ritualised sense) deep into the twentieth century. Although the number of people involved in violence became small ('a few hundred'),[92] sectarian problems had long been endemic:

> In Liverpool, the fabric of working life was permanently scarred by open sectarian violence ... To come home at night and find a brother, father or sister bleeding and battered after a fight over 'religion' was a traumatic experience which entered into the family stock of stories and prejudices, to be embroidered over time ... it was not simply the large-scale riot which set the tone of inter-communal dialogue; it was the thousand and one quarrels and fights, many unreported, which established animosity in the streets, public houses and workplaces.[93]

---

[86] *Cilla* (2014), three-part ITV television series.

[87] *Billy Boys* (1995), Channel 4 documentary on the breakaway group, the 'Independent Orange Order' of Liverpool.

[88] *Alexei Sayle's Liverpool* (2008), three-part BBC 2 television documentary series.

[89] 'Orange Day' or 'the Glorious Twelfth' is the main Protestant marching day of the Orange Institution.

[90] Bullough, 1990: 7.

[91] Ibid., 18, citing Gallagher.

[92] Neal, 1988: 244.

[93] Ibid., 251–2.

As sectarianism diminished during the twentieth century, disturbances continued on the 'Twelfth' into the 1970s, and sectarian resentment lingered. 'The Troubles' in Northern Ireland did not help matters, seemingly acting as the reason for the curtailment of Irish community presence on Liverpool's streets toward the end of the 1960s, which 'saw the demise of St Patrick's Day parades', owing to 'fears that growing civil unrest would transport itself to the streets of Liverpool'.[94] 'The Troubles', however, did not outweigh factors that were diluting animosity. Resentment subsided as the century progressed, and, by the twenty-first century, apart from isolated incidents, was virtually defunct.

The origin of sectarian division can be said to have been economic and xenophobic, as well as religious, owing to 'one workman frequently regard[ing] another as a jealous competitor rather than as a colleague in a common struggle'.[95] In conditions of scarceness, and amid a struggle for regular work, 'all the frustration arising from poverty, overcrowding and unemployment broke the surface and found [an] outlet in sectarian violence at the readiest "legitimate" excuse'.[96] For the English Protestant, the Irish were scapegoats, regardless that Catholic and Protestant bore comparable levels of deprivation, most residing in 'dark, dilapidated, and comfortless dwellings, lacking sanitary conveniences and even taps and sinks'.[97]

In these conditions, Irish Catholics, whose arrival had significantly contributed to the overcrowding, were perceived as alien intruders and economic rivals in a situation where competition for work was already fierce. Those who opposed their presence considered themselves the natural and rightful inhabitants of Liverpool. Amid ethnic and religious disunity, the Orange Order became attractive to the Protestant working-class, which desired an organisation that offered its own welfare schemes and mutual fellowship, comparable to what their Irish counterparts found in the Roman Catholic Church. In combining to 'resist' Catholicism, Protestants were encouraged by the denunciations of 'Rome' by strident clergymen, such as

---

[94] *Cairde na hÉireann Liverpool*, 'Under Pressure: A Report into Far-Right and Loyalist Attacks against Irish Community Parades/ Marches in Liverpool during 2012. Liverpool: Cairde na hÉireann Liverpool, 2013, p. 4.

[95] Waller, 1981: xvii.

[96] Neal, 1988: 231.

[97] Briggs, 1956: 181–2, citing D. Caradog Jones and Colin G. Clark, *Housing in Liverpool: A Survey, by Sample, of Present Conditions*. London: Royal Statistical Society, 1930.

Hugh McNeile and George Wise, and by the perception that the Catholic Irish were inherently inferior: 'more like squalid apes than human beings'.[98]

The Catholic clergy's obsession with 'safeguarding the souls' of their young caused much resentment among Protestants in Liverpool, and a bitter battle often ensued to ensure that a child was brought up in the 'correct faith'; the Catholic stipulation under the 1908 Ne Temere decree. In addition, the message from some Catholic clergy suggested that association with 'non-Catholics' would condemn one's 'soul to purgatory or limbo'.[99] This rhetoric would both scare their own flock and anger Protestants. The philosophy of 'better together', most associated with the Anglican Bishop David Sheppard and the Catholic Archbishop Derek Worlock from the 1970s, constructed new relations based on ecumenical partnership, but it was a long time coming.

Moreover, Liverpool sectarianism had a strong political manifestation. As the Conservatives and their partners in the Protestant Party played on the 'fear-fattened prejudices of people who were, at best, notional Protestants but who were very definitely opposed to Irish Catholics',[100] they enjoyed overall control of Liverpool City Council for much of the nineteenth and twentieth centuries, their efforts aided by the Working Men's Conservative Association (WMCA) and the Orange Institution. In contrast, Catholics elected an Irish Nationalist MP to represent them until 1929. Thus, sectarianism in Liverpool engulfed religious, political, and economic spheres. As Neal argues, 'The [Protestant] Clergy genuinely believed that Catholicism was evil, the Tories wanted to use it [sectarianism] for political power at voting time, and the working class resented all these paddies and wanted a punch up'.[101]

In 1909, Liverpool was said to have been 'comparable to Belfast'.[102] The sectarian disturbances of that year left a legacy which remained for decades in the form of residential segregation. In 1910, The Times declared that 'The Roman Catholics have driven the Protestants from the Scotland Road area; the Protestants have swept Netherfield Road clean of Roman Catholics. It is almost incredible in regard to a great English City, but these clearances

---

[98] Kinealy, 1994: 331, citing J.A. Froude, writing in 1841.

[99] Susanne Loughlin, 13 February 2013.

[100] Lane, 1987: 138.

[101] Frank Neal, 12 February 2010.

[102] Neal, 1988: 230, citing Leonard Dunning, Head Constable of Liverpool, 1902–11, who made the comparison in a letter to the Home Office.

are affected by actual violence'.[103] Neal suggests that, 'though the situation never approached the excesses of Belfast it was a near thing'.[104] Bullough's appraisal, based on a study of Orange processions between 1919 and 1939, stated that, 'sectarian strife and disorder on Merseyside were a ritualised dilution of the Ulster Capital'.[105] Inter-communal relations in Liverpool were certainly sour, on a par with, if not greater than, rivalries experienced in Glasgow.

Politically, socially, demographically, and economically, Liverpool is now transformed. Although Orange parades persist, they are of a much reduced size. Several very small Irish republican parades also take place annually in Liverpool. Churchgoing has declined markedly. In 1982, when Pope John Paul II visited Liverpool, 'attendance at mass regularly totalled 150,000 across the city; now that number is 60,000'.[106]

Some kind of case could be made that problems have remained evident: a protest from Loyalists and Orangemen prevented a St Patrick's Day parade from taking place in 1996. In 2010, Catholic Bishop Tom Williams stated that 'you do not have to scratch far beneath the surface to uncover sectarian resentment in Liverpool'.[107] In 2012, three Irish parades were targeted by 'Far-Right groups together with elements of Liverpool's Loyalist/ Orange community'.[108] In 2013, a tricolour was set ablaze by the *Apprentice Boys of Derry* on the grounds of the Loyal Provincial Orange Club on Everton Road.[109] These events indicate residual difficulties, although they were predominantly 'anti-Irish republican', and, possibly to some extent, anti-Irish events, not the anti-Catholic episodes of old. Religious sectarianism, in terms of Protestant versus Catholic loathing, is devoid of any real significance in Liverpool and is virtually defunct. The following chapters will explain why this has come to be the case.

---

[103] *The Times*, 26 November 1910, cited by Belchem, 2007: 193.
[104] Neal, 1988: 231.
[105] Bullough, 1990: 10.
[106] Granada Reports, Granada Regional News, ITV, Liverpool, 21 January 2011.
[107] Roman Catholic Bishop of Liverpool, Tom Williams, 23 March 2010.
[108] *Cairde na hÉireann Liverpool*, 'Under Pressure', 3.
[109] The malefactors were named as the *Apprentice Boys of Derry*. The event was reported as a 'hate crime' by several members of Liverpool's Irish community.

1

The Rise of Sectarianism

The Impact of the Irish Famine: Slums and Poverty

The growth of sectarianism owed much to the rapid influx of Irish immigrants and the economic dislocation, social upheaval, and religious antipathy which followed this mass arrival. Much of the emigration from Ireland was due to *an Gorta Mór*, or the 'Great Hunger', caused by a potato blight, which 'robbed more than one-third of the population of their usual means of subsistence',[1] and contributed to the death of one million people. Two million people emigrated from Ireland between 1845 and 1855, with Liverpool, as the nearest port, permanently transformed by this influx.

The dynamics of Liverpool sectarianism were already in place even prior to the new arrivals.[2] However, the hundreds of thousands of Irish who arrived in Liverpool during this period did much to shape and strengthen sectarian attitudes amid economic rivalry. There was 'a large and permanent increase in spending on Irish destitution in Liverpool' but employers 'benefited from the large pool of unemployed Irish to the extent that Irish labour was widely used, and the presence of so many people looking for work could not fail to influence the wage levels paid to labourers'.[3] The religious affiliation of the majority of the immigrants, Roman Catholicism, was already despised by many Protestants. These economic and religious factors, coupled with racist attitudes perpetuated by the local and national media, meant that the Irish Famine gave sectarianism powerful motivations.

---

[1] J. Donnelly, 'The Irish Famine' (last updated 17 February 2011). Available at: http://www.bbc.co.uk/history/british/victorians/famine_01.shtml.

[2] The relationship between Revd Hugh McNeile (an influential anti-Catholic orator), the local Tory hierarchy, and the Orange Institution had ensured that sectarian tensions were already a factor of Liverpool politics by the mid-nineteenth century.

[3] Neal, 2010: 107–8.

Liverpool's proportion of Irish-born multiplied in the nineteenth century: 5,000 in 1800, 11,000 in 1820, and 35,000 in 1840.[4] By 1841, about 20 per cent of the total Irish in England and Wales were to be found in Liverpool.[5] The scale of famine-based immigration into Liverpool hugely exacerbated pre-existing tensions. Even though, of the 500,000 Irish who entered Liverpool before July 1848, many re-emigrated, by spring 1847, 105,000 remained and the Select Vestry[6] of Liverpool complained to Parliament that 'this increase was not one of the people of all classes, but of the poor'.[7]

In the nineteenth century, Liverpool, as the gateway to the world, and the leading port of the British Empire, was the obvious destination for those who wished to escape the hardship of rural Ireland. Pauper families sometimes 'travelled for free as human ballast on empty coal ships, while others were given fare money by Landlords hoping to get rid of them cheaply',[8] a point studied in detail by Donald MacKay.[9] Despite attendant dangers, the Irish knew that in Britain they would probably not starve to death, as, 'unlike Ireland, food hand-outs were freely available throughout the country. The quality of food was also superior to the meagre rations handed out in Ireland's soup kitchens and workhouses'.[10]

The majority of the Irish influx concentrated in already established areas of Irish settlement and 'by 1841 immigrants were most concentrated in the north end political wards, specifically Vauxhall, Exchange, Scotland, and St Pauls, close to the docks'.[11] Although the Irish settled on both banks of the Mersey, the majority of Irish clustered in these northern and western wards of Liverpool, and also in the dockside area of Bootle. These ghettos soon became cramped, overcrowded, and unsanitary, as '1,500 passengers each day were landing from the packets from Dublin ... many thousands of cellars which the authorities had already condemned as unfit for habitation were brought back into use to house the crowds of people ... Scotland Road soon became a vast sprawling slum'.[12] By 1851, such was the scale of rapid

---

[4] Waller, 1981: 7.

[5] Kelly, 2003: 2.

[6] The Select Vestry were Poor Law guardians elected annually by the ratepayers.

[7] Waller, 1981: 7.

[8] Kerrigan, 2009: 219.

[9] MacKay, 1990.

[10] Kerrigan, 2009: 219.

[11] Neal, 1988: 11.

[12] Cooke, 1987: 19.

immigration, that 'the Irish-born population of Liverpool exceeded that of any Irish town except Dublin, Cork, and Belfast'.[13]

Between 1847 and 1853, '1,500,000 Irish landed at Liverpool's docks'. As a result, 'the north end of Liverpool became the most densely populated area of Irish immigrants in mainland Britain'.[14] By 1851, 22.3 per cent of the city's population was Irish-born.[15] This astonishing rate of alteration triggered a reaction. The 'native' felt invaded, as Irish communities 'grew too quickly for easy assimilation'.[16] The sheer numbers of Irish entering Liverpool at this time was enough on its own to breed contempt from the locals. As Neal suggests, 'to the poverty stricken Protestants living in, or near, the numerous streets filled by Irish newcomers the town must have seemed like part of Ireland'.[17]

Given their poverty, the Irish were distinct: 'in their rags, and malnutrition, in their missing teeth, matted hair, body smells, and in other visible signs which clearly set them apart'.[18] The majority 'dwelled in sordid conditions in the appalling slums',[19] amid 'every conceivable kind of filth'.[20] Yet, the Irish weren't the only group who lived in these conditions. The 'native' Protestants enjoyed only slight relative advantage, but this marginal superiority, allied to the perceived threats to jobs and conditions posed by the immigrants, led to considerable rivalry and much disdain towards the newly arrived Irish, stereotyped (relatively accurately) as 'a floor of poor, unskilled and mainly destitute people flooding into the city's slums in search of any menial poorly paid work'.[21] Added to the Irish were the Scottish and Welsh, 8 per cent of the city's population in 1871. The mix was not conducive to harmonious relations, not least because the majority of Welsh and Scottish were Protestant and the Irish were Catholic, but also as many of the immigrants were economic competitors.

The problems created by mass immigration 'elicited little national sympathy, many believing, like the Earl of Wicklow, that Liverpool, having "benefited more by their Irish commerce than by that of all the rest of the world together,

[13] Neal, 1988: 10.
[14] Boyce, 1999: 278.
[15] Pooley, 1989: 74.
[16] Davis, 1991: 148.
[17] Neal, 1988: 11.
[18] Kerrigan, 2009: 220.
[19] Muir, 1907: 8.
[20] Hocking, 1879: 12.
[21] Herson, 1989: 84.

should bear the burden".[22] Nonetheless, Liverpool's authorities found it difficult to facilitate the arrival of such a massive influx of often destitute Irish.

Much rancour was based on pecuniary consideration. Concerns were raised about 'the rapid increase in the numbers of Irish receiving poor relief ... and complaints were made of fraudulent claims by the resident Irish poor'.[23] The city's ratepayers solidified in a decidedly anti-Irish direction as the cost of poor relief amplified. With 'over 173,000 persons, probably 95 per cent Irish, receiving poor relief in Liverpool from the 18th to the 26th January 1847 alone',[24] The Times suggested that 'every English working man carries an Irish family on his shoulders'.[25]

Employers saw the crisis as an opportunity to distribute paltry wages, as any 'trouble maker' could be quickly replaced in the largely unregulated dock-pen system.[26] Philip Ingram wrote of proceedings:

> The result of this intense immigration in the first half of the nineteenth century was an overstocked labour market which, whilst it suited the employers' needs by allowing for sudden inexpensive expansion and contraction of his labour force, left the population working at the docks with permanent uncertainty in an atmosphere of ever-present competition for work.[27]

By 1851, 47 per cent of the people in both Vauxhall and Exchange political wards were Irish born, while 30 per cent of Scotland ward residents had also been born in Ireland.[28] These wards were all located close to the docks at the north end of Liverpool. Of the other central wards, also located on the periphery of the docks, the Irish-born population accounted for approximately 25 per cent of the inhabitants.[29]

It is claimed by Walsh that, 'While many dockers were Catholics, none of the shipbuilding firms would employ a Catholic. All ships' builders were members of the Orange Lodge'.[30] For a period, the Twelfth of July was known

---

[22] Cited by Waller, 1981: 7.

[23] Davis, 1991: 153–4.

[24] Waller, 1981: 8.

[25] Neal, 1988: 109, citing The Times, 6 May 1847.

[26] In 1842, a study showed that out of 2,628 labourers in Vauxhall only 17 were employed 5 days a week (Finch, 1986). As late as the 1960s, dockers were still 'picked off the pen'.

[27] Ingram, 1987: 30–1.

[28] Neal, 1988: 11–12.

[29] Ibid.

[30] Walsh, 2011: 25.

as 'Carpenters' Day'. Yet, in context, Liverpool had only a brief significance as a shipbuilding centre. By 1850, shipbuilding had passed to Birkenhead, leaving Liverpool with the more modest occupation of ship repair carried out by a much less skilled workforce. As Gallagher suggests,

> Nineteenth century Liverpool was a mercantile and commercial port rather than an industrial centre. The occupational structure of the city included a far higher percentage of unskilled and part time jobs for which the Irish *were* in a position to compete. So to a greater degree than in Glasgow (second only to Liverpool as a reception-centre for Irish immigrants), sectarian friction stemmed from economic competition and was a more intense and unpleasant kind.[31]

As Mark O'Brian writes, 'competition for day-labouring work between Catholic workers and unskilled Protestant workers was intense and pervaded all areas of life'.[32] However, a stress upon economic rivalry is not to discount racial and religious aspects. As MacRaild stresses,

> No amount of urban decay, workplace competition or poverty and hardship could explain the extraordinary passions that were inflamed by Irish migration. A more potent explanation is the fact that ... the dominant Protestant religion was vehemently anti-Catholic, and this acutely affected the reception that awaited the much despised 'Paddy' ... Irish Catholics in Britain were guaranteed a rocky reception because the native population viewed anti-Catholicism as a mainstay of their Protestant identity. Negative attitudes were endemic, dangerous and malevolent features of British cultural life.[33]

Added to this, some 'Irish' habits, such as 'faction fighting',[34] seemed alien to the English Protestants. The widely spoken Gaelic language added to the sense of 'invasion' and helped to solidify separateness.

Reference to Irish Catholics as 'the dregs of society' and even as an 'inferior race' by journalists, local officials, and Protestant clergy were akin to

---

[31] Gallagher, 1987: 14–15.

[32] Mark O'Brian, 'From the Ground Up: Radical Liverpool Now', in Belchem and Biggs, 2011.

[33] MacRaild, 1999: 155, 187.

[34] Organised fights between opposing factions were a feature of early nineteenth-century Ireland, a feature continued by some in Liverpool. See Doonbleisce.com (website), 'Faction Fighting: "They Fought for Sheer Love of Fighting"'. Available at: www.doonbleisce.com/faction_fighting.htm.

'full-blooded racial and religious condemnation'.[35] An article in the *Liverpool Herald* in 1855 describing, 'Not English but Irish papists' as 'wretches', 'the lower order', and 'the filthiest beings on the habitable globe', is claimed, by Davis, to have been an attempt to explain away social problems as 'weakness of character'; asserting that, 'In playing on fears of unemployment, and in targeting the Irish presence as an explanation of social problems like housing and crime,[36] the authorities relieved themselves of the responsibility to find practical solution'.[37]

As Neal suggests, 'the sheer pressure of population produced results that placed Liverpool at the head of every list of indices of bad living conditions'[38] and the concentration of disease amongst the dockland emigrants was such that Liverpool was described, in 1847, as 'the hospital and cemetery of Ireland'.[39] By 1845, 'figures of death by fever had raced to an appalling height ... [in 1846] an epidemic of scarlatina carried off fifteen hundred, mainly children, and then came cholera with a death roll of six thousand'.[40] David Charters describes the mortality rate in areas where many Irish resided, 'In the bad years 80% of children born off Scotland Road died before they were ten ... In 1847, 2,303 men, women, and children were buried in St Anthony's ... In the same year, 7,219 paupers were buried in a mass graves in St Mary's'.[41] 'Death from starvation' was another 'regular outcome of post mortems carried out on those from Irish districts',[42] as 'dirt, disease, and malnutrition flourished'.[43] Of the 21,000 people who had died from typhus in 1847, 87 per cent were Irish[44] and 'life expectancy became the lowest in the country'.[45]

Belchem states that, 'every step was taken to prevent the spread of fever beyond the "low Irish": at one point, no fewer than 88% of sick persons under

---

[35] Davis, 1991: 154–5.

[36] Lamb and Smallpage (1935: 64) contended that 'Violence and crime to a great extent was caused by evil conditions, and improvements were certain to bring about a lessening of some of the worst offences.'

[37] Davis, 1991: 155–6, citing *Liverpool Herald*, 17 November 1955.

[38] Neal, 1988: 2.

[39] *Liverpool Mail*, 6 November 1847, also *Liverpool Albion*, 1 November 1847, cited ibid., 94.

[40] Lamb and Smallpage, 1935: 62.

[41] Charters, 2003: 42–4.

[42] Neal, 1988: 85.

[43] Crawford, 1997: 137.

[44] O'Neill, 2010: 83.

[45] Boyce, 1999: 278: 280. See Swift and Gilley, 1989.

the care of the health authorities were Irish'.[46] The greatest incidence of death occurred in 'the recognisably Irish districts – the death rate in Vauxhall was 1 in 17 compared with 1 in 228 in the middle class Rodney ward'.[47] The town was 'helpless to adapt itself to its new conditions, and to perform its duty of providing the means of a humane existence for its citizens'.[48]

Nonetheless, many in Liverpool had little sympathy for the Irish plight. The outbreak of disease was blamed on the refugees, the accusation being that they had brought illness with them from Ireland: their 'disgustingly filthy'[49] habits being responsible for the 'Irish Fever'. The Catholic tradition of wakes[50] for the recently deceased was a custom little understood by the 'native' Protestants, but vital for many devout Irish Catholics, if unwise considering the high risk of infection from corpses.

In Liverpool, the Irish 'faced poverty inconceivable in England today'.[51] As Lamb and Smallpage wrote, 'Overcrowding was unbelievable, fifty or sixty living in one house of three or four rooms while forty or more are known to have slept in one cellar. Naturally disease developed under these abominable conditions and spread to other parts of the town ... ships had to be anchored in the river for use as hospitals'.[52] During this period, which Cooke describes as, 'the worst crisis in the city's history',[53] the 'teeming' Irish-filled 'lodging houses were breeding grounds for disease'[54] and Liverpool 'was recognised as the worst [place] in the country for ill health and malnutrition'.[55] The spread of disease in 'Irish quarters' of the town is not surprising given the deplorable circumstances the Irish had abided. The conditions the emigrants endured while crossing the Irish Sea were described as 'disgraceful, dangerous, and inhuman',[56] while in the Liverpool slums, 'germs bred freely around narrow courts [where] ... pools of stagnant water lay on the floors and there was rarely any drainage except into open cesspools'.[57]

[46] Belchem, 2000: 60.
[47] Neal, 1997: 129.
[48] Muir, 1906: 8–9.
[49] An 1847 Registrar General report, cited by Neal, 1988: 94.
[50] A wake is the custom of keeping a vigil or watch over a body from death until burial.
[51] Cooke, 1987: 19.
[52] Lamb and Smallpage, 1935: 60–2.
[53] Cooke, 1987: 19.
[54] MacKay, 1990: 262.
[55] Cooke, 1987: 19.
[56] MacKay, 1990: 201.
[57] Lamb and Smallpage, 1935: 60.

These years of squalor were pivotal in shaping relations between communities in the city: the new Irish Catholic arrivals blaming the local British for the conditions in which they found themselves, while the native Protestant believed that it was the Irish who introduced the contagions. The slum habitations of the 'Irish' wards were perceived as reflecting the deficiencies of their dwellers. Although most Irish had no alternative but to 'herd' into 'shocking dark, damp, dirty places'[58] such as cellars with 'absolutely no place of deposit for [human] refuse',[59] the Irish emigrants 'association with poverty, dirt, and disease created an uncomfortable and unpalatable impression on the mind of the host community'.[60]

In 1847, the Poor Law Removal Act emerged to alleviate some of the pressure on the municipality. It was estimated that 40,000 Irish were to be removed, but many stopped claiming relief in order to avoid deportation, further adding to their own desperate circumstances. In that year, '15,000 poverty stricken Irish people were sent back to Ireland,'[61] yet, given that it was 'simply impossible to police such a policy', some may have returned.[62] Meanwhile, as hostility between native and newly arrived grew, 'Liverpudlians gained a reputation for their predatory and vicious reception of immigrants'.[63] As MacKay states, 'When Irish emigrants were not robbed outright on the streets, they were overcharged for lodging houses and food',[64] and many scams and tricks also stripped the Irish bare of what little they had.[65]

Largely on account of the arrival of famine Irish, the population of Liverpool more than doubled from 220,000 in 1837 to 488,845 in 1871.[66] The inward migration of the Irish had a major effect. As one example of the growth of a Liverpool ward, in 1815, there were 1,222 inhabitants of Everton; by 1851, this figure was 25,508, and a decade later the population almost doubled to 54,848. By 1921, it was 124,414,[67] despite the forced

---

[58] Kinealy, 1994: 333, citing *Liverpool Mercury*, 11 March 1847; also *Liverpool Times*, 3 April 1847.

[59] Tyndale Harries, 1946: 85–6.

[60] Kinealy, 1994: 332, citing *Liverpool Times*, 15 April 1847.

[61] Kerrigan, 2009: 223.

[62] Neal, 1988: 131.

[63] Waller, 1981: 8.

[64] MacKay, 1990: 201.

[65] Kerrigan, 2009: 221–2.

[66] Tyndale Harries, 1946: 84.

[67] Figures cited by Rodgers, 2010: 28.

eviction of Catholics in 1909. Many people evicted from Everton settled in the already established Irish stronghold of the Scotland Road district, near the docks.

The sheer numbers of Irish arriving meant that working-class Protestants felt a sense of dislocation. As Waller suggests, 'the question seemed less of Liverpool absorbing the Irish, as of Liverpool resisting absorption by the Irish'.[68] In contrast, the Irish Catholics felt betrayed by an 'occupying' power that had allowed its people to starve in their millions, whilst still exporting food from Ireland. Furthermore, they felt ill-treated by a UK government that seemed to begrudge giving them even basic relief upon arrival. Liverpool's authorities seemed more concerned about the strain on the ratepayer than the pressures upon immigrants.

The Development of Protestant Orange Versus Catholic Green

Irish Catholics required assistance from the Church during famine years and the Catholic Church became central to the lives of the immigrant Irish. MacRaild claims that, 'In Liverpool, as the city reeled under the effects of Famine influx, many of the poor Irish ... saw few outsiders other than their priest'.[69] A 'philanthropic initiative spurred on by sectarian competition'[70] emerged to generate a 'charitable safety net for the Catholic communities'.[71] 'Community Catholicism'[72] developed as organisations, such as St Vincent de Paul's, provided a form of social security for the Irish Catholic community, with receipt conditional upon regular appearance at Mass. Such a system developed out of necessity, both for the destitute 'flock' and the Church, which hoped to retain allegiance. As Kanya-Forstner states,

> In response to the willingness of Irish Catholics to turn to competing religious organisations for assistance, some of which demanded their conversion to Protestantism, Catholic parish churches in Liverpool made a determined effort to provide a relief network which would isolate poorer parishioners from the city's other charitable agencies ... secure the

[68] Waller, 1981: 25.
[69] MacRaild, 1999: 89.
[70] Kanya-Forstner, 2000: 170.
[71] MacRaild, 1999: 93.
[72] Hill, 93: From Belchem and Biggs et al. 2011.

allegiance of poor Irish Catholics, and reform their religious and social behaviour in the process.[73]

As the numbers of Irish Catholics increased, Catholic churches began to proliferate: from only two Catholic parish churches at the start of the nineteenth century, Liverpool had twenty-one by 1886, two-thirds clustered in the Scotland, Vauxhall, and Everton areas.[74]

Just as the term 'Catholic' became interchangeable with the word 'Irish', anything overtly Protestant in nature would become synonymous with Orangeism. In Liverpool, the Orange Order became an influential organisation. Throughout the latter half of the nineteenth and first half of the twentieth centuries, the Order affected the success of the Protestant Party and the Conservative Party in national, local, and even School Board elections.[75] Membership of the Orange Order was seen as perfectly 'respectable', and the character of many businesses and institutions in Liverpool were affected due to individual allegiance, location, or custom. Some advertised jobs for which 'Catholics need not apply',[76] and public houses were often (officially or unofficially) designated as either 'Green' or 'Orange'.

Catholicism would come to epitomise much of what it was to be a 'Scottie Roader', and Orangeism was a central aspect of the lives of the residents of the Netherfield Road district. As the number of Irish in Liverpool increased, so did the membership of the Orange Order. While Catholicism 'agitated educated Protestants, simply by its theological claims',[77] for many Protestants, Catholicism was but one of several reasons (albeit an important one) to hate the Irish. Increased competition for jobs, the view that the Irish were more criminal in nature (as 'Catholicism robbed them of any morality'),[78] and the steady creation of a ghetto system that inevitably led to tribalism resulted in the Orange Order flourishing. In turn, 'Orangeism fuelled anti-Irish and anti-Catholic bigotry'.[79] This worked to the benefit of Conservative politicians, who would 'use the Lodge for muscle at election time'.[80] Historians of socialism have argued that 'in Liverpool political

---

[73] Kanya-Forstner, 2000: 173.

[74] Boyce, 1999: 282–3.

[75] See Waller, 1981: 93.

[76] Bullough, 1990: 16.

[77] Frank Neal, 12 February 2010.

[78] Neal, 1991: 162.

[79] Members of the Merseyside Socialist Research Group, 1992: 164.

[80] Neal, 12 February 2010.

forces, whether Tory, Orange or openly fascist, attempted to prevent the growth of class unity by inflating the existing divisions within the working class'.[81] Stanford suggests that, 'it suited the city's wealthy elite to see their workers distracted by religious hatred'.[82] By the turn of the century, as the Liverpool Irish were becoming more anglicised, Catholicism replaced Irish as the primary identifier of the 'rival' community in Liverpool.

One of the reasons that attention shifted from Irishness towards Catholicism was that, despite the huge Irish diaspora still residing in the dockside community, the Catholic Church refused to promote 'Irishness'. The perception of Liverpool's Irish as 'alien' was eventually tackled by the Church's education policy which did not promote 'foreign' allegiance, notwithstanding the origins of many of its flock. The Liverpool Catholic Bishop Tom Williams claims that 'lots of Irish people in Liverpool never knew about the Irish famine, they wouldn't have a clue about Irish Nationalism, and wouldn't have a clue about the Irish civil war'.[83] Furthermore, the make-up of the Roman Catholic Church in Liverpool was not distinctly Irish.[84]

Despite support for Irish nationalism (demonstrated in the election of an Irish Nationalist MP, T.P. O'Connor, until 1929), it has been claimed that, 'in Liverpool, the English Catholic hierarchy had proven itself to be particularly outspoken against the Irish nationalist cause'.[85] For example, 'from the end of the 1860s, the Church tried to quell the usual drunken rowdiness of St Patrick's celebrations by encouraging gatherings which were self-improving in tenor'.[86] While 'some priests defied the hierarchy of the Church and supported political initiatives like Home Rule and Fenianism', such efforts were swiftly curtailed.[87]

With such a large proportion of the congregation in Liverpool being Irish or of Irish descent, why did the Roman Catholic clergy in Liverpool not attempt to exploit their support by promoting Home Rule? Bishop Tom Williams puts it simply: 'The Church in Liverpool was never Irish. It

[81] Members of Merseyside Socialist Research Group, 1992: 163.

[82] *The Tablet*, 10 January 2004.

[83] Tom Williams, 23 March 2010.

[84] Kennedy and Kennedy (2007: 903) explain that most Liverpool priests were ordained in Lancashire or were foreign missionaries.

[85] Ibid.

[86] MacRaild, 1999: 96.

[87] Ibid., 89.

was English.'[88] Furthermore, perhaps, with so many incumbent difficulties already stacked against the Liverpool Irish, adding fuel to the fire of sectarianism was inadvisable. As such, Catholic clergymen did not openly air grievances in the same way as some Protestant orators (often connected to the Orange Institution).

Rather than involve itself in Irish politics, the Catholic Church opted to play a considerable role in the lives of its flock, providing a repository of care which engendered strong loyalty from parishioners. The Church worked alongside the Hibernian benevolent and friendly societies in Liverpool, as a welfare support network for the Catholic population. Yet, as Belchem describes, by making Irish Catholics dependent on the Church, it was perhaps counter-productive to what the Church was trying to achieve in nineteenth-century Liverpool:

> Allied to its spiritual purpose, Catholic welfare provision – like its denominational education – sought to prepare the Irish poor (as the hierarchy wished) for citizenship in conformity with dominant (English) notions of respectability ... In seeking to reform the 'residuum', however, the Catholic Church constructed a self-enclosed network of 'improvement' which, for all its commitment to Victorian 'respectability', served to underline Catholic apartness ... Catholics kept apart, determined to look after their own (whether 'deserving' or 'undeserving').[89]

Moreover, despite the Church's refusal to promote a distinctly Irish identity among the immigrant population in Liverpool, the theological claims of Catholicism promoted hostility from the indigenous population.

Catholic affirmation of transubstantiation, purgatory, and the veneration of saints were (and still are) rejected by Protestants, as is the alleged centrality of the Roman Catholic Church to Christianity. The Latin Mass was also distinct from the English spoken to Protestant congregants, who viewed the Latin Mass as suspicious (potentially misleading) and archaic. Additionally, priests, to Catholics, were considered mediators between God and man: a proposition rejected out of hand by Protestants believing in a 'Priesthood of all believers'.[90] MacRaild states that 'Anti-Catholics loathed the priesthood as something which held an incomprehensible mystical

---

[88] Tom Williams, 23 March 2010.

[89] Belchem, 2000b: 125.

[90] Religion Facts (2014) 'Comparison Chart: Catholic and Protestant Christianity'. Available at: www.religionfacts.com/christianity/charts/catholic_protestant.htm.

control over parishioners. The confessional, for example, was lambasted as a forum in which unmarried men could pry into the intimate lives of their female charges. Yet for tight-knit Irish communities, the confessional was very important'.[91] Boyce attests that 'regular Confession was timetabled during normal school hours ... frequent Communion and Confession were expected and priests were quick to visit families whose attendance at Mass was thought to be lax'.[92]

Additionally, Jesse Buck suggests that the Roman Catholic Church's position on 'mixed' marriage did much to further sour relations between the two denominations, as the 1908 *Ne Temere* decree required children of mixed marriages to be raised Catholic.[93] This act of 'Papal Aggression', as it was seen by many of the Protestant community, antagonised the already turbulent situation in Liverpool. Moreover, Kanya-Forstner states that Catholic welfare provision in effect was 'a tool for reshaping the behaviour of Irish Catholics in Liverpool ... the Catholic Church imbued its image of womanhood, and especially motherhood, with an explicitly Catholic meaning: good Catholic women had to attend to their own religious duties and as mothers were required to ensure the religious allegiance of future generations'.[94] Lambert's study found that 'Irish Catholic women generally kept up their religious practices in Lancashire, for social as well as spiritual reasons ... Catholic women either married Catholic men or ensured that their husbands be converted to Catholicism before marriage'.[95]

Another issue was the denominational school system. Public funding of Catholic education antagonised Protestants. When the Catholic Bishop of Liverpool, in 1895, proclaimed, 'the right of denominational schools to an equal share with Board Schools of public money',[96] cries of 'Rome on the Rates!' was the retort. Throughout the nineteenth and deep into the twentieth centuries the public funding of Catholic schools repeatedly caused controversy in Liverpool.[97] And denominational schools added to division. As one anecdotal example from Doris Bennett reveals:

---

[91] MacRaild, 1999: 89.
[92] Boyce, 1999: 284, 286.
[93] Buck, 2011: Abstract.
[94] Kanya-Forstner, 2000: 168–9.
[95] Lambert, 2001: 101.
[96] Ibid., 156, citing *Liverpool Courier*, 15 July 1895.
[97] Presentation by Ian Henderson in Bootle Protestant Free Church, 27 October 2012. Various Protestant Party election materials also talked of 'grants to Roman Catholic Schools' and 'Priestly control of education'. See Roberts, 2015: Appendices 3.1, 3.4, 3.7, and 3.8.

You used to have a lot of nuns in schools. A friend of my mothers had married a Church of England man, but her daughter still went to a Catholic school. A particular nun had it in for her. During prayers one time she opened her eyes. This nun saw her, clapped her hands and shouted, 'Stop prayers! We've got a Protestant in the class!' So I think the [Catholic] Church caused a lot of the trouble. These days it wouldn't be said, because it wouldn't be allowed.[98]

Bennett also recalls that her friend's brother 'was born on the twelfth of July and the priest told their mother that they had to tell everybody that he was born on the thirteenth!'[99]

As such, and although a case can be made that the Roman Catholic Church, in suppressing Irish nationalism in Liverpool, did more to halt sectarianism than encourage it, the Church is not bereft of blame. It was not uncommon for members of the clergy to declare Protestant Churches 'in error' or 'null and void', in bold assertions of Church doctrine. In 1855, an article in the *Catholic Institute Magazine*, which articulated the central place of the Church in the life of Irish Catholics in Liverpool, criticised Protestants who carried on a missionary campaign aimed at the town's Catholics: 'as for sending their spiritual labourers into our fields it is simply insanity at a moment when their own vineyard is thus deserted, weedy, fruitless and unprofitable'.[100] The article had been in response to a survey carried out by the *Liverpool Mercury*, which found that the established church 'could not fill its pews', whereas Catholic attendance at mass at its height ran at nearly three times over the amount of seating available to the congregation.

In 1909, a *Catholic Herald* article, entitled 'The Decay of Protestantism', claimed that 'the number of [Protestant] communions, baptisms, and church marriages are rapidly diminishing ... Protestantism has no clear message concerning the hereafter ... There is no expansion in its shrivelling and dying sects. The war is now one between Rome and the Unbelief'.[101] The *Herald* also goaded Orangemen in an article entitled 'King William's "Holiness" Examined': William had 'lived in adultery ... the Bible condemns adultery and makes no exception for royalty'.[102]

[98] Doris Bennett, 15 March 2013.
[99] Ibid.
[100] *Catholic Institute Magazine*, 2(1) (November 1855), cited by Neal, 1988: 127–8.
[101] *Liverpool Catholic Herald*, 31 July 1909.
[102] *Liverpool Catholic Herald*, 24 July 1909.

If Protestant labourers were 'indifferent to the claims of the established Church, the claims of Orangeism struck a much more responsive nerve'.[103] As Graham Maddocks describes, by 1914, both the 'indigenous descendants of Anglo-Saxon[s]' and the 'large ethnically Irish population' still lived in 'grinding poverty and horrific slum conditions ... in an age when there was only charity or religion to alleviate their social distress'.[104] Maddocks' observation highlights why organisations such as the Catholic Church and Orange Order were so important. Divisions were rarely simply about religious doctrine for Liverpudlians, and much more about belonging, pride, and loyalty. The Orange Order and the Catholic Church played substantial social and charitable roles in their respective communities. This is not to dismiss the role that the Anglican Church played, but it was more aloof from its flock than the Catholic Church, and had less of a working-class connection than did the Orange Order.[105] The Order offered a stout defence of Protestantism and a measure of status to its members, whilst also acting as a mutual aid society. Orangemen regarded Catholicism as 'the natural enemy' and excluded Catholics, spouses of Catholics, and those 'sponsoring' a child baptised Catholic from their membership.

In turn, Catholic publications denounced Orangeism. In 1900, the *Catholic Herald* referred to Orangemen as 'a lawless banditti'.[106] Another article, in response to widespread sectarian disorder in 1909, entitled 'The Orange Lambs of Liverpool', caused controversy when it referred to 'hordes of blackguards assembled every 12th of July for a drunken orgy', and the 'intolerant and tyrannical spirit' of Orangeism.[107] Upon receipt of an objection declaring, 'in your slandering you have told what is not the truth about thousands of its members', the newspaper's editor mocked the response as 'typical Orange logic', replying, 'fancy the Belfast or Liverpool lodges drumming-out the ruffians. What would become of the noble Order if the head-crackers and nut-throwers and cowardly assailants of nuns were expelled!'[108]

[103] Neal, 1988: 127–8.
[104] Maddocks, 1991: 13, 15.
[105] For example, in 1853, 90 per cent of Catholic worshippers in Liverpool were designated as working class, in contrast to 45 per cent of Anglicans. Likewise, the working class were 'most numerically significant' in the Orange Order. Neal, 1988: 127; 1990–1: 23.
[106] *Liverpool Catholic Herald*, 6 July 1900: a 'Special' article by P. Donnelly on 'The Dawn of Orangeism'.
[107] *Liverpool Catholic Herald*, 26 June 1909.
[108] *Liverpool Catholic Herald*, 3 July 1909.

A further objection perturbed the Catholic periodical sufficiently to prompt a satirical illustration of Orangemen.[109]

Sectarian tensions were particularly high at the height of the Orange marching season and around St Patrick's Day. Pat O'Mara's *Autobiography of a Liverpool Irish Slummy*, first published in 1933, illustrates how he and his Catholic school friends on 'the Seventeenth of March' 'were looking for battle', and would ask, '"I" or "O" (Irish or Orange: the challenge to strangers on St Patrick's Day)'.[110] Yet, he describes his 'first taste of actual religious battle ... not on St Patrick's Day but on the Twelfth of July':

> 'King Billy's Day', the day on which the Protestant boys sung: 'St Paddy was a Bastard' ... [we went] down toward Netherfield Road to witness the Orangeman's parade ... when we got within the enemy's gates ... and perceived just what we were up against, we rather repented our daring. A huge crowd of our worst enemies (the "O's") with bands and banners carrying inscriptions that made our blood boil, surged around us. Orange everywhere and not a bit of green! I had always been brought up in the belief that Protestantism was a dying cult, and its adherents cowards; but this mob up here ... didn't look frightened at all.[111]

O'Mara goes on to state how he and his compatriots, as a result of vocal support for a Catholic protestor, 'were set upon by the Protestant youths in the parade ... booted all over the place', and made to sing, "We are the sons of Billy and the hell with Popery": a humiliation they later rescinded with an utterance of, "King Billy's mother runs a whorehouse in Hell!"[112] The repeated use of the term 'enemy' is important. For the Irish Catholic community of Liverpool, the cultural nemesis, certainly at the start of the twentieth century (O'Mara was born in 1901) was Orangemen. That children in the Catholic heartlands of Liverpool were being instructed that 'Protestantism was a dying cult' is also illuminating of the direction of the Roman Catholic hierarchy in the city during this period, especially when it is considered that such a proposition couldn't have been much further from the truth.

Orangeism developed from modest foundations into a major facet of Protestant life in Liverpool. As Neal notes,

---

[109] *Liverpool Catholic Herald*, 10 July 1909.

[110] O'Mara, 1933: 64, 66.

[111] Ibid., 65.

[112] Ibid., 66.

[The Orange Order] produced a strong working class culture, with its own music, songs, traditions and social organisation of benefit clubs, burial societies and quasi-religious ceremonies. It continued to be faced by a huge Catholic population increasingly well led, still identified with Ireland, poverty, charity, a burden on the rates, competition for jobs, etc.[113]

The extent of 'Romanism' and 'Irishness' that confronted Liverpool Protestants encouraged those who feared displacement to join the Orange Order. Within its lodges, Protestants found like-minded individuals who considered themselves as the rightful inhabitants of Liverpool with first claim on jobs and welfare. In terms of religious opposition, the Protestant working class was fed by a plethora of anti-Catholic (and anti-Irish) propaganda by militant Anglican Clergy, such as Hugh McNeile, and later George Wise, who connected better to ordinary citizens through their demagoguery than more moderate Anglicans. The appeal of Wise was increased by his membership of the Orange Institution.

Orangeism flourished in Liverpool more than any other city in England. Its appeal stretched across class boundaries, although it would be correct to assert that working-class Protestants made up the majority of its ranks. Via the Order, Liverpool Protestants would proudly represent their half of the divide, and on the Twelfth of July, when their streets were decorated in orange, they would feel a sense of local pride, national patriotism, and religious righteousness. Although predominantly working-class, the Order succeeded in uniting the casual unskilled labourer with the skilled manual labourer, who contributed aid to poorer counterparts. With Irish Catholics seen as economic, religious, and national rivals, it is not surprising that the Orange Order became such an important part of Protestant identity in Liverpool. Belchem suggests:

The Orange Order offered an alternative way of identifying and affiliating oneself based on faith. The two key characteristics of the Orange Order are that first and foremost you are Protestant and second you are British. Thus, it emphasises religious affiliation above an ethnic or national one.[114]

As the Protestant working class filled Orange lodges, the 'heresy' of Catholicism was something which had to be opposed. The Orange Order

---

[113] Neal, 1988: 244.
[114] John Belchem, 25 February 2010.

was always 'Protestant first'. This oppositional stance to the Catholic Irish was played out politically, fracturing the working class on ethno-religious lines. Protestantism and Conservatism became interlinked, an alliance which became increasingly strained as Liverpool's hegemonic position as an industrial and trading city ebbed during the twentieth century. As Waller notes, 'the Orangemen's Conservatism was conditional on the Conservative's Orangeism'.[115] The hostility between Orange Protestants and Catholics had many violent episodes. When the opportunity presented itself, Orangemen indulged their hostility to the Irish 'invaders' and 'upheld their creed with their fists, feet, and swords'.[116] On the 'Twelfth', Roman Catholics would hurl verbal abuse and various types of missiles at the Order as they marched past in the morning.[117] In the evening they would often gather in groups, and attack Orangemen upon their return to Liverpool. Bullough argues that 'the air of expectancy and danger that surrounded parades of the Liverpool Orange Lodges added an edge of excitement to the 12th July ... Disorderly behaviour had become part of the ritual of the Twelfth [and] stones, bottles, and swords were the staple weaponry'.[118]

By 1910, sectarian violence between Orangemen and Roman Catholics in Liverpool had resulted in a public inquiry, and was attracting national newspaper coverage.[119] The public inquiry in part blamed the Orange bands for stirring up disorder and prompted the Liverpool Corporation Act, 1912, which regulated meetings and processions.[120] The Act was a mitigating measure designed to remove some of the animosity from the Twelfth of July processions and other similar rallies throughout the city. Although this legislation succeeded in changing the planning and make-up of public meetings and parades, those marching still acted as the symbols of sectarianism, and violence and bitterness continued.

The 'Twelfth' became arguably the most important day in the Liverpool Protestant calendar, marked by ritual, symbolism, and often, towards its close, naked sectarian violence. Its colourful aspects became a source of

---

[115] Waller, 1981: 96.
[116] Ibid., 58.
[117] Ron Bather, 15 March 2010.
[118] Bullough, 1990: 63.
[119] *The Times*, 26 November 1910.
[120] Bullough, 1990: 29 – The act prohibited insulting or abusive actions directed against the religious beliefs of any section of the community, required notice of any meetings or processions, and all of the details of the event, including the music to be played or sung and the emblems, weapons, and books to be used or carried.

Protestant pride, and extensive displays of decoration in the Orange areas of Liverpool signified strength and allegiance. Orangeism became part of the culture of being a Liverpool Protestant. According to Bullough, 'for the working class the "big day" provided a means with which to throw off the shackles of everyday life and preparation and decoration contributed another form of enjoyment'.[121]

For Catholics, St Patrick's Day was an opportunity to exhibit their 'colours'. Similar preparation and decoration was portrayed in the 'Irish districts', and Catholic parades and signs of allegiance were met with similar disdain by Protestant Liverpudlians. As Bullough suggests, 'militant Protestants may have had little conception of doctrinal religion but in the Roman Catholic faith they saw the antithesis of their established way of life'.[122] Clashes on St Patrick's Day, whilst not as inevitable, nor as fierce as those on the 'Twelfth', nonetheless also became an expectant feature of city life.

The Orange Order and the Roman Catholic Church were the most visible bastions of religious division in Liverpool. Mass migration from Ireland during the 'Great Hunger', and the ethno/religious ghetto system that followed, ensured that, by the time the rest of England had largely stopped worrying about Catholicism, religious, cultural, and tribal divisions had become entrenched in Liverpool. By the early twentieth century, the port was firmly established as England's last 'sectarian city', a title it did not easily shed.

Sectarian Violence and Liverpool's Protestant Orators

The topic of sectarian violence is important in determining the severity of tensions on Merseyside. However, having already been dealt with by Neal (1988) it will be outlined relatively briefly in this section. Nevertheless, it is important to denote these aspects of life in Liverpool, especially in helping to demonstrate and explain the decline of sectarian enmity. A practical means of assessing the waning of sectarianism is by considering the level of violent or riotous behaviour. Although many violent skirmishes over 'religion' may have been unreported or not reported as 'religious' disputes, the level of street violence in both the nineteenth and twentieth centuries visibly declined. While sectarianism has a much wider reach than

---

[121] Ibid., 83.
[122] Ibid., 65.

physical confrontation, some comment on the extent of violence in Victorian Liverpool is necessary.

Community tensions were often intensified by the grandiloquence of certain clergymen and the actions of quasi-religious organisations, such as the Orange Order. Indeed, as early as 1835, tensions arising from Irish immigration were exacerbated by the sermons of the Reverend Hugh McNeile, who denounced the religion of the new arrivals. This role of clerical aggravator would later be adopted by George Wise, John Kensit, and Harry Longbottom, all of whom regularly denounced the 'evils' of 'Romanism'.

Disentangling the impact of these religious firebrands from the racially inspired hostility amongst the working class is not easy. There were regular accusations of the 'natural inferiority' of the 'Celt'. This in part was a response to a demand for Home Rule, prompting suggestion that the Irish would not be able to govern themselves. Equally questioned by the indigenous population, abetted by hostile local media, were the morality and loyalty of the Irish. Due to their race and religion, some considered the Irish to be unreliable and disloyal, Ireland and the Vatican seen as their repositories of allegiance. Protestants felt these notions were vindicated by a range of factors, ranging from the disproportionately high numbers of Irish Catholics in crime statistics,[123] to, much later, Ireland's official neutrality in the Second World War. The Irish were also deplored because they were competitors for jobs and resources. Catholicism, more than race or economics, was the focus for some of Liverpool's Protestant Clergymen, whose inflammatory and divisive sermons would often result in breaches of the peace. As a result, 'sectarian disturbances were far from unique [and] Liverpool had nastier and more enduring sectarian conflicts than any other city in the United Kingdom save Belfast'.[124]

In 1819, an Orange procession, attributed to 'Manchester men', caused Liverpool's 'first Orange–Catholic riot'.[125] Orangeism was underdeveloped locally at this stage, having no particular value to wealthier Protestants. Indeed, Liverpool had only one Orange lodge in 1815, mainly comprising army personnel whom had served in Ireland. Even by 1830 this number had grown to only three.[126] The attack on the 1819 parade by Irish Catholics did not dissuade Orangemen, and processions took place in 1820 and 1821. Yet

[123] See Neal, 1991.
[124] Bohstedt, 1992: 202–3.
[125] Neal, 1990–1: 17.
[126] Ibid., 19, 40. Counterintuitively, Waller (1981: 12) states that Liverpool contained

following this no further Orange processions were held until 1842. Yet the 'Twelfth' was marked, even without processions, by disturbances, which occurred in public houses on that date on an annual basis from the 1820s. Concurrently, Irish Catholics made their presence known by high attendance at St Patrick's Day parades, of up to 12,000 people.[127] Lamb and Smallpage claim that 'riotous disorder' was often attendant to such occasions.[128]

In 1835, fallacious rumours of an Orange parade on the 'Twelfth' prompted a riot involving 2,000 Irishmen, requiring over 500 police and 200 troops to preserve order.[129] The riot provided an opportunity for the Tories to challenge local Liberal hegemony, utilising the negative image of the Irish for electoral purposes. Davis suggests that, 'sectarian violence was encouraged by militant Protestants for political ends. The legitimacy afforded to racial and religious bigotry by council officials, clergymen, and in newspapers, served to endorse street violence and indiscriminate attacks on Irish Catholics'.[130] The Conservatives became apt at establishing religion as a potent weapon in political affairs after the 1835 reform of local government meant that the fight for political control of Liverpool was open to a wider electorate.

Also in 1835, the Reverend Dr Hugh McNeile formed the *Liverpool Protestant Association*. McNeile was an educated man who came from a wealthy Irish Family. He was an Anglican, and became the most prominent voice (in a competitive field) of anti-Catholicism in nineteenth-century Liverpool. His reputation was such that virulent anti-Catholic attitudes became known as 'McNeilite attitudes'.[131] He had allies in the Orange Order and the Liverpool Conservative Party and heavily influenced the political divide. Partly because of McNeile, 'Protestantism became the Tories' electoral charm'.[132] In the 1840s, the Conservatives 'demanded that no prayers should be recited in the Council schools save those to be found in the Anglican liturgy, and that no teachers should be appointed outside those who professed the Protestant faith as defined by Dr McNeile'.[133] It was

thirteen Orange lodges in 1830. However, Neal cites a Select Committee report detailing the locations and dates of meetings in an appendix.
[127] Neal, 1988: 40–1.
[128] Lamb and Smallpage, 1935: 59.
[129] Neal, 1988: 41–2.
[130] Davis, 1991: 156.
[131] Waller, 1981: 12.
[132] Ibid., 11.
[133] Burke, 1910: 67.

claimed that 'no potential Tory councillor could hope to achieve public office unless he was established, in McNeile's eyes, as a "sound Protestant"'.[134] The provocative clergyman was 'a brilliant controversialist, intelligent, eloquent and pugnacious, and he was utterly opposed to Roman Catholicism'.[135] His 'no-popery' sermons captivated an attentive protestant audience, and although he preached against the Catholic hierarchy rather than individual Catholics, the subtlety of that distinction was often lost on his audience. His role in Liverpool was such that Gilley describes him as, 'the city's Ian Paisley' who 'bridged the gap between the middle-class *Protestant Association* and the working-class *Protestant Operatives*, thereby confirming the city's immersion in a long and bloody [sectarian] civil war'.[136]

In 1844, the *Catholic Club* was founded by Robert Sheil to counter McNeile's *Protestant Association*. As Bohstedt suggests, 'the low pay and casual work of the docks created a vacuum of "traditional" labour organizations, and that vacuum was filled by sectarian organisations which provided both the social services and the emotionally satisfying solidarities found elsewhere in the labour movements'.[137] These early 'sectarian organisations' portrayed a visible divide among the working classes and helped establish religion as a *badge* of identity, as 'marchers with green and orange ribbons were flaunting their allegiance … rather than their belief'.[138]

McNeile and his followers set out to politicise and 'make religious' the Protestant working class in Liverpool; first by a tirade of 'non-stop lectures and sermons on the evils of popery, including the thesis that there was a conspiracy to overthrow the Church of England', and secondly by alleging that 'Liberals were Catholic sympathisers [and] urging those with votes that it was their Christian duty to vote for Conservative candidates'.[139] Although it could be argued that the Tories were simply using religion as a useful tool for electoral dominance, the same sentiments cannot be directed at McNeile, who genuinely detested Roman Catholicism. The *Liverpool Mercury* claimed that McNeile stated, 'He hated popery, he was born and bred to hate it. He hated it through life and he would continue to hate it through death'.[140]

---

[134] Day, 2008: 274.
[135] Neal, 1988: 44.
[136] Gilley, 2000: 159.
[137] Bohstedt, 1992: 203.
[138] Waller, 1981: 12.
[139] Neal, 1988: 49.
[140] Ibid., 50, citing the *Liverpool Mercury*, 24 April 1842.

McNeile died in 1879, but his sermons and political influence had helped establish the divide in both Liverpool politics (election day in 1837, for example, had been marked by rioting) and among Liverpool's working classes.

By 1842, the Orange Order had grown significantly enough to begin regular Twelfth of July parades in Liverpool. By this time sectarian violence was very much a feature of life. In July 1845, an Orange funeral procession, which marched down Scotland Road, 'sparked a four hour riot, described by police as one of the worst (thus far) with peace eventually achieved only when Catholic priests persuaded the Irish to stop fighting'.[141] By this point, according to Macilwee, 'sectarian mobs, drawn from Orange and Catholic communities' were 'united by a common religious cause [and] became galvanised by their hatred for each other'.[142]

By the late 1850s, the Twelfth of July parade was marked annually by disturbances. Orangemen had started carrying pistols, and often discharged them in the air when passing Catholic areas. Several sectarian shootings resulted in fatalities.[143] It could be claimed that some Orangemen where carrying pistols for protection, as the Irish often attacked processions and individuals. For example, in July 1851, 1,000 Irishmen 'launched an attack' and in retaliation 'pistols were fired by Orangemen'.[144] Sectarian disturbances were by no means confined to the 'flagship' dates of the Twelfth of July and Seventeenth of March. Notable other examples included the 'papal aggression' riot in Birkenhead in 1850 and street violence in the slums of Liverpool between 1850 and 1860, whilst there was also the Fenian campaign in 1867,[145] a failed attempt by two 'Fenian' Irishmen to blow up part of Liverpool Town Hall on 10 June 1881,[146] and the Home Rule riots of 1886.[147]

---

[141] Neal, 1988: 62.

[142] Macilwee, 2008: 14.

[143] For example, in 1850, Henry Wright (an Orangeman) was charged with 'having shot at and wounded John Sangstar, thereby causing his death'. The article headline was 'Riot between Orangemen and Irish in Chadwick Steet – Four persons shot'. *Liverpool Courier*, 17 July 1850.

[144] Neal, 1988: 134–5.

[145] An ill-fated insurrection aimed at toppling British rule and establishing an Irish Republic.

[146] *The Colonist*, 25 (2925) (5 August 1881), 'Attempt to Blow up the Liverpool Town Hall', cited by Papers Past. Available at: http://paperspast.natlib.govt.nz/cgi-bin/paperspast?a=d &d=TC18810805.2.11&e=-------10--1----0--.

[147] For an in-depth description of these occurrences, see Neal, 1988.

Between 1886 and 1889, 'thirty instances of riot occurred'[148] and MacRaild suggests that by this point 'Liverpool was more divided than it had been forty years earlier, when the Famine and the Protestant agitator Hugh McNeile had helped shape the cultural terrain'.[149] McNeile's role of Protestant orator and rabble-rouser was taken up by another man: Pastor George Wise.

Wise, a Protestant and Conservative, moved to Liverpool in 1888, aged thirty. He became known as the 'anti-infidel lecturer' and would later come to 'dominate Liverpool'.[150] Wise was to become much loved by the Protestant working class in the city, so much so that when he decided to contest the School Board Election in 1902 he not only won but polled 107,063 votes.[151] He was later elected local councillor for Kirkdale ward in 1903, standing as an independent Protestant. He resigned from the council three years later to maintain his position as pastor of the Protestant Reformers' Memorial Church, which he had founded, a post he retained until his death. Wise's sermons were often replicated in the *Protestant Standard*, broadening his appeal to those who did not attend his public lectures as well as the upper echelons of Liverpool Protestant society. In 1891, The *Standard* described Wise as a 'gifted and eloquent lecturer'.[152] Conversely, he was labelled as 'The Everton mob-leader'[153] by the *Liverpool Catholic Herald* in 1909, as his inflammatory speeches often resulted in sectarian disturbances. Perhaps most aptly, the demagogue was identified as a 'Protestant crusader and menace to authorities'.[154]

Upon arrival in Liverpool Wise's focus was on organising an excess of public speeches intent on highlighting and eradicating 'popish' elements of the established Protestant Church. In 1898, Wise established the *British Protestant Union*, the aims of which were to fight 'Romanism, Ritualism and Infidelity'.[155] In this, he gained support from the Orange Institution, whose leadership were appalled at the 'ritualistic abuses within the Church

---

[148] Waller, 1981: 92.

[149] MacRaild, 1999: 179.

[150] Waller, 1981: 117.

[151] Henderson, 1967: 7: 'George Wise of Liverpool, Protestant stalwart, twice imprisoned for the Gospel's sake'.

[152] *Protestant Standard*, 18 July 1891.

[153] *Liverpool Catholic Herald*, 17 July 1909.

[154] Waller, 1981: 517.

[155] Neal, 1988: 201.

of England'.[156] Wise's 'anti-ritual warfare',[157] therefore, was an attractive proposition, if only a prelude to a series of vehement anti-Catholic sermons. His Protestant demonstrations could attract up to 15,000 spectators.[158] Wise's '"Protestant Crusade" led to clashes with Roman Catholics ... winding up tensions by arranging a series of public lectures that, because of their location and content, were bound to arouse Catholic passions'.[159] Acting as the 'mouthpiece' for the Orange Order, he would make public protests directed at Roman Catholicism. These demonstrations, often staged in close proximity to Catholic areas, resulted in civil unrest. When faced with police opposition to plans for future meetings 'Wise turned the issue into a defence of the principle of free speech ... enmities [created by Wise] survived long beyond [his] death'.[160]

In August 1902, John Kensit (Junior) came to preach in Liverpool, launching an anti-Ritualist campaign. The orator's popularity in Liverpool had been secured by addresses he had made in the city prior to his permanent arrival. In 1899, the strength of Kensit's support was suggested by the *Standard*, which claimed that the venue (Hope Hall) 'cannot be expected to hold one twentieth of the part of those who will wish to hear Mr Kensit [speak on anti-Ritualism]'.[161] For many, Ritualism was synonymous with Catholicism.

In 1902, Kensit's public rhetoric prompted public disorder, and he was imprisoned for 'refusing to be bound over to "keep the peace", which meant not holding open air meetings'.[162] The attendant press coverage and the protest meetings of Orange lodges and the Working Men's Christian Association (WMCA) alerted George Wise to the potential of martyrdom, and he was jailed in 1903 and 1909, blaming 'Popish mob rule' for his fate. As with Kensit, public meetings and processions followed Wise's impris-onment.[163] Prior to this, however, John Kensit (senior) travelled to Liverpool to lead the campaign for his son's release. Kensit (senior) himself became a 'martyr' when, on 25 September 1902, a two-foot (60 centimetre) iron file was thrown at him on a Mersey landing stage in Birkenhead. As a

---

[156] *Protestant Standard*, 15 July 1899.
[157] *Protestant Standard*, 16 July 1898.
[158] *Protestant Standard*, 9 July 1898.
[159] Bullough, 1990: 26
[160] Ibid., 27.
[161] *Protestant Standard*,15 July 1899.
[162] Henderson, 1967: 7.
[163] Bullough, 1990: 28.

result of public protest, 'the Home Secretary ordered the release of Kensit (Junior) from prison, but not before his father had died from the injuries he had received'.[164] Meanwhile, the *Catholic Herald* complained, 'wherever the [Protestant] lecturers go they seem to be followed by the rousing of angry passions and the stimulating of sectarian bitterness'.[165]

Throughout the period there was anticipation and almost an appetite for sectarian violence: a distraction from the tedium of everyday life in the Liverpool slums. Pat O'Mara described a serious sectarian riot almost as though it was an annual sporting event. The term 'opposition', which would today more commonly be used in relation to a football match, was utilised in and entirely different sense by O'Mara, who describes how 'the opposition [made] a serious mistake ... The little child who impersonated King Billy on his white charger had his head staved in with a brick, falling off the horse bleeding and screaming with pain'.[166]

Liverpool's most vicious sectarian disturbances took place in the summer of 1909, when 'sectarian civil war' was manifest.[167] The Provincial Grand Lodge arranged a counter demonstration to a Catholic procession and a fierce riot ensued. The fighting and animosity that took place in the weeks following the procession were unparalleled in Liverpool's history. Hundreds were arrested for violent assaults and vandalism, as each denomination intimidated the other out of 'their' areas: 'Houses were marked to denote the creeds of their inhabitants, and beatings and looting ensued as partisans aimed to enforce religious segregation in the Netherfield and Scotland areas a monopoly of faith'.[168] What occurred was a form of ethno-religious cleansing, as thousands of Catholics and Protestants were intimidated out of their homes and into areas where their own denomination was dominant. This segregation and the religious ghettos that the riots had reinforced persisted until the slum clearances of the 1960s.

In an attempt to repair shattered community relations, the city council requested a Government Inquiry.[169] In the report, released in March 1910, Roman Catholics had attributed sole responsibility for the riots to George

---

[164] Henderson, 1967: 8.

[165] *Liverpool Catholic Herald*, 24 July 1909.

[166] O'Mara, 1933: 66.

[167] Waller, 1981: 237.

[168] Ibid., 238.

[169] Midwinter, 1971: 174, citing Ashton, 1910 ('The Liverpool Religious Riots. The Commissioner's Report').

Wise, with the Commission broadly in agreement. Wise had been sentenced to four months' imprisonment in 1909, with 100,000 people accompanying him to the prison,[170] although it also stated that Orange Order activities were to blame (a point addressed in the following chapter). Additionally, Protestant accusations of police partiality towards Catholics were dismissed.[171] Ironically, the police had also been under intense scrutiny in the mid-nineteenth century for alleged Orange bias. Despite Ron Henderson's suggestion that 'the final report was of a most pacificatory character',[172] Wise's inflammatory sermons were held responsible for much of the turmoil; Catholics testified that they could 'live in peace with Orangemen and other Protestants, but found Wise's particular artistry with insults intolerable as it kept alive bitter sectarian feuding'.[173] Yet, as Waller attests, 'Wise did not cause Liverpool's sectarianism; he activated it'.[174] George Wise died in 1917, but his influence was such that as late as the 1960s, Neal recalls talking to Roman Catholics who didn't refer to Protestants, they referred instead to Wiseites.[175]

In 1919, Reverend Harry Longbottom, who had been invited to Liverpool by Wise in 1913, assumed responsibility for the Protestant Reformers Memorial Church.[176] Like Wise, Longbottom held his post in the Memorial Church until his death. He maintained the taste for open-air 'debates', stating that, 'Protestantism is an open air plant. It thrives in strong winds of opposition'.[177] As such, he continued much of Wise's work, including the 'Cromwell Club' debates, one of which was entitled, 'Ireland and the war – can she be trusted?'[178]

Tensions re-arose in the build-up to the partition of Ireland. The Orange Order in Liverpool had bitterly opposed Irish Home Rule; for many Protestants, this was simply a synonym for 'Rome Rule'. To Liverpool's

---

[170] Bohstedt, 1992: 187.

[171] Neal, 1988: 238–40.

[172] Henderson, 1967: 15.

[173] Bohstedt, 1992: 191.

[174] Waller, 1981: 240.

[175] Frank Neal, 12 February 2010.

[176] Upon Wise's death, the relatively moderate Pastor T.B. Wilmot briefly took control of Wise's church, but, following a drastic curtailment of the open-air work, divisions arose. Wilmot left and Longbottom returned as the haranguer.

[177] Henderson, 1978: 9.

[178] Ibid., citing accounts from the Minute Book of Cromwell meetings, held by Ian Henderson.

Orange Loyalists, Longbottom denounced 'the "alien priesthood" stirring up war in Ireland', and supported Councillor John Walker (Orangeman and Protestant Party councillor), who, on the same platform as Longbottom, added that 'if necessary, the Liverpool brethren would fight with their Ulster colleagues'.[179]

Professor Diarmaid Ferriter cites that, around the same period, the Liverpool Battalion of the IRA had 'about 130 active volunteers', who 'smuggled arms, set fire to property in Liverpool and attacked the homes of Black and Tans whose addresses had been secured by raiding the mail in Ireland'.[180] This is actually a surprisingly low figure given the potential recruitment base for Republican volunteers in the city[181] and may owe something to the Anglicisation policy of Liverpool's Roman Catholic hierarchy. While, by 1918 there was 'an extensive network for trafficking arms out of the Clyde and the Mersey to Ireland ... the exertions of Sinn Féin largely passed by the Liverpool Irish, for whom moderate constitutionalism (advocated by the city's Irish Nationalist politicians) had become both accepted and successful'.[182] Nonetheless, this era was potentially explosive. Some Liverpool Irish volunteers had fought in the Easter Rising in Dublin in 1916 and a local battalion of Óglaigh na hÉireann (soldiers of Ireland) were active during the Irish War of Independence.[183] As such, and given the sectarian volatility in the port, it is feasible that any civil war between Protestants and Catholics in Ireland (particularly in Ulster) could have spilt onto the streets of Liverpool.

Longbottom benefited from such tensions. In 1922, he was elected to the Board of Guardians (Poor Law administrators) as an independent Protestant. and from 1926 he served on the council as a member of the newly established Protestant Party. He also enjoyed a stint as Lord Mayor in 1950–1, as well as presiding as Grand Master of the Orange Order from 1946 until 1956. Longbottom became the new voice of militant Protestantism in Liverpool, leading the opposition against the sale of land on Brownlow Hill, where the Catholic Cathedral now stands. He infamously stated, 'I would sooner have a poison germ factory than a Roman Catholic Cathedral on the

---

[179] Bullough, 1990: 44–5.

[180] Ferriter, 2004: 225.

[181] The 130 IRA volunteers in Liverpool contrasts starkly with a reputed 4,000 IRA volunteers in Glasgow during the same period: MacRaild, 1999: 152.

[182] Ibid., 152–3; O'Connell, 1971: 238.

[183] *Cairde na hÉireann Liverpool*, 'Under Pressure', 3.

site. After all, a poison germ factory can at worst only poison the body ...
such a Cathedral would poison the mind as well'.[184] Nevertheless, the Pastor
would operate during a relatively more peaceful period in the city's history
than had Wise.

As Boyce asserts, other than during ritualised trouble on 'Orange Day'
and St Patrick's Day, 'by the 1930s, sectarian street violence had almost
disappeared'.[185] Although sectarianism was still a ubiquitous issue in the city,
and 'Longbottom's political position depended on surviving sectarianism',[186]
it would never again reach the excesses experienced in 1909. Longbottom
died in 1962, making him perhaps the last of Liverpool's 'Protestant Popes'.[187]

Academics generally agree that in the nineteenth and early twentieth
centuries Liverpool experienced a higher and 'more bitter and chronic'
level of Protestant–Catholic violence than any other area on the British
mainland.[188] Nonetheless, it is noted that different accounts of the past can
prompt divergent perspectives. Whilst the Catholic Bishop Tom Williams
recalls, 'we [Liverpool] were in danger of becoming like Belfast in the
1960s',[189] Bullough believes Liverpool to have been but a 'ritualised dilution
of the Ulster capital'.[190] The city's experience of sectarian violence must be
put into perspective. In terms of sectarian atrocities it is difficult to make a
serious parallel between the two cities. As Quiery contends, 'sectarianism in
Liverpool was never as violent as in Belfast. Somebody was beaten to death
in Liverpool in 1909, but at the same time people were being crucified on
their back doors in Belfast with hammers and nails'.[191] Nonetheless, from
the 1820s until at least the 1960s, sectarianism was a disturbing and often
defining feature of Liverpool life.

[184] Ian Henderson, Presentation in Bootle Protestant Free Church Saturday, 27 October
2012.
[185] Boyce, 1999: 282.
[186] Waller, 1981: 303.
[187] Midwinter (1971: 187) claims that 'Pastor Wise saw himself in a twin reincarnation
between Martin Luther and William III'. Longbottom certainly mimicked Wise in this
respect.
[188] Belchem, Bohstedt, Gallagher, McRaild, Neal, and Waller contend this point.
[189] Bishop Tom Williams, 23 March 2010.
[190] Bullough, 1990: 10.
[191] Greg Quiery, 25 March 2013.

2

The Influence of the Orange Order

The main purpose of this chapter is to explain the prominence of the Orange Institution on Merseyside. In so doing, it is necessary to portray how Orangeism was established in England and how Liverpool became the focal point of its powerbase, before chronicling how Orangeism eventually declined in the second half of the twentieth century. The following chapter analyses the decline of the Orange Order, and assesses to what extent the decline of the Orange Institution on Merseyside contributed to the overall decline of sectarianism. How much did a shift of focus away from religious and constitutional issues by the Merseyside populace impact on the size and strength of the Order and what further effect on intercommunal relations was yielded by the decline of the Institution?

The Development of English Orangeism

In November 1688, in Exeter Cathedral, the 'first Orange meeting' took place, in the presence of William, Prince of Orange.[1] It was here that the first 'Orange Association' was formed to assist William 'in defence of the Protestant Religion and the Liberties of England'.[2] The first subscribers to this Orange Association vowed to join the prince in his fight against the Catholic monarch, James II, and swore allegiance to God, William and each other to 'stick firm to the cause ... and never to depart until our religion, laws and liberties are so far secured to us in a free Parliament that they shall be no more in danger of falling into Popery and slavery'.[3]

---

[1] Rodgers, 1881: 8; Orange Pages (website), 'The First Orange Association'. Available at: www.orange-pages.tk/histindex.htm?http://www.orange-pages.tk/whatis.

[2] Independent Loyal Orange Institution, 'History'. Available at: www.iloi.org/history/.

[3] Rodgers, 1881: 8.

Orangeism was 'perpetuated through a loose confederation of Orange societies and clubs',[4] but in the eighteenth century 'Orangemen were few',[5] a small concentration of affiliates in various districts of Ireland where the Protestant Ascendancy held. It was not until the last decade of the eighteenth century, following disturbances in County Armagh, that 'the Orange Order, as we know it, was formed ... after the Battle of the Diamond in 1795'.[6]

The rules and regulations were first published for the Grand Lodge of Ireland in 1801,[7] authenticating its role in issuing warrants for the formation of lodges, a practice in which it was already well versed owing to its 'organisational structure [based] on the freemason system of lodges'.[8] In the first decades of the nineteenth century the principal centre for Orangeism in England was Manchester.[9] On 13 July 1807, an Orange parade in the city was attacked by Irish Roman Catholics, and a riot subsequently ensued, requiring the army to intervene.[10] This event has been cited as 'the English equivalent to the Battle of the Diamond',[11] as it acted as the precursor to the formation of the Grand County Lodge of Lancashire in 1807, and the Grand Lodge of England in 1808, both based in Manchester. From thereon, 'the original Irish warrants were cancelled, and henceforth the English lodges obtained their credentials from the new Grand Lodge [of England]'.[12] The English Grand Lodge kept up the Irish tradition of issuing military warrants to individual soldiers.[13]

By 1811, there were twenty-three Orange lodges in Manchester, by far the highest concentration in the country. Most lodges in England were

[4] Orange Pages, 'The First Orange Association'.

[5] Rodgers, 1881: 18.

[6] Grand Orange Lodge of Ireland (website), 'The first 100 years of Orangeism'. Available at: www.grandorangelodge.co.uk/history.aspx?id=99485.

[7] *Liverpool Catholic Herald*, 6 July 1900.

[8] Gray, 1972: 15, 52.

[9] Herbert, M. (2010) 'Rioting between the Orange Order and the Irish in Manchester', Manchester's Radical History (website). Available at: http://radicalmanchester.wordpress.com/2010/03/31/rioting-between-the-orange-order-and-the-irish-in-manchester/.

[10] Manchester Orange (website), 'History of the Orange Order in Manchester'. Available at: www.manchesterorange.co.uk/History/manchester-orange-order-history.

[11] Ibid.

[12] Herbert, 2010.

[13] Orange Lodge (website), 'L.O.L. 2123, Hamilton', Ontario. Available at: http://orangelodge.com/app/directory/113/l-o-l-2123-hamilton.

located in 'places of industrial unrest',[14] and Orangemen were allegedly used 'as spies to infiltrate meetings of workers'.[15] This point supports the supposition that 'the Orange Order was a useful organisation ... to deploy against ... radicals and reformers'.[16] MacRaild believes that in the early 1800s, owing to a 'revolutionary threat ... and the historic strength of anti-Catholicism', the Orange Order was viewed 'in quite instrumental terms', as 'Orangeism could be employed to divert working-class activities from Luddism, or general political insurrection, through anti-Catholicism and popular Protestantism towards patriotism and loyalism'.[17] As such, it is feasible that 'the possibilities of the Orange Order for counter-revolutionary activities'[18] were key considerations for those who established the English Grand Lodge.

For ordinary Protestants, the value of the Order was its role as a benefit society and burial club, the provision of recreational and social activities (often via meetings in public houses), coupled with an increased degree of job security, as 'lodge officials were often foremen or employers in the locality'.[19] There was also an 'element of genuine working-class Protestantism on the part of many members, separate from middle-class concerns over the establishment'.[20] Another attraction was the esteemed company that the Orange Order bestowed upon its working-class members, friendly relations with prominent clergymen and Grand Masters an advantage of membership. As Neal notes, 'For the less educated working men the Orange lodge offered conviviality, companionship, colour in its ceremonies ... In Liverpool the Orange Association and Institution gave relief to members who fell on hard times, not only Liverpool men but Orangemen from all over England while they were in Liverpool'.[21]

In 1819, a convoy from Manchester bolstered Liverpool's solitary lodge in its first Twelfth of July parade. Two thousand Irish Catholics attacked the parade and the port's first sectarian riot ensued. The band of Orangemen (even when bolstered with support from Manchester) is reputed to have

---

[14] Neal, 1990–1: 16.

[15] Ibid.

[16] Herbert, 2010.

[17] MacRaild, 1999: 111.

[18] Neal, 1990–1: 14.

[19] Ibid., 17.

[20] Ibid., 18.

[21] Neal, 1988: 171.

numbered only ninety,[22] a comparatively small amount paralleled to the many thousands who presided in the rest of Lancashire at this time. Despite this, neither Liverpool Orangemen, nor their Manchester compatriots, were deterred by the attack upon their parade, and another procession and riot occurred the following year. These early occurrences of sectarian disorder, in highlighting what was perceived as the 'threat' of Irish Catholicism, 'brought Protestants into the Orange Order'.[23] Nonetheless, in 1830, of Lancashire's seventy-seven lodges, only three located in Liverpool.[24]

By 1835, fears that the Duke of Cumberland, Grand Master of England, might displace the King with the help of the military lodges of the Orange Order, led to the establishment of a House of Commons Select Committee inquiry into Orange Lodges in Great Britain,[25] the results of which are concisely described by Michael Herbert:

> The report condemned the Order for provoking trouble between Protestants and Catholics and in response the [Duke of] Cumberland formally dissolved the organisation. It soon reappeared, however, in two forms – the *Orange Institution* and the *Orange Association* – which eventually united in 1874. In the wake of the Irish Famine and the huge Irish emigration into Lancashire the heartland of the movement moved to Liverpool, although there continued to be branches in Manchester and nearby towns.[26]

The Select Committee had stated that Orange parades excited 'one portion of the people against the other [and made] the Protestant the enemy of the Catholic and the Catholic the enemy of the Protestant' giving rise to 'breaches of the peace and bloodshed'.[27] What followed was 'a wave of negative publicity and the leadership dissolved the Order's official structures'.[28] It was not merely the adverse publicity of the report that led to

[22] Liverpool Province Loyal Orange Lodge (website), 'Liverpool History. Liverpool has a Turbulent History'. Available at: http://archie844.tripod.com/liverpoolprovinceoran-gelodge/id8.html.

[23] Orange Pages, 'The First Orange Association'.

[24] Neal, 1990–1: 19, citing figures from a 'Report on Orange Lodges (GB)' (1835). (Appendix 19 in Neal's study.)

[25] Committee on the Origin Institutions in Great Britain and the Colonies, British Parliamentary Papers, 1835, XVII (605), XV–XVI, Append. 204–20; CMSIED 9508167.

[26] Herbert, 2010.

[27] Neal, 1990–1: 21, citing British Parliamentary Papers, 1835.

[28] MacRaild, 1999: 112.

the dissolution of the organisation, but also 'a threat of legal sanctions'[29] and a loss of respectability for the Order.

Following this suspension, and in the interim period before its official restoration, a rechristening of de facto Orange lodges, as 'Operative Conservative Associations', helped ensure the survival of Orangeism in England. A Manchester newspaper carried a leading article claiming that such associations 'were Orange lodges in disguise'.[30] The move fortified an already sturdy link between the English Orange Order and the Conservative Party.

In May 1836, the survival of Orangeism was ensured as 'Orangemen from all over the country attended a meeting at the Ramsden Arms, near Huddersfield. The outcome was a new organisation called the Grand Protestant Confederation'.[31] By 1841, the Grand Protestant Confederation was transposed by the Orange Institution (Liverpool based) and the Orange Association, a broadly national body. The two factions would unite in 1874, supplementing the strength of English Orangeism, the nucleus of which was now firmly rooted in Liverpool.

As MacRaild notes, 'from well before the Famine years, Liverpool led the way for British Orangeism. No other town or city could match either its unique Irish composition or the great weight of its Orange tradition'.[32] By 1842, the year of Liverpool's first formal Orange procession for twenty-two years, the concentration of Orange strength had shifted from Manchester. Throughout the 1820s and 1830s, 'Irish Catholics [in Liverpool] by force of number and/or reputation were able to prevent the Orange Order from [regularly] taking to the streets on the Twelfth of July'.[33] This situation had changed by the mid-century owing to the growth, in size and stature, of the Liverpool Institution.

As the perceived threat of revolution began to rescind, the use of the Institution for Lancashire mill owners became less obvious and the focus of Orange activity switched to Liverpool sectarianism. The 1835 Select Committee report had also made the organisation less appealing to the aristocracy, and the tendency for Orange processions to turn ugly put off some middle-class Protestants. By 1875, Liverpool had two Orange lodges

---

[29] Neal, 1990–1: 21.
[30] *Manchester Guardian*, 5 September 1835, cited ibid.
[31] Neal, 1990–1: 22–3.
[32] MacRaild, 1999: 113.
[33] Belchem, 2000: 90.

for each one in Manchester. By the end of the nineteenth century, this ratio was four to one.[34] The last riot in Manchester in connection with an Orange procession occurred in 1888.[35]

In Liverpool, anti Irish-Catholic hostility 'retarded the development of a labour movement into the next century'.[36] In its place was a bond between the 'muscle' of Orangemen and the influence of the Conservative Party which would yield mutually profitable dividends.[37] The local Conservative political machine of Archibald Salvidge (1863–1928) was 'underpinned by the violent street culture of no-popery zealots such as John Kensit and George Wise, who could whip up Orange-Protestant violence in an instant'.[38]

The Strength of Liverpool Orangeism

Liverpool Orangeism was not limited to a collective of expatriate Protestant Ulstermen. In contrast, it was 'pan-nationalistic',[39] the Institution 'recruiting strongly among workers with no Ulster connections'.[40] Although its core strength lay in its working-class membership, admission was unrestricted in respect to social standing. The only prerequisite was that the applicant was a 'Protestant in reality and truth' and not married to nor parent of a member of the 'Church of Rome'.[41] The Orange Order was 'aggressively anti-Irish Catholic and reflected the virulent anti-Catholicism of Victorian Great Britain'.[42] Faced with a numerically large and predominantly Catholic Irish diaspora, putting pressure on both the rates and labour market, the Liverpool Orange Institution enjoyed considerable backing. It was thus claimed:

[34] Lodge statistics cited by Reginald Chadwick, Master of Loyal Orange Lodge, 184.
[35] Herbert, 2010.
[36] Neal, 1990–1: 23.
[37] Liverpool Province Loyal Orange Lodge (website), 'Liverpool History. Liverpool has a Turbulent History': 'In the nineteenth century the [Orange] movement became very closely linked to the dominant Conservative and Unionist Party.'
[38] MacRaild, 2002–/3: 105–6.
[39] Ibid., 108.
[40] Belchem, 2000b: 124.
[41] Loyal Orange Institution of England, 'Laws and Constitution Enacted by the Grand Lodge of England', 11 January 1975. Liverpool, L.O.L., 36.
[42] Neal, 2006: 69.

Liverpool has long had a reputation of being an 'Irish city', and in purely numerical terms this was so ... But, numbers aside, it would be more accurate to describe Liverpool as an Orange city ... The 1841 general election had the *Liverpool Mail* sporting the headline, 'No Popery on the Rates' ... Also in that year, 60 of the 390-member police force declared themselves to be members of the Orange Lodge ... In 1848, Orange paranoia really set in and the St Patrick's Day march saw 3,455 Special Constables sworn in along with troops of the 11 Hussars, 60th Rifles and the 52nd Regiment besides the entire police force which was now said to be 70% Orange.[43]

By 1854–5, 86 per cent of the English Orange Order members belonged to Liverpool lodges.[44] By 1860, 'the Orange Institution was almost entirely a Liverpool affair. At the Grand Lodge of the Institution, held in July 1860, of the thirty-four officials who attended, twenty-eight were from Liverpool.[45]

An early portrayal of Orange strength came in the form of direct opposition to the building of Catholic places of worship. New chapels became the focus of Orange aggression. It is telling of the strength of anti-Catholic sentiment in the port, even as early as the 1820s, that some of these churches were being built in the style of 'Nonconformist chapels', ostensibly to 'appease the local Protestant population'.[46] Nonetheless, Orangemen invariably directed their attention to anything remotely 'Fenian' in complexion.

On Park Lane, in the Dingle area of Liverpool, stands St Patrick's Chapel (an example of such a 'Nonconformist' styled church), opened in 1823 to accommodate the amassing Roman Catholic population. The western wall is dominated by a statue of St Patrick and, added much later, a large Celtic Cross memorial to the ten 'Famine Priests' who died during the typhus epidemic (or, as it was then described, the 'Irish fever') of 1847. Throughout the famine years, 'the Orange Lodge repeatedly attempted to storm the chapel in order to bring down the statue of Patrick'.[47] Of the instances, Burke wrote that, in 1841, 1844, and 1848, 'again and again, with ladders

---

[43] Saoirse – Irish Freedom (website), 'Orangeism and the Irish in Liverpool'. Available at: http://homepage.tinet.ie/~eirenua/mar99/saoirse4.htm.

[44] Day, 2011: 61, citing Phelan, 'Orangeism Resurgent' (Loyal Orange Institution of England).

[45] Neal, 1988: 172, citing the *Liverpool Herald*, 14 July 1860.

[46] Crowley, 2012: 139, citing Sharples, 2004: 271.

[47] Crowley, 2012: 119–20.

and ropes, the Orangemen of Toxteth sought to pull down the statue',[48] purportedly leaving their mark as a rope broke off one of the effigy's fingers. Although magistrates sought to curtail such attacks,

> The police seemed quite indifferent to performing an obvious duty. The Grand Master of the Orangemen sat on the Watch Committee [the regulatory body of the local constabulary], and too many of the humbler members of the force had secured appointment by joining the Orange organisation ... Under the guidance of the Orange Grand Master, the Watch Committee ... took measures to find out the religion of every member of the force, with the object of removing Catholic policemen.[49]

Another imposing Catholic church, St Francis Xavier, was targeted in 1853, when 'the congregation were startled by the sound of angry voices outside, followed by volleys of stones driven through the windows'.[50]

In 1842, the local Watch Committee decreed that 'Orangemen must either leave the Order or leave the police', but two years later 'the mayor received a complaint that sixty policemen were members of Orange lodges'.[51] Further evidence of partisanship occurred during the Orange parade of 1851, when 'Orangemen in the procession fired pistols in the air and police [reputedly] cheered'.[52] More notably, after the disturbances, in which 'Orangemen had beat several Irishmen to the ground while the police looked on ... seventy people, remarkably enough all Irish, had been arrested and taken into custody [while] no Orangemen were charged'.[53]

Although it was not always to the taste of the Orange hierarchy,[54] members had no problem in preparing themselves for confrontation. In July 1850, in response to an 'unprovoked attack' upon his property, following a riot between Orangemen and Irishmen, 'four persons were shot' by Henry Wright (an Orangeman).[55] In 1900, some amongst the ranks of the Twelfth of July procession were said to have been 'carrying swords' and called

[48] Burke, 1910: 92.
[49] Ibid., 76–7.
[50] Burke, 1910: 113.
[51] Neal, 1988: 61, 139, citing *Liverpool Mail*, 21 September 1844.
[52] Ibid., citing *Catholic Standard*, 26 July 1851.
[53] Neal, 1988: 136.
[54] 'Many of the leading officers restrained from taking part in the procession owing to a desire to put an end to them': *Liverpool Daily Post*, 13 July 1870.
[55] *Liverpool Courier*, 17 July 1850.

upon the '___ Papists' to come on.[56] In 1930, 'disturbances arising out of Orange Day procession scenes occupied the greater part of proceedings the following morning in the ... Liverpool Police Court'.[57] During the procession, a 'terrified crowd' watched as 'policemen had to draw their batons and form a line between the parties in order to prevent a fight'.[58] Roy Hughes, a former leader of the Liverpool Protestant Party, recalls joining a lodge in Heyworth Street, colloquially referred to as 'The Fighting Ivy', who 'quite literally would fight their way in and out of Liverpool on the Twelfth of July', adding 'it suited my temperament at that time. I wanted to fight for the cause'.[59]

That desire to 'fight for the cause' indicated the strength of Orange identity. The requisite of exhibiting 'party colours' was such that some people who could not afford to flaunt an orange ribbon or lily would 'simply wear orange peel to show which side they were on'.[60] A similar practice was also utilised by Roman Catholics, who, to display their affiliation, 'would wear watercress or mustard cress, in place of a shamrock'.[61]

It has been estimated, by the Grand Master of Liverpool, that as late as the 1940s the membership of the Orange Institution on Merseyside was approximately 50,000[62] (this figure contrasts with a cited Liverpool membership of 20,000, in 1909),[63] while throughout most of the twentieth century its annual Twelfth of July parades could consistently attract upwards of 10,000 participants and spectators.[64] In 2006, the *Orange Standard* claimed that, 'as recently as the 1950s the Liverpool Orange parade was around 10,000 strong, while in the 1930s it was twice that number'.[65] In fact, in 1960, the parade was said to have attracted 'nearly 30,000 Orangemen',[66] and, as late as 1985, 20,000 people were reportedly still being enticed to the annual event.[67] The strength of the Orange

---

[56] *Liverpool Catholic Herald*, 20 July 1900.

[57] *Liverpool Echo*, 15 July 1930.

[58] Ibid.

[59] Roy Hughes, 13 November 2012.

[60] Ibid.

[61] Susanne Loughlin, 13 February 2013.

[62] Telephone correspondence with Billy Owens, 29 August 2013.

[63] Jenkins, 2010: 169, citing 'Police (Liverpool Inquiry) Act. p. 176'.

[64] Appendix 3, 'Twelfth of July Parade Attendance Estimates'.

[65] *Orange Standard* (October 2006).

[66] *Liverpool Echo*, 12 July 1960.

[67] *Liverpool Daily Post*, 13 July 1985.

Institution in Liverpool however, is perhaps best demonstrated not in its parading numbers but in its influence.

Crowley notes how, 'Liverpool was run for a long time by the Tory-Orange Order hegemons'.[68] This statement has much merit and is echoed by Joan Smith, who suggests, 'Liverpool politics were dominated by the ruling Orange Tory bloc and the subordinate Irish Nationalist organisations'.[69] Certainly, to espouse Orange convictions in nineteenth-century Liverpool, and the early part of the twentieth, could enhance one's political prospects. The Orange membership acted as a sizeable army of 'campaigners' to be deployed for electoral operations, a factor which greatly added to their political sway. In 1867, the strength of Liverpool Orangeism was demonstrated when 'local Orangemen were able to pressure the Tory Lord Mayor, Edward Whitley into banning a protest against the public hanging of the Fenian "Manchester Martyrs"'. Whitley wrote to the Home Secretary stating, 'Liverpool is a very exceptional place owing to the Orange element prevailing to a large extent'.[70]

John Houlding, the founder of Liverpool FC, was one of many men who joined the Orange Order, arguably in pursuit of his own political ambitions. At the Twelfth of July rally in 1885, Houlding was 'received with cheers on being introduced as the probable Conservative candidates for Kirkdale'.[71] Of Houlding and Mr T.B. Royden (both prospective Conservative candidates), the speaker announced:

> Orangemen were duty-bound to work tooth and nail, heart and soul, to return them top of the poll. [Houlding and Royden] had never forsaken the Orange body in the past and the Orangemen would not forsake them now … The uncompromising support which both candidates had always given to Protestantism and Conservatism warranted them in relying on the support of every member of the Orange body.[72]

Royden claimed that 'the Conservative party were allied with the great principles which animated the Orange body'. Houlding 'returned thanks and hoped that would not be the last meeting of the kind he might have the pleasure of attending'. An impressive list of gentry and public officials felt the need to offer apologies for not attending the event, saying much of the

[68] Crowley, 2012: 136.
[69] Smith, 1984: 33.
[70] *Irish Post*, 27 January 1996.
[71] *Liverpool Daily Post*, 14 July 1885.
[72] Ibid.

Order's public standing. Lord Randolph Churchill wrote that he 'regretted not joining the gathering, but assured the Orangemen of [his] sympathy'.[73]

At the General Meeting of the Grand Lodge of England in 1898, it was announced that the Bootle MP, and impending Grand Master of England, Colonel Thomas Sandys, 'is to bring in a bill to remedy the evil in the Church [of England]'.[74] The 'evil' referred to was 'ritualism', or the tolerance of 'romanish practices' in the Anglican Church. It is telling of the strength of Liverpool Orangeism that the Member of Parliament for a neighbouring (and predominantly working-class) constituency was a Grand Master of the Institution.

The working relationship between the Conservative Party and the Orange Institution was a product of an Orange, Anglican, Conservative caucus, orchestrated in part by Hugh McNeile, which had ensured a mutually profitable relationship by the Protestant partners who collectively acted in opposition to Roman Catholicism. McNeile 'founded the Protestant Association to link middle-class Anglicans with the Orange Order and with the Tories. Liverpool Tories also maintained links with the Protestant working class through Orange lodges'.[75] Each organisation influenced the other in pursuit of its own ends; the physical strength of the syndicate resting with the Orange Order, who provided muscle, as well as core voting power, whilst the Order enjoyed political favour in return.

After the expansion of the voting franchise in 1832 and 1867, of the electoral strategies adopted by Liverpool's Conservative Party, 'sectarianism proved the most successful'.[76] The rank and file did not solely resent Catholicism. Racism was equally prevalent, as, 'to the working-class Orangemen, partic-ularly after the famine influx, they might well have felt they were living in Ireland'.[77] The Gaelic tongue was the principle discernible feature of their social and economic rivals. The Conservatives were attentive to this, as 'when allied to ethnicity, Protestant sectarianism provided a solid base for popular Tory support, addressing workers' fears not of Rome or reform but of Irish migration'.[78] The Orange leadership, however, was more virulently opposed to Catholicism. As such, the Conservative and Unionist leadership,

[73] Ibid.
[74] *Protestant Standard*, 8 July 1898.
[75] Day, 2008: 274.
[76] Belchem, 2000: 158.
[77] Neal, 1988: 31.
[78] Belchem, 2000: 159.

assured of Protestant cooperation should they appease Orange concerns, voiced their, often quite genuine, contempt for popery. The extent of the Orange Order's political footprint in Liverpool is described by Belchem and MacRaild:

> The successful penetration of Liverpool's political culture by a strong Orange tendency was unmatched anywhere in Britain. Orangeism became part of Liverpool's civic culture in ways that even Glasgow did not match ... Liverpool's Orange networks ran both laterally and vertically: they reached out across the city from north to south, and also penetrated upwards into the ranks of the local power elites.[79] Orangeism fell squarely into line with Archibald Salvidge's Conservative machine ... Loyal foot-soldiers, Orangemen contributed much to the electoral dominance of Conservatism in Liverpool.[80]

A leading article in the *Morning Post*, in November 1921, declared of Sir Archibald Salvidge [leader of the Liverpool Conservatives], that his 'whole political career has been dedicated to the indefatigable support of the Union, and especially Protestant Ulster. The powerful political organisation which he controls and directs – and by virtue of which he has attained from a local and national reputation – is held together by its strong Orange fibre'.[81]

The courting of the Orange vote by Liverpool Conservatives was already well established by the end of the nineteenth century, but with the ascendancy of Salvidge to the local Conservative leadership in 1898 'more of the upper echelons of Liverpool Conservatism joined the Orange Order [and] W.W. Rutherford M.P. became Grand Master of England in 1912'.[82] The strength of the Orange municipal connection was also demonstrated in February 1923, when the Lord Mayor of Liverpool, Councillor G.A. Stone, accepted an invitation from the Protestant Reformers Church to perform the opening ceremony of a 'huge Protestant Bazaar', which took place in St Georges Hall on 22 March 1923. The Bazaar had followed a large Protestant parade and pageant in the city. The preceding year, Reverend Longbottom and three other men had been elected as 'Protestant' or 'Protestant and Unionist' candidates to the Board of Guardians on the

---

[79] Belchem and MacRaild, 2006: 328.

[80] Ibid., 343.

[81] Salvidge, 1934: 206, citing an article entitled 'Salvidging Ulster' from London's *Morning Post*.

[82] Neal, 1988: 200.

city council.[83] Pastor George Wise had also joined the Orange Institution following his arrival in Liverpool in 1898. The religious tone to the city's politics was now solid.

Indeed, as late as the 1960s, Orange credentials were still flaunted in local elections. Both Councillor H.W. Blower and Councillor Roy Hughes of the Protestant Party cited their belonging to the Institution on their electoral pamphlets along with their patriotic and religious credentials, which would appeal to the Orange membership. Blower's material stated that he had 'served with the Royal Navy, [was] an active member of the Loyal Orange Institution [as well as] a keen Church worker'. Articles on Hughes emphasised his role as an Orange lodge drummer, stating that he was 'a fresh faced Orangeman [who] bangs the big drum for the Protestant Volunteers concertina band' and highlighted that he 'holds several offices' in the Loyal Orange Institution. In an article entitled 'The Merseyside Paisleyites', Ernest Dewhurst wrote that Hughes, having given his son the middle name of Carson, gave one of his daughters the middle name of Lilian, 'for the Orange lily'. The article also stated that all sitting Protestant Party councillors are 'in the Orange Order'.[84] Indeed, although there were long-standing Orange–Protestant–Conservative alliances, it was the Protestant Party which acted as the direct political outlet of Orangeism for a considerable part of the twentieth century.

Such was the importance of the Orange Order that it was in 'a packed church', in Hamilton Road, in 1960, where former Protestant Lord Mayor and Grand Master of England, Reverend H.D. Longbottom, suddenly collapsed 'whilst defending his position before hundreds of rank and file Orangemen'.[85] Longbottom had fallen foul of the Orange leadership 'because of allegations he had made about a high official in the Order visiting the Pope and he was subsequently expelled. This broke his heart'[86] and he died shortly afterwards.

The Order comprised of a bulky ensemble of prospective political activists, while the lodges, in turn, provided a social and economic support structure to Orange members. The draw of the Institution to its working-class members was not necessarily political or theological. For many, it was

[83] Presentation by Ian Henderson at the Bootle Protestant Free Church, 27 October 2012.

[84] See Roberts (2015), Appendices 2.3, 2.7, 2.10, and 3.3.

[85] Ian Henderson, Presentation in Bootle Protestant Free Church, Saturday, 27 October 2012.

[86] Ibid.

simply practical. Reginald Chadwick, the current Master of Loyal Orange Lodge (L.O.L.) 184, echoes this sentiment, remarking on the significance of the role of the Liverpool Institution to its members:

> At its height in Liverpool the various lodges would have been an integral part of their local communities, giving the community cohesion and direction, encouraging the members to help one another and co-operate in times of difficulty both practically and morally. The Orange Institution would have instilled in its members from a very young age the need to read the Holy Scriptures and encouraged members to live their lives in a Christian manner, endeavouring to instil a belief in the forces of law and order, pride in their country, and an adherence to the ideals and principals of the Reformed Faith. At its height in Liverpool, the various Orange lodges would have been the hub of the communities to which they belonged.[87]

This associational efficiency, described by Chadwick, was, it is suggested by Belchem and MacRaild, testament partly to the high proportion of women in the Liverpool Institution,[88] which, in turn, increased the social appeal of the Institution to its core, working-class, male membership. Female involvement in the Institution has been notable since its infancy in Liverpool. As early as 1860, a 'respectably dressed woman', Mrs Warham, was 'charged with being drunk and disorderly', on the Twelfth of July, while supervising her child, an infant, adorned 'in party colours, the prevailing colour being orange'.[89] Another spectator, on the return of the Twelfth of July convoy in 1900, commented:

> What struck me most about the Orange procession was the inordinate proportion of hard faced, brazen looking women and girls who, for the honour of humanity and the exigencies of common decency, I regret to say, had showed evident signs of having 'celebrated' not wisely but too well.[90]

The high degree of female participation is telling of the wider appeal of Orange culture to Protestant Liverpool. By 1915, the city had more than

---

[87] Reginald Chadwick, 9 August 2013.
[88] Belchem and MacRaild, 2006: 344.
[89] *Liverpool Daily Post*, 14 July 1860.
[90] *Liverpool Catholic Herald*, 20 July 1900.

forty female lodges.[91] However, it was not until 1960 that the Ladies Grand Committee was formed, allowing women to 'play a full part in the organisation'.[92]

Female participation in the Institution increased its appeal to young men, many families created by parents who met through an Orange lodge.[93] Inevitably, the children of members were introduced to the Orange Institution at a young age. In its own way, the Institution itself became a 'family' to many of its members, who would look out for each other. Owing to the family lineage of Orangeism, its appeal was part of a routine socialisation process. Upon reaching a certain age, membership of the Institution was expected, rather than encouraged.

Orange officials had the ability to rally together substantial numbers for various assemblies and demonstrations. Such influence was demonstrated in the build up to one of the more infamous sectarian riots of Liverpool's history. In June 1909, an 'organised Orange attack',[94] as described by the *Liverpool Post and Mercury*, took place on a Catholic procession as a result of an advert placed in the *Liverpool Evening Express* by officials of the Order. The advert stated:

> Loyal Orange Institution of England (province of Liverpool) – the male members of this province are earnestly requested to attend a monster demonstration … for the purpose of preventing any illegal procession taking place in the city of Liverpool. Wake up Protestant England! We must have no compromise and no surrender.[95]

There was general consensus amongst commentators that the Roman Catholic procession was neither illegal nor 'unduly provocative to non-Catholics'. Moreover, the agreed 'route [was] limited almost exclusively to what may be described as a Roman Catholic quarter'.[96] Regardless of this, the *Evening Express* advert had the desired effect; the 'Orange appeal [was]

---

[91]   Belchem and MacRaild, 2006: 344.

[92]   *Liverpool Echo*, 12 July 1960.

[93]   Lynn and Dave Hughes met through their lodge. Roy Hughes too met his wife through an Orange lodge. There are countless examples of this occurring in Liverpool.

[94]   *Liverpool Daily Post & Mercury*, 21 June 1909.

[95]   Cited by *Liverpool Catholic Herald*, 26 June 1909. *Liverpool Daily Post & Mercury* cites the same advert. In specifically requesting 'male members' the Orange hierarchy seemingly anticipated/desired a physical confrontation with Irish Catholics.

[96]   *Liverpool Daily Post & Mercury*, 21 June 1909.

met with a hearty response from members of the Order'.[97] Huge numbers of local Orangemen gathered and 'rumour [had] it that a contingent of Orangemen [was] brought over from Belfast for the purpose of swelling the forces'.[98] As early as 1886, the *Liverpool Mercury* had seen the potential for an Orange vigilante group 'to put down all lawlessness', should the police not 'maintain order'.[99] It would seem, owing to their influence and weight in numbers, this was how the Order was coming to view itself. Certainly, given the events that followed, many Orangemen had put by the wayside Orange rules stating 'no person do persecute or upbraid anyone on account of his religion'.[100]

As a result of the *Evening Express* article, 'the authorities had taken every precaution',[101] and 700 constables, supplemented with plain clothed and mounted police, were gathered to prevent a breach of the peace. The Catholic procession numbered only 2,000, and it is testament to the perceived threat of an Orange attack that such a large number of police officers was deemed necessary to protect a relatively small Catholic procession. Nonetheless, extensive disturbances took place, resulting in forty-six arrests on the Sunday, mostly Orangemen, and forty more the following day.[102] The scene was described as 'one of complete disorder and typical of the riots which have occurred in Belfast'.[103] Interestingly, the *Herald* claimed that 'the attentions of the [Orange] mob were not confined solely to Catholics, but were also bestowed upon respectable Protestants, several of whom stated that they had been left practically destitute for the crime of not belonging to an Orange lodge'.[104]

If it had not been for the repeated intervention of the police, 'there is not the slightest doubt that many lives would have been lost'.[105] As part of the sectarian rioting, churches, presbyteries, and schools were attacked. Clergymen were amongst those targeted,[106] and skirmishes spread to the

---

[97] Ibid.

[98] Ibid.

[99] Neal, 1988: 187, citing *Liverpool Mercury*, 9 July 1886.

[100] Clause in Orange rules, cited by Gray, 1972: 79.

[101] *Liverpool Daily Post & Mercury*, 21 June 1909.

[102] *Liverpool Catholic Herald*, 26 June 1909 and *Post and Mercury*, 21 June 1909.

[103] *Liverpool Catholic Herald*, 26 June 1909, citing a 'London daily paper' in its article, 'The Orange Lambs of Liverpool'.

[104] Ibid.

[105] Ibid.

[106] *Liverpool Catholic Herald*, 24 July 1909.

workplace.[107] Moreover, under threat of attack, people began to move from their homes to areas occupied by residents of their own faith. One of the actions directly attributed to an Orange lodge was a death threat received by an Irish Nationalist councillor, Thomas Kelly, representing the Scotland District, which declared:

> Lodge No. 126. June 23rd 1909 – Sir, you were very sure about the furnishing of Papist schools by Protestant ratepayers' money. Let me tell you that not one penny of Protestant money will ever be given to the Papist school furniture. We stopped your illegal, idolatrous, Romish processions and we will stop priests and nuns getting our money to help breeding places for Papist vipers. Get your own funeral furnishing arrangements ready, we are going to be revenged for the savage attacks on our Protestant brothers and sisters in your ward, which is a disgrace to this Protestant town. We will make a swoop someday; don't you forget it. Remember Derry. No Surrender. No Papist schools. God save George Wise. To hell with popery, priests, priestcraft and Jesuits. We will give you a call.[108]

Days prior to the rioting, a master of a Catholic school received a letter 'full of filthy abuse … threatening to "shoot him on sight" should he venture to parade his children'[109] during the Catholic march.

Practices which were akin to a form of 'ethnic cleansing' were well under way by the middle of the week, and 'in the three weeks following the June riot, 110 Protestant families had to leave the Anglican Parish of St Martin's, between Scotland Road and Vauxhall Road, through fear and intimidation. The attacks on Catholics living in or near predominantly Protestant areas were even more widespread':[110]

> Amongst Catholics living in even the best streets in the Orange portion of Everton there has been a perfect epidemic of terror, practically every one of them having had notices sent to them by post, or thrust in their letter boxes and under their doors, warning them to clear out of the district with the greatest possible dispatch, or take the consequences. In many cases the notices have been impressed with a bloody thumb-mark, to make the warning more emphatic.[111]

---

107 Neal, 1988: 232.
108 Letter printed in *Liverpool Catholic Herald*, 3 July 1909.
109 *Liverpool Catholic Herald*, 26 June 1909.
110 Neal, 1988: 233.
111 *Liverpool Catholic Herald*, 3 July 1909.

For nuns who 'would have to pass through or by any portion of the Orange district it was considered advisable that they should be escorted by police'.[112]

On the Tuesday of the riots Orange women, 'wildly brandishing their husband's swords' rushed into All Souls Catholic schools and assaulted teachers and students. Catholics, in retaliation, 'invaded the council school in Roscommon Street'. The education committee was hastily summoned to meet and, as a measure of precaution, decided temporarily to close all schools in the affected districts.[113] In late June, acting on advice from the Chief Constable, the Lord Mayor prohibited 'sectarian processions'. Amongst those tried and convicted for the riots were three officers of the Orange Order who 'had summoned the majority of Orangemen together',[114] each fined heavily and bound over to 'keep good behaviour for six months'.[115]

The scale of these events is significant insofar as they demonstrate the influence wielded by the hierarchy of the Orange Order. The riots had been brought about by an advert in one local newspaper, although rhetoric used by Pastor George Wise exacerbated the situation. Wise was also a leading official in the Orange Institution and was also tried for his role in the riots.

Three years after the disturbances, the extent of Orangeism in Liverpool was again demonstrated with the arrival of Edward Carson to the port, with,

> Up to a quarter of a million said to have turned out. As Orange bands blared out their redoubtable tunes, Salvidge [leader of the Liverpool Conservatives] welcomed the leading Unionists from across the water ... Sheil Park was chosen as the setting [to hear Carson and his entourage speak] for fear of violence in a city-centre venue ... The total volume of people made this Orange gathering one of Liverpool's biggest-ever crowds.[116]

Upon his arrival in Liverpool, Salvidge was there to 'shake [Carson] by the hand', who was 'visibly moved' by the 'great crowds of Liverpool people who

---

[112] *Liverpool Catholic Herald*, 26 June 1909.

[113] Ibid.

[114] *Liverpool Catholic Herald*, 3 July 1909.

[115] Ibid.

[116] Belchem and MacRaild, 2006: 343–4.

had gathered in the landing stage to greet him'.[117] Jackson also commented how, of the 'quarter of a million' Protestants who had greeted Carson, 'many of them [were] members of the Orange Order, infused with an almost religious fervour, and [gathered] under the auspices of the Conservative and Unionist Party ... to protest against the proposal to grant Home Rule to Ireland'.[118]

Liverpool Orangeism retained its influence for the first half of the twentieth century. It also maintained its relationship with Liverpool Conservatives. One lodge member declared: 'you had the Protestant Party [who openly supported the Conservatives politically and who were all members of the Orange Institution[119]]; prior to that, lots of Conservative councillors were in Orange lodges'.[120] This relationship became more turbulent as the century progressed, Day claiming that 'in 1928 the influence of the W.M.C.A. [Working Men's Conservative Association] and the Orange Order over the Conservative Party ... was reduced following the death of Archibald Salvidge ... their influence, while not quite dying with Salvidge, was severely curtailed'.[121] Orange districts, for some time, remained politically blue, and both Bessie and Jack Braddock, committed socialists and dominant Labour figures, 'needed a strong police escort to enable them to speak in the Orange heartland of St Domingo in Everton'.[122] Mike O'Brian, a former resident of the area, recalls one occasion where Bessie Braddock came to talk in the district, and 'the girls and women of the area threw stones and bricks at her'.[123]

Despite post-war slum clearance and depopulation of Liverpool, the Orange Institution maintained its ability to organise protests into the 1980s. On 7 December 1981, 'about one thousand Protestant militants marched into the Anglican Cathedral and occupied [it] for ninety minutes'.[124] The protest was 'against Pope John Paul II's scheduled visit [the] next year. The protesters [were] wearing orange sashes of the Orange Order ... Police were asked not to intervene [by] the dean of the cathedral, [who] said, "We were determined to avoid confrontation ... If we had stood up to them

[117] King, 1965: 19.
[118] Day, 2011: 65, citing Jackson, 2003: 101.
[119] See Roberts, 2015: Appendices 2.1 and 2.2.
[120] Day, 2011: 75, citing an anonymous Orange lodge member/official.
[121] Ibid., 65–6.
[122] *Irish Post*, 27 January 1996.
[123] Correspondence with Mike O'Brian, 16 October 2013.
[124] *New Straits Times*, 8 December 1981.

there could have been trouble.'"[125] On 8 May, the following year, 2,000 Orangemen 'opposed to Pope John Paul II's planned visit to Britain marched peacefully through central Liverpool led by fife-and-drum bands of the Orange Lodge'.[126] By this time, the Orange hierarchy was firmly committed to non-violent methods and no attempt was made to disrupt the Papal visit itself: 'We are dedicated to peaceful protest against the Pope's visit and will not condone troublemakers', said Richard Roberts, the Liverpool-based Grand Master of England. During the papal tour, a telephone caller to the police, saying he represented the 'Orange Lodge Action Committee', took responsibility for a fire started at St Mary's of Angels Catholic Church, the caller threatening: 'Next time it will be a bomb'.[127]

In October 1988, following the split of the English Order 'over the issue of support for the paramilitary groups', it was claimed that, 'The Ulster Volunteer Force (UVF) enjoys considerable support amongst Liverpool's large loyalist community'.[128] Loyalists were accused of collecting money for the UVF, whilst the newly formed *Independent Orange Association*, then led by the late Steve Bell (former master of Lodge 200, in the north end of the city), 'proudly carried UVF banners and flags in a separate four hundred strong march in Newbury, Merseyside'. Around this time, Trevor Cubbon, from Liverpool, and Albert Watt, from Canada, were sentenced to four years' imprisonment at Liverpool Crown Court, for 'plotting to smuggle weapons from Canada to Northern Ireland through Liverpool in hollowed-out diesel engines'. The trial revealed that the arms shipment had been organised in the Orange Order's Derry Club in Everton.[129]

Measuring the Decline of Liverpool Orangeism

There is a general consensus that the influence of the Orange Institution on Merseyside has markedly receded. Moreover, as will be noted, the Order

[125] Ibid. On this point, Ron Bather, Grand Master of England, comments that it was the second of such occurrences, and was more in protest against the Cathedral's ecumenical stance and refusal to hold a Reformation service than about the Pope's visit (Ron Bather, 1 November 2013).
[126] *New York Times*, 9 May 1982.
[127] Ibid.
[128] Birtill, 1988.
[129] Ibid.

itself, numerically, is nowhere near the force it once was.[130] Nonetheless, measuring this retreat is not straightforward. It has been stated that 'the Orange Order in Liverpool has not been good at recording its own history'.[131] In addition, owing to an unwillingness of the Institution to publicise its membership statistics, combined with a tendency of journalists to 'estimate' (i.e. guess) when reporting the size of Orange parades, there is no wholly reliable way of measuring decline. While this is problematic, this section will nevertheless attempt to analyse various reports and statistics relating to the size of the Liverpool Orange Order, and combine them with testimony from Orange members and officials to quantify the extent of reduction. Having interviewed a plethora of Orange members and affiliates, nobody connected with the organisation has denied that there has been a discernible attenuation of Liverpool Orangeism. This section will demonstrate how this is the case.

Perhaps the most obvious way of measuring the strength of an organisation is by looking at its membership statistics. However, officials of the Grand Lodge of England do not consider themselves at liberty to disclose such information, as the Institution has 'never done so in the past'. The Provincial Grand Master of Liverpool, Billy Owens, declares that, 'since our establishment we have never disclosed such information. Neither do the Grand Lodge of Ireland or Scotland'.[132] However, in recent years the Grand Lodge in Ireland has published membership figures, claiming to have held 98,000 members in 1968, but fewer than 40,000 today. However, in Northern Ireland, far more come out on Orange parades (many bands contain members not formally belonging to the Orange Order) on the 'Twelfth', and the veracity of these figures is difficult to confirm, given the lack of central membership records (local lodges hold such records).[133] Owens claims that current lodge membership across Merseyside stands at approximately '20,000 – though they obviously all don't come out on the Twelfth of July anymore'.[134]

This figure is far higher than other sources suggest, and seems unlikely given it would represent half of the figure right across Northern Ireland, whose population is only 400,000 greater than that of Merseyside. The

[130] Day, 2008: 273.
[131] Ibid., citing 2004 email correspondence with Donald MacRaild.
[132] Telephone correspondence with Billy Owens, 4 October 2013.
[133] See McAuley, Tonge, and Mycock, 2011.
[134] Telephone correspondence with Billy Owens, 29 August 2013.

Grand Master of Bootle Province, Tom Buckley, estimated that there are approximately only 120 members in Bootle today,[135] a significant decline from the 1960s, a figure Keith Allcock put at roughly 700–800 members.[136] Both the *Liverpool Echo* and *Daily Post* put local Orange membership at 3,000 at the end of the twentieth century, but there are problems with this figure in terms of what area was being covered.[137] In 2006, the Grand Lodge of Ireland wrote in its monthly publication that, 'the Liverpool membership is still substantial, but is not on the same scale as it was some years ago'.[138] Membership has at least held up better than in Toronto, where the 'Twelfth' parade has dwindled to a few hundred participants, and the Order's once-huge local political influence has vanished. On Merseyside at least, the Orange 'Twelfth' parade remains one of the region's larger public non-sporting annual gatherings, although it is now significantly smaller than the Glasgow event held on the Saturday before the 'Twelfth' – which was not always the case.

Dave Hughes, Master of District 92, the biggest District in Liverpool, claims that membership was once as high as 65,000,[139] whilst Owens suggests a figure of 50,000 in the 1940s.[140] Orangeism was a mass movement for more than a century in the city. However, these numbers are not backed by any firm statistical evidence. As such, they can be considered speculative rather than authoritative. More importantly, as Neal insists, membership statistics are only one indicator, albeit an important one, of the strength of Orangeism:

> It is important to note that Orangeism was more widespread than membership of the Orange Order. The early rules of the organisation specifically laid down that Orangemen should love all men, including Catholics. Orangeism however, as a set of negative attitudes towards Irish Catholics based on Orange songs and history, was adopted by many anti-Catholics not members of the Orange Order, and who often

---

[135] Tom Buckley, 12 March 2013.
[136] Keith Allcock, 12 March 2013.
[137] *Liverpool Echo*, 12 July 2000; *Liverpool Daily Post*, 13 July 2000. It is unclear whether this figure applies to all of Merseyside, as 'Liverpool' could be said to apply to the Liverpool City Region, which includes the Wirral, Knowsley, Sefton, and Halton.
[138] *Orange Standard*, October 2006.
[139] Dave Hughes, 24 January 2013.
[140] Billy Owens, 29 August 2013.

became involved in street fighting, beyond the control of concerned Orangemen.[141]

Thus many Protestants in Liverpool might once have considered themselves 'Orange', even if they were not necessarily 'Orangemen'. They would be ready and willing to fight for the 'cause', and would often walk alongside Orange processions as supporters, but if they caused trouble they were beyond the jurisdiction of the Order. This tendency has not fully disappeared. As an example, in 2010, the *Southport Visiter*, reporting on the 'Twelfth' parade in the town that year (lodges march in Liverpool and Bootle and then in Southport, which hosts their day out) noted:

> The march costs the taxpayer £3,600 to police. [In 2010] nineteen people were arrested for drunk and disorderly and drugs possession offences as scores of officers were out in force to tackle antisocial behaviour ... Liverpool Lodge leader Billy Owens said antisocial behaviour and criminal offences were 'nothing to do with the parade members'. He added: 'the arrests that were made were people following the parade and unfortunately we have no control over them – we wish we could have'.[142]

The problem of distinguishing members from followers is hardly new. Peter Day has cited figures from an 1854–5 Lodge Directory putting Liverpool membership at 1,100 and national membership at 1,333.[143] This, he points out, is contrasted with a reputed 'procession following' in 1859 of 20,000 during the Twelfth of July celebrations.[144] It would seem, therefore, that acquaintances and supporters of the Institution, who were not members of the Order, greatly increased the stature of Orange processions as well as the Orange traditions and culture of Liverpool. As such, it is necessary to look at other ways of measuring the decline of Orangeism, external to analysing speculative membership statistics.

One alternative measure is to examine accounts of the numbers on Twelfth of July Boyne commemoration parades. Figures 2.1 and 2.2 offer approximations of parade attendance, reported in various newspapers

---

[141] Neal, 1990–1: 23.

[142] *Southport Visiter*, 1 October 2010.

[143] Day, 2011: 61, citing Phelan, 'Orangeism Resurgent' (Loyal Orange Institution of England).

[144] Neal, 1988: 172, citing a procession estimate from the *Liverpool Herald*, 'a-pro Orange newspaper'.

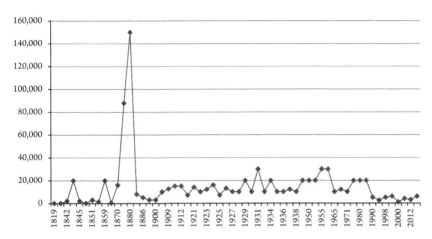

Figure 2.1   Twelfth of July Parades: Highest Attendance Estimates, 1819–2013

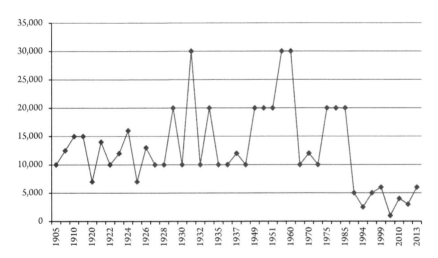

Figure 2.2   Twelfth of July Parades: Highest Attendance Estimates, 1905–2013

Sources: Bullough, 1990, Neal, 1988, Smith, 1984, *Daily Courier, Liverpool Chronicle, Liverpool Echo, Liverpool Forward, Liverpool Herald, Liverpool Mercury, Liverpool Mail, Liverpool Daily Post, Liverpool Post and Mercury, Liverpool Standard, Liverpool Times, Southport Visiter.* See Appendix 3 for specific details.

between 1819 (Liverpool's first 'Twelfth' procession) and 2013. The graphs demonstrate that there has been a visible decline in estimated parade sizes from 1990 onwards. Figure 2.1 offers a huge spike in attendees in the late nineteenth century, due to a unification of the *Orange Association* and the *Orange Institution*, although it is difficult to verify these figures and they may be suspect. Another important point is that no formal parade took place in Liverpool between 1821 and 1842. Between 1843 and 1905, parade estimates can be described as sporadic. Notably, there is a jump from an estimate of 200 in 1850 to 3,000 in 1851, and, remarkably, there is a huge drop from an alleged 20,000 in 1859 to 400 in 1860.[145] It should be noted that it is not always clear whether the attendance approximation is exclusive to those marching in full Orange regalia, or inclusive of supporters and spectators of the parade. This, to a large degree, accounts for such diverging estimates, although parade attendance was also dependent on a variety of other factors: weather, location, day of the week, political climate, prominence of attendees (word of a VIP could attract a large following), and how well advertised or supported the procession was.

Another aspect to be considered is the fallibility of reporters' observations of the processions. In 1870, a journalist for the *Daily Courier* highlighted such complications and was one of few who set out his calculations:

> It is difficult to estimate the numbers, but to set down the processionists who left the Dingle at 2,000, and those who mustered at the Botanic gardens at 1,000, is fairly within the mark. This would make the number of Orangemen represented, 3,000, while the friends and sympathisers on foot were nearly twice as numerous.[146]

The writer concludes that those present, at the 1870 procession, numbered 9,000. A correspondent for the *Daily Post*, however, reported that the procession comprised of 16,000 people.[147] Moreover, these estimates, even when offering some depth (the latter reporter cited 6,000 marchers and 10,000 spectators), only took into account those present at the parade, and not all those involved in the day's celebrations.

The problems of calculations of nineteenth-century parades are exacerbated by the existence of two regulating bodies until 1876: the *Orange Institution* and the *Orange Association*. It was not always clear which authority

---

[145] See Appendix 3 for precise estimates and sources.
[146] *Daily Courier*, 13 July 1870.
[147] *Liverpool Daily Post*, 13 July 1870.

had organised which parades, or whether individual lodges had simply opted to march autonomously. Often a variety of Orange celebrations would take place in Liverpool which did not always involve a parade. Individual lodges at this time were large enough to hold their own functions. Owing to a likelihood of violence should a parade take place, some of the more 'respectable' lodges often decided not to parade, opting instead for a private party or dinner. For a time, Orange processions were not always universally supported by Orangemen. In 1860, the *Liverpool Mercury* noted:

> There was a very small muster compared with previous occasions, arising, as we understand from circumstances that many of the more respectable members of the Orange societies kept aloof from this portion of the proceedings. The number in the procession was not more than about 300 or 400.[148]

The relatively small number of processionists was not necessarily indicative of the strength of its support. The same article reports that the parade was 'followed by an immense mob of men, women, and children, most of them wearing orange'.[149] In 1870, again highlighting a lack of unity in relation to holding a parade, the *Courier* reported:

> Although the idea [of a procession] was opposed by some of the local leaders, it found general favour, and the members of the Order turned out in unexpected strength. Processions ... have often brought unmerited disgrace upon the whole Order, and probably for this reason the Liverpool Orangemen, who number no less than 4,000, have for the last few years 'demonstrated', so to speak, in detachments.[150]

The 1876 merger of the *Orange Association* with the *Orange Institution* yielded the *Loyal Orange Institution of England*. The Twelfth of July Procession received cohesive and resolute backing by the newly united leadership. On the first 'Twelfth' after the merger, it was reported that up to 88,000 Orangemen marched from the city's boundary to Lord Derby's estate in Knowsley. This parade was described as 'an illustration of the increased strength of Orangeism and a demonstration of voting power which no politician could ignore'.[151] The parade was bettered four years later, when in

---

[148] *Liverpool Mercury*, 13 July 1860.
[149] Ibid.
[150] *Liverpool Courier*, 13 July 1870.
[151] Neal, 1988: 184.

1880 the largest ever recorded English Orange procession took place in Hale Park, south of Liverpool. Colonel Blackburne MP 'placed his peaceful park unreservedly at the disposal of the Orangemen',[152] and 'the anticipation of the leaders of the Loyal Orange Institution ... that the [procession] would eclipse all previous demonstrations ... were more than realised'[153] when an estimated 150,000 people attended.[154]

Figure 2.2, although it repeats some of the data in Figure 2.1, provides a higher degree of clarity on procession attendance over more recent times. Although in the nineteenth century we are presented with much more turbulent estimates, since 1905 it is clear that parade attendance consistently hovered above 10,000 before a sharp decline approaching the last decade of the twentieth century. Parade crowds dropped markedly after 1985, and have never recovered. The mean attendance figure between 1905 and 1985 is 15,015. Between 1990 and 2013 the mean dropped, by nearly three-quarters, to 4,063.

Amid these overall trends, considerable variation in attendance is the norm. Moreover, talk of declining attendances is not new. In 1890, the *Liverpool Daily Post* commented, 'Even the most enthusiastic supporter of the "Order" would not venture to expect on 12th July such monster attendance as was secured years back, when the Orange men and women assembled literally in their tens of thousands'.[155] That year, the Order held their annual rally in Halton Castle, an area closer to Liverpool than Hale. This procession attracted 'not more than 3,000 men, women and children',[156] while the procession held in 1900, which took place in Buckley, north Wales, again attracted a relatively paltry 3,000 participants.[157] A year earlier, at the annual Conference of the Grand Lodge of English Orangemen, 'It was decided to affiliate with the Imperial Protestant Federation',[158] a prominent nationwide Protestant association, aimed at fighting ritualism,[159] to 'add

---

[152] *Liverpool Daily Post*, 30 July 1880.

[153] *Daily Courier*, 13 July 1880.

[154] *Liverpool Daily Post*, 30 July 1880. Hale sits relatively close to the port, on the same embankment of the River Mersey. *Daily Courier*, 13 July 1880 stated that 'at least 100,000 people' made the short journey to the exurbia.

[155] *Liverpool Daily Post*, 15 July 1890.

[156] Ibid.

[157] *Liverpool Daily Post*, 13 July 1900.

[158] *Protestant Standard*, 15 July 1899.

[159] Kilcrease, B., University of Notre Dame DeSantis Lecture Series, 4 March 2011, 'Britons, Boers, and the Pope: The Great Church Crisis and the Second Anglo-Boer War'.

strength to the Orange backbone'[160] and advance a national Protestant crusade against 'Romanism, Ritualism and Infidelity'.[161] Consequently, by 1910, the July procession numbered 15,000.[162] No parades were held in wartime years,[163] and in the early twentieth century, various destinations (often in north Wales or the Wirral) were utilised for well-attended Twelfth of July processions, whilst after the Second World War, processions in Southport following the early morning assembly in Liverpool and Bootle, eventually became the norm.

As has been identified, procession statistics are by no means infallible. As such, auxiliary formulae are also necessary to quantify the diminishing of Liverpool Orangeism. Conveniently, Twelfth of July processions also afford a number of other methods of measurement. Useful indicators of parade size and support often appear in press reporting of the 'Twelfth'. The number of bands, lodges, and special trains offer a means of measuring parade numbers. Moreover, the length of the procession and the amount of time the procession takes to pass are, perhaps, usable gauges. Table 2.1 offers such measurements. The Table presents figures from press reports on Twelfth of July parades. An obvious limitation to this data is its intermittency. No dataset is consistently reported. In addition, some of the claims which form Table 2.1 are also vulnerable to the same problem of 'guesstimates' as parade estimates. Nonetheless, despite stated limitations, these datasets are still useful as indicators of the strength of Liverpool Orangeism.

The 1880 'Twelfth' parade required, in addition to thirteen special trains, 'one every ten minutes from 7.30 until 9.30 and over 100 cart loads of men and women',[164] the most of any procession. This makes sense considering that a reputed 150,000 were in attendance. Of the 20,000 reported to have taken part in the Southport procession a century later, in 1980, 11,000 are said to have travelled to Southport from Liverpool in the six special trains laid on by British Rail.[165] Many would take part in the parade itself, although it was often the case that 'normal service trains' would also

Available at: www.academia.edu/1691181/Britons_Boers_and_the_Pope_The_Great_Church_Crisis_and_the_Second_Anglo-Boer_War.

[160] *Protestant Standard*, 15 July 1899.

[161] Neal, 1988: 201, citation. For the politics of anti-Ritualism in Liverpool, see Waller, 1981: chapters 11, 12 and 14.

[162] *Liverpool Daily Post & Mercury*, 13 July 1910.

[163] *Liverpool Echo*, 12 July 1940.

[164] *Daily Courier*, 13 July 1880.

[165] *Liverpool Echo*, 12 July 1980 and *Southport Visiter*, 15 July 1980.

Table 2.1   Reported Features of Selected Orange Order Twelfth of July Parades, 1850–2010

Year of Parade	Number of Bands	Number of Lodges	Number of Special Trains/Coaches	Length of Parade	Time the Parade Took to Pass
1850		'only a few'			
1870				quarter of a mile	
1876		160			
1880		150	'special trains every ten minutes (7.30–9.30) and over 100 cart loads of men and women'		2 hours
1885	40	90			
1886		98		three-quarters of a mile	
1890	12	70			
1900	15	80	'several'		
1905				2 miles	
1909	30	156	6		
1910	24		9		1 hour
1920		60			
1939	40	50	7		
1949	30		7	2 miles	'well over one hour'
1950		129	6		
1951	40	60	6		
1955			11 plus 'added coaches to regular trains'		
1960	50	250	13		
1970			12		
1971			9		
1975	50				
1980	40		6		1 hour
1985			'fleet of 60 buses'		
1990	30				
2010			30 buses		

Sources: Bullough, 1990, Neal, 1988, Smith, 1984, *Daily Courier, Liverpool Chronicle, Liverpool Echo, Liverpool Forward, Liverpool Herald, Liverpool Mercury, Liverpool Mail, Liverpool Daily Post, Liverpool Post and Mercury, Liverpool Standard, Liverpool Times, Southport Visiter.* See Appendix 3 for specific details.

take Merseyside supporters to Southport to watch the procession.[166] The contingent of 11,000 Orange men, women, and children from Liverpool were supplemented 'with kilted contingencies from as far north as West Kilbride and coachloads as far south as Plymouth'.[167] Although it is not indicated how many spectators in attendance were, incidentally, either Southport residents or tourists unconnected with the Order, the article headline: '20,000 in a friendly invasion',[168] could indicate that a significant proportion of the spectators had been attracted to Southport specifically to watch the Orange procession.

If it is assumed that six special trains account for 11,000 Orangemen (this figure seems high) then it might be calculated that the eleven special trains that transported the Orangemen from Liverpool to Southport in 1955 accounted for approximately 20,000 of the 30,000 in attendance at that year's Twelfth of July procession. Yet the 1955 *Daily Post* article also reported that 10,000 Merseyside Orangemen had travelled on the eleven special trains, which seems a more plausible figure than 11,000 on six trains.[169] Although the article also states that 'the service to Southport was strengthened by adding coaches to the regular trains',[170] it is evident that there is considerable inconsistency in terms of numbers of Orangemen travelling on trains between 1955 and 1980.

In 1909, six special trains were put on with 'the railway company [having] received a guarantee of 10,000 excursionists'.[171] Assuming that the 'guarantee' would have accounted for members of the parade, it is suggested that fluctuations in attendance may have owed more to spectators than Orange walkers. The 30,000 Orangemen and supporters in 1960 also required thirteen special trains.[172] The *Southport Visiter*, however, put the number of Orange 'participants' at 10,000.[173] This may suggest that the additional 20,000 were spectators rather than marchers. To account for the surge of spectators, 'extra trains had been laid on by British Railways and as

---

[166] *Liverpool Echo*, 12 July 1971. It is still the case today that the Liverpool to Southport trains transport significant numbers of Merseyside supporters, despite Orange processionists themselves travelling by coach.

[167] *Southport Visiter*, 15 July 1980.

[168] Ibid.

[169] *Liverpool Daily Post*, 13 July 1955.

[170] Ibid.

[171] *Liverpool Weekly Mercury*, 17 July 1909.

[172] *Liverpool Echo*, 12 July 1960.

[173] *Southport Visiter*, 14 July 1960.

well as special steam trains, the electric Southport–Liverpool service was also extended'.[174]

Parades with a larger estimated attendance have tended to warrant mention of the number of 'special trains' put on for the day. However, the most important figures from this dataset are presented after the Order had to substitute trains for coaches. In terms of calculating a recent decline in parade attendance, the number of hired coaches has halved from sixty in 1985[175] to thirty in 2010.[176]

In terms of lodge presence, it should be noted that not all lodges in attendance come from Merseyside. The Twelfth of July parade in Southport is the official parade of the Loyal Orange Institution of England. As such, it welcomes bands and lodges from the rest of England, not just Merseyside. The English parade is also regularly attended by bands and lodges from Scotland,[177] and has also hosted lodges from Northern Ireland.[178] Therefore, the number of lodges present in Southport is not an entirely straightforward indicator of Merseyside Orange strength, although it is highly indicative. Nonetheless, the 250 lodges present at the 1960 parade, regardless of where in the UK they came from, tell us something regarding individual lodge size. If we take it that 10,000 present were processionists and 20,000 were spectators, then we can break the former figure down to give an approximation of lodge members involved in the 1960 parade. If the number of processionists is divided by the number of lodges, it can be projected that the average number of attendees from each lodge present was forty. This indicates that each lodge in 1960 had, on average, at least forty members.

The datasets on length and time of a parade are important indicators of a decline in precession size. In terms of length of the procession there has been a clear decrease. The researcher witnessed the parade annually from 2010 to 2014 in Southport. If the Bootle procession, Independent procession, and Provincial Procession were joined end to end they would come to no more than 250 yards (230 metres). For scale, that is approximately the

[174] Ibid.

[175] *Liverpool Daily Post*, 13 July 1985.

[176] *Liverpool Echo*, 13 July 2010.

[177] *Liverpool Echo*, 12 July 1971.

[178] *Liverpool Echo*, 12 July 1980, In 1994, as one example, Lee Barrow, 92 District lodge secretary, said: 'People have come down from Scotland and come over from Ireland especially for the occasion', *Liverpool Echo*, 12 July 1994.

length of two and a half football pitches. To put this into context, the 'quarter of a mile'[179] approximation of the parade in 1870 suggests the procession was roughly four and a half football pitches long (400 metres). The 1886 estimate of 'three-quarters of a mile'[180] is roughly thirteen football pitches in length (1.2 kilometres), while the 1905 and 1949 citations of 'two miles'[181] are approximately the size of thirty-five football pitches in length (3.2 kilometres). Whilst the 1905 and 1949 figures are almost indisputably exaggerations, the current length of parade represents a very large retraction in the scale of Orange marches since their heyday.

Of all 'datasets', 'the time it takes for a parade to a pass by a point' has been most utilised by individuals describing the decline. Yvonne Fearnehough, born in Liverpool in 1959, first walked in an Orange procession when she was two years old. She marched with the Old Swan Concertina Band until she was eighteen, got married, had a child, and put her daughter in the Institution. She comments on the decline of the Twelfth of July procession:

> Years ago, to watch a full Orange parade you were talking two or three hours, going back to the late sixties, early seventies. Each district had about ten bands and lodges in it, and you're talking about ten or fifteen districts. Now you're lucky if you get two bands in a district. Now it takes about half an hour, if that [to go past]. You're talking, twenty odd thousand [processionists] going down to a couple of hundred.[182]

Dave Hughes, also born in 1959, and a lifelong lodge member, comments on the procession: 'It would take two or three hours [to go past], now it takes twenty minutes'.[183] Roy Hughes, born in 1943, stated, 'In the north end of Liverpool you'd be waiting from 8.30 a.m. until 11a.m. until the parade had passed. Today the whole procession can pass in fifteen minutes'.[184] Ian Henderson, born in 1948, suggested it used to take 'one to two hours to pass a point', whereas now it takes 'about twenty minutes'.[185] Doris Bennett, also born in 1948, and former member of Bootle Village True Blues, L.O.L. 12, gave the highest estimate of time:

[179] *Liverpool Courier*, 13 July 1870.
[180] *Liverpool Daily Post*, 13 July 1886.
[181] *Liverpool Daily Post & Mercury*, 13 July 1905 and *Southport Visiter*, 14 July 1949.
[182] Yvonne Susan Fearnehough née Fogg, 23 January 2013.
[183] Dave Hughes, 24 January 2013.
[184] Roy Hughes, 13 November 2012.
[185] Ian Henderson, 27 October 2012.

In the sixties, early seventies, even up to the late seventies, you could stand on Stanley Road [Bootle] for an hour to an hour and a half, and watch the Lodge go past. Now it's gone in ten minutes. In Liverpool, you could wait four hours for the parade to go past, and when Bootle and Liverpool marched together, in Southport, some people would be getting ready to go home as others were just starting off. You could wait five or six hours, because it was that big.[186]

Dave Hughes verifies a point made by Bennett on the scale of the pageant, claiming he could 'remember watching half the parade going before it was our turn to get into the parade, it was that big'.[187]

Keith Allcock, Tom Buckley, and Billy Tritton, officials of Bootle Province, commented on the decline in stature of the Bootle march, traditionally held separate from the Liverpool procession. In a joint interview, Tritton, who joined the Orange Institution in 1932, commented, 'It used to take Bootle's parade a good half an hour to forty-five minutes to go past'.[188] Buckley also stated, 'when I first joined, the Bootle parade would take something like three quarters of an hour to pass, now don't blink!'[189] – 'Five minutes and its gone',[190] added Allcock.

Allcock's observation was apt. When measuring the length of time it took for the Twelfth of July processions to pass by in Southport in 2013, Bootle's parade, which marched first and was supplemented with lodges from Manchester, Bolton, Pendle, and Blackpool, took exactly five minutes to pass by. The Independent Orange Order, who were also supplemented by the 'Manchester Independents', took an even smaller space of time to march past: only four minutes. The Provincial Order, comprised of mostly Merseyside lodges, but also lodges from Glasgow, Northern Ireland, Brighton, and Wales, took fifteen minutes to pass by. Collectively, the three processions took less than twenty-five minutes to march past, a far cry from the processions of the past. This dataset, therefore, presents another useful indication of the decline of Orangeism. The time it takes for a procession to pass by has fallen from a cited 'one hour' in 1980[191] to under half an hour today.[192]

---

[186] Doris Bennett, 5 March 2013.
[187] Dave Hughes, 24 January 2013.
[188] William John Tritton, 12 March 2013.
[189] Tom Buckley, 12 March 2013.
[190] Keith Allcock, 12 March 2013.
[191] *Liverpool Echo*, 12 July 1980.
[192] In 2014, 'Orange Day' fell on a Saturday (with good weather), when perhaps a large

A less quantitative, but no less important, approach in measuring the reduction of procession sizes can be extracted by looking at a change in accounts of the parades. Of the 1870 procession, the *Liverpool Courier* wrote,

> Park-road was continuously thronged for about two hours by a stream of pedestrians and successive lines of spring cars, heavily freighted with Orangemen, Orange women, and Orange babies, all, not even excepting the babies, profusely dressed out with orange silks, orange lilies and rosettes ... the glare of the lily was almost universal.[193]

In 1880, 'besides the arrivals by train, hundreds of cart loads of men and women came to the starting place and swelled the already numerous throng'.[194] In 1905, 'from an early hour the streets of the city were thronged for the great annual gathering'. Orangemen 'assembled at various headquarters and proceeded in throngs and groups to their great meeting' at Wirral Park, Bebington. 'At the neighbourhood of the [landing] Stage there was an immense crowd and many boats were packed by the "Exodus"'.[195] In 1909, 'the thoroughfares contiguous to Exchange Station and the precincts of the station itself were thronged with people who had assembled to witness the departure of the great army of Orange'.[196] The repetition of the word 'throng' is suggestive of the sheer mass of people present to support the parade and is revealing of the strength of Orangeism at this time.

In 1910, 'vast numbers marched. Hundreds followed in their wake and the [Liverpool] station approaches were crowded ... Though the first party reached Southport at 9.30, it was not until twelve o'clock, so great was the crush, that the last contingent arrived'.[197] When the parade was held in Barnston, in the Wirral, 'there was a queue stretching from the [Liverpool] Landing stage to the top of James Street', while, 'across the river [in] Barnston ... the streets and the footpaths were packed with people'.[198] In 1929, on account of the 'big Orange invasion ... excursion trains [to Southport] were well filled and the road traffic was very heavy'.[199] A year

turnout might have been expected, but the Independent, Provincial, and Bootle lodges collectively took 23 minutes to pass, one minute less than the previous year.

193 *Liverpool Courier*, 13 July 1870.
194 *Liverpool Courier*, 13 July 1880.
195 *Liverpool Daily Post & Mercury*, 13 July 1905.
196 *Liverpool Weekly Mercury*, 17 July 1909.
197 *Liverpool Echo*, 12 July 1910.
198 Ibid.
199 *Southport Visiter*, 16 July 1929.

later, 'Liverpool was painted orange when over ten thousand members of the various lodges marched in procession to Exchange Station via St Georges Plateau ... In addition to those who travelled by train, hundreds of supporters travelled by road'.[200] This point highlights the difficulty in assessing how many supporters journeyed to Southport from Liverpool. Even in the 1930s, train passengers did not account for the entire Mersey contingent.

In 1939, at the last Twelfth of July celebration before the Second World War, there was an 'elaborate and colourful' procession, 'consisting of 50 lodges, 100 banners, and 40 bands'.[201] 'William of Orange was charmingly represented every few hundred yards or so. Bands of every description were in attendance ... as one set of music had faded into the distance another one immediately appeared. Princes Park [in Southport] was soon a "hive of activity"'.[202] In 1950, 'thousands of holidaymakers lined the streets to watch the procession go by [and] there was a massed meeting, with children's games, in Princes Park during the afternoon'.[203]

In 2013, the author journeyed to Princes Park, the much-cited location of Orange festivity. As the final destination of the Southport procession, it has traditionally been filled with Orange men, women, children, and supporters. One member of the Order recalled how 'the park used to be packed. It was a sea of orange. There was music, dancing, speeches, and all sorts'.[204] In 1950, the *Southport Visiter* stated that, 'Princes Park became a seething mass of humanity'.[205] A decade later, the same paper commented:

At Princes Park the scene was reminiscent of a war-time invasion. Nearly a hundred tents and marquees had been erected to house officials of various lodges and also to act as rest centres for tired children ... [There were] hundreds of lodge banners and Union Jacks [and] hawkers did a brisk trade selling orange coloured souvenir hats, ribbons, flowers and scarves.[206]

---

[200] *Liverpool Echo*, 14 July 1930.

[201] *Liverpool Echo*, 13 July 1939.

[202] *Southport Visiter*, 13 July 1939.

[203] *Liverpool Echo*, 12 July 1950.

[204] A discussion with an elderly member of the Orange Institution at Princes Park, Southport, 12 July 2013. In addition to the stated entertainment, 'public meetings and religious services were held in the park', *Southport Visiter*, 14 July 1949.

[205] *Southport Visiter*, 13 July 1950.

[206] *Southport Visiter*, 14 July 1960.

By 2013, although the grounds still hosted a sizeable contingent of Orange processionists and spectators, it was by no means 'packed'. Instead of a 'sea of orange', there was a considerable share of green on show – on account of great portions of unoccupied field. Orangemen nowadays celebrate in the Southport hostelries rather than the park, but even taking this into account the area appeared a shadow of the 'hive of activity' it once was.

As late as the early 1970s, reports on Orange processions were still regularly describing the great crowds which accompanied them: 'As the procession marched down Bold Street to Church Street thousands of sightseers marched beside them, and eventually there was a moving mass of people, shoulder to shoulder, stretched right across the roads and foot-paths'.[207] In 1951, 'long before 8 a.m. in spite of showers thousands of children, parents and spectators assembled at the many marshalling points ... in Liverpool, Bootle and Birkenhead to see the start of the procession ... Traffic in the centre of Southport was brought to a standstill [as] thousands of holidaymakers lined the pavement to watch the procession go by'.[208] In 1960,

> From an early hour, Orange music blared from record players in homes throughout the city as the 250 lodges of the Institution assembled ... Nearly 30,000 Orangemen arrived in Southport – seven special electric trains and six special steam trains. Over 8,000 people took part in the colourful procession. Bright sunshine brought hundreds of holiday makers crowding around the procession route. At times they lined the pavement five deep.[209]

For the same parade, the *Visiter* put the Orange processionists at 10,000, adding that 'the Bootle lodges were taking part for the first time in a number of years and their party alone topped the 2,000 mark'. They agreed that 'crowds five-deep lined London Street and Neville Street', while, 'business in local offices and shops practically stopped as shop girls and employees hung out of upstairs windows, or joined the crowds on the pavement'.[210] The significance of the 'invasion' was noted in that the procession was for Southport public houses their 'busiest day of the year'.[211]

[207] *Liverpool Echo*, 12 July 1950.
[208] *Liverpool Echo*, 12 July 1951.
[209] *Liverpool Echo*, 12 July 1960.
[210] *Southport Visiter*, 14 July 1960.
[211] Ibid.

In 1971, the *Liverpool Echo* described how 'the streets of Liverpool city centre today echoed to the sound of drum, fife and concertina bands as over 10,000 members of the Orange Lodge marched through the streets ... Crowds lined the streets to watch the march and in Moorfields and Tithebarn Street at Exchange Station spectators were five to six deep'.[212] In 1985, Provincial Grand Master of Liverpool, Mr Ronald Mather, said, albeit probably exaggerating, of the alleged '20,000 Loyalists [who] marched through the city', 'I think it is the biggest turnout ever'.[213] This was to be the last procession of such a scale in the twentieth century. The *Liverpool Daily Post* remarked that 'the streets of Liverpool were well lined with spectators [although] Princes Park was less crowded than usual probably due to a number of heavy rain showers'.[214]

A few years later the Orange Institution split and many members were lost from both camps in the turmoil.[215] With an ageing membership unable or unprepared to travel to meetings,[216] and a lack of interest from younger members leading to their exit,[217] Twelfth of July procession attendance fell markedly. In newspaper coverage, full-page procession reports of the past were substituted by much humbler articles, whilst the special edition of the *Liverpool Echo*, sometimes entitled 'Magic of the March' to boost sales to revellers, disappeared. Sometimes the report was just a small column, often stating simply that a parade had taken place, with no mention of attendance, nor any other means of measuring the size of the parade.[218]

The numbers of lodges in Liverpool have also fallen to their lowest level in over a century, as Figure 2.3 shows. The number of lodges in Liverpool Province has fallen from 177 in 1974 to 91 today. The slight rise in 1974 was owed to the incorporation of 23 newly established lodges in the two new Districts of Speke and Kirkby.[219] Since then, the number of lodges in Liverpool Province has fallen rapidly. The decline in lodge numbers is not

---

[212] *Liverpool Echo*, 12 July 1971.

[213] *Liverpool Daily Post*, 13 July 1985.

[214] Ibid.

[215] Interviews with Dave and Lynn Hughes, 10 March 2013, and Yvonne Fearnehough, 23 January 2013.

[216] Billy Owens and Ron Bather, 15 March 2010.

[217] Yvonne Fearnehough, 23 January 2013, and Doris Bennett, 5 March 2013.

[218] *Liverpool Echo*, 13 July 2004, 12 July 2005, and 12 July 2006. These short reports mention only that a 'peaceful' parade had taken place. Only a brief mention of traffic disruption in 2005, owing to the 'parade and two car crashes', says anything of its scale.

[219] Day, 2011: 98.

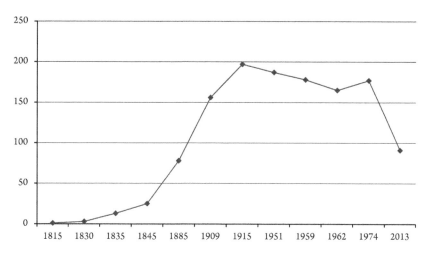

Figure 2.3   Number of Orange Lodges in Liverpool, 1815–2013

Sources: Day, 2011, MacRaild, 2002–3, Neal, 1988, Orange Institution: Bootle Province, and *Liverpool Weekly Mercury*. See Appendix 2.1 for specific details.

exclusive to Liverpool. Bootle Province has seen its lodges fall from 32 in 1959 to 14 in 2013.[220]

In 1885, average lodge membership was 100.[221] If the same average was used today, then by joining the number of lodges in Bootle and Liverpool Province it can be calculated that the membership of the Orange Institution on Merseyside is approximately 10,500. However, in considering the stated decline of the Twelfth of July procession, it can be assumed that the average lodge membership has, at least, halved. It can therefore be said that the membership of the Orange Institution stands at roughly 5,250. Even if another 2,625 (half of the original amount) were added to this number to account for the members of the Independent Orange Order, and this overall figure was doubled to incorporate those who do not attend the annual Boyne celebrations, it would still stand that Owens' membership total, of 20,000, is a considerable overestimation. When Billy Tritton recalled that there were roughly 'sixty or seventy' in his Juvenile lodge in 1932, Keith Allcock commented that, today, the same lodge has only 'six or seven' members.[222]

---

[220] See Appendix 2.2.
[221] Neal, 1988: 185.
[222] William John Tritton and Keith Allcock, 12 March 2013.

In summary, declining parading numbers are but one indicator of the fall of Orangeism on Merseyside, but they offer a quantifiable measure. By 1990, the annual Twelfth of July parade attendance for the Order's day out in Southport had fallen rapidly from a stated attendance of 20,000 as recently as 1985,[223] to a mere 5,000.[224] 'Twelfth' attendance has not risen above 6,000 since. Once a central feature of Liverpool religious, political, and cultural life for many, Orangeism has been relegated to the margins, a cultural artefact still of significance in small pockets of the city, but of very modest or even no significance beyond. This section has charted the decline, the next chapter offers explanations.

---

[223] *Liverpool Daily Post*, 13 July 1985.
[224] *Liverpool Echo*, 12 July 1990; *Liverpool Daily Post*, 12 July 1990.

3

Explaining the Decline of Orangeism

The previous chapter charted the rise and fall of the Orange Order on Merseyside. This chapter explains why decline occurred. It assesses the possible explanations of population decline, slum clearance, secularism and changes in lifestyle, a reduction in family sizes, the loss of interest among young people, and the split which divided the Orange Order on Merseyside. It will demonstrate, both quantitatively and qualitatively, the key reasons behind the diminution of Orangeism in Liverpool, and challenges the conventional proposition, in the very limited existing literature, that slum clearance was almost exclusively accountable.

Between 1931 and 2008, Liverpool's population fell from 846,100 to 434,900. As such, 'any study of Liverpool post 1945 has to take account of this dramatic fall'.[1] The 1960s saw 'an exodus of 100,000 of the conservative minded [from Liverpool] leaving the city, never to return'.[2] Yet, counter-intuitively, neither the surveyed membership, nor the current Orange leadership, holds population change to be as important a determinant of decline as other causal factors.

The orthodox perspective on the deterioration of Liverpool sectarianism is that the breaking up of close-knit Protestant communities, as a result of post-war slum clearance, is the foremost factor in the loss of Orange sway.[3] This position is supported by the Grand Lodge of Ireland:

> The declining membership in Liverpool resulted in a large measure from the policies of the city council which many Protestants believe was designed to break up the traditional Orange strongholds and disperse

---

[1] Day, 2011: 73, citing figures from Office of National Statistics documents.

[2] *Irish Post*, 2 February 1996.

[3] This argument was made by Imperial Grand Master Ron Bather and Provincial Grand Master Billy Owens on 15 March 2010. Owens has also restated this position to the author during discussions on 29 August and 4 October 2013.

the population to the suburbs. Great Orange areas like Netherfield Road, Everton, and Kirkdale were flattened and thousands of families moved to Kirkby, Cantril Farm, Skelmersdale, and other new suburbs. New lodges and bands were formed in these areas, but the dissemination of the famous traditional inner-city areas was significant.[4]

Reginald Chadwick, Master of L.O.L. 184, echoes this point:

I do not think that the redistribution of the population helped in number retention ... With the demolition, members were scattered much further afield and probably found it harder to recreate the same feeling in a new environment, with many members losing touch and drifting away. As the Lodge was not such a big part of their new community, it may not have been quite as important to the members in their new environment as it was in their old one.[5]

Chadwick adds that 'there are those who would argue that this was an intentional ploy to weaken the Orange Institution'.[6] Dave Hughes stresses this point:

Orangeism in Liverpool declined because Protestant strongholds were ethnically cleansed ... The whole of Netherfield Road was a massive Orange area. The community was broken within its strongholds. The area then got regenerated, and from the regeneration they moved families in that weren't of the Protestant persuasion.[7]

This point, although plausible given the hostility to the Orange Order among some of Liverpool's secular or Catholic Labour elected representatives, is difficult conclusively to attest.[8]

Whatever the case, the loss of local Protestant/Orange strongholds had an effect on the ability of the Institution to retain its members. Owens states that 'since slum clearance, people have moved out and of course some people have left because they couldn't be bothered getting the bus and coming back down'.[9] Buckley echoes this observation: 'slum clearance played a large part in the decline of the Institution because a lot of people

[4] *Orange Standard*, October 2006.
[5] Reginald Chadwick, 9 August 2013.
[6] Ibid.
[7] Dave Hughes, 10 March 2013.
[8] This point is considered in more detail by Day (2008; 2011).
[9] Billy Owens, 15 March 2010.

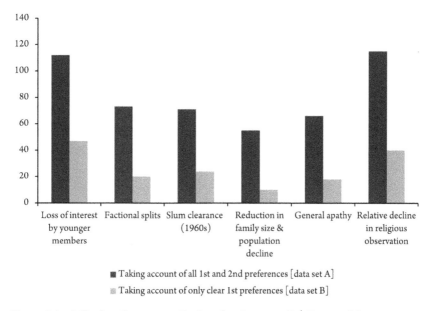

Figure 3.1   Why has Orangeism Declined in Liverpool? (all ages of Orange Order members)

went up to Netherton and other areas and it meant they had to travel. You get "it's too far" or "it's too cold", even if they've got a car'.[10] In a survey of Orange members conducted by Peter Day, '60% expressed the view that the slum clearance programme was the single most significant cause of declining numbers of members'.[11] This outcome does not tally with the larger survey of 215 Orange respondents for this research (around four times the number undertaken in the Day study).

Dave Hughes, Master of District Lodge 92, outlined five reasons which he believed contributed to the decline of Orangeism on Merseyside:

1. The nucleus was split in the atom. It went everywhere: Runcorn, Kirkby, Winsford, Skelmersdale. It got split up all over the place [post-war slum clearance].

2. Families weren't as big as what they were, so people didn't have brothers and sisters keeping them in it.

[10] Tommy Buckley, 12 March 2013.
[11] Day, 2011: 88.

3. We had the split that took a big number away from us.

4. We had a situation with [a decline in] the junior movement. New technology came on the scene.

5. I think apathy came into it with a lot of people.[12]

Based on these points, with the addition of a choice about a decline in religious observance, a questionnaire was constructed and distributed amongst randomly selected Orange lodges on Merseyside. Five hundred question-naires elicited 215 replies, a response rate of 43 per cent. The questionnaire was anonymous, although there was a section for the respondent to indicate their age and their district. The questionnaire asked the respondent to rank the choices 1 to 5, with 1 being the most important reason for the decline of Orangeism and 5 being the least important. Figure 3.1 provides the results.[13] Slum clearance was not indicated as the main reason for the decline of Orangeism by the majority of respondents. By contrast, a loss of interest by younger members and a relative decline in religious observance are presented as the most important reasons for the fall in numbers, whilst a reduction in family size and population decline is viewed as the least important reason.

In dataset A, which takes account of all 1st and 2nd preferences, 'relative decline in religious observance' just outscores 'loss of interest by younger members' by less than 1 per cent, the former attaining 23.4 per cent of 1st and 2nd choices and the latter attaining 22.8 per cent. Dataset B, taking account of only clear 1st preferences, however, puts 'loss of interest by younger members' as the most important reason. It achieved 29.6 per cent of first choices while 'relative decline in religious observance' attained 25.2 per cent. In both datasets, slum clearance achieved approximately 15 per cent of the vote, 14.4 per cent of 'all 1st and 2nd choices' and 15.1 per cent of 'only clear first choices', on each occasion lower than a decline in religious observance and a loss of interest by younger members. It is important to consider both outright and joint first preferences to give an accurate portrayal of opinion,

---

[12] Dave Hughes, 24 January 2013.

[13] For precise figures for the Orange Order survey, see Appendices 4.1 to 4.4. During analysis it became clear that many respondents had indicated multiple 1st or 2nd preferences. The questionnaire had asked for only one of each preference to be indicated. However, not to discount these outcomes, it was decided to present two sets of results. One set presents 'all indicated 1st and 2nd preferences' (dataset A) and another set presents 'only clear 1st preferences' (dataset B). For the latter results, any multiple indications were discounted. The technique paid dividends as both sets of results appeared generally to mimic the other.

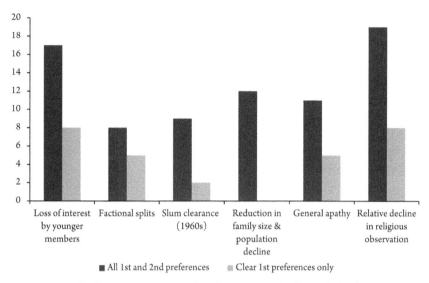

Figure 3.2   Why has Orangeism Declined in Liverpool? (25 or below)

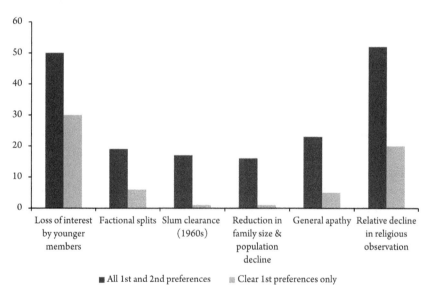

Figure 3.3   Why has Orangeism Declined in Liverpool? (26–49)

as there were 492 1st and 2nd choice selections, but only 159 respondents offered clear first preferences in terms of explaining decline, indicating a sizeable number felt explanations were multi-faceted.

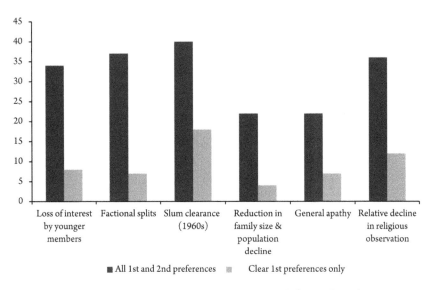

Figure 3.4   Why has Orangeism Declined in Liverpool? (50 and over)

When the results were further broken down to take account of age, it became clear that older respondents did, in general, believe slum clearance to be a more important factor than younger respondents, who had different opinions. Results are shown in Figures 3.2, 3.3, and 3.4. The graphs clearly show that those aged 49 or under do not see slum clearance to be as important a reason for the decline as other elements. Dataset B for Figure 3.2 (25 years of age or below) holds that slum clearance is the second least important factor behind reduction in family size and population decline, while the same dataset in Figure 3.3 (repondents aged 26–49) suggests that slum clearance is the least important factor of all. In contrast, datasets A and B for Figure 3.4 (respondents aged 50 plus) contend that slum clearance is the most important cause of the deterioration of Liverpool Orangeism.

The figures show a clear division between older members, who consider slum clearance to be the most important factor, and younger members, who do not recall the 'golden age' of close-knit Orange communities and believe a lack of religious observance, lack of interest among the young, factional splits, and general apathy to be more important factors in the decline of Orangeism. It should be noted that, for those aged 49 or under, of those with a clear first choice, only 3 per cent thought slum clearance was the main reason for the decline of Orangeism. Of respondents aged 50 or above, almost one-third of those with a clear first choice believed that slum clearance was the main reason for the decline. Of all the first and second choices of the 253 selections from those aged 49 or under, only 10 per cent believed slum clearance to be the main explanation for Orange decline. For those aged 50 or over, of their 191 1st and 2nd choices, 21 per cent support slum clearance as the key variable, which, although the largest category, is not an overwhelming choice. Nonetheless, it is clear that those with a memory of slum clearance and its impact are more likely to hold it responsible for the retreat of Orangeism than those born after the clearances.

Overall, whilst age of respondents is an important variable, the results suggest that a loss of interest by younger members and a decline in religious observance are the most important factors in the decline, while a reduction in family size/population decline and general apathy, of the choices offered, are least important. Depending on which dataset is used, slum clearance and factional splits are 3rd or 4th most important reasons for the decline of sectarianism. Crucially, no one choice is way above the rest, suggesting that all points have their validity. Even the least two supported reasons for the decline had respectable backing. As such, each can be said to be a contributory reason for the decline of Liverpool Orangeism.

'General apathy' is perhaps the least distinctive reason, part of a broader picture of diminished social capital.[14] Asked why attendance had declined, Keith Allcock replied, 'Apathy: people just don't have the commitment to the Institution nowadays. There is just so much for them to do they're just not interested in it now'.[15] Declining membership is not simply a problem affecting the Orange Institution. Trade unions, political parties, and youth organisations, despite an increasing general population, have experienced a decline, a point made by Billy Tritton; 'You used to have Boys Brigades and Scouts. They had lots [of members] in them. They're not as strong as they were years ago'.[16] A 59-year-old respondent from Anfield mirrored this point: 'Society has changed, making things like the Orange Order, [trade] unions etc. less important'.[17] Amid more demands on a finite proportion of spare time, people have tended to shy away from groups such as the Orange Institution. Moreover, with a relative increase in economic wealth, families

---

[14] It is noteworthy that the leading exponent of theories of diminished social capital, Robert Putnam (2000) was invited to address the Grand Lodge of Ireland on this topic in 2009.

[15] Keith Allcock, 12 March 2013.

[16] Billy Tritton, 12 March 2013.

[17] See Appendix 4.6.

may not be as dependent on the lodge's local charity (which in turn may be impossible to provide).

The Orange Institution, which is essentially a political, theological, and social organisation, has suffered as a consequence of diminished political partisanship, secularisation, and social atomisation. One senior member also complained that there is a 'lack of understanding about [the Order's] history',[18] but many people may simply no longer care about the Order's history. Falling family sizes and a declining local population have also hacked away at the Institution's numbers, circumstantial blows added to more ideological or apathetic reasons for the depressed numbers of adherents.

The 'failure' of the Orange leadership to organise against the Papal visit in May 1982 during the event itself (there were Orange protests prior to the visit) was a precursor to the split in the Institution, sections of which wished to 'kick the Pope's ass'.[19] The extent of anti-Catholicism and how much it contributes to an unfavourable image for the Order, deterring recruits, is contested. Doris Bennett declares:

> Being in the Lodge, people used to say to me 'Why do you hate Catholics so much?' I'd say, 'I don't hate Catholics. Some of my best friends are Catholics!' You're not against them. It's the religion you're against, not the people. I've now got two Catholic sister in-laws and I love each one of them, but the teachings are different. With the Catholic religion it's the teachings of the Church. With the Protestant religion it's the teachings of God, and that's the way it's looked on, but then, if Catholicism is what you're brought up with, you can't help it.[20]

Provincial Grand Master of Liverpool, Billy Owens, states: 'I think if you speak to anybody who walks on parade, or who is in the Lodge, or anyone in this building tonight, we have all got friends and possibly some of us have got family who are Roman Catholics'.[21] Buckley, Provincial Grand Master of Bootle, remarks: 'when we lived in our old house, most of our neighbours were Catholics. I got on great with them. Even now my next door neighbour is Catholic. I worked on the docks and we used to have gangs of eight men, and the other seven fellas were all Catholics, but we

---

[18]   Ibid.

[19]   Quote from Independent Orange Order member, *Billy Boys* (1995), Channel 4 documentary.

[20]   Doris Bennett, 5 March 2013.

[21]   Billy Owens, 15 March 2010.

got on fantastic'.[22] In addition, the Grand Master of England, Ron Bather, stresses: 'I had Catholic neighbours and lads who I still know now. We used to play football and cricket together'.[23] Like Bennett, Dave Hughes recalls how people would judge him for being in the Orange Institution, while stressing, it is the Roman Catholic religion, not individuals, to which the Provincial Order take umbrage:

> I work alongside Roman Catholics. I have been a lifeguard. If somebody is drowning do I shout, 'What religion are you?' You don't. I became a senior manager in the City Council and got on with a lot of people, and when they found out I was in the Orange Order, their attitude changed towards me. People say, 'You Orange bastards! You hate Catholics!' We do not hate people. We disagree with the Roman Catholic religion. We disagree with its teachings and we disagree with a hell of a lot that goes on within it. First and foremost, we do not believe that the Pope of Rome is God's mediator on Earth. We believe he is the antichrist![24]

In contrast to the fairly circumspect expressions of the Loyal Orange Institution of England, a 1995 documentary on Liverpool's Independent Orange Order highlighted starker attitudes. The Channel 4 *Billy Boys* documentary on the Independent Order revealed some hard-line attitudes from their members. One affiliate controversially stated: 'It is a great privilege to walk in the Black and Tan uniform'; while another commented: 'Protestant Ascendancy, that's what we celebrate today!' A more temperate statement suggested, 'we hear it from the media and the Catholics that we're a bigotry band and that we're out to cause trouble, and that's not the case. We've got no objections towards the Catholic side. We just want to enjoy ourselves. If they want to kick up the fuss, so be it. We can give as good as we can take'. Another individual offered a somewhat less sedate statement.

> We're here because we stand for the UVF ... We don't go round playing silly tunes. We go round kicking the Pope's ass, and that's what it's all about. Our tunes basically are against the IRA and obviously the Catholics, but it's not so much the Catholics as the IRA. [He later added], Catholics, they're all right. I couldn't eat a whole one. They don't bother

---

[22] Tom Buckley, 12 March 2013.
[23] Ron Bather, 15 March 2010.
[24] Dave Hughes, 24 January 2013.

me because they know what I am. I don't go round looking for them. I don't expect them to come round looking for me.[25]

Attitudinal difference between members of the Provincial and Independent Institutions, particularly over support for the UVF, underpinned their separation. Although both organisations regard some of the specific details of the split as highly secretive, there is general agreement, in both camps, that the pivotal event was the displaying of a paramilitary (UVF) flag at a juvenile parade in the 1980s. This occurrence contravened directives from the Grand Lodge of England and resulted in the expulsion of a significant number of members. There were also some personal disagreements accompanying some of the politics of the dispute.

A sizeable number of survey respondents highlighted the significance of the split in diminishing Orangeism. One even described it as the 'the break-up of the Orange Order',[26] whilst others attributed the split to 'too many leaders looking after their own interests',[27] or blamed 'the running of the Orange Order [and] the divides that are put in place by the higher authority'.[28] It was not just in Liverpool that members left. Some from Bootle Province also joined the Independent.[29] The division brought out a large degree of sullenness in some of the members of both camps. Yvonne Fearnehough gives one interpretation of this:

> We [the Provincial Lodge] didn't want any trouble. The other part of the Lodge wanted to tell people that their beliefs were stronger, with the paramilitary flags and uniforms. The Independent became very bitter towards us. On parade we would either go first or they would go first, so to avoid any clashes. Sometimes if we walked when they'd already done their parade, we'd get booed by them. You still get a bit of friction now.[30]

A member of the Independent, who wished to remain anonymous, expressed his grievance towards the Provincial Order: 'I'd been a member for 36 years, and I was asked to leave. We hadn't done much wrong. It was "if you don't agree with the rules, go." There was no chance to change them, so we had no

---

[25] *Billy Boys* (1995), Channel 4 documentary.
[26] See Appendix 4.6.
[27] Ibid.
[28] Ibid.
[29] Dorris Bennett, 15 March 2013.
[30] Yvonne Fearnehough, 23 January 2013.

choice. We had to go.'[31] Doris Bennett, a member from Bootle at the time, insists, 'the Independent wouldn't go by the rules. They wanted to cause trouble. That was what the Independent was for. They wouldn't abide with the rules, so they made their own rules and left'.[32] Whatever the case, there was a sizeable portion of paramilitary sympathy from members of the Independent Institution.[33] One of the members from Liverpool, speaking on the *Billy Boys* programme, admitted previous involvement during 'The Troubles' in Northern Ireland.[34]

The split in the 1980s was perhaps inevitable because of the stark difference in opinions on paramilitary organisations. Nonetheless, as described by Dave Hughes, the split damaged Merseyside Orangeism as a whole:

> Paramilitary Loyalism and Orangeism are miles apart. They have the same arrow head, but their beliefs along that path are completely different ... The Independent Order started up and we lost a hell of a lot of people, and nobody won. The Orange Order lost because when those people left for this new Institution and found it wasn't for them, they left but didn't come back to us. We lost families. Families went against each other. Consequently, the institution, numerically, lost out big time.[35]

Yvonne Fearnehough also comments on how damaging the split was:

> A lot of things happened ... people just started coming out and said 'end of!', and didn't want to know anymore. If they came out, their spouse also came out, and so did their children ... We were losing a lot of people. I wish they would all come back together and make it one big Institution again, the way it was in the sixties, seventies, and keep our culture going. We were stronger when we were united.[36]

---

[31] Member of the Independent Orange Order, Interview held at the Beaconsfield Club, Everton Brow on 11 July 2013.

[32] Doris Bennett, 5 March 2013.

[33] Birtill, 1988.

[34] *Billy Boys* (1995), Channel 4 television documentary. The Independent Orange Order member claimed: 'I've seen the killings and bombings in Northern Ireland. I used to go over very often. I was right in the middle of IRA country ... I was picking up a gun. That's what I went away for [to prison] you take the consequences ... I still had the same strong views then as I have now.'

[35] Dave Hughes, 24 January 2013.

[36] Yvonne Fearnehough, 23 January 2013.

Yet the 1980s split, although the most significant, was not the only occurrence of internal division and fragmentation of Liverpool Orangeism in the twentieth century. In 1963, after Longbottom had been expelled from the Orange Institution, there was a rupture of the 'natural' Protestant Party–Orange Order link. Roy Hughes claims that 'all the [Protestant] councillors in the Orange Order left':

> I came out of the Institution in the 1960s. I was always on the evangelical wing of Orangeism. The Orange Institution officially applied for a drinking licence for the Orange headquarters in Everton Road. I said, 'I don't think the Orange Institution, as ostensibly a very Christian organisation, should get involved in the liquor business' ... The leadership took a different stance, and Ronnie Henderson [another former leader of the Protestant Party] was expelled from the Orange Institution, because we fought the application in the courts ... As there was no provision in law for such an internal dispute against a drinking licence, there was 'no provision for Mr Henderson and others like him to object', and therefore it was found in favour of the Grand Lodge. As such, we all resigned from the Orange Institution over the issue.[37]

Given that nearly one in six Orange members deemed 'factional splits' as the first or second most important reason for the decline of Orangeism, intra-Orange factionalism may clearly be seen as damaging, a quarrel with wider ramifications.

The 1980s split in the Institution was undoubtedly a contributory factor in the falling membership of the Order. Accusations of paramilitary sympathies, despite the Grand Lodge's repeated refutations, did not assist the Order's reputation. Yet municipal influence had already disappeared. In a 1996 article for the *Irish Post*, Tony Birtill highlighted the Order's reduced circumstances:

> [The Order's] Influence was at its height in 1903 when the then Lord Mayor, W.W. Rutherford, was an Orangeman and the Conservative administration carefully courted the Orange vote. This influence lasted right up to the seventies.

In 1903, 5,000 supporters marched with George Wise to the gates of Walton Prison. Rutherford, the Orange Mayor, was heavily involved in organising the petition to the Home Office for Wise's release ... In all, petitions

---

[37] Roy Hughes, 13 November 2012.

containing 63,569 signatures were presented to the Home Secretary, a far cry from the 375 which the Orange Order were able to muster [in December 1995] in protest at the plan to twin Liverpool and Dublin.[38]

Beyond broader societal reasons and intra-Orange feuds, non-political, pragmatic explanations are sometimes offered for diminished parading numbers, although these reflect, rather than explain, the Order's diminished influence. Even the change from trains to buses as the mode of transport to the 'Twelfth' demonstration is cited as a reason for a loss of atmosphere and consequently a loss of involvement on 12 July. Tommy Buckley recounts:

> When you got the train it was your train, so you'd have all the bands playing, people singing, it was a great atmosphere. The bit I used to enjoy was walking up the tunnel at Seaforth Station because it's enclosed, and being a drummer, the noise was tremendous. It was fantastic. The whole procession used to love it. Trains to Southport stopped in the eighties because they got so expensive and they couldn't guarantee that the Lodge could have specific trains.[39]

After the reserved special service had carried the bands and lodges to Southport, those attracted by the procession in Liverpool would often follow in their wake on the regular service. In 1950, the *Liverpool Echo* reported that 'thousands more joined in the march through Liverpool to Exchange Station [while in Southport] the London Street excursion platforms were brought into use to deal with the 17,000 celebrants, before marching in procession to Princes Park'.[40] Hughes comments on the impact of losing the train service:

> You can imagine what it was like at Moorfields Station getting that many people on the trains. When the trains improved and new lines went in, we went on the buses and a lot of atmosphere went. A lot of the banners, that used to be carried, could not be carried because we couldn't get the poles on the bus.[41]

Increasingly negative publicity, presented in newspaper reports, may have also put people off attending Twelfth of July processions, although highly publicised sectarian confrontations of previous eras did not appear to deter

[38]   *Irish Post*, 27 January 1996.
[39]   Tommy Buckley, 12 March 2013.
[40]   *Liverpool Echo*, 12 July 1950.
[41]   Roy Hughes, 13 November 2012.

people and negative publicity is nothing new for the Orange Institution. As early as 1860, the *Liverpool Mercury* said of the Orange parade:

> Notwithstanding the repeated remonstrances of the authorities against processional displays, a section of Orangemen still persist in their determination to perpetuate these senseless and ridiculous exhibitions. As the law forbids them to parade the streets of Liverpool, they are driven to the localities beyond the boundary, which have now been the scene of these unseemly proceedings for several years past.[42]

Likewise, in 1949, an incensed contributor to the *Southport Visiter*, wrote:

> Please allow me to vent my disgust at the so-called Orange Day Procession, which brings with it a blot on your very beautiful and select town ... Drunken and ill-behaved people ... who sing and brawl ... brought a stigma to Lord Street, and the general opinion heard all around was 'why isn't something done about keeping them in their own town of Liverpool?'[43]

This opinion has been repeatedly expressed over the last two decades by contributors to the *Visiter*. In 1995, as lodges marched 'to the cries of "no surrender" from Protestant spectators',[44] Southport resident, Dave Scully, complained:

> The Orange Lodge parade through Southport is no longer appropriate, certainly not for a forward-looking resort ... The display of Celtic, or rather Rangers, tribalism is at best odd in an English town ... and at worst a provocation which does nothing to further ecumenical relations or encourage the peaceful coexistence of residents and holidaymakers. Elements attach themselves that make it an unwelcome prospect.[45]

In 1998, the *Southport Visiter*'s editorial opined: 'the issue of whether the Order should be allowed to march to the streets of Southport has been raised once again ... It is being claimed that stores lost upwards of £250,000 in business during 1997 ... "Hangers on" misbehave, causing trouble'.[46] On 17 July of the same year, a Mr Wareing wrote to the paper stating that

[42] *Liverpool Mercury*, 13 July 1860.
[43] *Southport Visiter*, 14 July 1949.
[44] *Southport Visiter*, 14 July 1995.
[45] *Southport Visiter*, 21 July 1995.
[46] *Southport Visiter*, 10 July 1998.

'the only fair way to decide on a "welcome" or a "ban" [for the Orange parade] is a ballot. Every ratepayer should be allowed to vote, similar to a by-election'.[47] In 2010, the *Visiter* cited a report stating that the parade was responsible for a '20% drop in profits for Southport traders'.[48] An abundance of correspondence through the years commented on the costs, number of arrests, and the level of anti-social behaviour associated with the Southport Orange parade.[49] Negative reports have not been exclusive to Southport papers. In 1966, a Liverpool paper asked, 'should the police and commerce continue to have this strain imposed on them? Has not traffic reached such proportions that procession through the heart of Liverpool, colourful though they are, can only be admissible at weekends?'[50]

While, for most of the twentieth century, but decreasingly so, negative reports had been outnumbered by the positive comment on 'the sea of colour'[51] and business that the parade brought to Liverpool and Southport,[52] negative articles have increased both in virulence and frequency. In 2000, a letter to the *Liverpool Daily Post*, urging Orangemen to 'put away their ancient garb', states, 'these annual marches clearly boast victories and bloodshed of centuries gone by, marching over the very doorsteps of whom they deem to be vanquished … We can no longer bear to see the Union Jack in the hands of thugs, hell bent on destroying all this country has tried so hard to resolve in Northern Ireland'.[53] The issue received national attention. In 2007, Will Hutton, writing for the *Observer*, commented:

> On the Southport-Wigan train [I witnessed] marchers from the day's Liverpool Orange Order parade in Southport. 'Fuck the Pope', they drunkenly sang, amid ever coarser, more explicit anti-Fenian songs.
>
> The boys from the Orange Order parade were most obvious about their motivation. They were simply getting pissed and showing an intense, animal, masculine togetherness; the best and most enjoyable way they could bond was by asserting their unity against the other – in this case

---

[47] *Southport Visiter*, 17 July 1998.

[48] *Southport Visiter*, 1 October 2010.

[49] Some examples of reports can be found in *Southport Visiter*, 16 July 1999; 14 Jul 2000; 14 July 2010; 16 July 2010.

[50] Date understood to be 11 July 1966 (the article gives details of traffic disruption owing to a World Cup game at Goodison Park).

[51] *Liverpool Echo*, 12 July 1994.

[52] *Southport Visiter*, 30 July 1999.

[53] *Liverpool Daily Post*, 12 July 2000.

Irish-Catholic republicanism. It felt more like supporters at a football match than a political/ religious fraternity. This was not about argument; it was about identity.[54]

The following year, a reporter for *The Times* opined:

> Each year the lodges parade through the town with their Lambeg drums [this is incorrect – there were no Lambeg drums on the parade] and banners before enjoying a day of alcohol fuelled naked sectarianism. Southport breathes a sigh of relief when they board the trains back to Liverpool and begin to sweep the debris under the carpet. The Orangemen swear that it is a great occasion, but the town is a little uncomfortable that it is the bigots who are banging the drum for the resort. But few others do.[55]

In addition to this negative publicity of the Orange parade, suggestions of a ban on the procession have grown. In 2011, Southport's (Catholic) MP, John Pugh, responding to complaints about the march, stated, 'The additional costs of any damage caused by the Orange parade have to be accepted by organisers ... If it is going to be a riotous occasion then it does not have a future'.[56] In 2013, Tony Dawson, a senior caseworker at Pugh's office, stated:

> I have personally made repeated and detailed investigations to see whether it is possible to prevent the Orange Lodge marches. Unfortunately, the laws and rules relating to these marches are the same as those which relate to the right to demonstrate, which I would think few would wish to curtail. As long as the organisers comply with police and council direction they have as much right to march down any street in the UK as you or I have to drive our car down that same road.[57]

Southport councillor, Terry Jones, said, 'most people I know avoid the town centre on this day. The town centre looks like a war zone and it scares tourists'.[58]

It seems that far gone are the days when the Orange Institution could rely on municipal support. Rather, today's politicians are displaying open hostility towards the Order. Negative publicity and a change in people's

54   *Observer*, 15 July 2007.
55   *The Times*, 17 July 2008.
56   *Southport Visiter*, 14 July 2011.
57   *Southport Visiter*, 18 July 2013.
58   Ibid.

attitudes may be keeping the public away from the processions. The Institution is also facing an increasing threat of legislative action to restrict marches.[59]

However, Orange respondents to the distributed questionnaire indicated that it was not a negative image but apathy – a 'lack of interest by younger members' and a 'relative decline in religious observance' that were more important reasons for the decline of Liverpool Orangeism.[60] These points are made by several members of the Institution. When asked what the most important reason was for the decline of the Institution, Lynn Hughes, a lifelong Orange member responded:

> The kids today don't want to know. They're not interested. There's nothing for them. I was put in the Institution under the proviso that once we reached a certain age we could decide to stay in it or not. I stayed in because it interested me. My brother left. We had the same stipulation with our children and both of them came out. They're not interested the same way we were years ago.[61]

Keith Allcock explains the problem:

> As people are getting older and unfortunately die off there's no new people coming in. They have so many things to do nowadays. In the sixties and seventies there wasn't much for them to do, so … they'd make the most of youth clubs and junior meetings that were run by the Institution around that time. Because they have so many things to do it's not a priority for them now.[62]

Although her parents were not in the Institution, so great was the social appeal of the Order in Bootle that Doris Bennett recalled of herself, friends, and family members, 'we were all in it when we were kids … I think we lived so close to Bootle Village [an Orange area] and we just got talking to people. The meetings were well packed'.[63] It is telling of the lodges' appeal

---

[59] *Liverpool Echo*, 15 July 2013: 'Mayor Anderson [is] refusing to rule out using legislation to restrict future marches if the situation deteriorates.' In response, Billy Owens commented that if such restrictions were put in place, the order would 'get everyone down from Scotland and Northern Ireland and we'd occupy the city centre.' Telephone correspondence with Billy Owens, 4 October 2013.

[60] See Appendix 4.6.

[61] Lynn Hughes, 10 March 2013.

[62] Keith Allcock, 12 March 2013.

[63] Doris Bennett, 5 March 2013.

as community organisations that people joined who did not necessarily have family connections with the Order. With so many modern pastimes, Orange lodges do not appeal to young people as they once did. This point was made by Yvonne Fearnehough:

> As I grew up I noticed the membership of the Orange Order declining. In my day people joined because they wanted to, but increasingly people's parents put them in the Lodge when they were younger and when they reached sixteen they didn't want to be in it any more. They wanted to do their own thing. That's when a lot of the lodges broke up and it wasn't as big as what it was in the 1960s, 70s.
>
> Our generation was put in it and brought up with it, but the younger generation think it's boring. We used to go to Church on a Sunday morning and Sundays School at night and then whatever the lodge had.[64]

Points like this were repeatedly made in the 'other' reasons section on the membership questionnaires. A fifty-three-year-old respondent, from Walton, wrote, 'The younger people don't want to get involved anymore'.[65] Another contributor, from Fazakerley, aged twenty-eight, commented, 'younger people need to show more interest',[66] while a 61-year-old respondent, from Bootle, highlighted the role of 'underestimating the feelings of younger members (20–30-year-olds)' as a contributory factor to the Institution's decline.[67] On the feelings of younger members, Fearnehough comments, 'there has been a cultural change as they've grown up. The young ones don't want to know now. They don't want to be sitting in lodge rooms or going on parade. They want to be going out clubbing it!'[68] The Institution itself admits that the 'junior movement is declining'.[69] Relating to this loss of the youth wing another contributor from Bootle, aged 51, contended that 'schools teach too much about foreign religions'.[70]

The inference that a loss of religion is connected with the loss of younger members is an important proposition. Ron Bather, Grand Master of England, contends that, 'We might not be as big as what we were thirty years ago,

[64] Yvonne Fearnehough, 23 January 2013.

[65] See Appendix 4.6.

[66] Ibid.

[67] Ibid.

[68] Yvonne Fearnehough, 23 January 2013.

[69] Discussion with Billy Owens and Dave Hughes at the Orange Headquarters, Everton Road, November 2012.

[70] See Appendix 4.6.

but this is a question of how society has changed ... the principles of the Orange Institution are the same today as they were in 1795, when it was first formed'.[71] Importantly, these principles may not match up with those held by today's youth. Reginald Chadwick, Master of L.O.L. 184, gives his view on the decline of Orangeism in Liverpool:

> Arguing and falling out amongst each other does not help, but that happens in all organisations ... I put the decline down to the changing demographics of the population in Liverpool and the moving away from Christianity of many of the inhabitants of these Islands, which, as such, does not just affect the Orange Institution as is shown by the dramatic decline in those classing themselves as Roman Catholics in the Republic of Ireland. Most of today's population do not have the same moral and religious beliefs that were held in the past and so organisations, such as ours, they believe, are meaningless to them.[72]

Tommy Buckley states that 'religion isn't a priority for people anymore. Otherwise the churches would be full. Nearly all churches are empty now'.[73] Doris Bennett makes the point that religion is no longer important for young people; 'these days religion is second thought to everything, especially with younger people. A lot of children now don't even know the Lord's Prayer! That was the first thing we learned when we were children ... It's took second place'.[74] The decline of Orangeism has coincided with rejection of religion by many. Few young Liverpudlians are concerned with Orange principles of honouring Scripture, rejecting the doctrines of the Church of Rome, and observing the Sabbath.

Another potentially fractious dynamic is the Order's official political position. On their website, it comments, 'today, Orange Order members in Liverpool lean towards the policies and thinking of the Conservative Party with regards to Loyalism and a pride in the Union'.[75] Although many of Liverpool's younger citizens can be said to be generally politically disengaged, many, regardless of anything else, know they're 'not Tory'. Politically, Liverpool appears solidly red and even the Orange Order admits

[71] Ron Bather, 15 March 2010.
[72] Reginald Chadwick, 9 August 2013.
[73] Tommy Buckley, 12 March 2013.
[74] Doris Bennett, 5 March 2013.
[75] Liverpool Province Loyal Orange Lodge (website), 'Liverpool History. Liverpool has a Turbulent History'.

their political position is 'a difficult one to explain in a "Socialist City"'.[76] With these things considered, it is not surprising then that Liverpool's young people are not breaking down the doors of Orange clubs to become members. Even younger members who have a tradition of Orangeism on the side of each parent are deciding to cut short their involvement with the Institution. This point is made by Lynn Hughes:

> Years ago, the older ones took more interest in it. They believed in how it was done. They taught you and you learnt from them. Now those older ones have passed away and with our generation, even though some of us will tell the younger ones what's good, the other half of us will say, 'well if you don't want to stay in, don't stay in. If you want to marry a Catholic, marry a Catholic'.
>
> Our kids, after leaving the Lodge, have turned round to us and said, 'If I want to marry a Catholic, I'll marry a Catholic'. I've said, 'well you shouldn't really' and he'd [husband] go, 'you're not!' As it's turned out they both have Protestant partners, but if they'd have married Catholics there's nothing we could do. My brother married a Catholic, got divorced and then married another one, and my dad (who had been in the Institution all his life), his outlook changed then. He said, 'well if that's what he wants'.[77]

Bennett makes a similar claim to Hughes on the decline: 'a lot of people used to get skitted in school and they'd get embarrassed about it and leave, then a lot of old ones died and there was nobody there to replace them, and then, of course, you've got a lot of mixed marriages'.[78] Fearnehough stated that, 'In the sixties you weren't allowed to marry a Catholic, or have anything to do with a Catholic, because if you were found to then you were thrown out of the Institution. These days now they just go and marry them, they come out of the Institution'.[79] Doris Bennett believed that mixed marriage was the most important reason for the decline of Orangeism:

> The decline of the Institution is mainly mixed marriages. Years ago, before you married ... they were vetted. They didn't ask what their name was ... just 'What religion is she?' If a man met a girl and she was a Catholic, his parents would say 'get rid of her ... She's not coming into

[76] Ibid.
[77] Lynn Hughes, 10 March 2013.
[78] Doris Bennett, 5 March 2013.
[79] Yvonne Fearnehough, 23 January 2013.

this family'. It was like some sort of plague! The same thing happened on the Catholic side.

If inter-marriage occurred families wouldn't speak. It happened on my mum's side. My grandfather's brother married a Catholic and he was never spoken about ever again in the family. It was hushed up. If you married outside of your religion you were cast out. It wasn't done!

Back then sons and daughters would take notice. These days, parents don't ask about religion. They're not really interested. That was a big part of the decline ... I think people started saying, 'OK, if I can't marry her, I'll come out of the Church and I'll come out of the Orange Institution and I'll marry her anyway'. I think that's a lot of what started to happen. They put themselves and their lives and their love before the Lodge.[80]

The divisions that could occur over mixed marriage in Liverpool were well documented and even featured in the Alan Bleasdale film, No Surrender.[81] Dave Hughes would take mitigating measures by asking, 'What school did you go to?' so as to ascertain religion, before considering bringing a girl home. He pointed out that, 'in them days it was serious business ... only one member of the family married a Roman Catholic (my mum's sister) and it was frowned upon to the extent that none of the family went to the wedding'.[82]

The hard-line sectarian attitudes of Liverpool's past have been continually demonstrated throughout this research and were still very much in evidence in living memory, Bennett stating that, 'years ago, in the Lodge, you weren't allowed to go into a Roman Catholic church. Friends of ours, from the Institution, couldn't even go to a family wedding because of the way it was'.[83] The diminution of this sectarian animosity is apparent even among Orange leaders. Tom Buckley, Grand Master of Bootle Province, commented:

One of my granddaughters goes to a Catholic school. She went there because the Protestant school she was in, she was getting bullied and they weren't getting any joy, so they moved her to a Catholic school. We just say 'when you do prayers you don't cross yourself'. Whether she goes into the actual church, I don't know.[84]

[80] Doris Bennett, 5 March 2013.
[81] Alan Bleasdale (1985) No Surrender. Palace Pictures/Video UK.
[82] Dave Hughes, 24 January 2013.
[83] Doris Bennett, 5 March 2013.
[84] Tommy Buckley, 12 March 2013.

When asked, 'Does that bother you that she goes to a Catholic school?' Buckley replied, 'No! As long as my granddaughter gets a good education I don't care what it is, especially if it means she's not getting bullied. She's eight years old and I think she's a bit too young to grasp the situation ... Her mum's a Catholic and my son is not'.[85]

Conclusion

This chapter has demonstrated that a variety of factors, not just slum clearance, were responsible for the decline of Liverpool Orangeism. Although slum clearance undoubtedly played a part by breaking up solid Orange areas and it is suggested by Grand Lodge officials (and by a very slight majority of older members) as the main reason for the deterioration of the Orange Institution, the membership as a whole do not view this to be the case. They acknowledge the importance of slum clearance, but highlight broader social factors at work beyond a bulldozed demographic. As has been demonstrated, the Liverpool Institution continued to be able consistently to attract July Twelfth attendances above 10,000 for decades after the initial clearance programme in inner-city Liverpool. As late as 1985, 20,000 were still being attracted. It is therefore likely that splits in the Institution in the late 1980s had a big effect on the deterioration of Orangeism, as did other stated factors such as general apathy, a decline in religious observance, the prominence of mixed marriage (itself linked to diminished religiosity), and, crucially, a loss of interest by younger members who saw the Order as a dated anachronism and sought alternative sources of cultural satisfaction. Dave Hughes contends that:

> The principles of the Orange Institution were lost within the kids. Because they left at an early age and because people weren't putting their kids in the Lodge, they weren't brought up with the Orange family and they weren't brought up with the principles, the motives, and the actions of what we should be doing. The concept of being brought up an Orange Protestant has been lost.[86]

Liverpool remains an important city in relation to the international Orange tradition, if somewhat marginalised in the city itself. In July 2000 and 2015,

---

[85] Ibid.
[86] Dave Hughes, 24 January 2013.

it hosted the Orange Order's World Council conference and is still regarded as a key stronghold of British Orangeism. Nonetheless, it is symptomatic of the relative decline of Orangeism (and that of a general societal change of attitudes), that the city's annual gay pride event attracts a palpably larger audience than the Orange procession. In 2013, *Liverpool Pride* attracted 50,000 people,[87] whilst the Twelfth of July Orange parade enticed 6,000.[88] In 2014, the Orange procession attendance figure shrank again to 4,000.[89]

Although the Orange Institution has declined, both in size and influence, is it the case that this degeneration prompted the same to occur to general sectarian tensions or did the latter have more of an effect on the former? What of cause and effect? A reciprocally reductionist relationship was evident: as sectarianism waned so did the Order. Sectarianism had provided meaning to people's often monotonous and deprived existence in communities where little else was on offer, and for a small but diminishing number Orangeism's band culture still offers excitement and commands loyalty. The Orange Order was the organisational repository for sectarian views of Catholicism (as distinct from anti-Catholic sentiment, although perceptions could be blurred). As other loyalties than Protestant-Orangeism commanded local affections, so the Order went into decline, unable to offer a sufficiently large broader social role to arrest decline. With changing circumstances, socially, economically, and demographically, the same building blocks of resentment would not be in place to reignite religious sectarianism even if the Order staged an unlikely revival. The echo of the old religious tensions has lain in clashes over republican marches in the city in recent times – but they concern Loyalism versus Republicanism rather than Protestantism versus Catholicism. Many of the elements of traditional Liverpool sectarianism are missing (see Figure 1.1). Moreover, the numbers involved are incredibly marginalised relative to clashes of old. Importantly, the Twelfth of July Orange celebrations in modern times have been relatively passive affairs. Amid a general decline in religious observance, coupled with other distractions, priorities have changed.

---

[87] *Liverpool Echo*, 3 August 2013: an annual event to celebrate lesbian, gay, bisexual, transgender, and a variety of other cultures in the city.

[88] *Liverpool Echo*, 16 July 2013; *Southport Visiter*, 18 July 2013.

[89] *Southport Visiter*, 16 July 2014.

4

Sectarian Dividing Lines and Post-War Slum Clearance

The geography of sectarianism had considerable reach on Merseyside. As its most northerly point, the town of Little Crosby existed as an almost exclusively Catholic enclave. Just north of Liverpool, Bootle's religiously defined areas included Marsh Lane (Catholic) and Bootle Village (Protestant).[1] County Road in Walton was a 'strong Orange area',[2] while Tony Birtill recalls the lodge bands deliberately playing loudly down his predominantly Catholic street in Walton.[3] Anfield was said to have been very Welsh and Protestant,[4] while the religious areas closest to Liverpool city centre are well known as Everton, St Domingo, and Netherfield Road (Protestant) and Scotland and Vauxhall wards (Catholic). In 1971, Frank Shaw wrote that the district encompassing the Adelphi Hotel, in the city centre, had been 'a predominantly Irish area'.[5] Bullough writes that Toxteth had 'Orange' and 'Green' streets,[6] and Alf Mullins recalls the same denominational distinctions in areas of Garston, south Liverpool.[7] Although these cited examples of 'Catholic', 'Protestant', 'Green', or 'Orange' streets are revealing of the wider remit of sectarianism in Liverpool, the religious heartlands were clearly designated in Liverpool northern dockside wards as two distinctive areas divided by Great Homer Street, as described by Pat O'Mara:

[1] Stated by Joe Benton MP, Cllr Jimmy Mahon, Doris Bennett, Susanne Loughlin, Tom Buckley, et al.

[2] Dave Hughes, 24 January 2013.

[3] Tony Birtill, 29 October 2012.

[4] Jean Hill, 26 October 2012.

[5] Shaw, 1971: 40.

[6] Bullough, 1990.

[7] Mullins writes that Byron Street and Shakespeare Street were Orange while Saunby Street and Vulcan Street were mostly Catholic.

The slums – a bit of Ireland united, save in religion … The Catholic elements have their stronghold in Scotland Road along with a goodly segment of the southern end of the Dock Road. In the South, the Protestants have Clive Street and Jerry Street, and in the North, Netherfield Road – scattered bits grouped under the name of Orange River. The religious issue is sharply defined and anyone foolhardy enough not to heed it gets scant sympathy from the English bobbies when trouble ensues. Connaught is Connaught and Ulster is Ulster and never the twain shall mix – save in desperate battle on St Patrick's birthday and on the eventful day when Prince William of Orange crossed the river Boyne.[8]

The Embedding of Two Cultures: The Liverpool Catholic Irish and the Liverpool Protestant British

Charters writes that although 'the popular image of Scotland Road as "little Ireland" grew after the potato famine of the 1840s, the Irish population had been quite large before that. The first big influx followed the [Irish] rebellion at the end of the eighteenth century'.[9] Thus, there was longevity in the area's connection with Ireland, which had already helped solidify an Irish, identity in the locality. It is evident that many 'Scottie Roaders' maintained Irish allegiances until deep into the twentieth century. Michelle Chambers recalled this connection: 'it seemed to me at the time that Scotland Road was very much an Irish Catholic stronghold which you couldn't easily live in if you weren't from that background'.[10] Father William Lupton, who presided in St Anthony's (the largest parish in the Scotland Road district) between 1941 and 1947, noted, 'The people were conscious of the age of the place and the history tied to the place, especially the Irish element. You had to be very careful about what you said – as an English, Lancashire priest. I was tolerated. It was far more Irish than English. When I delivered my first sermon there, I was petrified'.[11] Father Lupton's successor, Father Clifford Murphy (St Anthony's Parish Priest, 1947–52) commented:

When I first went there, they all thought I was Irish because I was a priest – but I have no Irish ancestors … There were about 8,000 Catholics in

[8] O'Mara, 1933: 7.
[9] Charters, 2003: 40.
[10] Michelle Chambers, 7 April 2013.
[11] O'Neill, 2010: 235.

St Anthony's … Great Homer Street was very much a border between ourselves and the King Billies. The parish, I would say, was roughly one quarter of a square mile, very compact. I know there were forty-one pubs because I counted 'em.[12]

There were a reputed 246 pubs 'serving the congregations of 14 Catholic churches on Scotland Road and its immediate vicinity' at the beginning of the twentieth century, and still 158 in the 1950s.[13] This high concentration of public houses, which along with the churches, acted as community hubs, may have been a factor which helped to solidify people's identification with the locality. The pub culture and a lack of integration with the 'King Billies' evidently played a role in keeping Irish and Catholic issues at the heart of Scotland Road politics.

This attitude was not isolated to the dockland community. Much like those in Scotland Road, who considered themselves Irish rather than Liverpudlian, many Protestants on 'the hill' would identify separately. In 1967, John MacDonald (former Great Homer Street business owner) commented, 'years ago, before the Second World War … we all looked on ourselves as being Lancastrians rather than from Merseyside'.[14] Thus, 'beyond the ritual clashes on the streets, the ethno-sectarian formations – both Orange and Green – remained firmly entrenched, offering collective mutuality and support, through pub, parish, and informal networks, to those of the requisite faith'.[15]

Scotland Road was distinct not just culturally, but also politically. As Bernard O'Connell's work denotes, from 1875, Liverpool's Irish Nationalist Party had 'developed a stable foundation on continuous electoral victories in two "Irish" wards, Scotland and Vauxhall'.[16] In addition, Scotland ward was to elect England's only Irish Nationalist MP (1885–1929): T.P. O'Connor. In 1887, core 'Catholic' streets in the Scotland Road area such as Lace Street, Crosbie Street, and Marybone were described as 'as Irish as any part of Dublin'.[17] The first generation of 'Liverpool Irish', as Neal refers to them, although born in England, still identified with their parents' native

[12] Ibid., 247.
[13] Charters, 2003: 41. Cooke, 1999: 15 found that in 1899 there was one pub for every 156 people in Scotland and Vauxhall wards.
[14] Rodgers, 2010: 122, citing John MacDonald.
[15] Belchem and Biggs, 2011: 8.
[16] O'Connell, 1971: 238.
[17] *Catholic Times*, 4 November 1887, cited by Belchem, 2007: 56.

land. Moreover, by the mid-twentieth century, even as the area became less discernibly 'Irish', it was still distinctly Roman Catholic.

In the early twentieth century, many people in Liverpool (whether born in the country or not) maintained a very strong link with Ireland. Agnes Cowper recalls, 'a surging mass of humanity' gathering when 'the many local Irish Societies' welcomed an Irish regiment passing through Liverpool during the Second Boer War (1899–1902).[18] Such strong affiliations ensured support for the Irish Nationalist Party until the 1920s.[19] Despite such 'Green' association, as time progressed, and as the proportion of Irish born in the area lessened, it was Catholicism, rather than Irishness, that became the main emblem of discernment and hostility from their Protestant, Netherfield Road counterparts.

The working class in Everton and Netherfield Road, living in their 'densely packed terraced streets'[20] (like those abounding the Scotland and Vauxhall residencies) developed a strong sense of community. Although, in relative terms, Scotland Road can be said to have been the poorer of the two districts, this was by no great margin. As late as the 1920s, 'hunger and mass unemployment still darkened the landscape'[21] and school comprised of 'boys with bare feet [sitting] sixty to a class'.[22] Limited and sporadic employment, the lack of a 'living wage', the 1930s recession, and the decline of the docks meant that, as late as the 1950s, for many people, the pawn shop was still 'the only way to beat poverty'.[23]

When former residents of both sides of Great Homer Street talk about this period, it is not uncommon to hear the remark, 'our doors were always open'. One local resident, Kevin McMullen, claimed, 'doors were never shut around here. I didn't know anyone who locked their doors and it wasn't just because we had nothing to steal. If someone robbed a gas meter and they were found out, they would be ostracised in every way'.[24] Everton artist, Billy Schwartz, comments, 'we were very safe because people then had a

[18] Cowper, 1948: 84–5: The 'homecoming' was the Irish Battalion of the King's Liverpool Regiment.

[19] See O'Connell, 1971.

[20] Rodgers, 2010: 48.

[21] Unwin, 1986: 7.

[22] Ibid., 105.

[23] Cooke, 1999: 24: 'In 1880, it was estimated that there were 190 pawnshops in Liverpool taking 50,000 pledges each week.' The continuation of this practice into the thirties is cited by Rodgers, 2010: 71–3.

[24] Rodgers, 2010: 111, citing Kevin McMullen.

great sense of community spirit and were very protective of their areas'.[25] It was not until the latter half of the twentieth century, however, that this sense of community began to transcend the sectarian divide.

Liverpool developed its own brand of sectarianism for much of the twentieth century, part of the socialisation undertaken by the city's inhabitants, for whom they now form part of a personal historical narrative. A causal factor relating to sectarianism was the relationship between deprivation, alcohol, and violence. As Unwin demonstrates, this relationship was not isolated to occasions of religious fervour: 'Only the toughest [police] were used on the dreaded beat [of Scotland Road] ... The men lived in shocking conditions, and when they'd had a few drinks they became aggressive and violent ... the Morning Star [a local hostelry] was known as the "Blood Pub".[26] When religious antagonism was added to this mix, the battle lines were drawn, and combatants, often fuelled by drink, converged for their annual altercations. The Twelfth of July parade and other Irish and Orange marches reminded people that, no matter how similar their structural conditions, they were still different. Religion at this time did much to maintain the existence of the 'two working classes' in Liverpool.

One could be forgiven for assuming that the world wars would have united the two communities, but, although those fighting side by side may have begun to see things differently, back home not much had changed. Still isolated in their ghettoised slums, 'Catholic- and Protestant-only' air raid shelters are reported to have existed.[27] During the Blitz of the Second World War, Bootle and Liverpool were the most bombed areas outside of London. A local resident, Terry Cooke, acknowledged the thawing of religious division in some quarters amid the collective suffering endured in the Second World War, whilst noting that unity was still far from evident:

My view is that any religious problems were inbred and that it was the older group making sure that hatred and contempt continued. Then the 1939/ 45 War broke out, and lads who might not have crossed Greaty [Great Homer Street] to meet each other were suddenly fighting side by side and giving their lives for their country. If you are wounded and being dragged to safety, you don't ask the person who is helping you what religion he is. After the War, more people from the west side of Everton

[25] Ibid., 123, citing an interview with Billy Schwartz.
[26] Unwin, 1983: 63–4.
[27] Bullough, 1990: 20.

went out with people from the East side. Old habits and views began to be forgotten. People inter-married and it was a breath of fresh air. But the gulf between the Orange and the Green still existed, and anyone born in the area who claimed anything different is not telling the truth.[28]

Jim Elliott recalled the 1940s invitations to children's parties, 'over the bridge in Scotland Road'. There was no bridge in Scotland Road. 'Rather, this was an expression which demonstrated the territorial gulf which separated the Catholic community from the Protestant Community'.[29]

Following the end of the war, and Labour's landslide victory in the General Election, the newly established welfare state had the effect of lifting many in Liverpool out of absolute poverty. Yet, with employment at the docks becoming scarcer and Liverpool's unemployment languishing above the national average, economic competition remained an issue between the two areas, whilst religious differences remained strong. Win Lawlor, born in the Wirral and raised in a strong Irish Catholic household, recalled 'people would say "Don't go to Liverpool. The Orange marches are on today" and mum wouldn't let us come over for St Patrick's Day, because of a fear of being attacked'.[30] As Rodgers notes, 'putting aside any Protestant and Roman Catholic rivalries is easier to do these days than in the fiercely partisan fifties',[31] an era when Patricia Fitzsimons (footballer Wayne Rooney's grandmother) has 'memories of running away from the King Billys [Orangemen] on the Twelfth of July',[32] reiterating just how sectarian Liverpool was until [relatively] recently. Sectarianism was fuelled by the strength of religious organisations. Countering the Catholic Church was a strong Orange Order in the city. At the end of the 1950s there were forty-six Orange lodge bands in the city centre, a number which today stands at fourteen.[33]

Segregation was not confined to the ghettoes of the Netherfield and Scotland Road areas, As the Orange Order's Grand Master, Ron Bather, recalls:

---

[28] Rodgers, 2010: 135, citing an interview with Cooke.

[29] Elliott, 2006: 19.

[30] Win Lawlor, 21 February 2013.

[31] Rodgers, 2010: 129.

[32] 'Rooney is part of a generation Irish "on the inside"'. *Irish Independent*, 1 October 2006. Available at: www.independent.ie/irish-news/rooney-is-part-of-a-generation-irish-on-the-inside-26359427.html.

[33] Figures cited by George Green (Honorary Deputy Grand Master of the Liverpool Orange Lodge), Rodgers, 2010: 131.

> Back into the sixties ... if you were Protestant you could only get a job in certain companies and that was the same if you were Roman Catholic. There were certain companies that would only employ one religion. I started work in 1968 and one of my first jobs was in a garage for a haulage company. In this garage there was my Lodge Master, there was the two sons of the Lodge Secretary, I had two uncles there, who were both in the Lodge and there were two other Lads who were working there who were both in the Lodge club and there was no way a Roman Catholic was getting a job in that company.[34]

Religious affiliation was a badge of separateness. Cherry Simmonds recalls 'rarely being acknowledged during the priest's visits', as she 'was never considered one of his flock' due to her enrolment at the Protestant primary school, that was much closer, despite being a Catholic.[35]

Overt doctrinal observance was an extremely important part of life in Catholic Liverpool and the (Latin-orientated) ritualism of the Catholic Church heightened the sense of separateness. The Catholic Church made considerable demands upon its flock, enforced through the segregated schooling system. The experiences of Bryan Kelly provide one such example:

> The school register kept tabs on our attendance at school and the Mass register kept track of our religious devotions over the preceding weekend. We were obliged to go to confession, Mass, Holy Communion and Benediction. In my un-blinkered view, I firmly believed that religious instruction took precedence over normal education ... The catechism was a questionnaire with answers on the doctrines and principles of Roman Catholicism, and had to be studied each day, the answers memorised and answered in parrot fashion when asked to by the teacher or priest.[36]

The centrality of the Catholic Church had diminished little by the 1960s. As Cherie Blair reminisced, 'Sunday Mass was an important ritual. It wasn't simply our weekly appointment with God; it was the weekly get-together of the various branches of the family'.[37] When recounting the day her father, Tony Booth, announced the arrival of his new child (to another woman) in the Crosby Herald, Blair portrays how identity bound upon religion still retained its supremacy in 1960s Liverpool:

[34] Ron Bather, 15 March 2010.
[35] Simmonds, 2000: 18.
[36] Kelly, 2006: 38–9.
[37] Blair, 2008: 31–2.

It is difficult to overestimate the humiliation – to my mother, to his mother and, of course, to us, his children. This was 1963, in the heart of Catholic Liverpool. People didn't get divorced, or if they did they didn't talk about it. Girls who got pregnant were sent away to convents to have their babies who were then offered up for adoption. As for 'single-parent', it was a term that hadn't yet been invented. To blazon your sins to the world by placing an announcement in the local paper that everybody could read was a crime against society, against the Church, against everything that any decent-minded person stood for.[38]

Although religion evidently remained a central facet of Liverpool life, sectarian violence had been steadily declining for some years. Alf Mullins recalls that, despite Garston having religiously partisan streets, there wasn't 'any real animosity between them, other than on the day of the Orange 'Twelfth' or the Seventeenth of March [St Patrick's Day], Mum would say "don't go over there today"'.[39]

Although overt sectarianism was diminishing, as late as 1958, 'Archbishop (later Cardinal) John Heenan was stoned by a Protestant mob waving Orange flags in a side street off the main Scotland Road, while he made his way to visit a sick member of the parish of St Anthony's'.[40] Heenan's visit had provoked excitement amongst local Catholics who had gathered in numbers, antagonising Protestants on the other side of the divide. Jean Hill recalls her father telling her about being present during the stoning of Archbishop Heenan:

> He told me it was dreadful and brought Protestants into ill-repute. My parents, who were quite seriously religious, said, 'This is awful. This has got nothing to do with religion' … [The stoning of Archbishop Heenan] didn't seem to have very wide repercussions. It was a weird one-off incident.[41]

This is telling of a decreasing sectarian fervour. At the start of the twentieth century, such an event could have easily triggered a serious riot. Nonetheless, the incident indicated that the 1950s were by no means bereft of religious hostility. Liverpool journalist Ken Rodgers describes his experience of witnessing clashes between the two communities during these years:

[38] Ibid., 25–6.
[39] Alf Mullins, 14 May 2012.
[40] Stanford, *The Tablet*, 10 January 2004.
[41] Jean Hill, 26 October 2012.

I was brought up in heartland Netherfield Road North where the lodges marched with a passion, every year on the 12th July, and where the Protestant Orange and the Catholic Green lined up on opposite sides of the divide to hurl abuse at each other and make their own religious points. Sometimes people overstepped those boundaries along the route, often within sight of the Roman Catholic Bull Ring near London Road, where the skins of the 'Proddy' drums pounded even longer and louder in the name of King Billy. If you ever brought a girl home, the first question one of your parents would ask her was: 'What school did you go to?' It was only slightly less subtle than blurting out: 'What religion are you?' It seemed this is the way it had always been.[42]

Rodgers also spoke to Nancy Flanagan, who came from a Roman Catholic family living on 'Greaty'. She described her experience of events surrounding 'Orange Day':

All year round the kids loved my father, but on the 12th July, Orange Lodge day, all the Protestant kids would throw green cabbage leaves at him ... They would also shout, 'Paddy is a bastard' ... Other kids would grab you and say 'are you a Proddy Dog or a Catholic?' ... On Greaty itself, they knew we were Roman Catholics and they used to come down and ram the door. It was very political and very bitter, with Great Homer Street the dividing line between the Orange and the Green ... When I was little, I would be hiding under the table at our house in Greaty. My mam would put a big blanket over us and we stayed under the table, all crying. In those days, your whites would all be boiled in a bucket. Mam would have that bucket of boiling water at the top of the stairs, should anyone break in ... We would be confrontational in return, when the bands got by the Catholic Bull Ring in town.[43]

Increasingly, 'Orange Day' and 'Paddy's Day' became the lone elucidations of sectarian aggression: two days of confrontations which extended northwards out of the city to Bootle. Councillor Jimmy Mahon, a Roman Catholic, recalls 'Orange Day' confrontations in Bootle's 'religious ghettos':

Malice, you're talking parades! Marsh Lane was the Catholic part of Bootle. Now the Orange Lodge deliberately had their route through the area and as they marched past we'd throw bricks at them, not

---

[42] Rodgers, 2010: 128.
[43] Ibid., 130.

worrying about the kids in the parade. I was only a kid myself, but I was getting taught by the older kids this is what you had to do. This would happen every Twelfth of July and the same thing would happen every Seventeenth of March. They'd throw stones at us when we were marching, but it slowly died down. It's got to a point now, when they march, nobody bothers.[44]

Yvonne Fearnehough, from a strong Orange family, also recalls fighting at the infamous London Road 'Bull Ring'. In doing so, she highlights how individual attitudes began to change as the century progressed: 'My Auntie Brenda used to always be fighting near the Bull Ring. If they [Catholics] threw something at us [the Orange procession] she'd go after them. She'd end up in the back of a police van, but she married a Catholic! We all went down to protest against it and her sisters threw tomatoes at her. She still married him'.[45]

Dave Hughes, an official of the Orange Institution, reflects on both the past violence associated with the annual Orange parade and how it was diminishing by the 1980s:

In today's age of walking on the road with the Orange Institution there are virtually zero problems. You get idiots these days. You don't get collective mobs. On the twelfth of July, coming home, I could tell you every hot spot. I have seen some trouble – some terrible things going on! This was in the sixties and seventies. It started petering out in the eighties. I remember twenty years of running a gauntlet, but the gauntlet got less and less as the eighties came in.[46]

The Contribution of Slum Clearance to the Decline of Sectarianism

The most prominent reason advanced as the cause of the near-disappearance of sectarianism is slum clearance. The rehousing programme of the mid-twentieth century is perceived by many as the key to understanding the fading of tensions between two rival communities. As Brenda O'Brian succinctly puts it, 'I think the destruction of the communities had a lot to do

---

[44] James Mahon, 24 April 2012.
[45] Yvonne Fearnehough, 23 January 2013.
[46] Dave Hughes, 24 January 2013.

with it [diminution of sectarianism]. When they moved to new locations it was never the same'.[47]

Waller's account of sectarianism on Merseyside concluded: 'in the slums removed for the highway for a second Mersey tunnel, sectarian identities were buried'.[48] Peter Stanford, although also acknowledging that other factors such as politics and religion played an important role in dispelling resentment, states: 'the need to rebuild after the wholesale destruction caused by German bombers, led to the break-up of the old sectarian ghettos'.[49] Alf Mullins, a resident of Garston (south Liverpool) at the time, comments, 'when they decided to demolish the slum areas, I think it was that which dissipated a lot of sectarianism ... Anyone who was in the Garston lodge, when they first moved us all to Halewood (because that's where we all got moved to) would journey back, but people would gradually say; 'No, I don't think I'll bother this week'.[50] The Orange Institution themselves believe that slum clearance was an intentional ploy, by the Labour-led city council, to 'clear the Protestant strongholds'.[51] Belchem's research also insists that slum clearance played a significant role in the decline of animosity. In relation to the motivation behind it, however, he disagrees that it was a deliberate policy to hamper 'sectarian' institutions:

> I think that slum clearance is an incredibly important factor. It was a changing of the social ecology of Liverpool ... The whole point about slum clearance is that it removes the infrastructure that upheld sectarianism. I mean it removes the parish and the pub, and until you replant both of those, it's pretty difficult to get that type of sectarian associational culture going again ... In terms of motivation, however ... I didn't see it in terms of a [potential] policy of ethnic cleansing. In my innocence, I had thought [slum clearance] was a self-fulfilling prophecy for both [sides] ... I genuinely think that the slum clearance programme was socio-economic rather than ethno-sectarian.[52]

Despite differences over the motivations behind relocation after slum clearance, it is acknowledged in most assessments that it diminished

[47] Brenda O'Brian, 12 November 2012.
[48] Waller, 1981: 349.
[49] Stanford, *The Tablet*, 10 January 2004.
[50] Alf Mullins, 14 May 2012.
[51] Ron Bather, 15 March 2010.
[52] Professor John Belchem, 25 February 2010.

sectarianism. Although promoting many more reasons for the decline, Andy Burnham MP concedes 'I think [slum clearance] would have played a part. There is no doubt about that'.[53] The Roman Catholic Bishop Tom Williams articulated this view:

> Great Homer Street: that would be the dividing line. Netherfield Road was where you had all the Orange Order churches. Everyone in these houses, all this side [Netherfield Road area] were Orange Lodge. All that side [Scotland Road area] was Catholic. All the tradesmen were this side [Netherfield Road area] and all the labourers were that side [Scotland Road area]. That was the reason for the sectarianism in some ways; the protection of jobs. So when they decided to demolish all these streets … that in many ways was the end of sectarianism.[54]

Thus it can be said that the orthodox view on the relapse of religious tensions is that the slum clearance programme simply 'bulldozed it away'.

Approximately 161,000 people, almost one-third of Liverpool's population, were 'forced to leave' the city.[55] In the Liverpool Scotland constituency alone the electorate fell from 56,000 people in 1955 to 25,000 people in 1971.[56] One of the main areas of resettlement was Kirkby, whose population had already exploded from 3,000 to 52,000 in the space of ten years, by 1961.[57] Kirkby's population, however, was set to swell again. A report from the *Liverpool Daily Post* in 1957 mapped out the 'Blueprint for Exodus': 30,000 more people would head for Kirkby, 48,000 people would go to Skelmersdale, 18,000 to Widnes, 19,350 to Halewood, 6,000 to Cantril Farm, and 3,500 to Formby.[58] Tens of thousands more would relocate in Runcorn, Ellesmere Port, Winsford, and within the city in areas such as Norris Green and Speke.[59]

---

[53] Andy Burnham, 28 March 2013.

[54] Bishop Tom Williams, 23 March 2010.

[55] 'Slum Clearance from 60s Liverpool', BBC television. Available at: www.youtube.com/watch?v=oq_Zkishh1Q.

[56] Figures cited by Waller, 1981: 349.

[57] Figures cited by Dudgeon, 2010: 312.

[58] *Liverpool Daily Post* article and figures cited by Rodgers, 2010: 163–4.

[59] Lane (1987: 157) writes: 'By 1961 Liverpool City Council had entered into overspill agreements involving a total of more than 100,000 people with Ellesmere Port (20,000), Skelmersdale (37,500), Runcorn (30,000), Widnes (14,000), and Winsford (1,600).' Norris Green and Speke are cited as areas of resettlement by Dudgeon (2010) and Rodgers (2010) respectively.

This vast movement of people is referred to by J.P. Dudgeon as 'wholesale demolition ... the ethnic cleansing of the working-class Irish ghetto of Vauxhall and Everton, the old waterfront communities, site of the original nineteenth-century conurbation, and of the tribal culture that had shaped life over the preceding two hundred years'.[60] Although it is not the case that this 'tribal culture' had been a factor of Liverpool life for all of 200 years, nor that Everton was part of the 'Irish ghetto', Dudgeon does articulate an argument, shared with many members of the contemporary Orange Institution in Liverpool, that the slum clearance of the 1960s was a form of 'ethnic cleansing' undertaken by the city council to dismember Protestant strongholds.

Day's research into the decline of Orangeism in Liverpool found that 60 per cent of Orange Order members said that the decline of the Orange Institution in Liverpool was principally due to the breaking up of the communities by slum clearance and rebuilding which began in the late 1950s. Some went on to claim that this was a deliberate policy of 'ethnic cleansing', the council policy initiated under the leadership of the (atheist, socialist, and supposedly anti-Orange) Bessie and Jack Braddock.[61] According to Day, very little official evidence exists which suggests that slum clearance was a 'deliberate policy' to combat Orangeism. He does, however, identify one phrase in the planning statement which could be interpreted as a wish to undermine the strength of the ghetto system:

> Concentrations of residents of one particular social class or religious denomination have important local effects ... The redevelopment of practically the whole area ... while presenting enormous opportunities, has certain inherent dangers ... great care will have to be taken to secure that a balanced population structure is achieved in new development.[62]

The term 'balanced population structure' is a relatively ambiguous phrase. Palpably, transformation of the city's housing stock was an imperative necessitated by the state of Liverpool slums after the 1940–2 Blitz. Bessie Braddock had paid special attention to the slums as early as 1945 during her Maiden Speech in the House of Commons, referring to them as 'bug-ridden, lice-ridden, rat-ridden, lousy hell-holes'.[63] Although Bessie Braddock is said

---

[60] Dudgeon, 2010: 308.

[61] Day, 2008: 277.

[62] Information from the slum clearance planning statement, ibid., 278.

[63] Day, 2008: 277.

to have regarded Pastor Longbottom as an 'out and out Protestant bigot',[64] her otherwise non-religious (and non-sectarian) approach was evident when she declared that despite having a large proportion of Roman Catholics in her constituency she 'would not watch their Catholic interests at the expense of the working-class interest as a whole'.[65] Her secular approach proved appealing as, having already served as a popular city councillor, she retained her parliamentary seat until her death in 1970.

Unofficially, de-sectarianisation and community integration may have been intended outcomes, but not the primary ambitions, of the slum clearance programme. The destruction of the ghetto system would, no doubt, have been a useful accompaniment to anticipated improvements in housing stock for the city's socialist politicians. Neal believed that such a policy had to remain unofficial due to the effect sectarianism had in splitting the Labour Party in Liverpool. Moreover, as he states, 'Bessie Braddock in political terms would oppose the Orangemen, because they tended to be Tories'.[66] Former Liverpool MP for Walton, Peter Kilfoyle, supports this claim:

> It's logical when you think about it. There was a political imperative to break working people away from sectarian politics to politics based upon economics or based upon class ... there was ... a long and consistent effort that was made by people in the [Labour] Party [to break people away from religious sectarianism] and it wasn't necessarily a conscious effort itself, pro-Catholic or anti-Orange or vice versa. It was just because they could see that both on the local and on the national level that the sectarianism was doing tremendous damage to Labour.[67]

Day writes that although 'no evidence has been uncovered to suggest that [Bessie Braddock] was anti-Orange any more than she may have been "anti" any religiously based group ... the Orange Order was determinedly anti-Braddock'.[68] He notes how, in 1958, when Hugh Gaitskell visited Liverpool to open high-rise flats named after Jack and Bessie, 'the booing, singing and shouting from the Orangemen and women, accompanied by the waving of Union Jacks, completely drowned out speeches by Gaitskell

---

[64] Rees, 2011: 24.

[65] Ibid., citing Roberts, 1965.

[66] Professor Frank Neal, 12 February 2010.

[67] Peter Kilfoyle, 23 January 2012.

[68] Day, 2008: 277–8.

and the Braddocks'.[69] Ron Bather, Grand Master of England, explains the antipathy:

> There was set areas that would have been predominantly 100% Protestant and these were the first areas to get demolished. Bessie Braddock did say when she became an MP that she would 'clear the Protestant strongholds' and during her time in office that did happen, and yet she was brought up as a Protestant.[70]

When asked if Bessie Braddock was 'trying to look beyond religion, to unite the working classes?', Billy Owens responded, 'Well she was a socialist, but having said that, she didn't do it to Scotland Road and move them all out. So you can look at it whichever way you wish, but from our point of view, we think our comments are right, because Scotland Road is still basically intact'.[71] Allied to the belief that the Braddocks were anti-Orange is the charge that the slum clearance programme disproportionately affected areas where Protestants were in the ascendancy, rather than Catholic-dominated districts.

Grand Master Bather concurred in respect of the attitude of the Braddocks to Protestant strongholds but offered an alternative explanation of the huge population movement, based upon a perception of greater Protestant determination to succeed:

> This is not an anti-Roman Catholic statement, so don't take it the wrong way, but when the council started making the plans for demolishing the areas round here, they dangled the carrot of better housing conditions, and our people were more apt to moving away and settling into a new environment. Whereas, the likes of your Scotland Road, they said 'yes you can knock our houses down but when you rebuild in that area we want to come back' ... I think it is a bit of a Protestant ethic that if you can expand and diversify that's what you do.[72]

Despite this observation, it would be flawed to conclude that the Scotland Road district remains largely as it was prior to slum clearance, or that the Roman Catholics in that area were not also shipped to various locations in and around the city. Roy Hughes, a former leader of the Protestant Party, who

[69] Ibid., 278, citing *The Times*, 23 September 1958.
[70] Ron Bather, 15 March 2010.
[71] Billy Owens, 15 March 2010.
[72] Ron Bather, 15 March 2010.

campaigned vigorously on the slum clearance issue,[73] comments, 'It broke up both communities. Many people from Scotland Road, for the building of second Mersey tunnel, arrived in Kirkby and people from Netherfield Road arrived in Kirkby. So for the first time in many of these people's lives, their next door neighbours were from the other side'.[74]

Although Kirkby's Protestant residents set up their own Orange lodges, they were joined in the area by a significant proportion of residents from the predominantly Catholic dockside community. Many Catholic schools, churches, and social-clubs were also constructed in the overspill areas, alongside the former Netherfield Road Protestants, who previously would not have been accustomed to these institutions directly on their doorstep, certainly not without the boundary of Great Homer Street dividing them. Thus, the argument that Scotland Road, relative to its Netherfield Road counterpart, remains 'basically intact' is not supported by the empirical evidence. As the (Catholic) former MP Peter Kilfoyle noted of Scotland Road, 'there's hardly anything left!'[75] Only two pubs remain on Scotland Road compared to 41 in the Parish of St Anthony's in 1952.[76] According to one of the few remaining inhabitants of the area, the slum clearance programme 'wrecked the greatest community in Liverpool':[77]

> There was just this parade of people along Scottie, and the same thing was being played out along Greaty and, to a certain extent, Netherfield Road ... This all continued up to the 1960s when slum clearance finally began to take the heart out of the district ... The reality was that when the pubs went, everything went. Also, when they demolished tenement blocks that had five landings with 120 families and 500 people, they replaced them with seven or eight small bungalows. The impact on the area was immense. Suddenly there were no people to service the local shops or support the pubs. The shops died and many of the pubs closed. It was disastrous.[78]

The 1960s housing programme relocated Scotland Road's inhabitants to Kirkby, Walton, Aintree, Fazakerley, Norris Green, Croxteth, Skelmersdale,

---

[73] See Roberts, 2015: Appendices 2.4, 2.5, 2.6, 3.1, 3.6.
[74] Roy Hughes, 13 November 2012.
[75] Peter Kilfoyle, 23 January 2012.
[76] O'Neill, 2010: 247, citing Father Clifford Murphy.
[77] Rodgers, 2010: 112.
[78] Rodgers, 2010: 110–11, citing Kevin McMullen.

and other areas. The depopulation of the Scotland Road area is apparent from census and electoral data. According to the 2001 census, the Vauxhall district of Liverpool, which incorporates the Scotland Road area, has a population of only 6,699.[79] In the 1964 Liverpool Scotland by-election, covering broadly the same area, the turnout was 18,242. Thirty-three years earlier, turnout for the same constituency was 27,444, which represented only 68.7 per cent of those eligible to vote.

Post-war slum clearance was not isolated to Liverpool. As Tom Buckley explains, 'there was houses here [Bootle town centre] but the council knocked all the houses down and built their offices. The old Bootle Village and Marsh Lane were cleared and they just scattered everybody to Netherton and all over the place'.[80] Bennett echoes this point: 'I think a lot of it [reduction in religious tensions] was the areas coming down. Bootle Village came down and a lot of people moved. Bootle Village was virtually flattened in the sixties–seventies. A lot of people went back when the new place was built, but a lot of people moved to Skelmersdale, Kirkby, and all different places. Then they started meeting new people'.[81] Marsh Lane was predominantly Catholic and was renowned as a hotbed of tension on the Twelfth of July, a situation which was to calm after housing relocation. Billy Tritton recalls, 'people would try and break through to the procession. We used to get pepper thrown at us. We used to get stones and grass sods thrown at us at Marsh Lane but that's stopped now'.[82] Bennett adds, 'We moved out of Bootle Village, off Hawthorne Road, in 1971. We had lived there from 1954. It all came down, so did Marsh Lane and all flats went up. I'm not saying there wasn't any trouble afterwards but at one time you couldn't walk down Marsh Lane. You'd get buckets of piss thrown over your head!'[83]

Although there tends to be general agreement that slum clearance was an important factor in the decline of sectarianism, and the contentious issue is the motivation behind the decision by the city council, the idea that slum clearance was the main reason for the decline of sectarianism appears

[79] Office for National Statistics, 2001 census, Liverpool Vauxhall Ward, www.ons.gov.uk/ons/guide-method/method-quality/specific/population-and-migration/pop-ests/local-authority-population-studies/local-authority-studies/liverpool.pdf?format=contrast.
[80] Tom Buckley, 12 March 2013.
[81] Doris Bennett, 5 March 2013.
[82] William John Tritton, 12 March 2013.
[83] Doris Bennett, 5 March 2013.

to be assumed rather than proven. There is some evidence of community integration before the relocation programme. Mullins says of Byron Street (a predominantly Protestant area) of Garston:

> Though there were a couple of Catholic families ... on Orange Lodge Day it was all decorated up. There'd be Union Flags up and everything. It was a ghetto area, in a sense, but there was a big community spirit. I don't think that the Orange just looked after their own. There was a woman at the end of our street. Her name was Larkin, which tells you what religion she was. Her husband came round in the middle of the night knocking on the door and my mum went round and delivered her baby. There was no 'she better get somebody from her side'. It wasn't sectarian in that way, not under the bridge [Garston].[84]

Although senior Orange Institution figures lean towards the slum clearance hypothesis, this idea is not shared by all of their members. It has already been demonstrated in this book that more members believe a decline in religious observance and a lack of interest by younger members to be the most important factors in the decline of Orangeism.[85] Although it was observed that a slight majority of older members believe housing relocation to be the most important factor in the decline, this is not universal. When 94-year-old Billy Tritton (a lifelong Orangemen) was asked 'if slum clearance had played a major part in the decline?', he replied, 'No, I don't think so.'[86] Moreover, even in Bennett's testimony that the demolition of the old 'Orange' and 'Green' areas of Bootle played a part in the waning of tensions, she also hinted that the perception of the youth was already changing, 'going into the sixties, I can't describe it really. It was more the older ones. As the young ones were growing up they didn't seem to bother anymore.'[87]

There was a broader hostility to slum clearance, with a common view that the planners had 'got it wrong' by splitting up communities and not providing sufficient amenities. This is a version of events which seems to dominate in Liverpool. Likewise, the belief that slum clearance resulted in vandalism and a gang culture is generally accepted. Merseyside residents do, however, seem to take solace in the idea that, although slum clearance may have destroyed communities and resulted in various social issues, at least it managed to sort

---

[84] Alf Mullins, 14 May 2012.
[85] See Chapter 3.
[86] William John Tritton, 12 March 2013.
[87] Doris Bennett, 5 March 2013.

out the religious problem. This conviction is partly summed up by Brother Ken Vance, Parish Administrator for St Francis Xavier's Church:

> On the 12th July, we had to be in school by 8 a.m., well in advance of the lodges passing by at 9 a.m. We were then locked in until the lodges had all gone. I suppose we felt in a state of siege … When the lodges were marching it was Catholics and Protestants, them and us … I suppose the only good thing to come out the 1960s slum clearance in Everton was that ghettos were broken up.[88]

Likewise, O'Connor states:

> The widespread demolition meant the break-up of old communities but this is not entirely to be mourned. Religious divisions had been rife … Serious rioting and fighting had been regular occurrences on St Patrick's Day and on the 12th July but as the areas were cleared and the communities dispersed from the 1950s such incidents have, fortunately, been much less frequent.[89]

This view, suggesting that slum clearance was the main reason for the moderation of hostilities, although widely accepted, does not necessarily convey the entire picture. It fails to recognise that sectarianism was not confined to the Scotland and Netherfield districts. As Bullough has suggested, streets in Toxteth were designated Green and Orange. Likewise, sectarian trouble had been evident in Birkenhead. Large Irish Catholic populations also existed in Little Crosby, Litherland, Walton, Kirkdale, and Bootle, with the last location witnessing occasional sectarian trouble on the 'Twelfth' into the 1970s.

Joe Benton, MP for Bootle and devout Roman Catholic, rejects the notion that slum clearance was the sole causal factor in the attenuation of religious friction on Merseyside, highlighting education and ecumenism as more significant dynamics:

> The decline of sectarianism is not just merely attributable to breaking down of so-called 'ghettos' and the harbouring together of different communities. I think that also, through education and, in certain respects, religious enlightenment, there has been a movement that has created a far, far better notion of tolerance and understanding between

---

[88] Rodgers, 2010: 134, citing Bro. Ken Vance.
[89] O'Connor, 2013: 92 (originally published 1986).

people who do not necessarily have the same views. I think the tolerance factor ... had more to do with it than the breaking up of ghettos. There is no doubt about it. So many people now seem to reject such notions [of prejudice] ... People still hold onto their religious beliefs, but it's with a degree of tolerance.[90]

Where slum clearance took place, it did not entirely remove all sectarian tension; the remaining populations continued some aspects of the divide. The emasculated Scotland Road and Netherfield Road areas are visually almost bereft of the sectarianism that once dominated. Yet, there remain Orange clubs in the district. Loyalist flags and bunting still adorn lamp posts in the Netherfield Road area in the run-up to the Twelfth of July. 'King Billy' posters are visible in some windows during this period and parties are held in the area on the 'Twelfth'. Peter Aughton, also writes that, 'in the St Domingo and Breckfield area graffiti proclaiming "No Surrender" and obscenities regarding the Pope can sometimes still be seen'.[91]

In the Scotland Road area, tricolours are flown on St Patrick's Day and a republican band parade passes through the district. Isolated examples of religious/sectarian graffiti, ranging from 'God Bless Our Pope' to support for 'RIRA' (the Real IRA) have been seen. The Orange Order is still not permitted by the police to march past St Anthony's Catholic Church on Scotland Road.

The argument which suggests that sectarianism was demolished along with the slums also fails to recognise that Orange lodges were established in the new suburbs of the city. The transfer of sectarian cultures to new locations on Merseyside is not the death of sectarianism. Twenty-three new lodges had been established in Kirkby and Speke by 1974.[92] Moreover, the reductionist argument that slum clearance was responsible for burying sectarianism fails to explain why such a process could work only in Liverpool. Slum clearance also took place in both Glasgow and Belfast, areas which retain strong sectarian traditions to this day. In 2006, *The Orange Standard* made this point:

The number of new houses and flats put back in Netherfield road was only a fraction of the number which had existed before. The same thing, of course, has happened in Belfast and Glasgow, and we all know the

90 Joe Benton, 18 May 2012.
91 Aughton, 2008: 271.
92 Day, 2011: 98.

difficulties caused for the Loyal Orders by the 'rape of the Shankill', and the controversial redevelopment housing schemes which ripped the heart out of the great Protestant districts ... Much the same thing happened in Glasgow, but the Orange Order in Scotland [and Northern Ireland] has proved highly successful in following the scattered families and forming new lodges.[93]

One of the reasons, not mentioned in this report, for the relatively better survival of Orangeism in Glasgow is its (informal) affiliation with Rangers Football Club,[94] while Belfast has an entirely different set of circumstances not relevant to the Liverpool experience.

This suggests that other factors may have played an important role in the decline of sectarianism. Waller concedes that his original assertion that slum clearance simply removed Liverpool's sectarian problems may have been overly simplistic. He admitted to now

finding unsatisfactory and insufficient the argument that sectarianism was simply bulldozed away by slum clearance. Instead, I should be inclined to look at the changing character of the local political parties, and their relations with their national counterparts; likewise, at the changing character of the churches ... How new interests and issues came to overlay and supersede the old must be the key.[95]

Waller had also hinted at alternative explanations, in 1981, by stating that, 'increasingly, people were discovering alternatives to, or surrogates for religion'.[96]

This chapter has contended that in removing the infrastructure that upheld sectarianism, slum clearance played an important role in its decline. However, it has also highlighted that it is tenuous to suppose that slum clearance expelled sectarianism in itself. The most literal consequence of the post-war clearance programme, in terms of diminishing sectarianism, was the demise of denominational supremacy in geographical concentrations, thereby removing the ability for political candidates to be consistently elected on religious labels. In new locations, neither the Conservatives nor the Protestant Party could outweigh support for Labour.

[93] *Orange Standard*, October 2006.
[94] This point will be expanded in Chapter 9.
[95] Email correspondence with Professor Phillip Waller, 12 May 2011.
[96] Waller, 1981: 350.

5

The Diminishing Politics of Sectarianism: How Class Politics Displaced Identity Politics

The Politics of Sectarianism

In Liverpool, sectarianism and xenophobia became useful tools to gain power. By feeding on prejudice directed towards the Irish 'invaders' and their offspring, fear and economic rivalry became entities that local politicians would exploit for electoral success. For the Irish, their politics was centred neither upon the conditions nor the town in which they found themselves. It was instead focused upon factors relating to their homeland. As a result, Liverpool politics became quickly 'impregnated with religious-cum-national stereotypes'.[1] David Kennedy paints a portrait of Liverpool's unique political landscape:

> Like no other mainland British city, Liverpool reflected the contours of the on-going struggle in nineteenth century and early twentieth century Ireland between Unionism and Nationalism over the matter of Home Rule for Ireland ... The local Labour Party struggled to gain a commanding foothold in the city until well into the twentieth century. 'Liverpool', the frustrated Labour leader, [Ramsay] MacDonald, wrote in 1910, 'is rotten and we better recognise it'. The local Home Rule supporting Liberal Party and, more especially, the Conservative–Unionist Party were more adept at competing for civic power by recourse to ethno-religious politics.[2]

[1] Waller, 1981: 18.
[2] D. Kennedy, 'Red and Blue and Orange and Green?' Everton Season 2009–10. Available at: www.toffeeweb.com/season/09-10/comment/fan/RedBlueGreenOrange.pdf.

Aughton comments that, 'politics in the city ... had a very distinctive local flavour ... religion played a major role. Orangeism, still a powerful force up until the Second World War, was strongly linked to Unionism and the Tory Party ... the city's socialists were seen to be linked to Catholicism'.[3]

MacRaild states that, 'from the 1830s politics [in Liverpool] was coloured by an Orange and Green palette',[4] yet much of the political outworking of religious antipathy began with the formation of the WMCA in the late 1860s. This organisation was interconnected with both the Orange Institution and Conservative and Unionist Party. As many of its members were also Orangemen, it acted as a link between the two organisations and helped provide 'an influential working man's voice within the Tory apparatus'.[5] The WMCA 'took as its emblem the maintenance of Protestantism',[6] and was an important component in the local Conservative leadership's 'long-term strategy of courting the working man's vote as a defence against Liberal (and later Labour) advances'.[7] Waller suggests that the WMCA (along with some prominent evangelists and the Orange Institution) helped convince Liverpool's Protestant working class that Protestantism evoked 'personal independence, material prosperity, and all civic virtues',[8] whereas Catholicism brought 'priest-ridden superstition, lawlessness, and economic fatalism'.[9] As Neal comments:

> Among the factors most responsible for virulent anti-Catholicism three stand out. They were an ultra-Protestant Conservative caucus on the town council and their supporters; the coterie of Irish evangelical clergy who held livings in Liverpool and Birkenhead, led by Hugh McNeile, and, lastly, the Orange Order. Membership of these groups overlapped after 1835. Some Conservative councillors were members of the Orange Order, all were Anglicans, some of the Anglican clergy – though not McNeile – were Orangemen and all were Conservatives.[10]

The populist rhetoric used by the Liverpool Conservatives was articulated in 1874 by one Conservative Association ward chairman. He announced to a

---

[3] Aughton, 2008: 271.
[4] McRaild, 2000: 55.
[5] Kennedy and Collins, 2006: 769.
[6] Waller, 1981: 18.
[7] Kennedy and Collins, 2006: 769.
[8] Waller, 1981: 18.
[9] Ibid.
[10] Neal, 1988: 38.

cheering crowd, that Protestant ascendancy 'was the ascendancy of truth over error, of light over darkness, of freedom over slavery'.[11] In 1875, Conservative posters highlighted the importance of the 'Irish Question', urging 'loyalty to Queen and Constitution ... and not Home Rule dictation'.[12] Although the Tories were perhaps most notable for using religious divisions and sectarianism for political gain, they were not in isolation.

In nineteenth-century Liverpool, Liberal candidates would often stand on an Irish ticket to gain electoral support. The Liberals 'used their commitment to Irish Home Rule to appeal directly to many Irish voters. By forging an alliance with the local Irish [Nationalist] Party, the Liberal agenda tended to be synonymous in most people's eyes with defending the rights of Catholic voters in the city'.[13] The 'Home Rule' candidate was a regular phrase adopted at election time. Many Irishmen supported Liberal candidates who 'combined Home Rule sympathies with labour causes'.[14]

The division between the Liberals and Conservatives on the 'Irish question' would later be displayed in the boardrooms of Everton FC and Liverpool FC: Everton's Mahon, Wade, and Baxter (two Methodist, one Catholic – all Liberals) favouring Home Rule for Ireland, while Liverpool's Houlding and McKenna (both Protestant Orangemen and Conservatives) were virulently opposed to Irish Home Rule.

Liverpool's sectarian divisions continued to influence local political agendas for a sizeable portion of the twentieth century. The Irish Nationalist MP for Liverpool Scotland, T.P. O'Connor, kept his seat until his death in 1929. The consistent support for the Irishman (44 years as member for Scotland Division) led him to become Father of the House of Commons. As Charters comments, 'his advocacy of Irish Nationalism, though unpopular in other parts of the UK, stood him in good stead in his constituency. In the General Election of 1918, two years after the Easter Rising, Tay Pay [colloquial name for O'Connor] was elected unopposed, which tells us much about the sympathies of people in that part of Liverpool'.[15]

O'Connor was succeeded by David Logan, who, although representing the Labour Party, had been endorsed locally because of his Irish nationalist background and his Catholicism. Logan had a Scottish father and Irish

---

[11] Waller, 1981: 18.

[12] Ibid., 32.

[13] David Kennedy, 'Red and Blue and Orange and Green?'

[14] Waller, 1981: 60.

[15] Charters, 2003: 48.

mother. He also married an Irish schoolteacher and had been a Nationalist councillor until he joined Labour in 1923. Logan would often vote against the Labour party if policy contravened his deep-rooted Catholic principles and clashed with his left-wing and religiously sceptical fellow MP in neighbouring Exchange, Bessie Braddock. Braddock, who opposed the Nationalist–Labour caucus on the council, took her seat from a Conservative in 1945, midway through Logan's time in office. Braddock advocated 'more homes, not more Priests'.[16] As Waller wrote, 'Liverpool's Labour party was a bipartite creature, whose Catholic and secular halves often clashed ... Arguably the Catholicism of many electors and elected came before their socialism. Labour inherited rather than won Nationalist seats'.[17]

Logan remained in office until his death in 1964 and was very much a product of his constituency, as had been the Irish Nationalist councillors who maintained a presence on the Liverpool City Council until the 1920s.[18] One such councillor, 'Dandy' Patrick Byrne, was landlord of the Morning Star pub on Scotland Road, avowedly used to shelter the Irish Nationalist leader, Éamon de Valera, on his way to the USA after escaping Lincoln prison in 1919.[19]

Members of the Protestant Party or the Conservatives represented most of Protestant Liverpool until deep into the twentieth century. The former MP for Liverpool Walton, Peter Kilfoyle, described this as, 'working class Protestants being skilfully recruited and manipulated to vote Tory',[20] a point challenged by Belchem, who suggests that the Protestant working class were not simply 'passive instruments ... manipulated at will by the Tory caucus'.[21] Bohstedt also states that, 'Sectarianism was not simply elite manipulation of the masses. The elites did not create it. Plebeian Protestants used the Conservative bosses to advance their own interests more than vice versa'.[22] Indeed, as Belchem and Biggs assert, 'the progressive potential of class-based Liverpool labour was not to be realised' before the First World War',[23] nor would it fully be realised until 1964 when the city at large finally substituted its Conservative representatives for Labour MPs.

---

[16] Belchem, 25 February 2010.
[17] Waller, 1981: 323–4.
[18] *Irish Post*, 27 January 1996.
[19] Charters, 2003: 48.
[20] Peter Kilfoyle, 23 January 2012.
[21] Belchem, et al., 1992: 11.
[22] Bohstedt, 204; ibid.
[23] Belchem and Biggs, 2011: 8.

Irish Nationalism and the Liberals

Irish Catholics in Liverpool had long association with the Liberals, partly because they were the antithesis to the Tory–Protestant caucus, but also as Liberals were the only real alternative until the first electoral success of the Irish Nationalist Party (INP) in November 1875.[24] The INP thereafter remained an electable force in Liverpool until 1922. Nationalists and Liberals were often united over Home Rule, but this link came under strain. 'Irish issues' (specifically over public funding for Catholic schools) created disharmony in the Liberal Party. Liberals opposed denominational education, and the party's backing for non-sectarian educational provision 'threatened their Catholic support'.[25] Belchem also makes this point that, 'in seeking emancipation, Catholics identified with the Liberal project of civil and religious liberty, but this was called into question by subsequent Catholic defence of denominational education. On this recurrent point of tension, Catholics drew away from Liberals'.[26]

Liverpool's Irish nationalism[27] began seriously to grow in strength in the late 1860s, with the perceived failings of the Liberals, in terms of both state and municipal politics. Liverpool's Nationalist councillors were an electable force by 1870s. The party 'grew out of a quasi-religious base in that it splintered off the pro-Liberal Catholic Club[28] – essentially a lay organisation – and it developed a stable foundation on continuous electoral victories in the two "Irish" wards, Scotland and Vauxhall'.[29] Bernard O'Connell states that,

> The I.N.P. was a 'political party' in that it did provide candidates and did present issues under its own banner at elections, and did provide a channel of political representation whose aim was to acquire and maintain a degree of political control [although] there was no local executive in official terms – for the I.N.P. in Liverpool, for it had been designed to obey only the instructions of Parnell via the national executive.[30]

[24] O'Connell, 1971: 269; L. Connolly (Irish Nationalist) beat W. Williams (Liberal) by 928 votes in a municipal contest for Scotland Ward.

[25] Kennedy and Collins, 2006: 768.

[26] Belchem, 2007: 121.

[27] Muir, 1907: 304: 'There were Irish names among the burgesses as early as 1378'.

[28] Belchem, 2000a: 133.

[29] O'Connell, 1971: 238.

[30] Ibid., 238–9. For more information, see O'Connell's thesis, the authoritative work on the formation, and history of the Irish Nationalist Party in Liverpool.

Forty-eight Irish Nationalists sat on the Council between 1875 and 1929, 'potent electorally because of the concentration of Liverpool Irish in Scotland and Vauxhall wards'.[31] The Liverpool Irish followed Nationalist Party advice, to 'remember they were Irishmen first and Liverpudlian after' – a statement which, several Conservatives claimed, illustrated the Nationalists' 'improper attitude to municipal affairs'.[32] Nonetheless, not all had abandoned the Liberals: many of whom were still focusing on their Irish and Catholic credentials to gain election. Indeed, as Waller observes, 'several Liberal Ward Associations selected Home Rulers in 1876. One candidate combined a galaxy of titles – Liberal, Catholic, temperance, and Home Rule'.[33] Liberals and Nationalists collaborated on municipal affairs, but 'pressure increased to eradicate all vestige of patrician Liberal dependence, to provide self-sufficient protection for the Catholic working-class community'.[34]

The Liberal–Catholic alliance was not as durable as the Conservative–Protestant caucus. When 'Gladstone overturned the political world by embracing Home Rule ... considerable disaffection existed among Liberals ... [and] in May 1886 a Liverpool Liberal Unionist Committee was formed'.[35] The committee immediately numbered one hundred members and this figure was to increase. In Tory rhetoric, Liberal Unionists became known as 'Loyalists' and Gladstonians 'Disloyalists'. To complicate matters further, the Liberal Unionists formed a pact with the Conservatives and often stood against their Liberal counterpart. Birtill suggests that elements of 'the Liberal Party despised Orangeism and [thus] supported Catholic attempts to get involved in running the city, [as such] Liberal support for Home Rule in the 1880s helped cement the alliance between them and Irish nationalists'.[36]

By 1884, Catholics formed over one-quarter of the Liverpool electorate.[37] By 1885, Liverpool Scotland had become the only constituency in England to elect an Irish Nationalist MP. Belchem puts this down to 'the extensive parish and pub based infrastructure' located in the Irish wards.[38] Scotland and Vauxhall constituencies were both Nationalist targets, but, although both

---

[31]   Bohstedt, 1992: 205. From Belchem, et al., 1992.

[32]   Waller, 1981: 137.

[33]   Ibid., 31.

[34]   Belchem, 2000a: 141.

[35]   Waller, 1981: 72–3.

[36]   *Irish Post*, 27 January 1996.

[37]   Waller, 1981: 40.

[38]   Belchem, 2000a: 147.

boasted INP councillors, Vauxhall Nationalists could never achieve the same level of electoral success as their neighbour, given a higher predominance of Liverpool Irish in the Scotland area. Patriotic Irishmen in Liverpool had initially devoted their time to converting Liberals to the Home Rule cause, but the Liberal/Nationalist partnership was ultimately doomed to failure. The years 1892–5 witnessed the first Liberal administration in Liverpool for fifty years. The success of the administration, however, rested heavily on its affiliation with Irish Nationalists. The promotion of Nationalists to positions of authority within the council provided an ideal platform for the Conservatives to question the loyalty of the Liberals.

The Conservatives and the Protestant Party

When out of power, Liverpool Tories campaigned much more ferociously with the Protestant card. In 1893, Lord Randolph Churchill visited Liverpool, asserting three times that 'Ulster would fight and be right'.[39] The focus of the Conservative campaign, however, is more aptly demonstrated by Arthur Bower Forwood. A Conservative councillor from 1871 and MP for Ormskirk from 1885 until 1898, Forwood claimed that the Gladstonians were supported only by

> the lowest strata of society ... such as the Irish corner rough, too idle to work, too much of an inebriate to find employment and too impecunious to find a permanent home ... men who regarded the English as foreigners in Ireland, and whose countrymen in Liverpool were certainly foreign in many of their ways to the ideas and principles of his hearers.[40]

Welshmen and Scotsmen, he noted 'became good citizens', leaving their national fads outside the council chamber; 'but it was different with the body of Irishmen – (a voice: "Papists")'.[41] Forwood played on issues that would hit a nerve. He talked of how 'the influx of the Irish into Liverpool brought poverty, disease, dirt and misery, drunkenness and crime, in addition to a disturbance in the labour market and the cost to the ratepayers of an enormous sum of money'.[42] This scapegoating tactic was widely adopted

---

[39] Waller, 1981: 140.
[40] Ibid.
[41] Ibid., 141.
[42] Ibid.

by the Conservatives. Forwood's rhetoric offered credence to extreme Protestant orators such as John Kensit and George Wise, whose 'lewd assertions – for example, that priests "lived with harlots" and "rob the poor" to feed their bastards – incited disorder'.[43] Conservatives did not openly condone these views or the violence that followed, but encouraged and capitalised upon racial xenophobia and religious sectarianism.

Anti-Irish/Catholic rhetoric served two purposes for the Conservatives: first, it kept people distracted from the dreadful surroundings in which they found themselves and provided an alternative source of blame for these material conditions, as patriotism was utilised instrumentally as 'a force which could push to one side the significance of social and economic divisions'.[44] Secondly, it provided the Conservative party with considerable muscle in the form of the WMCA and the Orange Order come election time.

There were early tensions in the Protestant–Conservative relationship. In 1889, it was claimed that the Tories were becoming 'unappealing to masculine Orangemen', whose experience was 'of Conservatives snubbing them once they attained power'. Conservatives, the *Protestant Standard* reflected, 'would support the devil himself if he answered their purpose'.[45] The failure of the Tories to introduce a new church discipline bill to counter 'extreme ritualism' within the Church of England, coupled with 'Rome on the Rates' issues, in 1902,[46] served only to exacerbate disunity. As a consequence, in 1903, many disgruntled Orangemen turned to the newly created National Protestant Electoral Federation for guidance on candidates.[47] Orangemen did not have to look far for alternatives. The year witnessed a number of candidates stand as independent Protestants.

By January 1905, Protestants had returned their sixth councillor against Conservative opposition and the first proposals of an electoral pact were put forward in October, by 'Tory boss, Archibald Salvidge, [who] had used the Orange card to build the W.M.C.A. into an urban working-class machine'.[48] Local Conservatives indicated they would not oppose a Protestant candidate in St Domingo ward, if the Protestants allowed Kirkdale's Conservative

---

[43] Ibid., 200, citing *Liverpool Review*, 4 April 1903.

[44] Lunn, 2008: 90.

[45] Waller, 1981: 93, citing *Protestant Standard*,, 21 September 1889.

[46] The 1902 Education Act made public monies available to Roman Catholic schools.

[47] The NPEF, whose motto read 'Protestantism before Party', was established in Liverpool. Chaired by Thomas Massey, an Orangeman, the federation recommended the 'most Protestant' candidate, irrespective of party allegiance.

[48] Bohstedt, 204: From Belchem, et al., 1992.

councillor a clear run.[49] An agreement was eventually made which meant that Protestants would not stand in Tory target seats as long as Tories did not stand in Protestant target seats, an electoral pact which survived until the 1970s.

Despite this political covenant, George Wise tried to distance Protestants from the Conservatives. He argued for social reform and referred to himself as a 'worker's candidate', and even as a socialist. In 1905, he declared that, 'every Protestant should be a labour man'.[50] 'Independent Protestants', of which Wise was one, generally concentrated their activities in St Domingo, Netherfield, and Kirkdale. They stood four candidates in 1903, and the dissatisfaction with the Tories among the Orange rank and file was reflected when three of the four achieved office, Wise triumphing in Kirkdale before standing down three years later to become Pastor of the Protestant Reformers Church in Netherfield Road. Protestants demonstrated against the Liberals' Education Bill introduced in the House of Commons in 1906. The bill (had it not been rejected by the Lords) would have been damaging to denominational schools and their powers of religious instruction. Ironically, the Protestants sided with Roman Catholics on this issue as each wished to maintain autonomy when it came to the spiritual guidance of their flock.

Protestant and Conservative candidates were steadfast on religious and political issues. They vowed to support Ulster and to 'fight for the Liberty and honour of the British flag'.[51] William Rutherford, the Conservative MP for Kirkdale, told parliament that feelings in his constituency 'may rise to a point of danger from concern about Ulster's boundaries'.[52]

In December 1930, Pastor H.D. Longbottom, who, following the death of Wise, had headed the Protestant Reformers Church, started a newspaper, the *Protestant Times*, and in the same year won a three-cornered contest to become a local councillor for the newly formed 'Protestant Party'. In 1932, Longbottom's wife was also elected to the Council, also representing St. Domingo'.[53] The Protestant and Conservative presence on the council appeared secure.

[49] Waller, 1981: 212–13.
[50] Ibid., 213, citing *Protestant Standard*, 11 November 1905.
[51] Bohstedt, 1992: 199.
[52] Waller, 1981: 287.
[53] Ibid., 334.

Labour and Catholicism

By the 1930s, the main political adversaries of the Tories and Protestants were not Liberal, nor Irish Nationalist, but the Labour Party. The year 1892 saw the foundation of an Independent Labour Party and Fabian Society in Liverpool. These autonomous groups would eventually merge with the national Labour Party. Initially, Labour struggled in Liverpool. This was demonstrated in 1907 during the Kirkdale by-election. At the time, the election was designated 'the biggest fight in Labour's [short] history'.[54] By polling day, nearly twenty Labour MP's had visited the constituency, including Ramsay MacDonald and Arthur Henderson, but the WMCA had mobilised 500 canvassers for the staunch Protestant and Unionist candidate Charles M'Arthur, who polled 700 more votes than John Hill, the Labour candidate. During the election, Protestants had equated socialism with atheism. Ramsay MacDonald concluded that 'Labour would never progress in Liverpool until Orangeism was broken'.[55]

The proposition, offered by some Protestants, that socialists were atheists is ironic given that a regular simultaneous criticism of Labour was to allege, often not without merit, the Roman Catholic bias of the party's elected representatives.[56] In the early days, Liverpool's Labour leaders 'were invariably Home Rulers ... often Catholics or at least affectionately disposed towards Catholic interests, just as many Conservatives were traditionally champions of Protestantism'.[57] Although initially Irish Nationalists were suspicious of this emerging fifth party,[58] Labour would eventually succeed the Liberals as the Nationalists' allies on the council and then secure the majority of the Irish Catholic vote. Yet Labour's capture of Liverpool was slow and the party's internal problems considerable:

> In 1921 Éire came into existence. There was no longer any need for people in Liverpool to support Irish Nationalist candidates. So they all joined the Labour Party and immediately they split the Labour Party from top to bottom, because all the new members of the Labour Party had strong views on abortion, church schools, and divorce. So the Labour Party

[54] Waller, 1981: 233, citing *The Times*, 27 September 1907.
[55] Waller, 1981: 234, citing *The Times*, 28 September 1907.
[56] See Roberts, 2015: Appendices 3.1, 3.4, 3.6, 3.7, 3.8.
[57] Waller, 1988: 100, 340.
[58] Ibid., 136: 'Nationalists believed that a Labour candidate who fought a Home Ruler must be a crypto-Conservative'.

never had power in Liverpool until the 1950s, which is incredible in a
town so full of poverty, and the reason it didn't, of course, was because it
was split over religion.[59]

As Belchem puts it, 'as local leadership of the I.N.P. passed steadily into the
hands of second-generation (that is, Liverpool-born) Irish, it displayed less
interest in the fate of Ireland than in the intermediate needs of the local
Catholic community in housing and employment'.[60] O'Connell writes that,
'in Liverpool, the party gradually lost its "Irish Nationalist" identity in real
terms and became increasingly aligned to the social policies of the Labour
Party'.[61]

Sam Davies describes how 'Labour inherited rather than won Nationalist
seats':[62]

> After the formation of the Irish Free State in 1922, there was little support
> for the continuation of the I.N.P. in Liverpool … the Labour Party's
> sweeping gains in the general election of 1929 precipitated wholesale
> defections. Those councillors who subsequently represented the safe
> Catholic seats formed a numerical majority for the Labour group.[63]

Labour, thus, became 'a hybrid creature, whose Catholic and secular halves
often clashed'.[64] Division came to a head during the proposed sale of the
Brownlow Hill Workhouse in 1929–30 to the Catholic Church, to build a
Cathedral. As Davies suggests,

> It says something about the subtleties of the implicitly sectarian Toryism of
> the city that it was the ruling Conservative group that pushed forward this
> proposal. The effect on Labour was disastrous. Party policy, reaffirmed at
> the time, was that publicly owned land should not be sold into private hands.
> On the crucial motion approving the sale, 21 Labour councillors voted
> against [and] 37 voted for selling to the Catholic Church. Significantly,
> of the Catholic members of the Labour group, only one supported party
> policy, while 27 others supported the cathedral proposal.[65]

---

[59] Frank Neal, 12 February 2010.
[60] Belchem, 2000a: 141.
[61] O'Connell, 1971: 240.
[62] Waller, 1981: 324.
[63] Davies, 1996: 70–1.
[64] Waller, 1981: 324.
[65] Davies, 1996: 69.

In the aftermath, the Party was formally split in the council chamber, prompting the National Executive Committee to intervene and restore order. The legacy of the Cathedral site controversy 'was an apparently endless feud in which Labourites hated each other far, far more than they hated the Tories'.[66] Councillor Duffy, the only Catholic to oppose the sale of the land, was deselected by his ward in Scotland North. Conversely, Councillor Mrs Hughes, who had supported the sale, was deselected in St Anne's ward, and replaced with Bessie Braddock, before re-standing against Braddock as an 'Independent Labour' candidate, gaining 40 per cent of the vote.[67] All of this played into the hands of the Conservatives and the Protestant Party.

Shortly after the affair, Labour suffered in the municipal elections, losing five seats to the Conservatives and one to a Protestant Party candidate. Within Labour's ranks, there were fierce divisions over the desirability of religious influence. The atheist Labour councillor (and later MP) Bessie Braddock, in supporting the City Council's wartime resolution permitting cinemas to open on Sundays, demonstrated her religious indifference by responding to a call for Sabbath observance (from opponents from various denominations) with: 'Those who do not want Sunday entertainment can keep away'.[68]

The Persistence of Sectarian Politics

As Councillor Thomas White, the Liverpool Conservative leader from 1928 to 1938, suggested, 'sectarianism had triumphed over politics,' as even if a Party could 'shed their sectarian skin', in Liverpool, this would not have been advisable. He stated, 'Whether we like it or not … there are many thousands of electors in Liverpool who will, if the need arises, put Protestantism before their politics, and it would simply be madness on my part if I told the people of Kirkdale, Everton, or West Toxteth, that the Conservative Party has ceased to care for religion or for Protestant interests'.[69]

The Liberals tried to shed the shackles of religious sectarianism decades earlier. Liverpool's Nationalists withdrew formal co-operation in 1899, a

---

[66] Waller, 1981: 235.

[67] Davies, 1996: 70.

[68] Perrett, 1990: 120.

[69] Waller, 1988: 332, 339, citing Councillor Thomas White.

development which 'was a relief rather than an embarrassment to many'.[70] Liverpool's Liberals believed that, separated from the Irish, they would get some Liberal Unionists back and gain new support from less religiously committed electors. In 1921, under the leadership of Richard Holt, the Liverpool Liberals 'concentrated their efforts on the outer districts and rallied the better class of citizen against the Irish–Labour efforts to exploit the ratepayer and the Tory dictatorship', but this meant the party became a 'conservative, class-bound, suburban rump, excluded from all vital areas of power and interest in the city'.[71] Only long after the demise of sectarian politics, in 1998, did the Liberals (now Liberal-Democrats) come to control Liverpool Council.

The ethno-sectarian nature of politics in the city meant that once the ties with Irish Nationalists had been severed the Liberals ceased to be an effective force in Liverpool Politics for most of the twentieth century. It became clear that it is 'far easier to generate sectarian animosities than it is to calm them down',[72] while 'politicians might have wanted to quit the sectarians' arena, sectarians would not quit the political arena'.[73]

Lane sums up the exceptional nature of Liverpool politics:

> It was certainly a strange English city that could return an Irish Nationalist MP for one of its constituencies, from 1885 until 1929. It was no less strange for having a Protestant Party which even in 1971 had four councillors in the Town Hall. In the nineteenth century Liverpool stayed almost continuously Tory when other cities were far more likely to be Liberal. In the twentieth century it was a city which remained Tory when others were becoming Labour ... When Labour eventually took over the direction of the city administration, in 1955, the Tories had enjoyed more than one hundred years' control of the city council.[74]

The question begged is how were ethno-political and ethno-religious sectarian rigidities removed?

---

[70] Ibid., 222.

[71] Ibid., 279.

[72] Project on Middle East Political Science, 'The Politics of Sectarianism', *POMEPS Studies*, 4 (13 November 2013). Available at: http://pomeps.org/2013/11/14/the-politics-of-sectarianism/.

[73] Waller, 1981: 29.

[74] Lane, 1987: 125–6.

The Slow Thaw of Ethno-Religious Political Affiliations

It has been demonstrated that religious 'ghettos' on Merseyside were by no means exclusive to the areas abounding Netherfield and Scotland Road. They existed in south Liverpool as far as Garston and the north as far as Bootle. In Garston, there were predominantly Protestant/Orange strongholds of Shakespeare and Byron Street, with Catholic areas closer to the docks such as Saunby Street and Vulcan Street.[75] In Bootle, the communities around Derby Road, Marsh Lane, and Strand Road were principally all Liverpool-Irish Catholic. The Bootle Village area was a section known well for its Orange Lodge activities. As Bootle MP, Joe Benton, explains, Derby Ward – now the 'safest' Labour ward – was once an aspiration for 'ambitious Tories ... because of the very strong Orange presence. It took in Bootle Village, the Orange quarter'.[76]

Although Bootle is today one of Labour's safest parliamentary seats (alongside the neighbouring constituency of Walton), this is a relatively recent phenomenon. Until 1945 it was a Conservative stronghold. The constituency's first Member of Parliament, Thomas Myles Sandys (elected in 1885) was a staunch Protestant who became the Grand Master of the Loyal Orange Lodge of England.[77] Sandys was succeeded by Andrew Bonar Law, later the Prime Minister. The parliamentary seat was Conservative for fifty-six years out of sixty, before it was won for only the second time by Labour in 1945.

Catholics made political progress despite, or because of, the sectarian backdrop. The local councillor for St Oswald's ward, James 'Jimmy' Mahon, recalls, 'when my great uncle Alderman Simon Mahon senior (1886–1961) became a member of the old Bootle Council he was a practising Roman Catholic ... Catholics and the Orange Order were at loggerheads, families fought over it! Simon was eventually voted in as mayor, in 1929. He was the first Catholic mayor of Bootle'.[78] Labour took the parliamentary seat during the same year, but only until 1931. Liverpool's first Roman Catholic mayor, Austin Harford, did not assume the role until 1942. Joe Benton highlights the difficulties Labour faced:

---

[75] Alf Mullins, 14 May 2012.

[76] Joe Benton, 18 May 2012.

[77] Colonel Thomas Myles Sandys (12 May 1837–18 October 1911). Available at: www.tutorgigpedia.com/ed/Thomas_Sandys, citing 'Obituary: Col. T. M. Sandys'. *The Times*, 19 October 1911.

[78] James Mahon, 24 April 2012.

In Bootle it was the Liberal and Tory Party that benefited from sectar-ianism ... When I was growing up, if we ever went near the fire, my Mum would say, 'Burnie for Bootle'. The [Liberal] MP was Major James Burnie ... it all emanated back to Gladstone and Home Rule for Ireland ... keep in mind that the Irish contingent in Bootle at that time represented a huge proportion of the electorate. In those days, because the Labour Party was still in its infancy, it always came down to a choice of Liberal or Tory.[79]

Labour held Bootle from 1945 onwards. There is a common narrative which suggests that the Second World War softened religious rivalries. Mahon contends that, 'with the people [both] fighting a war and people at home getting battered by bombs the community knitted together a bit. They must have started realising "what the hell are we doing fighting?"'[80] The unity via war thesis is appealing, but it is contested and there is dispute over which world war was more significant in heralding the beginning of the demise of sectarianism.

Andy Burnham MP supports the supposition that war changed perceptions in Liverpool (although he states that his grandmother still proudly played Irish rebel songs during the 1970s) but argues that the process began during the First World War. He recalled how he had read out a letter in the House of Commons which his great grandfather had written to his twin brother, Walter, in July 1918, shortly before his death in active service:

I had a good talk last night over Old Ireland. Walter, there are thousands of Irish boys here and I may tell you it is God help the Boche if they come across them. Then they say Ireland is not doing her fair share in this war.[81]

Burnham highlighted how people from Liverpool would have changed their opinions as they fought beside comrades of different creeds and religions during the world wars. Steve Rotheram, MP for Walton, also shares this perception: 'War was a massive reason for the decline. When you're fighting a common enemy, fighting side by side, when your life relies upon them, you'd see through false religious symbolism and see the quality of person'.[82]

---

[79] Joe Benton, 18 May 2012.
[80] James Mahon, 24 April 2012.
[81] Andy Burnham, 28 March 2013, citing a speech made in the House of Commons during a debate on veterans affairs, dated 9 June 2004.
[82] Steve Rotheram, 4 January 2013.

Roy Hughes of the Protestant Party also acknowledges that the Second World War 'altered mind-sets in many ways'.[83]

It is notable that in 1939 Liverpool had been a target of an IRA bombing campaign in Britain. During this campaign, the relatively small number of IRA volunteers in Liverpool bombed (with varying success) the external wall of Walton Prison, an electricity pylon, an army barracks, a railway station, a bank, and several other commercial and private properties. Most notoriously, on two occasions, tear gas was released in packed cinemas. Although more serious attacks occurred in other areas of Britain and no casualties were suffered in Liverpool, 'the attacks were met with widespread revulsion' and the 'city's Irish [re]assumed the status of folk devils'.[84] Yet, the IRA's bombing campaign, as Evans suggests, 'was soon overshadowed in scale – and consequently relegated in historical memory – by the altogether more destructive Luftwaffe bombardments of the Second World War'.[85]

More than 80 per cent of Bootle's housing was destroyed or severely damaged during the Second World War. There were 1,500 fatal civilian casualties in Liverpool, with the death toll nearly 4,000 across Merseyside. Some 150,000 households had properties destroyed or damaged, and 40,000 were made homeless in one week during the May Blitz.[86] It would seem odd if such cataclysmic events had not, at least temporarily, changed some people's attitudes. Yet it has been argued that, 'the war and Blitz fostered camaraderie, a community spirit, but did the affinity survive the Blitz? People soon reverted back to pre-war ways. The coming together was necessary but it was transitory'.[87]

The steady erosion of unwavering Orange support for Liverpool's Conservative Party may have been more significant than the direct effect of war. After the establishment of the Irish Free State in 1921, coupled with the exclusion of six of the nine Ulster counties, the protection of Ulster Protestants seemed to have been secured. From this point, it is contended by Stanley Salvidge, 'the solid phalanx of working-class voters, which at [Sir Archibald Salvidge's] bidding had marched steadily to the polls at every election since 1900, was never again quite the same reliable force. The old incentive of "Loyalty to Ulster" had gone, and more modern cries

---

[83] Roy Hughes, 13 November 2012.
[84] Evans, 2012: 25–46.
[85] Ibid.
[86] Garnett, 1995: 103, 107.
[87] Ibid., 115.

of a class-conscious Labour movement were reaching the ears of a younger generation'.[88]

The First World War had a significant effect on the WMCA, whose membership in 1917 was half the size as it had been at the turn of the century. Day states,

> Conservatives fared poorly in Liverpool elections in 1919 which was largely due to the silence and apathy of the Orange Order ... Many saw signs of Orangemen turning to the Labour Party at this time ... Tory jingoism, it seems, died on the First World War battlefields and the new generation were joining trade unions. In 1924 the WMCA approved candidate for the West Toxteth by-election was defeated by Labour and in the General Election later the same year Labour assumed the opposition to the Tories in Liverpool.[89]

The political allegiances associated with religion began to shift. As Benton comments, 'the ethos of Parties changed. Labour came more to the fore, so much so that some of my Orange friends were strongly Labour. Kenny Jones, for example, a former chairman of the Bootle Labour Party, was strongly Orange and a good friend of mine. He, his father, sister, and the rest of his family were all Labour Party members, all very strong Labour'.[90] Post 1945, it became more common for traditionally Orange areas to begin electing Labour councillors and Members of Parliament.

Reverend H.D. Longbottom's death in 1962 marked the passing of Liverpool's last populist anti-Catholic orator. It marked the beginning of the end for the Liverpool Protestant Party, whose last councillors would opt not to stand, so as not to be defeated, following boundary change in 1974.[91] As Roy Hughes put it, 'Once the hub of the community had gone, the Orange house of cards collapsed'.[92]

Although 'the Protestant Party continue to breath old life into new issues',[93] it struggled to maintain the old religious-political tie-up. Longbottom's son-in-law, Ronald Henderson, attempted to revitalise the party by aligning it to the British Constitution Defence Committee, allied with the Reverend Ian

---

[88]   Salvidge, 1934: 220.
[89]   Day, 2011: 65.
[90]   Joe Benton, 18 May 2012.
[91]   Roy Hughes, 13 November 2012.
[92]   Ibid.
[93]   Waller, 1981: 349.

Paisley, to 'resist Ulster being submerged into Éire and Britain in Europe'.[94] This was to no avail. Their support network had gone. Concurrently, the WMCA was in terminal decline, from a membership of some 8,000 at the turn of the century, to a body of fewer than 700 by 1936. One secretary opined that the WMCA was 'declining very fast due to working men showing more interest in socialism'.[95] In 1972, the Conservative Party urged the Protestant Party to merge into them (absorption) as the only means of survival. In 1974, with the Protestant strongholds having been depleted and a tendency for remaining constituents to opt for Labour, Roy Hughes, the last leader of the Protestant Party, opted not to stand for election.

At the 1992 general election, there was a forlorn, fleeting attempt to revive explicitly Protestant politics in the city in the Walton constituency. This area includes Everton (traditionally a Protestant heartland) and incorporates St George's Church, which for some is still considered the 'Orange Church'.[96] The constituency includes much of Liverpool's old 'Orange heartland' and it was testimony to the change that had occurred in the area that a 'Protestant Reform' candidate, D.J.E. Carson, gained only 393 votes compared to Labour's 34,214. To put this into perspective, 'Screaming Lord Sutch' of the Monster Raving Loony Party had secured a higher share of the vote in the constituency's by-election the preceding year, attaining 546 votes.

As the twentieth century progressed, people had begun to be 'steered' much more by class politics and trade union membership, as opposed to a politics based on religion. The tide had been turning in Labour's favour in parliamentary constituencies in the city for a long time, with the 1964 election a crucial point. That year, the constituencies of Kirkdale, Toxteth, Walton, and West Derby were all won by Labour having previously been safe seats for the Conservatives. Significantly, each of these comprised of mainly Protestant areas, with sizeable Orange contingents. Edge Hill and Exchange remained Labour, having been first won by the Party in 1945. Liverpool Scotland, an Irish Nationalist seat until 1929, had been Labour thereafter. Walter Alldritt, who held the seat in 1964 following the death of sitting MP David Logan, was a more secular MP than his predecessor. Logan was a former Irish Nationalist, who often put his Catholicism before his Party. Alldritt was a trade unionist who went on to become regional secretary for the National Union of General and Municipal Workers. His

[94] Ibid.
[95] Ibid., 350.
[96] Peter Kilfoyle, 23 January 2012.

successor, Frank Marsden, was challenged in a 1971 by-election by Peter Mahon, standing on a 'Labour and Anti-Abortion' ticket, a clear pitch for the constituency's Catholic vote, but Mahon was outpolled by more than six to one by his official Labour rival. Wavertree and Garston were held by the Conservatives in 1964, but Conservatism and Protestantism and their linkage were in sharp decline in the city.

The orthodox explanation of diminished sectarianism owing to slum clearance is unsatisfactory, as the clearance programme was only part way to completion in 1964. Moreover, the outer areas of the city, such as Knowsley, had been voting Labour since 1950 and continued to do so after dispersal from Liverpool to the area. Moreover, slum clearance had not entirely removed sectarianism, as the Prime Minister was aware. As Kilfoyle notes, 'Harold Wilson was very, very much aware [of sectarianism], having represented Huyton and Kirkby [1950–83], because, remember, particularly when he represented those areas, many of those people had only recently moved out from the city centre. So it still will have been raw with them the sectarianism. So he was very, very well aware of that'.[97]

The Growth of Labourism

It is important to note that two years after the worst sectarian riots in Liverpool's history, in 1909, 'religious sectarianism was [said to be] largely dormant during one of the most volatile and violent strikes ever in British history'.[98] John Bohstedt asserts that 'it was the trauma of the massive 1911 transport strike, not any melting sectarian animosities, that generated political will for a resolution ... The brush with anarchy and the spectre of working-class revolt finally galvanized the town fathers to give up sectarian conflict'.[99] The contention of sectarianism being 'largely dormant' is not entirely accurate, but it does hint at what was to come in terms of future unity.[100]

Liverpool's industrial confrontation of 1911 led Lord Derby, the Lord Mayor, to inform the Home Secretary that 'a revolution was in progress'.[101]

---

[97] Ibid.
[98] O'Brien, 2011: 153.
[99] Bohstedt, 1992: 212–13.
[100] See Bohstedt; O'Brien; and Waller for in-depth information of proceedings.
[101] Bohstedt, 1992: 255.

Over 2,300 soldiers, 4,000 special constables, a battleship, and a battlecruiser patrolled Liverpool. Waller states that, 'during labour disputes which paralysed Liverpool in the summer of 1911 … industrial violence and sectarian violence were connected'.[102] Notably, 'although unionised north-end Protestant carters had joined Catholic dockers to march hand-in-hand to a great rally … rioting of that night included much sectarian violence: as fierce Orange–Catholic fighting as had ever been seen in the city's history'.[103] Perhaps inevitably, with so much tension in the air, trauma struck: troops shot two workers, resulting in two funerals attended by mourners of both denominations. Religious feuds were temporarily forgotten and Orange drums were 'twined with orange and green ribbons'.[104] O'Brien states,

> It is not that the religious divide simply disappeared. Indeed, Labour politics retained a religious character in the city long after the strike. Still, the fact remains that the marginalising of the Green and Orange divide in 1911 created a point of reference for the syndicalist and socialist street agitators of that time and of the next generation that followed.[105]

While these events were important in helping to lay a foundation stone for the future Liverpool labour movement, and in demonstrating that in times of strife the two sides were capable of uniting, the events of this year, Bohstedt contends, were pivotally important in the short- and long-term cessation of sectarian riots:

> Sectarian violence finally subsided in pre-war Liverpool, not because ethnic antagonisms changed, but because community politics changed … the near-anarchy of the great transport strike of 1911 convinced the town's leaders they could no longer afford to permit sectarian disturbances, and they acted promptly to shut them down … [through] endorsement of a Special Act of Parliament, the Liverpool Corporation Act 1912, enabling the City Corporation to pass by-laws empowering the Watch Committee to regulate meetings, processions, and emblems, music and weapons … Control of processions and meetings finally reduced sectarian clashes.[106]

---

[102] Waller, 1981: 249.
[103] Bohstedt, 1992: 212.
[104] O'Brien, 2011: 145, citing Fred Bower (1936).
[105] Ibid.
[106] Bohstedt, 1992: 210, 213–14.

Thus, as Ingram attests, while helping to change only the 'manifestation' of sectarianism 'without threatening its existence', increased police powers 'made skirmishes between individuals or small groups the characteristic sectarian disturbance in place of the obviously more prominent riot involving thousands of participants'.[107] While such small clashes could go on with 'monotonous regularity without making news',[108] it was a growing unity, aided by a transcending political outlook, which began to threaten the existence of sectarianism.

The growth of labourism at the expense of religious sentiment did not arise from an organic process, the sudden dawn of class consciousness, or even the shared experiences of the Second World War. Rather, it involved the promotion of labourist affiliations over religious sentiment, without attacking religious fervour overtly, which might have offended the city's residents. The former Labour MP for Walton (1991–2010), Peter Kilfoyle, a Roman Catholic lifelong resident of the city, makes the point that there was a combined effort in Merseyside to defeat sectarianism and the Conservative Party:

> There was a sustained programme of education and agitation … getting a message across through the workplace, the trade unions, the schools or whatever … that the way forward for working-people was Labour representation. You didn't have to mention sectarianism, but implicit was obviously that what divided us, that sort of sectarian prejudice, was nothing compared to what united us: a class consciousness, a mutual interest to try and take on the employers or the Tories in Government, and generally a combination of both.[109]

In a similar vein, the Labour MP for Bootle (1990–2015), Joe Benton, adds credence to the argument that sectarianism had to be broken down through education, rather than simply allowed to flourish in the absence of a strong, united labour movement. Benton stresses the role of (non-sectarian) trade unions in uniting the working class:

> We did have sectarianism in Bootle, but it wasn't the breakdown of communities [that changed things], it was enlightenment. At one time if you were Orange you could be 90% certain that you were Conservative

---

[107] Ingram, 1987: 297–8.
[108] Ibid.
[109] Peter Kilfoyle, 23 January 2012.

as well. Later on I started noticing a lot more cross fertilisation. People from Protestant areas started voting Labour ... people became a lot more politically aware through education, enlightenment, but mostly through the Labour movement. Trade unions played a massive role in that.

As national politics began to take precedence over local issues and as Labour and (more importantly) the secular wing of the Liverpool Labour Party took control, generic working-class issues became much more important. Steve Higginson believes that, 'as the Wilson Government of the sixties had a beneficial effect on people, they started to reject the Conservative ethos, because of the successes of Labour Governments and what they stood for: an egalitarian ethos'.[110] Kilfoyle also makes this point:

> It makes sense that there was more of a national dimension and a focus on the leadership as opposed to what was happening locally ... Education was changing things generally. Television was bringing new sorts of attitudes ... It's a question of people sort of maturing and voting on grounds which were more in tune with the political exigencies, as opposed to sectarian/ religious influences.

As employment shifted from the 'pen system' at the docks towards more factory work and apprenticeship disciplines, there were greater possibilities for the development of trade union affiliation as vehicles of political education and class consciousness. The Liverpool working class began to show more solidarity and trade unionism helped to politicise the Liverpool electorate. Trade unionism contained the potential to diminish ethno-sectarian affiliations. Labour and trade union militancy was not merely a product of activism; it was a consequence of Liverpool's declining fortunes as a city. Andy Burnham MP argues that Liverpool became less sectarian as the city as a whole went into economic decline, stressing that with the loss of the 'second city of Empire' label, the 'strong Establishment feeling' – thus Conservative power – broke down. 'People's religious loyalties remain to this day, but the bigger problem became poverty and [the desire for] prosperity. That rode above the sectarianism'.[111] This economic decline would serve further to entrench negative stereotypes about the city in the minds of the rest of the UK. Conversely, Liverpool developed a defence mechanism in the form of a prevailing single identity: an identity which would help further to

[110] Steve Higginson, 11 February 2013.
[111] Andy Burnham, 28 March 2013.

erode sectarian tension in the city. Many became proud of being known as the city that 'dared to fight back'.[112]

Liverpool's docks and traditional manufacturing industries went into sharp decline. By January 1980, the unemployment rate had reached 12.7 per cent. Some 40 per cent of these had been unemployed for over a year. As Waller argues, the future of Liverpool 'now seemed not that of an expanding provincial capital, but a decline to the status of shanty town, unless the Government was induced to reverse the trend by an industrial strategy beyond short-term expedients'.[113] Between 1981 and 1991, 50,000 jobs, 20 per cent of Liverpool's total, disappeared'.[114] In the 1980s, the response to economic crisis transcended the religious boundary. Although the Labour Party had captured wards and parliamentary constituencies across Liverpool, local Labour parties were often small in number, a product of the city's reductions in population (due to slum clearance). Combined with increased militancy in response to the acute industrial crisis, this allowed the takeover of numerous Labour branches by the Militant organisation, a party within a party.[115]

Liverpool witnessed the stand-off between the Militant-led Labour council in continuing with a programme of council house construction and their refusal to set a rate, in defiance of Thatcher's government, which wanted to curb local authority expenditure. Militant's control of the city council had been preceded by the Toxteth riots of 1981, fuelled by mass unemployment and police tactics. Following the riots, Protestant Bishop Sheppard and Catholic Archbishop Worlock walked arm in arm through the area, indicative of how Catholic–Protestant religious hostilities had diminished. In the aftermath of the Toxteth riots, Geoffrey Howe advised Thatcher to abandon Liverpool to a fate of 'managed decline'.[116]

The 1980s most visibly demonstrated the transition from identity to class-based politics in Liverpool through the dominance of the Militant Tendency. The Militant Tendency was a Trotskyite entryist group within the British Labour Party.[117] They played a leading role in Liverpool City Council

[112] See Taafe and Mulhearn, 1988.
[113] Waller, 1981: 351.
[114] Dudgeon, 2010: 328.
[115] See Frost and North, 2013.
[116] 'Thatcher Urged "Let Liverpool Decline" after 1981 Riots'. BBC News, 30 December 2011. Available at: www.bbc.co.uk/news/uk-16361170.
[117] Belchem and Biggs, 2011: 8.

between 1983 and 1987. In 1985, they took part in the rate-capping rebellion along with Lambeth Council.[118] The campaign's tactic was that councils whose budgets were restricted would refuse to set any budget at all for the financial year 1985–6, requiring the Government to intervene. Labour's National Executive Committee subsequently suspended Liverpool District Labour Party in November 1985 and began an inquiry into the council's conduct. Ultimately, the rate-capping rebellion led to Militant's downfall and, after an audit, forty-seven councillors were expelled and surcharged.

Ken Taylor argues that the resistance to economic misfortune became the dominant image of the city, replacing that of little Ireland, or of a city driven by religious hostility, arguing that 'there is an inevitable harking back to the radical socialism that was a key component of the city's identity – especially during the 1980s … a local authority dominated by the Militant Tendency … This, along with the radical trade union activity throughout the city and the Toxteth riots of 1981, helped cast a view of Liverpool as a hotbed of revolutionary socialism that still persists today'.[119] Liverpool, a city that was once defiantly Conservative is now defiantly Labour.

Conclusion

Traditionally, in Liverpool, Orangemen had regarded the Conservative Party to be 'their' Party, because they wanted to preserve the Union, as opposed to the Irish Nationalists or Liberals who wanted to break up or substantially revise the Union. For part of the twentieth century, the local Labour Party too was considered 'too Irish', due to the ancestry of its members and their overt Catholicism. However, as secular Labour began to dominate, as local versus national government economic issues overrode local sectarian enmities, and as secularism began to develop as society opened up through new forms of media, people began to discover new horizons and think differently. Changes occurred on both sides. Catholics moved from Irish Nationalist and Liberal to Labour. Likewise, Orangemen, often influenced by their trade unions, began to become more politicised on class issues and question the historic link to the Conservative Party. There was a new battle to be fought, a battle not on religious grounds, but on class grounds; for some, indeed, a 'class-war'. Many Merseyside residents by this time had

---

[118] Frost and North, 2013: 95, 122.
[119] Taylor, 2011: 159.

realised, 'you don't have to have much of a commonality to have a common enemy'.[120]

To what extent then did the decline of identity politics contribute to the decline of sectarianism? What appears to be the answer is 'not very much', but the identities became less mutually exclusive in political terms. It became possible, even normal, to be Orange and Labour. It seems that the decline of identity politics was primarily a product of other factors affecting the decline of sectarianism. The Conservative Party had understood the futility of using religion for electoral gain in Liverpool by the 1970s. The Conservatives no longer wished to stir – or were capable of stirring – sectarian resentment. On the Labour side, the emergence of secular politicians like Bessie Braddock diminished the 'Catholic Labour' identity of local politics which had persisted with the transfer of Irish Nationalist votes to the Party. Amid economic crisis, it was secular Labour, in the form of Militant, which came to dominate the Labour Party (opposed by more moderate Catholics within the party). Class politics, not Orange versus Green, dominated Liverpool by the 1980s.

[120] Kilfoyle, 23 January 2012.

6

Ecumenism: 'The Great Mersey Miracle' and a Decline in Religious Observance

Beyond the impact of slum clearance, a further plausible explanatory hypothesis underpinning improved Protestant–Catholic relations is that which focuses upon improved inter-church relations. Strong religious and personal relationships developed between the Anglican Bishop of Liverpool, David Sheppard and the Roman Catholic Archbishop of the city, Derek Worlock. This relationship has been associated with the growth of ecumenism which eased the religious divide. The second part of this chapter will concentrate on a shift towards secularism and the decline of religious observance and attendant fervour. It is plausible that the churches getting on together helped their congregations get along, although it is just as plausible that denominational tensions declined because people simply stopped believing in God.

When David Sheppard was appointed as Protestant Bishop of Liverpool, in 1975, he was made aware of the 'long history of sectarian suspicion', 'bitterness', and the 'violence which lay behind the religious divide in the city'.[1] Such was the divide that as late as 1968 the Prime Minister Harold Wilson, a Merseyside MP, opposed the invitation of royalty to the consecration of the Catholic Metropolitan Cathedral, as the 'relationships between Protestants and Catholics, though they had calmed down, were too fragile to risk a royal presence at such a public Roman Catholic event'.[2] The following year, Sheppard's Roman Catholic counterpart, Derek Worlock, was appointed Archbishop of Liverpool. Worlock made it his ambition to 'close the gap between religion and life [in Liverpool], between what goes on in church and what goes on at work and at home'.[3] The ecumenical vision

---

[1] Sheppard, 2002: 164.

[2] Ibid.

[3] Furnival and Knowles, 1998: 169, citing Derek Worlock.

and conduct of Sheppard and Worlock was such that they would become affectionately known on Merseyside as 'fish and chips',[4] and in 2008 a bronze commemorative statue of the pair, paid for by public subscription, was unveiled on Hope Street. It is the view of many in Liverpool that these two figures did much to help calm spiritual divisions in the city. As Reverend John Williams suggests:

> The biggest impact on the decline [of sectarianism] was the Great Mersey Miracle. The great friendship, trust, and common bond shared between Sheppard and Worlock cascaded down to the ordinary parish clergy. 'If they can do it so can we', was the attitude. Their friendship shined down and set an example. I could go to Sheppard and say 'there's a problem with the Green and the Orange', and we would work together to sort it out. It didn't change the doctrine but we learned to respect each other's differences.[5]

Furthermore, the wider concentration of efforts of the two clergymen on the declining economic fortunes of the city meant that the two Church leaders gained much credence. The Church leaders had taken over during an economic recession, with Liverpool languishing consistently below the national average of unemployment statistics. The pair worked in tandem to tackle social and economic problems. As Longley notes, 'the demonstration of solidarity with those whose livelihood was threatened did much to cement bonds of affection and respect between the two episcopal leaders and the people of Merseyside. They made the Churches seem relevant to the real problems in people's lives'.[6] Cardinal Hume suggested, '[Worlock] made his home in Liverpool. He was concerned not only for the Catholic flock there but for Liverpool and all its people'.[7] Bishop Tom Williams recalls the effect the 'better together' philosophy had:

> I think we were in danger in the sixties of being like Belfast. It was always about resistance … There was always this bitter, 'you did that to us, so we did that to you' attitude, and people would keep that alive. So there was distrust and no attempt at reconciliation, no attempt at healing the

---

[4] P. Coslett, 'Statue for Two Bishops'. BBC (12 May 2008). Available at: www.bbc.co.uk/liverpool/content/articles/2008/05/12/faith_bishop_statue_feature.shtml. The pair were dubbed 'fish and chips' 'as they were always together and never out of the papers'.

[5] Revd John Williams, 17 November 2010.

[6] Longley, 2000: 314.

[7] Furnival and Knowles, 1998: 167.

wounds, and no attempt at forging partnerships. Some people believed that ecumenism was an attempt at making everybody the same, [but] we came to acknowledge that you had to start off meeting, getting to know one another, and being friendly. I think that was what started breaking down the barriers, the fact that people started meeting and talking. Now, in many ways, the sectarian element has gone.[8]

The importance of Worlock and Sheppard's partnership was also articulated by a recent Catholic Archbishop of Liverpool, Patrick Kelly, who reflects on how they became symbols of change: 'Could we have believed forty years ago that we would have a statue of our two former Church leaders (Anglican Bishop David Sheppard and Catholic Archbishop Derek Worlock) in Hope Street? People would have said, it cannot be, but it has happened and it is a declaration that things can change'.[9]

In order to authenticate the impact that Sheppard and Worlock had on sectarianism in Liverpool, it is important to gauge the situation the pair inherited when they arrived. It was not the case that division was at the same level as in the 1900s – a decade acknowledged as both that of the 'greatest wealth' for the port and the 'worst record of sectarian violence'.[10] Nor was it the case that sectarianism was largely theological. As Sheppard and Worlock acknowledge, 'there was a great deal of belonging which did not necessarily imply believing'.[11] There was, however, a lingering distrust and bitterness on Merseyside that the Church leaders thought it necessary to tackle.

Although the sectarianism which blighted Liverpool was seldom derived from devout religious observance, divisive religious rhetoric often inflamed tensions and played a key role in keeping animosity alive.[12] The respective 'flock' of each denomination jealously guarded its connections with a religious institution which had historically (particularly in the case of the Irish community) suckled them in times of need. For the Liverpool Irish, their identity was largely centred on their observance of Catholic principles, demonstrated by the respect afforded to their priests. For the Netherfield Road community, the prerequisite for joining the Orange Order or WMCA was Protestantism. In addition, the 'Orange' district benefited

[8] Bishop Tom Williams, 23 March 2010.

[9] *Liverpool Echo*, 16 January 2009.

[10] Sheppard, 2002: 164.

[11] Sheppard and Worlock, 1988: 57.

[12] This was the case in 1909. The public inquiry which took place the following year attributed much of blame for the disturbances on George Wise's anti-Catholic rhetoric.

from a range of local initiatives centred upon faith. *The Protestant Boys Drum-and Flute Band*, *The Liverpool Protestant Benevolent Society*, *Protestant Operative Associations*, and *Protestant Truth Society* are all testimony to this. Faith-based munificence also was prevalent in the predominantly Catholic Scotland Road district. Belchem describes the motivation behind this:

> The [Catholic] Church was extremely concerned to prevent leakage from the faith. It was very different from other forms of organisations or associations as it was not trying to expand the remit of its sector, but what it wanted to do was prevent leakage. In Liverpool you were not talking about the more fortunate recusant Catholics who lived in other parts of Lancashire. You are talking essentially about poor Irish migrants. Now unless the Catholic Church makes provisions for them, they are going to be very dependent upon local authorities, who, certainly in the nineteenth century, would be part of the establishment, i.e. the Anglican Church. So there was this great fear that if the Catholic Church itself didn't develop this whole form of faith-based welfare state, it's going to be losing people. It was very much in its interest to develop this wide-ranging umbrella cover for its people.[13]

The development of this 'welfare umbrella' coincided with the erection of many Catholic churches and schools. This scale of 'Romanism', coupled with the Catholic tendency to 'protect their own', prompted resentment. This religious divide was only partly down to doctrinal disagreement between the faiths. Underlying it was an economic and political stimulus. Most visibly, the Conservative Party was using religion and 'Rome on the rates' issues to distinguish between 'them' and 'us'. Superseding this was the role of the Liverpool Irish as economic competitors for jobs on the docks. The view of 'Paddy' as a 'parasite' benefited the Conservative Party, as did the ghetto system, which helped maintain ignorance of the 'rival' community. Sheppard and Worlock explained how these factors could act as reasons for sectarian resentment, declaring that 'bitter rivalry between one community group and another can be a distinctive feature in an area of deprivation, especially where there is competition for limited resources'.[14] Kilfoyle agrees, but adds credence to the political stimulus, arguing that, in Liverpool, 'religion acted as a useful tool to divide the working class'.[15]

---

[13] John Belchem, 25 February 2010.
[14] Sheppard and Worlock, 1988: 282.
[15] Peter Kilfoyle, 23 January 2012.

Nonetheless, whatever the underlying basis, religion was seen as a badge of identity and was zealously protected. This was picked up on by David Sheppard and Derek Worlock when they first arrived in Liverpool:

> First impressions of Liverpool include a fierce sense of identity ... It has to do with the most intense loyalties, which are themselves reflected in a strongly expressed possessiveness. Some of these loyalties have been inherited through many generations and are rooted in family ties ... The same intense loyalties are to be found with regard to churches, football teams, trade unions, districts, and recently with Merseyside as a whole. There is a strongly positive side to this sense of identity. Possessiveness is matched by a sense of belonging, responsibility for each other, generosity within the local community, and dogged persistence if it comes to a strike for survival. Solidarity may find expression in quickness, sharpness, wit and anger of a people united in vigorous response to an enemy. In the past that enemy might have been the new migrants on one hand, or the hostile host community on the other.[16]

That Sheppard and Worlock refer to the 'enemy' of 'the past', acknowledges the fact that by the time of their arrival on Merseyside much had already changed. The ghetto system had been largely reduced to rubble, as had the Conservatives' relationship with the Protestant Party. Consequently, identity itself had been in flux for a number of years as individuals and families tried to rebuild a sense of community in their new surroundings on the outer echelons of the city. 'Roman Catholic families [in the overspill estates], asked where they came from, still did not offer an address or name of their district but replied with the name of their parish of birth or upbringing in the inner city'.[17] Although identification with the new estates may not have developed for a number of years,[18] identification with 'Merseyside as a whole' was taking shape. Despite this, slum clearance and a change of political discourse could not do away with what Sheppard and Worlock described as the 'negative side' of identity: 'a fortress mentality' which 'aggressively defended "our group" whether right or wrong', 'a kind of tribalism which is inward looking, self-protective and exclusive'.[19] This segment of sectarianism was part of what Sheppard and Worlock aimed to break down.

---

[16]   Sheppard and Worlock, 1988: 42.

[17]   Ibid., 43.

[18]   Rodgers, 2010: 110.

[19]   Sheppard and Worlock, 1988: 42.

As Sheppard recalls, 'it was quickly clear to me that Protestant–Catholic relations were going to be more important than they had ever been'.[20] Worlock commented, 'one of the strongest impressions I received on coming to Liverpool … was that the intense loyalty of northern Catholics was directed primarily to externals, such as "our" parish, "our" priest, "our" archbishop and even "our" social club'.[21] Not far beneath this lay remnants of 'sectarian bitterness'.[22] Reverend John Williams remembers what he termed 'religious division' in Liverpool: 'There was great bitterness which often surrounded mixed marriages due to a sort of inbuilt hatred by family members'. He recalled how in the late 1960s and early 1970s there was 'no dialogue' between the faiths, whereas 'now the clergy is fraternal'. He also explained how in his first parish 'clergymen would walk on the other side of the road to each other and wouldn't speak'.[23] Reverend Williams explained how the willingness of the clergy leadership and rank and file to work together to solve social problems helped to put aside these differences:

> We started working together tirelessly to tackle social problems … people [Protestant and Catholic] started working together for the good of the community. Eventually friendships developed and out of friendship came trust. Catholics were not a threat any longer. We would talk about what united us, what we had in common. 'Us' and 'them' diminished. The lust for power diminished. Great friendships were made in time of strife. People began to grow out of the ghetto mentality, and when in the past a Catholic would not employ a Protestant or vice versa, times have changed. Business is not run like that anymore. The world got wider.[24]

Sheppard and Worlock were at the forefront of this new relationship, but although they appeared to be the main driving force between reconciliation of the two communities, it is important to recognise that building blocks of rapprochement had already been placed before the pair arrived in Liverpool. Leading clergymen of both faiths had attempted to shake off sectarian tension before the 1970s. Moreover, the preceding century had witnessed a spirited attempt on the Catholic side to shake off the badge of 'otherness'.

---

[20] Sheppard, 2002: 148.
[21] Ibid., 57.
[22] Bishop Tom Williams, 23 March 2010.
[23] Revd John Williams, 17 November 2010.
[24] Ibid.

Prior to the 1970s, other Church leaders in Liverpool had spoken out or taken action to oppose religious discord. When Richard Downey became Archbishop in 1928, he 'immediately forbade the use of the title "Catholic" to any political party and banned electoral activity by priests'.[25] This was in response to his predecessor Archbishop Keating, who had agreed to the formation of the *Catholic Representation Association* (the 'Catholic Party') eight years earlier. In response to the militant Protestantism of Wise and Kensit in the 1900s, Anglican Bishop Chavasse said, 'I am often ashamed of the unwise and unchristian conduct of some who call themselves Protestant'.[26] Moreover, there had been a long-standing Roman Catholic crusade in Liverpool to separate Irishness from Catholicism. An early account of this comes from Pat O'Mara, whose autobiography, *Liverpool Irish Slummy*, first published in 1934, sheds light on the Anglicisation of the 'Liverpool Irish' in Catholic schools:

> St Peter's School in Seel Street was, in a way, a new vista opening in my life. Here was an English school filled mainly with Irish-Catholic boys. But the tutors in this school, though all of them were Catholic, had been trained in England and all their teaching smacked of this English training. The Empire and the sacredness of its preservation ran through every text book like a leitmotif. Our navy and the necessity to keep England ruling the waves is another indelible mark left in my memory – though the reason for this was never satisfactorily explained. Pride in our vast and far-flung colonies and the need for their protection and preservation were emphasised, as was the confidence that in any given crisis the colonies and motherland stand as one. The British always won wars – not the English, but the British – giving the impression that we were all more or less brothers under the skin, the Irish, the English, the Welsh and the Scottish.[27]

These 'straight patriotic impressions', as O'Mara calls them, were the implementation of a deliberate policy by the Roman Catholic Church in England to, in the words of Neal, 'turn Irish men and women into good English men and women'.[28] He adds, 'Irish history wasn't taught in schools in the nineteenth century, and it was the English leadership of the Catholic

---

[25] Sheppard and Worlock, 1988: 55.

[26] Ibid., 53.

[27] O'Mara, 1933: 56.

[28] Frank Neal, 12 February 2010.

Church that set this about'.[29] There was, however, a slight problem with this policy, as O'Mara explains:

[The teaching of] religion was something else. Oliver Cromwell might have been a hero in Protestant St Michael's but not in our school. And so, with forthright Pastors like Father Twomey, it wasn't long before religion got to race, and from race to definite biases ... The best I can say is that what I derived from my elementary English-Irish schooling was an intense love for the British Empire and an equally intense hatred for England as opposed to Ireland. Our mothers and fathers, of course, were unequivocal in their attitude – destroy England, no less! But we children at school, despite the intense religious atmosphere of the Catholic school, were rather more patriotized and Britishized – until we got back to our shacks, where we were sternly Irishized'[30]

This 'paradox', as O'Mara put it, reflected what David and Peter Kennedy refer to as 'the ambiguous attitude of the Irish religious and political hierarchy towards the maintenance of a distinctively Irish identity [in Liverpool]'.[31] Nonetheless, as they describe, there was a very definite attempt to anglicise the Irish, and this went as far as 'vetting' potential Irish priests preparing to serve in England:

The Church's policy in Liverpool was to incorporate the immigrant Irish and their descendants into British mainstream life by denationalizing them of their Irishness, while maintaining their commitment to Catholicism ... the strategy the Church adopted involved a concentrated attack on Irish political culture by a re-education policy for the Irish population focusing on and celebrating dominant British values. In schools emphasis was placed on religious instruction, while secular studies made little reference to Ireland or its people's affairs.[32]

Bishop Tom Williams explains:

Liverpool Catholicism was never Irish. [The Catholic Clergy] was always a mixture. In the Catholic schools the syllabus was integration. Prior to the First World War I think there was a deal done with Bishops and the Education board, which said, 'right you can have your Catholic schools

[29] Ibid.
[30] O'Mara, 1933: 57.
[31] Kennedy and Kennedy, 2007: 895.
[32] Ibid., 902.

but you've got to teach English history, not Irish history'. So you've got the national spirit of England drummed in. You could be a Catholic but you still were English, not Irish. It was always an English Church. There was an Irish tradition. I mean some of the Clergymen were from Irish backgrounds. Two of my Grandparents were Irish, for instance. But there was no attempt to promote Irishness.[33]

Kennedy and Kennedy suggest that by the end of the nineteenth century the Liverpool Irish had begun the process of 'privatising their ethnicity'. Outside key dates in the calendar, 'such as celebrating St Patrick's Day or reacting to Orange Day parades on 12th July, they were increasingly less likely to formally demonstrate their ethnic distinctiveness in the manner in which large Irish Catholic communities in the towns and cities of Scotland and Northern Ireland continued to do'.[34] In this sense the Catholic Church in Liverpool had been successful in its attempt to dilute Irishness. However, as Neal suggests, 'though they were no longer distinctively Irish, they were still subject to hostility because they were Catholic'.[35] Stark states that the 'sect has ever been the child of an outcast minority'.[36] This 'outcast minority' in Liverpool were Irish Catholics. It follows that when this minority becomes an established part of the majority, the sect will dispel. This appears to be the line of reasoning the Catholic Church took when trying to play down Irishness. However, they seem to have misjudged that the insular nature of the Catholic district would maintain and foster animosity to the 'host' community. Catholicism itself became a badge of identity, as did Protestantism for their counterparts. The level of genuine observance to the doctrine was not the overriding factor. It was about identification and belonging.

When Worlock arrived in Liverpool on Sunday, 14 March 1976, having already been greeted by an 'enthusiastic crowd' at Lime Street, his first visitor to Archbishop's House was Bishop David Sheppard, who turned up, 'armed with a bottle of wine'.[37] When appointed as Liverpool's Anglican leader during the previous year, Sheppard's first telegram of congratulations had arrived from the soon-to-retire Catholic Archbishop of Liverpool, George Andrew Beck, Worlock's predecessor.

[33] Bishop Tom Williams, 23 March 2010.
[34] Kennedy and Kennedy, 2007: 911.
[35] Frank Neal, 12 February 2010.
[36] Stark, 1967: 5.
[37] Sheppard and Worlock, 1988, 19.

Sheppard recalled that whilst religious divisions needed to be addressed, 'the issue of unemployment was to fill the foreground for us – with Merseyside showing double the national count'.[38] Worlock arrived 'with the firm belief that the Pope had given him the task of addressing people's social and material needs and ensuring Liverpool, with its sectarian past, did not become another Belfast'.[39]

Liverpool, however, had changed unrecognisably in the previous two decades and the religious leaders acknowledged the de-ghettoisation:

> By the time of our coming to Liverpool many of the near-ghetto like segregations within the general community had largely disappeared ... The population of the northern end of the inner city of Liverpool was in many places no more than one tenth of what it had once been. The famous Jesuit parish of St Francis Xavier, which used to house thirteen thousand Roman Catholics, had through demolition and dispersal fallen to under nine hundred.[40]

Nonetheless, the physical removal of antagonistic communities had not removed the need to promote reconciliation. Sheppard recalls: 'On arrival in Liverpool, I made a point of asking advice about ecumenical partnership. The most frequent advice was, "Do be careful. Don't rock the boat"'.[41] This is testimony to the instability that still existed in relation to religion in Liverpool at the time. Nonetheless, Sheppard believed 'the Gospel was at stake in building bridges between Christian churches, and every opportunity should be seized to act in partnership with Roman Catholics'.[42]

This was a view shared by Worlock. Although 'it was still the Catholic style in England for Church leaders to look after their own',[43] this role was soon extended to that of city spokesman. Thus, 'in matters touching politics and society, Derek Worlock gradually established himself as one of the most thoughtful and outspoken Church leaders of his generation, of any denomination ... Given his ministry in Liverpool, this was not inappropriate. If any city did, this one needed some standing up for'.[44] Worlock and Sheppard

---

[38] Sheppard, 2002: 148.
[39] Furnival and Knowles, 1998: 170.
[40] Sheppard and Worlock, 1988: 44.
[41] Sheppard, 2002: 165.
[42] Ibid.
[43] Longley, 2000: 315.
[44] Ibid., 313.

would work together to help the people in times of economic and social hardship. This work included negotiating with big firms in Merseyside to ameliorate redundancies and walking hand in hand through Toxteth after the 'race riots' in the eighties.

One of the most symbolic public displays of partnership came with Pope John Paul II's visit to Liverpool, in 1982. The Pope visited both of the city's cathedrals, thereby publicly 'endorsing' the 'friendship and collaboration' demonstrated between Liverpool's Catholic and Anglican hierarchies. He also observed that 'ecumenism is not just intellect but also affections'.[45] The Pope's visit, however, was also marred by remonstrations from a group of anti-Popery protestors. Although Orange regalia were not worn and the Loyal Orange Order did not organise demonstrations, the protestors included both members of the Liverpool Orange Lodge and members of Paisley's Free Presbyterian Church, which had been gathering members in Liverpool during the previous decade. That the Orange Institution did not officially protest on the day demonstrated how times were changing. No longer was there the same apparent fervent desire for rupture.

Evidently, ecumenical efforts were not to everybody's taste. Former Protestant leader, Roy Hughes, said that Worlock and Sheppard's 'doctrinal truce' was 'an agreement of falsehood', as 'real, vital, everlasting issues were blurred by ecumenism'.[46] Such disapproval was not an exclusively Protestant sentiment. Devout Roman Catholic, Alice Thomas Ellis, in her book *God Has Not Changed*, repeatedly expressed her annoyance at the action of the Church hierarchy. She condemns, 'false ecumenism which requires us to put our brains in the cupboard under the stairs and embrace any old error for fear of giving offence'.[47] In contrast, Benton states, 'They weren't saying "abandon your beliefs", but closeness and a great deal of tolerance grew'.[48]

There is general acknowledgment that the 'better together' mentality, at the very least, had a positive effect in 'setting an example'. As Win Lawlor suggests, 'gestures are really important'.[49] The Sheppard–Worlock duopoly built on a broader improving inter-church situation, described by Joe Benton: 'In the fifties, early sixties there was still this [sectarian] thing lurking round ... when we got into the seventies and eighties there seemed to be a greater

---

[45] Furnival and Knowles, 1998: 212.

[46] Roy Hughes, 13 November 2012.

[47] Ellis, 2004: 42, 119, 180.

[48] Joe Benton, 18 May 2012.

[49] Win Lawlor, 21 February 2013.

enlightenment coming from all the Church leaders and the background to that, I would suggest, was Vatican II'.[50] Peter Kilfoyle agrees, arguing that Vatican II had a 'revolutionary effect'.[51] Vatican II not only took away some of the mystery behind Roman Catholic rituals (for example, adopting vernacular language in Holy Mass instead of Latin) but more importantly it consciously promoted ecumenical effort towards dialogue with other religions. As Power's research suggests, ecumenical efforts were not distinct to Liverpool, but were also taking place in Northern Ireland in the 1970s, where the Protestant and Catholic leaderships 'used their moral authority and influence to encourage mutual understanding within their communities' by engaging 'in joint displays of solidarity as well as making regular statements together'.[52] Yet the persistence of sectarianism in Northern Ireland indicates that ecumenical projects can only be part of the solution.

Worlock and Sheppard themselves acknowledge how their 'predecessors, Stuart Blanch and George Andrew Beck, had enjoyed good friendship. We hoped it would be the same for us. We agreed that we should try and build on that base'.[53] Yet, Worlock and Sheppard were distinct from what had come before. The ecumenism was certainly more overt, and they were demonstrating not just tolerance, but affinity for one another. Sheppard had asked Worlock's predecessor, Andrew Beck, 'if he thought we might work towards joint schools; he thought that was going too fast'.[54] Segregated schools remained and Merseyside has more faith schools per capita of population than anywhere else in England,[55] but Worlock and Sheppard oversaw the reorganisation of the Colleges of Higher Education in Liverpool. A federation of Catholic and Anglican colleges was established where once there had been separate institutions. Sheppard and Worlock helped pioneer the Liverpool Institute of Higher Education, the eventual successor of which was Liverpool Hope University (a unified ecumenical institution). The inclusion of the word 'Hope', it has been suggested, 'was very deliberately a reflection of the theme which Derek and David had made

---

[50] Joe Benton, 18 May 2012. The Second Vatican Council, known informally as 'Vatican II', took place in the 1960s (1962–5) and is regarded mostly for its ecumenical efforts and a modernisation of Catholic doctrine.

[51] Peter Kilfoyle, 23 January 2012.

[52] M. Power, 'Providing a Prophetic Voice for Peace? Church Leaders and Peacebuilding', at Power, 2011: 74.

[53] Sheppard and Worlock, 1988: 83.

[54] Sheppard, 2002: 165.

[55] See Appendices 1.1 and 1.2.

their own: encapsulated in the title of their book, but more importantly put into practice with regard to the life and unity of Liverpool and the region'.[56]

While the 'Mersey Miracle' is held, by some, to be of vital importance in the 'spiritual healing' of the city, the prominence of Worlock and Sheppard may have owed less to the taming of sectarianism than to its inevitable eclipse amid the broader social and economic problems Liverpool was facing at the time. Andy Burnham makes this point:

> Sheppard and Worlock [did] an important thing in setting a different tone, but the reason they worked in that way was because they were capturing the mood of the city. They didn't change it. They were responding to it. I don't think there was any great divide by the time they came to power in Liverpool. My gran talked about singing rebel songs in a way that my mum never would have done. It wasn't relevant to her generation. It had gone by then.[57]

Mike O'Brian made a similar observation:

> I'm not sure whether Sheppard and Worlock led it or they followed it. From what I can remember it was nowhere near as bad as what it had been. It could have been a mixture of both. People had learned sense, and Sheppard and Worlock just pushed it [ecumenism] to the front of the agenda.[58]

Both comments have pertinence. Without doubt, relations in the city were much tamer in the late 1970s than in the 1920s or even the 1950s, yet, both Bishop Tom Williams and Reverend John Williams express how clergymen from both denominations began to sit down and talk about ways they could help the community, as a result of the example set by the hierarchy. There is a line of thought which suggests that this would have happened with or without the example from the leadership. Nonetheless, it is most likely the case that the 'better together' philosophy did trickle down to denominational teaching practice. The religious leadership of the city facilitated a new respect for the religion of the other side amongst the wider population. Susanne Loughlin recalls being told not to go into 'non-Catholic' places of worship in the 1960s,[59] but such invitations became normal from the 1970s onwards.

[56] Furnival and Knowles, 1998: 212–13.
[57] Andy Burnham, 28 March 2013.
[58] Mike O'Brian, 12 November 2012.
[59] Susanne Loughlin, 15 October 2010.

Losing Faith

It is suggested that one key reason for the push for ecumenism and more 'legitimacy' in the lives of the congregations was that people were turning away from religion: ecumenism as a response to apostasy. Benton observed how it was not just Sheppard and Worlock who were pushing greater unity between the faiths, as 'the drive and initiative came from lots of things ... What we actually saw post Vatican II, coupled with similar philosophical and theological thinking by the Church of England, were the first steps towards the ideal of Christian unity: the Holy Spirit working towards the unification of Christendom'.[60] Yet ecumenical accommodation of rival faiths was being targeted at a population increasingly apathetic about any faith. As MP Steve Rotheram puts it, 'ecumenism may be too philosophical for the normal person in the street ... There are people who are fervently religious one way or another, but people, generally, don't care anymore'.[61]

J. Francis Hall wrote of the Liverpool 'habit' of 'going to church' in the 1860s.[62] In 1853, '50% of Catholics in the city' attended Sunday Mass, while the 'Anglican figure of church attendance was 40.7%' in 1851.[63] In 1873, the town was referred to as 'the stronghold of Catholicity', in a newspaper article commenting on 'the important position which the diocese of Liverpool holds' in Catholic England.[64] Protestantism paralleled such strength. In 1898, 15,000 attended a Protestant demonstration at St Georges Hall.[65] The article states that, 'The flow of the tide [in the city] is exceedingly strong in the Protestant direction'.[66] Cowper comments, 'One of the manifestations of corporate family life in Victorian days was the regular and organised attendance of families at Sunday-morning church service', with the regular accompaniment of 'the Church Parade', a practice 'not exclusive to Liverpool' but one 'which developed more fully in Liverpool than in any other large city' in England.[67] However, her work, published in 1948, also highlighted

---

[60] Joe Benton, 18 May 2012.
[61] Steve Rotheram, 4 January 2014.
[62] Hall, 1939: 38–48.
[63] MacRaild, 1999: 83–4.
[64] Burke, 1910: 208.
[65] *Protestant Standard*, 9 July 1898.
[66] Ibid.
[67] Cowper, 1948: 75.

'the virtual disappearance of the practice' of regular church attendance by the mid-twentieth century.[68]

Pastor George Wise's bible class reputedly had a regular weekly attendance of 1,000 people.[69] Another source puts this figure at 1,500.[70] Many of Wise's bible class were working men, but, as Hall writes, 'in mid-Victorian days church-going was the great outward sign of respectability, and Sunday after Sunday St. Nicholas [located in the city centre] drew its full quota from the *elite* suburbs of Liverpool'.[71]

Frank Boyce writes that, 'by the interwar years, each dockland parish had ... the church, presbytery, and elementary school all in close proximity to each other, evidence of the centrality of Catholicism within the community'.[72] Although not all residents of Scotland and Vauxhall were 'God fearing and devoutly Catholic',[73] religion was embedded as part of a Catholic upbringing.[74]

As Neal suggests, 'if you look at attendance at Mass after the Second World War it was very high, and now it's down very low. Most Catholics practise birth control. When I was a kid, Catholic families were big. Now they're just like any other family'.[75] The tendency for Catholics to use contraception or to be 'Catholic from the waist up' increased as the century progressed. People began to reject traditional doctrines, especially those imposing limitations in their personal lives. Susanne Loughlin, a Roman Catholic born in 1948 in Litherland, highlights how her attitude changed dramatically towards the Church as she got older:

> I think I was more brainwashed into being a Catholic when I was younger ... we saw a priest and we were in awe of them. You were afraid of the priests, but as you grew up and you got older and wiser and you knew how hard it was ... you think, I can't have people dictating my life, telling me how to bring my kids up. That's for me to do. You got sick of people trying to run your life and rule you.[76]

---

[68]   Ibid.

[69]   Henderson, 1978: 10.

[70]   Bohstedt, 1992: 183.

[71]   Hall, 1939: 41.

[72]   Boyce, 1999: 284.

[73]   MacRaild, 1999: 87.

[74]   For an account of such a Liverpool Catholic upbringing, see Woods, 1995: 2–3, 38, 106.

[75]   Frank Neal, 12 February 2010.

[76]   Susanne Loughlin, 13 February 2013.

Loughlin explained how, having married a non-Catholic, she resented being 'blackmailed' by the Church to attend Mass regularly in order to have her children christened so as to dispel 'Mortal Sin'. She refers to this as a 'dictatorship' and states, 'I rebelled, so I've got two Catholic and two Protestant [children]. I've known other people to not get their kids christened because they didn't want to do what the Catholic Church wanted and be hypocrites [go to Mass when they didn't want to]'.[77] When asked if her parents would have 'rebelled' in the way she had, Loughlin replied, 'no they wouldn't have'. Nonetheless, she recalls how,

> They [priests] used to come round every week and you had to give them money, no matter how hard times were. The priest never left your house without money. Though my gran once ran the priest up the road, because when my granddad died, when she needed him for a little bit of comfort, he never came near, but when he was buried, the priest came round knocking for his money and she ran him out the house and up the road.[78]

Brenda O'Brian also alludes to why priests, once respected and feared, lost much of their influence and admiration as the twentieth century progressed. She highlights how it may have been priests' own tactics which changed some people's minds:

> [Catholics] were terrified of them. They wouldn't say no to a priest. Religion was shoved down your neck when I was little. The priest used to come and visit your house and take the rent money off the fireplace. My mum went through all that. I mean she was Church of England all her life but in the neighbourhood they [priests] used to pop in and out the back doors and take the rent money, with the excuse 'there's poor in the Church'. She remembers a [Catholic] neighbour coming in crying, saying, 'he's [the priest] took the rent'. My mum used to lend her money.[79]

Attitudes on marriage, religious upbringing, and demand for 'Peter's Pence' were not the only factors causing controversy in people's minds in relation to the Catholic Church. Some of the claims by individual priests caused consternation amongst their own flock. Mike O'Brian, whose father was Catholic and mother was Protestant stated:

[77] Ibid.
[78] Ibid.
[79] Brenda O'Brian, 12 November 2012.

My dad never argued with my mum over religion. He used to have this
saying: he'd say, 'I'll fight for religion when it puts bread on the table',
but I remember once, in the mid-1960s, my dad got some weird jaundice.
He was in a ward in Walton Hospital. A priest came in and got talking to
him. He asked, 'Where did you get married?' He said, 'St Chad's Church
[Church of England]'. The priest said, 'Do you realise that you're not
married and all your children are bastards? You'll spend eternity in hell!'
and my dad said, 'It's all right, I won't be able to get near the fire for all
you bastard priests!'[80]

Bennett suggests that the decline of Church power was part of generational
change as younger citizens threw off the shackles: 'Both Churches were
going down in attendance. Older people, for whom religion really mattered,
were dying, families got busier, men and women worked longer, and, of
course, then you had a lot of mixed marriages, which years ago would have
been frowned upon'.[81] Bennett's observation is important. Many people on
Merseyside began to see past the narrow confines of denomination. If it
came to a choice between religion and contentment, religion increasingly
took second place. For families it also began to matter much less. Mike
O'Brian gives one example:

When my dad died, they had the Catholic Mass ... My mum was a firm
believer that if that's what he believes [Catholicism] that's what he's going
to be buried as. In fact, my uncle, on my mum's side, was there and he
was in the Orange Lodge. They said to him, 'It's in a Catholic church. You
can't go'. He said [to them], 'You can piss off! It's my brother in law. I'm
going!'[82]

As such, it is clear that religion's relevance as a 'badge of identity' (and,
more importantly, a symptom of division) began to wane as communities
transcended traditional communal boundaries.

As Séafra Ó Cearbhail states,

Religion is a territorial badge of identity if you've got sectarian fault
lines. If there's a sectarian conflict it's not a fight over different sections
of the Bible and interpretation of it. Religion is a badge overlaying other

---

[80] Mike O'Brian, 12 November 2012.
[81] Doris Bennett, 5 March 2013.
[82] Mike O'Brian, 12 November 2012.

identities, such as national identities [or geographic loyalties], but it's not really about religion, I would contend.[83]

It must be acknowledged that, relatively speaking, Liverpool is still more of a 'religious city' than most in the country. The 2011 census results showed continuing extensive affiliation to Christianity across the Diocese of Liverpool: '75.2% consider themselves Christian. This compares with a national average of 59.3%'.[84] In parts of old 'sectarian' north Liverpool, such as Kirkdale, over 90 per cent still identify as 'Christian'.[85]

Yet, affinity as 'Christian' and the continuing presence of large numbers of faith schools are not tantamount to religious fervour. It would certainly be difficult to envisage 1,000 people regularly attending a men's bible class in the city today. The Catholic Archbishop of Liverpool remarked sadly that 'churches closing has happened many times before' as the announcement of a further six closures was made in 2000, long after the depopulation of north Liverpool had taken place.[86] The fall in church attendances has resulted in the closure of both Catholic and Protestant churches in the city.[87] This trend extends to a national level as 'numbers in the pews have fallen to less than half the levels of the 1960s'.[88]

For Roman Catholics, the priest once 'offered them absolution: he married them, baptised them and buried them. The priest was friend, protector and sage'.[89] Similarly, '100,000 [Protestant] Liverpudlians' were said to have

[83] Séafra Ó Cearbhail, 14 March 2013.

[84] Diocese of Liverpool (website), 'Christianity Remains Strong in the Diocese of Liverpool'. Available at: www.liverpool.anglican.org/Christianity-remains-strong-in-the-Diocese-of-Liverpool.

[85] See DataShine (website), '2011 Census Map of Merseyside'. Available at: http://datashine.org.uk/#zoom=13&lat=53.42678&lon=-2.95403&layers=BTTT&table=QS208EW&col=QS208EW0002&ramp=RdBu.

[86] Scottie Press (website), 'Pastoral Regeneration in Liverpool', 'Holy Cross Church Now Closed! "End of an Era", 152 years'. Available at: www.scottiepress.org/projects/churches.htm.

[87] Granada Reports, Granada Regional News, ITV, Liverpool, 21 January 2011 (on the decline of Catholicism in Liverpool and the closure of Catholic churches); *Crosby & Litherland Champion*, 23 April 2014 (the newspaper headline reported on the closure of a prominent Protestant church).

[88] *Daily Mail* (website), 'Just 800,000 Worshippers Attend a Church of England Sunday Service' (22 March 2014). Available at: www.dailymail.co.uk/news/article-2586596/Just-800-000-worshipers-attend-Church-England-service-average-Sunday.html#ixzz39HTtlJRz.

[89] MacRaild, 1999: 91.

'look[ed] to Pastor George Wise as a political and spiritual leader'.[90] As Boyce states, religion was a 'fixed point in the life of the community and a badge of identity'.[91] This, as he describes, contrasts with the contemporary situation:

> Local priests claim about 10% of Catholics living in Vauxhall attend Sunday mass [*this area maintains the highest proportion of Catholics in the city*]. [Yet] Contact between some of the priests' parishioners seems minimal ... Catholics in the Vauxhall areas have, in the past, identified very closely with their parishes, and have looked upon their priests and sought guidance from them. With very few exceptions this tradition has died ... The influence of local clergy has been marginalised. While 'secular' organisations are facing the millennium with confidence ... [Liverpool's] vibrant devotional and social tradition now exists only in the memory of an older generation.[92]

In highlighting why sectarianism declined, Steve Higginson stated, 'Well, just look at the declining church attendances. Not many people care'.[93] Owing in part to the ecumenical movement, even those who do go to church do not regard those of the 'opposite' denomination as a 'threat'. In 1978, Ron Henderson complained about the religious 'apathy which permits reconciliation with the evil system of Rome to proceed unchallenged';[94] a complaint against growing ecumenism in Liverpool. As the trade union leader Billy Hayes puts it, 'Protestants, unless they're in the Lodge, don't really have an axe to grind'.[95]

Bishop Tom Williams offers a defence of religion in Liverpool: 'I don't think that the Catholic Church is declining, I think that less people go to Mass. It's like people who support Everton and Liverpool but don't go the match ... The idea of identity and faith were still important but they took on a different expression'.[96] Bishop Williams' argument, although indeed relevant, is debatable.[97] As Midwinter, having discussed Liverpool's sectarian

---

[90] Bohstedt, 1992: 189.

[91] Boyce, 1999: 190.

[92] Ibid., 296–7.

[93] Steve Higginson, 11 February 2013.

[94] Henderson, 1978: 28.

[95] Billy Hayes, 2 February 2013.

[96] Tom Williams, 23 March 2010.

[97] The point can be made that although a lot of Everton and Liverpool fans don't go to matches, they still wear their colours. At one time, ostentatious religious symbols

past, states, 'It is quieter now. Perhaps religion does not move the blocs of people as emotively as it used to. Tolerance, it has been cynically remarked, is indifference'.[98]

In concluding which was of greater importance in diminishing sectarianism – the 'better together' Sheppard–Worlock project or the onset of indifference, it is difficult to escape the conclusion that the latter was more important. The ecumenism of Sheppard–Worlock was not insignificant as it emphasised to religious adherents on either side that it was fine to embrace 'the other side'. Zealots looked marginalised when they saw religious leaders enjoying such cordial relations and this leadership may have smoothed the path towards integration via, for example, mixed marriage.

Yet the theological aspects of religious hostility were already in sharp decline, with the vanishing of the rabble-rousing preachers of old. What remained of the old sectarianism was residual suspicion and prejudice regarding the 'other' community. Church attendance and religious adherence – and attendant loyalty – were much weakened by the 1970s as a variety of political and cultural distractions discussed elsewhere in this book provided alternative repositories for action and adherence. This is not to suggest that Liverpool became entirely secular, as in terms of affiliation it remains, by some distance, England's 'faith city'. However, religious affiliation was largely divorced from activism.

characterised the streets of Liverpool, but this practice has significantly declined, replaced instead by displays of football allegiance.

[98] Midwinter, 1971: 172.

7

The Transfer of Racism: Did Liverpool's Black and Chinese Communities Become 'New Aliens'?

Sectarianism and anti-Irish racism were never Liverpool's only problems. During the nineteenth century, a wide variety of immigrant groups came to Liverpool: Irish, Eastern European Jews, Chinese, Asians, and Africans, the arrival of each grouping triggering some reaction. As Herson states, 'Liverpool's very cosmopolitanism contributed to its propensity to racism' as 'the city's society ... negatively marked out ethnic and racial differences and in so doing encouraged conflictual inter-ethnic relations'.[1] In the latter part of the nineteenth century, at least, the dominance of the conflict between Liverpool's native white community and the immigrant white Irish community, led to conflict between whites and other minority groups becoming overlooked amid the omnipresent main Protestant versus Catholic sectarian fracture. Herson acknowledges:

> It is questionable whether, in the nineteenth century, the mixture of immigrants in Liverpool actually created a cosmopolitan culture. Rather, the city was dominated by a fractured white majority from Britain and Ireland amongst whom various continental and overseas minorities inserted themselves.[2]

Prejudice and discrimination against Liverpool's other minority communities were a sideshow. This chapter concentrates on Liverpool's black and Chinese communities, primarily due to their position as the largest two minority groups in Liverpool throughout the latter stages of the twentieth century.

---

[1] Herson, 2008: 68.

[2] Ibid., 69.

Moreover, although the port has the 'oldest sizeable, settled African, South Asian and Chinese community in the country',[3] the black and Chinese communities have very different experiences due to the varying degrees of racist intensity they have experienced in Liverpool.

Liverpool's main social problem may have been sectarianism before its ostensible replacement by anti-black racism in the latter half of the twentieth century. However, Murray Steele highlights how Liverpool's main division may have added to an increasingly racist perception of black people:

> Liverpool evolved a distinctly imperial culture moulded by a local environment that made it unique amongst English cities. The religious sectarianism ... divided its working class and had the effect of giving the Conservative/ Unionist cause, traditionally the party of empire, a control over local politics that lasted until the mid-1950s. Liverpool's celebrations of empire thus received much official local backing: annual Empire Day observance in schools started as early as 1905 (on the late Queen Victoria's birthday of 24 May), well before it became official in 1916, while the imperial theme featured in successive coronations and other royal occasions.[4]

It has already been noted that Irish and Irish descendants were anglicised in Catholic schools in Liverpool.[5] Local councillor Mike Murphy recalls being told to take his Shamrock off by the Headmaster in his Catholic school 'because you are English!'[6] As such, Steele's comments are afforded credence. Protestant (or non-Catholic) schools in Liverpool naturally celebrated events like 'Empire Day', but Catholic schools also acknowledged these occasions. Therefore, both denominations began to conform to dominant British values and had developed a largely shared identity. Moreover, similarities between Catholics and Protestants increased as the proportion of Irish born in Liverpool began to diminish and with a lack of discernible external features to highlight their apartness, Irish descendants in Liverpool became more and more assimilated into a predominantly white host community, sections of which looked with hostility towards groups beyond the sectarian divide.[7]

---

[3] Preface by Ann Dummett, Runnymede Trust in Liverpool Black Caucus, 1986.

[4] Steele, 2008: 123.

[5] O'Mara, 1933: 56–7.

[6] Cllr Michael Murphy, 8 April 2013.

[7] It should be noted that many Irish or of Irish decent also integrated with Liverpool's black community.

Liverpool's Non-white Communities

Liverpool's black community is characterised by its longevity. Dating back to the 1700s, it is one of the oldest black communities in Europe, with many blacks the descendants of servants and slaves (plus some sailors from the West Indies and Africa). The black population of Liverpool, 0.4 per cent of the city's population by 1911, was established prior to any substantial immigration from the Commonwealth in the twentieth century. Moreover, as Frost notes, 'Liverpool had one of the largest biracial or mixed-race populations by the late twentieth century'.[8]

Conversely, new Commonwealth immigration had only added a meagre 0.3 per cent to Merseyside's population by 1969[9] and Liverpool had one of 'the least diverse ethnic communities by the late twentieth century in terms of recently arrived first-generation migrants'.[10] Indeed, that 'Liverpool developed from being one of the most ethnically diverse populations in the mid-nineteenth century to one of the least diverse at the time of the 2001 census'[11] is due to 'the well-known fact that relatively few migrated from the new Commonwealth in the 1940s and 1950s ... because of the city's depressed state'.[12] Lack of understanding of Liverpool's black communities and that of their relative isolation may have led some of the city's primarily white population to perceive Liverpool born blacks as 'foreigners'.

Much of Liverpool's success as a port was built on black servitude. For more than a century, Liverpool ships took nearly 1.5 million Africans from West Africa to work as slaves in the Americas.[13] By the end of the seventeenth century, 40 per cent of all slaves traded from Africa by all European countries were transported in Liverpool ships.[14] A significant proportion of Liverpool's grandeur and early trading wealth was a result of transatlantic slavery: a trade described as 'the pride of Liverpool', since it flooded the town with wealth.[15] 'The city's merchant elite was heavily involved [and] twenty-five Liverpool mayors [were] connected to the

---

[8] Frost, 2008: 144–5.
[9] Murphy, 1995: iii.
[10] Frost, 2008: 144.
[11] Ibid., 187, citing Liverpool 800.
[12] Ibid.
[13] Museum of Liverpool, 2012: 51.
[14] Gifford, Brown, and Bundley, 1989: 25.
[15] Ibid.

trade'.[16] Slaves were sold in the port, advertised in the 1700s in local papers such as the *Williamson's Liverpool Advertiser* and the *Liverpool Chronicle*.[17]

Negative views on mixed marriage abounded. Black men were said to 'insult and threaten respectable women in the street' and be 'over familiar with white girls'.[18] An experienced Liverpool policeman, talking about the cause of the 1919 'race riots' in Liverpool, stated: 'the Negroes would not have been touched had it not been for their relations with white women'.[19] Even in the latter half of the twentieth century, white women were ostracised for having relationships with black men. Councillor Anna Rothery recalls, 'There were a lot of women from the north end of the city that married African and Jamaican men. They were spat on in the streets. I remember as a child, seeing white women spat on. They were called things like "monkey lovers"!'[20]

Yet, at the same time, it was claimed that black people in Liverpool were not treated with the same degree of hostility as in other areas of the western world. In 1849, it was observed:

> In Liverpool ... the negro steps with a prouder pace and lifts his head like a man; for here, no such exaggerated feelings exist in respect to him, as in America ... the black cooks and stewards of American ships are very much attached to the place and like to make a voyage to it.[21]

Law believes that such attitudes 'may well have accounted for black sailors settling in Liverpool, particularly in the dock areas where they were relatively well received'.[22] Whilst areas such as Scotland Road were very definitely heartlands of Irish Catholic Liverpool, the Liverpool 1 area was home to a wider array of cultures, including that formed by 'runaway' slaves and servants and later bolstered in the nineteenth century by seamen and ex-servicemen. A larger black community developed in Liverpool 8.

The Liverpool Black Caucus has highlighted the uneven development of the black community in the city, arguing that this has occurred largely through processes of exclusion:

[16] Museum of Liverpool, 2012: 51.
[17] Cited by Law, 1981: 11.
[18] *Liverpool Courier*, 11 June, 1918, cited by Murphy, 1995: 46–7.
[19] Murphy, 1995: 46–7.
[20] Anna Rothery, 19 February 2013.
[21] Law, 1981: 15, citing Melville, 1969: 172.
[22] Law, 1981: 15.

> [There's] a clear situation of racial inequality in the allocation of council
> housing in Liverpool ... Black households are disadvantaged compared
> to white households ... [Black residents have] a lower quality dwelling
> overall; they have been excluded from sheltered accommodation ... and
> virtually excluded from the better quality environment of the suburban
> areas. Though Liverpool's black population is relatively small it is concen-
> trated in 5 contiguous inner city wards: Abercromby, Arundel, Granby,
> Picton and Smithdown.[23]

Jean Hill, brought up in Anfield in the 1940s and 50s, recalls how 'black
people were never seen', as they 'were all corralled into Liverpool 8'.[24] She
also remembers seeing provocative graffiti in Anfield in the late 1960s and
1970s: 'big graffiti', saying 'Anfield is white man's territory!'[25] Michelle
Chambers, a Liverpool-born black resident of forty years, added:

> There were some areas that if you went to you could expect trouble. At
> the time of my growing up, Kensington in Liverpool 7 was very much a
> 'no-go' area, also places like Everton, Netherley. In fact, the further you
> got away from the Toxteth hub was the more you could expect trouble
> when you went to those areas.[26]

The idea of there being 'white' and 'black' areas in Liverpool is widely
accepted. O'Reilly recalls this moving to Childwall Valley when she was
eleven: 'I remember asking my mum, when we moved up there, "Why is
everybody around here all white, mum?" and she said, "Because that's the
way it is."'[27] Billy Hayes, born in Liverpool and head of the Communication
Workers Union (CWU), states: 'There's definitely segregation in Liverpool.
No question about it: conscious or unconscious ... When they demolished
all the slums around Scottie [Scotland Road] ... hardly any black people
were dispersed [and] I would say, in terms of black people, the north end
[of Liverpool] is like a white only area'.[28] Tony Birtill, a freelance journalist,
who grew up in Walton, concurs: 'Very few black people come here at all.
[Walton, north Liverpool] is a white, working-class area'.[29] Walton MP, Steve

---

[23] Liverpool Black Caucus, 1986: 34–6.
[24] Jean Hartrick Hill, 26 October 2012.
[25] Ibid.
[26] Michelle Chambers, 7 April 2013.
[27] Maria O'Reilly, 15 March 2013.
[28] Billy Hayes, 2 February 2013.
[29] Tony Birtill, 29 October 2012.

Rotheram, remembers, 'When I went to school, [there were] very few black or minority ethnic faces, but I didn't think about it. You were used to what you were used to'.[30]

Racial Tensions in Liverpool: The Lack of Institutional Response

The development of Liverpool's black and Chinese communities was not accompanied by economic progress. The Toxteth riots of 1981 were followed soon after by the capture of the city's council by the far-left Militant Tendency in the 1980s, which merely heightened problems. Militant, opposed to black sections in the Labour Party as a distraction from class struggle, was criticised by the black community. The Liverpool Black Caucus[31] excoriated the city council for its approach, whilst Lynn[32] highlighted a lack of provision for the Chinese community by Liverpool City Council. The themes of both the Liverpool Black Caucus' *The Racial Politics of Militant in Liverpool* (1986) and Irene Lynn's *The Chinese Community in Liverpool* (1982) are of discrimination by omission, or a lack of understanding for their respective communities. Sections of the local black community believed Liverpool City Council, when controlled by the Militant Tendency, deliberately demonised them in order to discredit local representatives politically and curtail their non-compliance with Militant's approach.[33] The Anglican Bishop David Sheppard and Catholic Archbishop Derek Worlock supported this claim, recalling 'attempts by Militant to introduce extraneous elements into Liverpool 8 to discredit local community leadership'.[34] Concurrently, the Chinese community felt 'ignored by the makers of social policy' in Liverpool.[35]

Several works and personal accounts highlight how discrimination was commonplace in the economic life of the city. Connolly and co-authors claim that 'the impediments to the young black's progress extended beyond obstacles common to the entire Liverpool working class',[36] while Gifford

---

[30] Steve Rotheram, 4 January 2013.
[31] Liverpool Black Caucus, 1986.
[32] Lynn, 1982.
[33] Liverpool Black Caucus, 1986: 85.
[34] Ibid.; Sheppard and Worlock, 1988: 7 ('Foreword').
[35] Lynn, 1982: 7.
[36] Connolly, et al., 1992: 35.

and others, enquiring into race relations in Liverpool, highlight that 'black people in Liverpool have not, by and large, achieved even the limited advances in jobs, housing and equal treatment that had been gained by more recently arrived black communities in other major cities in Britain'.[37]

The Chinese community in Liverpool has traditionally been limited mainly to the catering sector. Although it is argued that this was a consequence of 'changes in eating habits of the British public' being 'met by Chinese immigration,'[38] it is also the case that, for much of the twentieth century, the Chinese community was limited to this sphere of employment, as they faced opposition from the white working class in Liverpool if they chose to compete in areas such as dock work, laundry work, or as merchant seamen.[39] The Liverpool Black Caucus highlights how businesses failed to hire members of Liverpool's minority communities.[40]

There was also growing evidence of discrimination by omission in the provision of services. One study, produced via Liverpool Social Services Department, highlighted the existence of 'personal prejudice, explicit racism and prejudicial ignorance, feelings of unease in working with black people which affect competence and quality of service, [and] explicit discrimination in the failure to provide "ethnic-sensitive" services, particularly for the Chinese and Muslim communit[ies]'.[41]

In addition, Torkington highlighted a similar distinction of direct and indirect racism within the provision of health care on Merseyside, claiming that certain groups of people in the [Liverpool 8] community are denied medical facilities to which they are entitled because of individual GPs' prejudices'.[42] Torkington also noted that health concerns were not helped by the fact that, 'generally, black people wait longer before being re-housed and when re-housed they tend to be given lower quality accommodation'.[43]

The problem of housing allocation and quality, however, was not an issue exclusively affecting Liverpool's black community. Lynn notes that, 'Chinese people lacked information on the availability of local authority housing and the existence of Housing Associations',[44] and although 'Chinese

---

[37] Gifford, Brown, and Bundley, 1989: 21.

[38] Wong, 1989: 5–6.

[39] See Lynn, 1982 and Wong, 1989.

[40] Liverpool Black Caucus, 1986.

[41] Rooney, 1987: 101.

[42] Torkington, 1983: 27, 32.

[43] Ibid.

[44] Lynn, 1982: 74.

people, white people, black people and Asians all [had] similar housing and social problems ... a Chinese family may not be fully aware of their rights and [the] services available and have problems articulating their needs'.[45]

The belief in racist structures in Liverpool was vocalised by Wally Brown in his Foreword to Ian Law's *History of Race and Racism in Liverpool* (1981), in which he claims that 'Racism is deeply ingrained in every brick of the city and its institutions'.[46] This perception was most strongly articulated by Liverpool's black community in respect of the police force, criticised for its alleged persistent harassment of blacks. The predominantly black 'Granby Triangle' was highlighted as a recipient of heavy-handed tactics employed by the police during the 1970s and 1980s. Police harassment of the black community in Granby is seen locally as the main reason for the Toxteth riots.

Nonetheless, it would be wrong to assert that Liverpool's police force, then headed by Chief Constable Ken Oxford (considered a 'racist' by many in the black community),[47] was universally bigoted. This was acknowledged by Margaret Simey, Chair of the Police Committee of the Merseyside County Council from 1981 (shortly before the riots) to 1986. She talked of the contrasting styles of policing in Liverpool 8:

> We have this utter folly for an official policy of softly, softly backed up by strong arm. The people do admire the local police for their courage. They're good friends ... But the minute there is trouble they are sent out of the neighbourhood, and what we regard as trained thugs are brought in to impose control.[48]

The 'trained thugs' to which Simey referred were the Operations Support Division (OSD), whose overt racism was such that they are quoted, on the beat, as singing 'We are the OSD. We will get you black bastards' and 'We are the OSD and we are nigger hunting tonight'.[49] David Copley, a Methodist Minister who experienced the riots at close hand, recalled:

> As pressure from the police was getting heavier and heavier towards black [people], particularly young boys, that sense of irritation and frustration grew into a real sense of anger ... part of their anger was that they were

---

[45] Ibid., 68–9.
[46] Wally Brown, 'Foreword', Law, 1981: iv.
[47] Liverpool Black Caucus, 1986: 42.
[48] Gifford, Brown, and Bundley, 1989: 164–5.
[49] Ibid., 172–3.

never allowed to feel at home ... Whereas a very strong feeling amongst [the youths] was this was their territory, their home ... these are their streets and the police are invading them.[50]

Anti-Irish Racism

It is arguably indicative of a reduced sectarian focus that, by the 1980s, institutionalised anti-black racism was a much more obvious component of the Merseyside Police force than hostility towards the Liverpool Irish. Allegations of anti-Irish racism were still evident – one interviewee, comparing the treatment of the Irish compared with loyalist, Orange, and far right groups, argued, 'The police in Merseyside are prejudiced and that's the bottom line!'[51] However, the allegation was more common in respect of the broader local Orange and loyalist population.

Because of 'The Troubles' in Northern Ireland, from the 1960s onwards, the Irish presence on the streets of Liverpool (in terms of marches and parades) 'virtually disappeared', owing to a fear of attack by Loyalists and amid expectations of harassment and a lack of protection from the police if such attacks were to take place.[52] Tony Birtill (and others at Liverpool Irish Centre) argued that the Merseyside police force offered insufficient concern for the local Irish community, evident when that community attempted to reappear on Liverpool's streets following the improvements in the situation in Northern Ireland in the mid-1990s.[53] This lack of protection led to loyalists successfully blockading the St Patrick's Day Parade in the 1990s.

In 1996, Merseyside Chief Constable, Jim Sharples, 'expressed concern over sectarianism and inter-community tension in Liverpool'[54] in response to a 'planned and agreed' St Patrick's Day procession being blocked by Orangemen. There were 'complaints that the police did not do enough to allow the properly organised and approved St Patrick's Parade to follow its agreed route and in effect sided with the demonstrators'.[55] Mary O'Neil,

---

[50] Cited by Frost and Phillips, 2011.

[51] Tony Birtill made this point at a public talk at St Michael's Liverpool Irish Centre (6 February 2013), hosted by *Cairde na hÉireann Liverpool*.

[52] The lack of Irish presence on the streets, and the stated reasons for it, were given by Séafra Ó Cearbhail, Neil Dulin and *Cairde na hÉireann Liverpool*, 2012, p. 4.

[53] Public talk at St Michael's Liverpool Irish Centre (6 February 2013).

[54] *Irish World*, 26 April 1996.

[55] *Irish World*, 29 March 1996.

of Huyton, who was in the parade, went further in her criticism in the *Irish Post*:

> The police in full riot dress stood menacingly in Hope Street … sizing up to a peaceful multicultural St Patrick's Day parade … they wouldn't move the loyalists blocking the street [who] were allowed to goad the marchers with obscene chants …. When a marcher protested about the change of route to a police officer, he told them to 'Shut up or we'll march you to the bleedin' boat'.[56]

What followed was a 'wave of support' for the Merseyside Irish, as local MPs Bob Parry and David Alton took on the police over the issue. Councillors who had been on the parade were 'outraged' and Parry was 'absolutely disgusted' by the police actions.[57] The Chief Constable of Merseyside Police, in a letter to Bob Parry MP, 'blame[d] the disturbances and the decision to re-route the parade on the hostility of the loyalist demonstrators'. He apportioned some of the blame to 'a small group within the parade displaying what could be interpreted as IRA placards [posters calling for the release of "political prisoners']'.[58] Yet, later that month, Merseyside Police had to apologise to the Liverpool Irish Centre when 'armed officers supported by a helicopter surrounded the premises' following an erroneous 'tip off' about two men on the roof, who were in fact checking the building's wiring.[59]

Journalist Tony Birtill refers to what he perceives as consistent examples of police prejudice against Liverpool's Irish community:

> The police launched on the Irish when they attempted to exercise their right to march: they [the OSD] were there all day, they didn't go anywhere near the fascists [Loyalists], but they were there to harass us! I have observed this from 1996 onwards. For any Irish parade (even if there was no opposition whatsoever) the police would be there taking our photographs, asking people their personal details and so on, a sort of low level harassment. Sometimes it was ridiculous. If you're Irish, you can't wear sunglasses. However, if you go along and throw missiles at an Irish parade, if you scream racist abuse, that's fine! They won't ask you your name. They won't do anything to you. The contrast is startling![60]

---

[56] *Irish Post*, 30 March 1996.
[57] *Irish World*, 29 March 1996.
[58] *Irish World*, 26 April 1996.
[59] See Roberts, 2015: Appendix 4.1.
[60] Tony Birtill, talk, 6 February 2013, *Cairde na hÉireann Liverpool*.

Following a similar debacle in 2012, when the Sean Phelan march was blocked from entering Liverpool city centre by Loyalists denouncing an 'IRA march', the police appeared to take a tougher line with counter-demonstrators and have ensured that more recent marches have taken their intended route.

The claims of analogous experiences of the Irish and black communities extend beyond policing. In relation to access to other social services, it is argued that prejudice directed towards Liverpool blacks was also felt by Irish people in Liverpool, who were subject to a similar unfavourable treatment. Descriptions of blacks as 'lazy' mirrored those of the Irish as 'slothful' as a comparable demeaning picture was painted of the two communities. Roddy Doyle famously referred to the Irish as the 'niggers of Europe',[61] highlighting the comparable experiences of the two populations. However, in Liverpool, it is argued that, unlike black people, the Irish could escape their labels by assimilation. The Liverpool Irish would often become indistinguishable from the 'host' community.

Testimony to the change in focus from sectarian issues to race issues might be seen in the accusations of racism that have been levelled at the city's two most prominent sporting institutions. In recent history, Everton FC has had allegations of racism directed towards its management team, while Liverpool FC has had allegations of racism directed towards its playing staff. There is also evidence of racist elements in the fan base of both teams. The former accusation is recalled and repudiated by Everton FC's most successful manager, Howard Kendall:

> I used to be criticised for not signing black players and that was totally wrong, because I left Everton the second time as manager because the board pulled out of a deal for Dion Dublin, which I'd agreed with Alex Ferguson. So that was an absolute load of nonsense, that there was anything racial in my signings or my team.[62]

The argument of racist motivation within Everton's management structure, although unsubstantiated, stems from the fact that Everton FC was one of the last teams in British football to sign a black player. There were also racist elements within the club's fan-base. Bananas were thrown onto the pitch, whilst a pocket of Everton fans delivered racist jibes to Liverpool FC's

---

[61] Roddy Doyle, *Roddy Doyle Quotes* (1987). Available at: www.allgreatquotes.com/roddy_doyle_quotes.shtml.

[62] Howard Kendall, 17 November 2010.

John Barnes.[63] In 2000, Everton topped the racist 'league of shame',[64] with more Everton fans claiming that they had heard racist remarks at football games than fans of any other club.

For Liverpool FC, the Luis Suarez affair in 2011,[65] and the club's subsequent defence of the player after he racially harassed Manchester United's Patrice Evra during a football match, caused much consternation.[66] The player's behaviour – refusing to shake Evra's hand in the next fixture between the two clubs – caused much embarrassment for Liverpool FC. The reaction of some Liverpool fans in defending Suarez on both occasions led to accusations of 'racist club' shifting across Stanley Park.[67] Claims of racism have long displaced those of sectarianism. Although it is acknowledged that both clubs have a wide-reaching and ethnically varied international support structure, fans from the city of Liverpool are largely white and working class and, unlike in Glasgow, not divided on sectarian lines. Fans of both teams have been arrested for racially abusing football players.[68]

The Evertonian MP and Shadow Minister Andy Burnham believes that racism within the support bases of Liverpool's two football clubs supplanted previous shades of sectarianism:

[63] M. Furber, 'Trying to Face Everton's Racist Past' (website). Available at: www.football365.com/f365-features/5062782/Trying-To-Face-Everton-s-Racist-Past.

[64] P. Brown and V. Chaudhary, 'Everton Fans Top Racist "League of Shame". *Guardian*, 7 January 2000. Available at: www.guardian.co.uk/uk/2000/jan/07/race.world.

[65] D. Taylor, 'Liverpool Furious as Luis Suárez Banned in Patrice Evra Racism Row'. *Guardian*, 20 December 2011. Available at: https://www.theguardian.com/football/2011/dec/20/liverpool-luis-suarez-patrice-evra.

[66] Mirror Football, 'New York Times Attack Liverpool over Suarez Conduct'. *Daily Mirror*, 12 February 2012. Available at: www.mirror.co.uk/sport/football/news/luis-suarez-racism-row-new-3308186.

[67] S. Cohen, 'Defending the Indefensible'. Goal.com (26 December 2011). Available at: www.goal.com/en-us/news/3824/steve-cohen/2011/12/26/2819070/steven-cohen-defending-the-indefensible.

[68] BBC, 'Everton Fan Guilty of Racist Abuse at Loftus Road' (21 January 2013). Available at: www.bbc.co.uk/news/uk-england-21129082; Mail online, 'Fan Arrested in Connection of Alleged Racist Abuse of Oldham's Adeyemi at Anfield' (7 January 2012) http://www.dailymail.co.uk/sport/football/article-2083680/Liverpool-race-row-Tom-Adeyemi-Fan-arrested.html; D. White, 'Merseyside Police arrest "racist" supporter after image of "monkey" gesture appears on Twitter'. *Daily Telegraph* (28 January 2012). Available at: www.telegraph.co.uk/sport/football/teams/liverpool/9047119/Merseyside-Police-arrest-racist-supporter-after-image-of-monkey-gesture-appears-on-Twitter.html.

Everton in my youth were definitely predominantly associated with Celtic and Liverpool were predominantly associated with Rangers … It started to diminish in the mid-eighties, and the racism was rife at Goodison in the eighties with John Barnes and everything. As the Celtic/ Rangers thing sort of melted away, a new thing came up, which was racism.[69]

The Supplanting of Sectarianism by Racism

Racial problems had long co-existed alongside sectarian divisions, but had been overshadowed by the greater pervasiveness of the latter. During the twentieth century, Liverpool experienced three 'race riots': in 1919, 1948, and 1981, although the lattermost also involved sizeable numbers of white rioters. In the summer of 1919, 'serious race riots' broke out near the docklands in Liverpool 1, as 'black men were attacked in the street by white mobs and fought back'.[70] Economic rivalry felt by unemployed and demobilised white ex-servicemen was one factor involved in the disturbances, whilst 'jealousy over sexual or marital relations between black men and white women … was also very evident'.[71] Initially, the riots were reported 'in terms of an indignant white backlash, following sudden, frenzied and unprovoked black violence'.[72] The *Liverpool Echo*, however, acknowledged that 'Negro Baiting' had taken place, and evidence from special court hearings (between 16 June and October 1919) suggests that 'many of the black people in the dock had responded to intimidation by white mobs'.[73] Of the twenty-one white people convicted for offences during the riots, most are thought to have been 'Irish or of Irish descent'.[74]

Liverpool's next 'race riot' coincided with the local economy hitting a post-war slump. By 1948, with unemployment 6.5 per cent (two and a half times the national average), Liverpool's black population stood at 8,000[75]

[69] Andy Burnham, 28 March 2013.

[70] Helmond and Palmer, 1991: 18.

[71] Liverpool Black Caucus, 1986: 14, citing *Guardian*, 12 June 1919.

[72] Murphy, 2001: 13.

[73] Ibid., 28, citing *Liverpool Echo*, 13 June 1919.

[74] Murphy, 2001: 31.

[75] Helmond and Palmer, 1991: 16, 'By 1911 census figures showed a black population of 3,000 against a total population of 750,000. After the First World War this had risen to 5,000 and by 1948 to 8,000.'

and appeared (as the Irish once had been) clear competition for scarce jobs.[76] Local media were expressing concern about what they perceived as the 'threat' of immigration, as Murphy notes:

> When the welfare state arrived in 1948, the National press chose the headline of 'security from cradle to the grave', but the *Liverpool Daily Post* on the same day preferred to launch a front-page attack on welfare 'scroungers' ... the 'coloured' stowaways who if able to prove British citizenship could not be deported and could obtain employment, receive dole, a ration book and even free clothing ... The new rhetoric about abuse of the welfare state ... enabled the local media to represent black people as not only 'racial' aliens but also as enemies of the working class.[77]

Whites and blacks clashed violently and black homes and businesses were attacked. The police arrested 'mainly black men'[78] and it was claimed that the white media were, in 1948, 'as unwilling to name white aggressors as the police were to arrest them'.[79] Murphy claims that 'in the years that followed 1948, the visibility of black people outside Toxteth visibly decreased' and that they were 'noticeably missing from almost all private sector jobs in the city centre which involved face-to-face contact with the public'.[80]

The lack of employment opportunities for black people was a problem throughout the twentieth century. The 'Fletcher Report', published in 1929, found that local firms were unwilling to employ 'half caste' youngsters, but nevertheless 'saw black people as the problem not the racist attitudes in society'.[81] A report in 1940 by Liverpool University Social Science Department traced 225 'coloured families' who were living in Liverpool. It found that '[black families] were found to pay higher rents than white people for similar accommodation. Of [black] adult males, 74 per cent were unemployed in 1939 compared with the figure of 34 per cent for white adult males. Consequently, the 'coloured' families fell much further below the poverty line than comparable white families. The report concluded

---

[76] Murphy, 1995: 59.

[77] Ibid., 126–7.

[78] Helmond and Palmer, 1991: 18.

[79] Murphy, 1995: 131.

[80] Ibid., 147.

[81] Helmond and Palmer, 1991: 18.

that unwillingness to employ, not unwillingness to work, maintained black poverty'.[82]

As the Liverpool Irish became assimilated into the local community, and to some extent anglicised, Liverpool's other minority communities became the subject of hostility from Liverpool's white working-class population. The Liverpool black community was 'rapidly becoming a distinct people,'[83] whereas 'the articulation of Irish identity down the generations was increasingly contested, and weakened'.[84]

While anti-black prejudice was demonstrated during the Toxteth riots, the deterioration of religious antipathy was highlighted as Protestant Bishop Sheppard and Catholic Archbishop Worlock walked together to view the destruction of the Granby district of the city.[85] The partnership of the Churches during the riots was not only a practical example of Sheppard and Worlock's 'better together' philosophy but was evidence of how inter-Christian rivalries had thawed in favour of a common stance against acute social conditions. The lack of significant opposition to this partnership was testament to the fact that, by 1981, religious attitudes had altered on Merseyside. The city, rather than particular religions, was being defended far more. The difficulties for Sheppard and Worlock now lay largely beyond religious sectarianism amongst their respective flocks and more in the overall state of Liverpool's economy. And amid that major problem, was a lack of concern amongst some whites for the especially acute difficulties experienced by Liverpool blacks. Racism had largely displaced religious sectarianism as the city's most pressing inter-communal issue.

Racism and the Isolation of the Black Community

The 'fear of attack' is widely acknowledged as a reason for the relative isolation of Liverpool's black community. Greg Quiery comments, 'There are plenty of accounts of [black people] feeling unsafe when they left their own home area. [Even] going to football matches was something that they wouldn't have felt comfortable doing'.[86] Knowsley councillor, Mike Murphy,

[82] Costello, 2001: 91.
[83] Ibid., 78.
[84] Herson, 2008: 73.
[85] See Power, 2014.
[86] Greg Quiery, 25 March 2013.

recalls blacks only drinking in selected pubs because they 'felt safe in there'.[87] The fear of attack acted as a strong deterrent for many of the city's black habitants. The study, *Black Youth in Liverpool*, notes:

> The expectation of encountering discrimination ... together with fear of racial harassment appeared to be creating ... social 'no-go' areas for Liverpool's young blacks ... Of the blacks who felt unsafe during the day, 81 per cent specified 'the north' of the city, the one-time hotbed of religious sectarianism, and 71 per cent stated that this was due to racial tension or fear of racial harassment or attacks in the streets or other public places.[88]

Another interviewee reinforced the point:

> The majority of the black population, which came to Liverpool in the sixties, settled in the Toxteth area and really never ventured out because of resistance they would face ... They found they would have a hard time if they went to areas which didn't have a group of black people already living there.[89]

One example of such resistance was recalled by Maria O'Reilly, when a black relative moved to a 'white' area: 'My uncle moved up from Berkeley Street [Toxteth] and he got a house in Rundell Street and the people got a petition to stop him moving in there with his wife. His wife was white. His children were mixed-race. They got a petition up to stop him moving in, but he moved in anyway'.[90] Another illustration of such resistance is recalled by Councillor Rothery: 'You could only go so far down Smithdown Road, down to Earl Road, and you'd have [white] skinheads coming up from the other side. There were daily battles going on between black and white communities'.[91] Connolly and co-authors contend that black people 'knew that they were at risk if they travelled outside Liverpool 8'.[92] As such, they 'controlled themselves and their lifestyles so as to avoid trouble'.[93] The Liverpool-born MP for Southport, John Pugh, a former Toxteth resident, acknowledges that

---

[87] Michael Murphy, 8 April 2013.
[88] Connolly, et al., 1992: 34.
[89] Michelle Chambers, 7 April 2013.
[90] Maria O'Reilly, 15 March 2013.
[91] Cllr Anna Rothery, 19 February 2013.
[92] Connolly, et al., 1992: 85.
[93] Ibid.

considerable residential segregation of the black community existed, but is not necessarily convinced that all segregation was enforced:

> I was not aware of black people being obliged to live there [Toxteth] ... If you moved to Kirkby, and you're the one black person in the road, you're probably going to get some difficulties. So whether [black] people were forced into [living together] or whether it was just more convenient to live in a place where being black was more 'normal', I don't know.[94]

Many black people in Liverpool were segregated in other ways, with the operation of '"colour bars" preventing them from mixing freely with other Liverpudlians'.[95] Costello argues that 'black settlers (who had retained the skin colour of their African ancestors) have been the group that, more than any other, remained ghettoised'.[96] He stresses that 'any isolation has never been voluntary'.[97] It should be stated, however, that within the areas of significant black settlement, Liverpool 1 and Liverpool 8, relatively harmonious relations between black and white residents have traditionally been apparent. The 1981 Toxteth riots often consisted of 'blacks and whites standing together against the police'.[98] Uncharacteristically for Merseyside, Liverpool 8 is highly mixed: '40% black; 60% white'.[99] It was asserted that 'the harmony existing between most black and white people in Liverpool 8 was no fiction ... it sustained the community there'.[100] Equally, however:

> There was a difference. White people within the ghetto could be as socially mobile as their life chances allowed; black people were still denied by their racialised identity the life chances that would have allowed them to complete equality. Black people belonged to Liverpool but Liverpool definitely did not yet belong to them.[101]

Prominent trade unionist, Billy Hayes, highlighted how job discrimination persisted:

---

[94] John Pugh MP, 22 March 2013.
[95] Murphy, 1995: iii.
[96] Costello, 2001: 100.
[97] Ibid., 5.
[98] Clarke, 2007: 368.
[99] Maria O'Reilly, 15 March 2013.
[100] Murphy, 1995, 147.
[101] Ibid.

In 1981 ... out of 4,000 postal workers we had one black postman, who delivered to Granby Street. We as a Union went to see the powers that be and it was like if you bring one person in there's a problem, so they brought in a critical mass. There was a bit of consternation in the branch. People were really angry about what we were doing, but we held our nerve and it started to improve things.[102]

Many black people who went for interviews knew 'that the problem is not of academic qualification but that of racism'.[103] Torkington recalls a speaker at the University of Liverpool, in 1982, making this point: 'For many of us with English surnames we get as far as the interview room before the employer realises that you are black. It is the eyes that give them away. You can tell just by looking at the eyes that you have lost the job even before the interview starts'.[104] The Liverpool Black Caucus talked of the 'continually devastating problem of massive unemployment facing the black community in Liverpool' and the 'continuing shame and scandal of Liverpool's abysmal record with respect to the employment of black people'.[105] In 1980, a year before the Toxteth riots, 'black unemployment was around 60% compared with 20% for the white population',[106] and by 1986, 'out of 911 people taken on in city centre stores since the riots of July 1981, only six were black'.[107] Jean Hill comments:

Certainly, black people were discriminated against ... you had the explosion of the Toxteth Riots because of all that; the attitude of the police, the employers and everything like that. They were suffering far more than any Protestants or Catholics were suffering in terms of jobs and police attitudes and everything.[108]

The Toxteth riots of July 1981 were thus seen as inevitable by some: 'the culmination of years of racism, poverty, unemployment, harassment, and heightened tensions between people in Liverpool 8 and local police. New stop-and-search laws, which allowed police to detain on suspicion of a crime,

---

[102] Billy Hayes, 2 February 2013.

[103] Torkington, 1983: 13.

[104] Ibid., citing a black speaker at a conference at the University of Liverpool, 7 January 1982.

[105] Liverpool Black Caucus, 1986: 8, 17.

[106] Ibid., 18.

[107] Ibid., 21.

[108] Jean Hartrick Hill, 26 October 2012.

prompted black and white residents to react, resulting in the worst civil unrest in peacetime Britain'.[109] The disturbances consisted of 'four nights of rioting, followed by six weeks of aftershocks,'[110] as 'police reinforcements were called from as far away as Cumbria, the West Midlands and even Devon in a desperate effort to control the burning streets'.[111] Frost's account notes:

> After four days of riots 150 buildings had been burnt down and countless shops looted, while 258 police officers needed hospital treatment and 160 people had been arrested. Six weeks later, when the disturbances died down, 781 police officers had been injured and 214 police vehicles damaged ... Injuries were of course also sustained by rioters ... When police vehicles were used to disperse groups of rioters, one young man was knocked down and killed, provoking another series of clashes.[112]

The Chief Constable, Ken Oxford, claimed by opponents to have been 'the most sinister and racist man you could ever have in charge of the police',[113] labelled rioters as 'thieves and vagabonds'.[114] A poster calling for his dismissal claimed: 'Oxford's own racism is an established fact [which] allows his officers to give expression to their racism and indulge in the harassment of the black community'.[115] The police were seen as 'a hostile force'[116] rather than as protectors: 'very colonialist'.[117]

In 1992, a study of the black population in Toxteth found that 78 per cent of black males reported having been subjected to stop and search tactics and 92 per cent of all black people sampled argued that 'not everyone receives fair and equal treatment from the police'.[118] Alienation was such that the Chair of the Police Authority, Margaret Simey, allegedly said that Toxteth's people would have been 'apathetic fools' if they had not rioted.[119]

---

[109] Museum of Liverpool, 2012: 87.

[110] Frost, 2011: 2.

[111] BBC, 'Toxteth Riots Remembered' (4 July 2001). Available at: http://news.bbc.co.uk/1/hi/uk/1419981.stm.

[112] Frost, 2011: 2.

[113] Claire Dove, ibid., 135.

[114] BBC, 'Toxteth Riots Remembered'.

[115] Liverpool 8 Defence Committee poster entitled 'Why Oxford Must Go', circulated on 25 July 1981, cited by Liverpool Black Caucus, 1986: 42.

[116] Connolly, et al., 1992: 85.

[117] Anna Rothery, 19 February 2013.

[118] Connolly, et al., 1992: 44.

[119] BBC, 'Toxteth Riots Remembered'.

After the riots, Toxteth became renowned as a 'no-go' area for many of Liverpool's white population. Liverpool-born, Conservative MP, Nadine Dorries recalls this:

> I used to live in Toxteth, Boswell Street, and I remember going back a few years later [after the riots] and being scared. It suddenly became as though there were parts of Liverpool that were slightly no-go [for white people] and had become almost ghettoised by immigrant communities ... it definitely became a bit scarier in areas, where before, it had just been fine to go to.[120]

Yet much of Liverpool was also regarded as 'no-go' by the city's black populace. The Liverpool Black Caucus argued:

> Where black people do move out of the Liverpool 8 area or own a shop or restaurant in a white suburb, they are frequently subjected to harassment, vandalism, abuse, even physical attack, whether by neighbours, gangs of youths or fascist groupings ... This form of racist abuse has meant that many areas of social space have been difficult for black people to enter ... many areas of Liverpool are felt to be out of bounds and a physical threat for black people.[121]

Steve Rotheram, MP for Walton, acknowledges that blacks endured 'in their face' racism, and that 'institutionalised and institutional racism was only slightly hidden', otherwise thriving in Liverpool.[122] Fellow MP, Andy Burnham, stated, 'I detect, sadly, higher levels [of racism] – stronger [yet] latent racism in Liverpool, than I do elsewhere, which worries me at times'.[123]

Recent years have seen claims that residual racism still features in Liverpool. As one example, the Liverpool actress, Phina Oruche, talked of being 'forced out of her dream job' as a presenter for BBC Radio Merseyside, as a result of 'racist', 'vile', and 'targeted' provocation.[124] Councillor Anna Rothery contended that 'racism, unfortunately, is alive and well in Liverpool, and faring quite well. It's not just covert racism ... it's deeply ingrained and institutionalised within the structures of the city'.[125]

---

[120] Nadine Dorries, 13 March 2013.
[121] Liverpool Black Caucus, 1986: 19–20.
[122] Steve Rotheram MP, 4 January 2013.
[123] Andy Burnham, 28 March 2013.
[124] *Liverpool Echo*, 10 April 2013.
[125] Anna Rothery, 19 February 2013.

The stereotyping and stigmatising of black people, as inferior, idle, criminal, and anti-authority, was similar to that endured by the Irish. In 1848, at the height of the Irish famine, the *Liverpool Mercury* wrote, 'There is a taint of inferiority in the character of the pure Celt'.[126] The same year, *Punch* magazine published pictures depicting 'The British Lion and the Irish Monkey'.[127] The Irish were often characterised as monkeys and gorillas in the nineteenth century and continued to be dehumanised in *Punch* illustrations in the twentieth.[128] Many newspapers in Liverpool, from the 'Orange' *Standard* to the 'liberal' *Mercury* portrayed the Celt as a lesser human than the Anglo Saxon.[129] The idea of a 'hierarchy of races' was coming to prominence and 'the Celt [was often placed] just above the Negro'[130] at the bottom of the scale.

In Liverpool, the outlook which labelled the black community as 'criminal' was initially held by the Irish. 'In 1854, 48% of the prison population was Irish. In 1876, 70% of all committals to Liverpool borough gaol were Catholics'.[131] Most offences were minor, such as drunken brawls. Moreover, Neal explains that the high indices of Irish criminality were down to the status of Irish Catholics as a low-income group, the demand for prostitutes (and the tendency for Irish Catholic girls to fill this role) and petty thievery. The lack of the discipline of the factory system, which was present in other Lancashire towns, 'made work for idle hands' as unemployed and mostly uneducated Irish Catholic boys would steal from the docks.[132]

Despite the impact of 'a negative unfamiliar and hostile environment',[133] 'there was general agreement among indigenous non-Catholics that Irish Catholics were more prone to criminal behaviour than the resident non-Catholic population. These attacks on Catholicism were widespread, persistent and long-lasting'.[134] The view which suggested that 'freed from Catholicism the Irishman could take his place in the civilised world' was

---

[126] Neal, 1991: 162, citing *Liverpool Mercury* (1848).
[127] *Punch*, 'British Lion and the Irish Monkey'. Available at: www.punchcartoons.com/History-and-Politics-Ireland-Cartoons/c273_351/p111/British-Lion-and-The-Irish-Monkey/product_info.html.
[128] *Punch*, 'Ireland Cartoons' (88 images). Available at: http://punch.photoshelter.com/gallery/-/G0000tcWkXyP4OHo/.
[129] Frank Neal, 12 February 2010.
[130] Ibid.
[131] Neal, 2006: 71.
[132] See Neal, 1991.
[133] Ibid., 194.
[134] Ibid., 162.

often undistinguished from the belief that 'the Celt is racially inferior to the Anglo-Saxon'.[135] As such, Irish Catholics faced prejudice and hostility, racial and religious, whilst their black counterparts were victims of acute racism without a religious addition.

The Liverpool Chinese and their Experience of Racism

Liverpool is home to the oldest Chinese community in Europe.[136] The Chinese can trace their Liverpool origins back to the late 1850s,[137] as Chinese sailors first began to settle around the middle of the nineteenth century,[138] owing to the *Blue Funnel Line* opening boarding houses close to the docks to accommodate workers on shore leave. In these boarding houses the Chinese seaman could stay with 'fellow countrymen, who spoke their own language'.[139] Some sailors 'jumped ship' and settled in Cleveland Square, Pitt Street, and Frederick Street. This area was to become the location of Liverpool's first 'Chinatown' and from the 1890s onwards 'Chinese people began to set up their own shops, cafés, and boarding houses to cater for the needs of the Chinese sailors'.[140]

By the beginning of the twentieth century, Liverpool's Chinese community 'was said to have been the largest in Britain'[141] as it grew to twice the size of that in London.[142] Even at this time, however, Liverpool's Chinese community was small, with 'just over four hundred Chinese-born people in the city'.[143] Nonetheless, in 2001, the Chinese stood alongside

---

[135] *Liverpool Mail*, 19 July 1851 and *Liverpool Mercury*, 1 August 1848, cited ibid.

[136] Wong, 1989; I. Herbert, 'Liverpool Pips its Arch Rival with Gateway to Chinatown'. *Independent* (30 March 2000). Available at: www.independent.co.uk/news/uk/this-britain/liverpool-pips-its-arch-rival-with-gateway-to-chinatown-5371968.html.

[137] Liverpool Chinatown (website), 'History of Chinatown'. Available at: http://web.archive.org/web/20160220023303/http://www.liverpoolchinatown.co.uk/history.php; Wong, 1989. Alfred Holt and Company's Blue Funnel Shipping Line was behind 'the first direct steamship link between Britain and China' and created 'strong trade links' between Shanghai, Hong Kong and Liverpool.

[138] Wong, 1989: 3.

[139] Liverpool Chinatown (website), 'History of Chinatown'.

[140] Ibid.

[141] Wong, 1989: 3.

[142] Museum of Liverpool, 2012: 129.

[143] Herson, 2008: 68–9.

the Irish and black communities as Liverpool's largest minority groups.[144] Although less prominent in terms of political controversies than the black community, the Chinese in Liverpool have also endured difficulties. In September 1945, 200 of its male members were removed from the city. One year later, '1,131 Chinese seafarers [were] forcibly repatriated to China, leaving their Liverpool families destitute'.[145] The men, many of whom had married or cohabited with local girls, 'left behind devastated wives and children believing they were abandoned'.[146]

Hostility towards the Chinese was not isolated to the English. Greg Quiery asserts that 'there was a time when the Irish community was hostile towards Chinese labourers, because cheap Chinese labour was being brought in and there are accounts of protests and processions [involving the Irish]'.[147] A cut-priced Chinese workforce was often at the centre of contention and the Chinese community was ostracised after strike-breaking during the 1911 seaman's strike, a position exacerbated by the 'Yellow Peril' propaganda of the mid-nineteenth century through to the 1940s.[148]

The Liverpool *Weekly Courier* carried complaints about the Chinese from readers; one, for example, complaining: 'we who are engaged in the laundry business are being literally driven out of it by the crowds of Chinamen who are coming into the city. To my own personal knowledge, over 30 laundry women … are now in Brownlow Hill Workhouse, living on the parish. And they have been sent there by the Chinese'.[149] A day later, a banner headline in a local newspaper proclaimed: 'Chinese Vice in Liverpool'. The article focused on the subjects of gambling, drug-taking, and sexual relations between Chinese men and white women.[150] Another editorial, in the Liverpool *Weekly Courier,* headlined 'Chinatown: A Transformed Region of Liverpool', crudely characterised the Chinese community as 'strange

[144] Office for National Statistics, Neighbourhood Statistics, Area: Liverpool (Local Authority), Resident Population Estimates by Ethnic Group (Percentages). Available at: http://neighbourhood.statistics.gov.uk/dissemination/LeadTableView.do?adminCompAndTimeId=21821%3A131&a=3&b=276787&c=Liverpool&d=13&r=1&e=13&f=27646&o=58&g=359393&i=1001x1003x1004x1005&l=1812&m=0&s=1368804596996&enc=1.
[145] Museum of Liverpool, 2012: 129.
[146] Ibid.
[147] Greg Quiery, 25 March 2013.
[148] Wong, 1989: 59.
[149] 'Mr Tudor', interviewed by a reporter from the *Weekly Courier,* 1 December 1906, cited by Wong, 1989: 61–2.
[150] Law, 1981: 23.

figures, moving with the stiff-jointed shamble of the orient, and gazing with impassive eyes, set aslant in Saffron, [with] mask like faces', reporting that 'gambling and opium smoking were two great vices of the Chinaman'.[151]

The subject of mixed marriage was typically contentious, with claims that 'Chinese communities have infiltrated British society through inter-marriage'.[152] By 1945, '[approximately] 300 sailors [had] married or cohabited with local girls, giving birth to about 900 Eurasian children'.[153] Relationships between Chinese men and English women were labelled 'abominations', 'mongrel affairs', and a 'dangerously promiscuous medley'.[154] The Chief Constable of Liverpool talked of the 'strong feeling of objection to the idea of the half-caste population which is resulting from the marriage of Englishwomen to the Chinese'.[155]

It was claimed that 'Chinese morality would have an adverse effect on the local community and that women and children were endangered by the presence of Chinese men on the city streets'.[156] It was also claimed that 'failing local authority action the people themselves would force [the Chinese] to leave'.[157] A Commission of Inquiry 'into the morals and habits of the Chinese as well as into the economic effects of their presence'[158] was established by Liverpool City Council in December 1906.

The Inquiry gave evidence that the Chinese Quarter comprised 224 residents and 132 transient Chinamen.[159] Whilst the habit of gambling was found to be prevalent, 'stakes were thought to have been small and as a rule Chinese gambled only amongst themselves ... Opium smoking was found to be more prevalent amongst seamen than residents and a statement to the effect that the Chinese were in the habit of giving sweets impregnated with opium to children [was] not confirmed by evidence'.[160] Allegations that Chinese laundries and lodging houses were used as brothels were also found to be unsubstantiated, and, ultimately, 'the Commission of Inquiry

---

[151] *Weekly Courier*, 1 December 1906, cited and described by Wong, 1989: 60–1.

[152] Wong, 1989: 65.

[153] Liverpool Chinatown (website), 'History of Chinatown'.

[154] Wong, 1989: 65.

[155] Law, 1981: 23.

[156] Ibid., 64.

[157] 'Mr Tudor', *Weekly Courier*, 1 December 1906, cited by Wong, 1989: 62.

[158] Law, 1981: 23.

[159] 'Report of the Commission Appointed by the City Council to Inquire into Chinese Settlement in Liverpool', 1906: 1744, cited by Wong, 1989: 62–3.

[160] Ibid., 63.

found favourably on the standards of Chinese residents'.[161] Overall, 'no difference was found between English and Chinese households and the general accusation of immorality was left unsubstantiated'.[162] In its report, the Council stressed that the Chinese were the 'embodiment of public order'.[163]

Law argues that after the inquiry 'a certain pattern of "accommodation" of the Chinese presence emerged in Liverpool. The Chinese were accepted in their place i.e. as seamen on the shipping routes to China and later on, in the restaurant business which took over as the main area of work in which they became involved'.[164] However, as the Liverpool Chinese developed 'a reputation among the host community for being a self-contained and self-sufficient community',[165] a stereotype developed about the Chinese community's 'insular' nature and their reputation for self-sufficiency. It is alleged that social services were not provided for the Chinese; services which were otherwise readily available to the general population. Maria O'Reilly highlights racism by omission:

> The Chinese were ignored. They were discriminated against in the way that people believed they were a closed society and that they kept to themselves and saw to each other, and it wasn't true. Because there was that attitude, nobody provided any services to the Chinese community or the Chinese elders. The Chinese people themselves have had to make their own services.[166]

By 1982, the discrimination to which O'Reilly refers was being recognised. Lynn's study argues that 'in many respects state agencies have tended to respond to the needs of the Chinese according to a stereotype and this ... constitutes a form of institutionalised racism'.[167] Lynn mapped out this stereotype: the Chinese are 'proudly independent, they like to stay apart from [the general Liverpool population], they hate interference. There is an extended family network which caters for the needs of the family'.[168]

---

[161] Ibid., 64.

[162] Law, 1981: 23.

[163] Minutes of Liverpool City Council, pp. 1739, 1753 (1906–07), cited by Law, 1981: 22–23.

[164] Ibid., 24.

[165] Lynn, 1982: 14.

[166] Maria O'Reilly, 15 March 2013.

[167] Lynn, 1982: 74–5.

[168] Ibid.

It is generally accepted that prejudice towards the Chinese occurred in Liverpool. This prejudice (although not limited to these spheres) was mainly concentrated in a moral attack on the Chinese, accompanied by stereotyping and assumptions of a 'self-supporting' Chinatown. Combined, this meant that Chinese people were at one time 'amongst the worst housed people in the city'[169] and were also at a disadvantage in schools, the employment sector (outside of the service industry), health provision and social services for the elderly, otherwise available for the host community.[170] Other minority communities, too, suffered in terms of these forms of direct and indirect racism. Moreover, in the main, prejudice against the Chinese has existed in a diluted 'piecemeal' format when compared with that ranged against the black and Irish communities. Chinese people in Liverpool nonetheless have suffered indignities, the terms 'Chink', 'Nip', 'Ching-Chong Chinese', and 'dirty-knees' having been 'in regular use'.[171]

It has been demonstrated that all three of the aforementioned communities have been affected by racism. The extent of this racism, however, has been experienced on different levels. Although the Chinese consistently suffered the pejorative label of 'Chink', Liverpool blacks seldom escaped scorns of 'Nigger' and 'Coon'. For the Irish, it has been difficult to shed the labels of 'Paddy', 'Fenian', 'Taig', and 'Papist'. Likewise, it has been alleged that all three groups have suffered from 'institutional racism' in terms of access to health care and social services, in gaining employment, and in terms of accessing higher-quality housing. Yet, Chinese relations with the police have tended to be good, whereas the black and Irish communities have accused the Merseyside police force of institutional racism.

Why were the Chinese viewed more favourably than the blacks or Irish? Nadine Dorries MP recalled, 'With the Chinese community, there was no difference. They were law-abiding and friendly. You didn't feel scared going to Chinatown. There was no problem there'.[172] Lynn argues:

> The British do not want another 'immigrant problem' and the Chinese are determined not to even hint at creating one. Thus, the Chinese labour force has not been incorporated into the wider job occupational structure. Chinese people have so far kept to the jobs they know, the places where people expect to find them – in service; with the result that

[169] Ibid., 73.
[170] For more details, see Lynn, 1982.
[171] Helen Owen, 27 March 2013.
[172] Nadine Dorries MP, 13 March 2013.

the indigenous workforce does not see them as a threat to their livelihood. They are not looked upon as a group that competes for scarce services and housing nor are they considered a burden on the wider community.[173]

Chinese community resident Helen Owen suggests that 'being ignored partly could be our fault, because we keep very quiet and we just get on and we don't kick a fuss and we don't protest'.[174]

In contrast, both the Irish and black communities are much more willing to respond to provocation. It has been noted that the first Orange procession in Liverpool, in 1819, was attacked by the Irish. Subsequently, many sectarian skirmishes and battles became a prominent feature of Liverpool life. Likewise, there has been a tendency for Liverpool blacks to respond to provocation. This was evident in the 'race riots' of 1919, 1948, and 1981. Furthermore, there is a tendency for the Irish (in particular) and black communities to parade, protest, and become involved politically. St Patrick's Day parades were once an annual celebration in Catholic Irish Liverpool. There was also a large 'Irish vote' to be captured. O'Reilly recalls how Liverpool blacks would protest against anti-black racism, recalling, as an example, protests over a gollywog being sold in a shop near the slavery museum.[175] The Liverpool Black Caucus also actively campaigned against the Militant Tendency in the 1980s. This was not the case for the Chinese, as John Pugh MP describes:

> There is a long-withstanding Chinese community in Liverpool, who have formed their own world, engage in a limited set of businesses (obviously, restaurants but other things as well), who have absented themselves from the political sphere altogether. So though there is quite a large Chinese contingent in Liverpool, they certainly don't politically engage. They don't vote. There is no point in you making a play for the Chinese vote.[176]

Another factor relating the Chinese is that there has seemingly been little pressure for them to integrate. Quiery comments how, 'the Chinese community have retained their own culture very strongly, particularly their own language, and lots of the Irish people had their own language and it was used in every day discourse, but the Irish have lost that'.[177] It appears that

---

[173] Lynn, 1982: 74–5.
[174] Ibid.
[175] Maria O'Reilly, 15 March 2013.
[176] John Pugh MP, 22 March 2013.
[177] Greg Quiery, 25 March 2013.

pressures which may have been present to assimilate the Irish were not there for the Chinese, perhaps indicative of a perception that Irish culture was less desirable than Chinese culture. This would appear to be the case today, as Chinese heritage is overtly celebrated throughout the city.[178] The Chinese Arch, which commemorates a twinning with Shanghai, was celebrated in 2000, contrasted with the twinning of Liverpool and Dublin, which fuelled a large Loyalist protest on the streets of Liverpool in 1996. According to Maria O'Reilly, the only time black heritage was officially celebrated in Liverpool was in the build-up to Liverpool Capital of Culture 2008.[179]

How Far Did Racism Displace Sectarianism?

Liverpool sectarianism has never been bereft of a sizeable element of racism. The sectarian element of the division between 'Orange' and 'Green' Liverpool related to a Catholic–Protestant split. Anti-Catholicism, however, was often interchangeable with anti-Irishness, just as, in its embryonic stage especially, antipathy towards Protestantism was coupled with hostility towards Great Britain and its Empire. The situation began to change as Catholics in Liverpool (the majority of whom can trace their ancestry to one or more Irish-born relatives) began to be anglicised in Catholic schools. Similarly, as the proportion of Irish born declined in Liverpool and the Liverpool Irish began to become less visibly set apart, due to the development of a shared accent, a familiar skin tone to their Protestant counterparts, a larger degree of 'inter-marriage' between Catholics and Protestants, and the lack of a physical separation, owing both to slum clearance and a common working environment, the two once competing sects began to see a new enemy in the 'outsider'.

These 'outsiders' were largely segregated in Liverpool 8 and visibly set apart by their colour. Furthermore, owing in part to their lack of association with the vast majority of Liverpool's white residents and their confusion with recently arrived immigrants from the Commonwealth, they would become the most obvious 'local outsiders'. This is not to say that anti-black racism is a new addition to Liverpool, nor that it entirely 'replaced' anti-Irish racism. The populace of Liverpool has never been single-minded in terms of its xenophobia. As Andy Burnham MP comments, 'It's not as if racism

---

[178] Liverpool annually celebrates the Chinese New year and other specific Chinese events.
[179] Maria O'Reilly, 15 March 2013.

wasn't there. There was always racism. Racism was there even when there was sectarianism'.[180] This statement has been supported throughout this chapter. Anti-black racism has been a feature of life in Liverpool since black people first began to arrive in the port in the eighteenth century. Indeed, Liverpool's success as a port was largely built on transatlantic slavery.

Racism was never directed exclusively to either the Irish or the black communities. Hostility towards any variant of immigrant has been evident in Liverpool. As Law comments, 'the potential of class and community alliances has constantly been fragmented by the overriding power of racism',[181] whether against the Irish, blacks, Chinese, or other ethnic minority groups. Nevertheless, after the 'Great Irish Hunger', for much of the nineteenth and twentieth centuries the huge proportion of Irish Catholics in Liverpool ensured that anti-Irish racism and sectarianism overshadowed bias directed at other communities, a point made by Herson:

> The concentration of the black population in the South Dock/ Park Lane area made it very apparent, but in sheer numbers it was small in relation to the city as a whole ... Liverpool's minority populations were highly visible in the localities they frequented ... Nevertheless, Liverpool's dominant social character was white and determined by its synthesis of British and Irish peoples.[182]

Prejudice held by Irish Catholics and Lancastrian Protestants was seldom reserved solely for their religious counterparts. During the 1919 'race riots', many white people convicted of attacking blacks were Irish or of Irish decent.[183] As O'Reilly suggests, 'just because you were Irish it did not mean you weren't racist'.[184] As the century progressed, descendants of Lancastrian Protestants and Irish Catholics would assimilate into a homogeneous body of predominantly white 'Scousers'. Blacks and Chinese were excluded. Helen Owen talked of how her children of dual British/Chinese heritage, who were born in Liverpool, are still, 'seen as Chinese, rather than English' and how they feel the need to 'put on the Scouse accent heavier'[185] when they're around their white friends from Liverpool. Herson also believes that the

[180] Andy Burnham, 28 March 2013.
[181] Law, 1981: v.
[182] Herson, 2008: 68.
[183] See Murphy, 1995: 31.
[184] Maria O'Reilly, 15 March 2013.
[185] Helen Owen, 27 March 2013.

notion of 'Scouseness' excluded black residents of the city.[186] The point is also made by Costello that white immigrants who once lived alongside black immigrants began to distance themselves:

> With the passing of time and improving conditions of the poor, more poor whites were able to pass into the middle classes. The increasing denial of this facility to poor blacks and, indeed, blacks of higher station as all blacks came to be seen in the same light, undoubtedly led to poor whites distancing themselves from their black fellows as they chose to identify themselves increasingly with the Anglo-Saxon ruling class.[187]

It has been noted that friendly relations between blacks and whites were evident in Liverpool 8. This was also the case with Catholics and Protestants in their new areas of settlement outside the religious ghettos of dockside Liverpool. Catholics and Protestants, once set apart by their respective religious ghettos, now grew up in the same neighbourhood and, although often still educated separately, worked together and shared similar interests and problems. The two once competing identities began to merge into one. Nonetheless, ethnic minority communities for the most part were excluded from these friendly relations. Owing to their concentration in specific areas of south Liverpool, black people encountered different attitudes from whites according to location, as Chambers notes:

> I think that different attitudes are only to be expected in the south end of Liverpool to the north end considering that people in the south end of Liverpool have in some part grown up with a black population around them they have grown up together, mixed with each other, formed friendships and respect for each other. That has never happened in the north end of Liverpool, because there has never been a black community established there.[188]

Bishops Sheppard and Worlock commented that, 'the life of Liverpool's long-established black community has always been largely unrecognised by the majority of the white population [who] remained steadfastly "colour blind" [and] for the most part unmoved by the obvious disadvantage' of the black community.[189] Although this can be attributed partly, as Chambers

[186] Herson, 2008: 73.
[187] Costello, 2001: 57.
[188] Michelle Chambers, 7 April 2013.
[189] Sheppard and Worlock, 1988; 'Foreword', Liverpool Black Caucus, 1986.

suggests, to a lack of contact between many blacks and whites on Merseyside, Connolly offers a different perspective:

> Racism has a long history in Britain. There are senses in which it has become part of white citizens' national culture and identity. Racist attitudes were consolidated during the decades of Empire. Non-whites were seen to be inferior, conquered peoples, and as such attitudes have been confirmed in metropolitan Britain by colonial immigrants' concentration in menial jobs and poor housing.[190]

Unsurprisingly, *Cairde na hÉireann Liverpool* mimic Connolly's remarks, stating that, 'the imperialist and colonial policies of Britain have been and continue to be the primary determinant of racism in this country ... racism is endemic and is interwoven into the culture, history and traditions of Britain'.[191] If this is the case, could racism have replaced sectarianism?

Jones states that, 'the religious divide between Protestants and Catholics which produced recurrent violence and was reflected in occupational barriers, had tended to die away by the 1930s. Also, the Irish were not permanently set apart by visible characteristics such as skin colour'.[192] It was noted by Reverend Vincent Glover of Liverpool that, 'there is a decided amelioration in the English-born Irish: the longer they stay, the more they improve'.[193] These statements suggest a change in emphasis from sectarianism.

Suspicion and hostility to the Irish were not displaced by other forms of racism and were exacerbated by 'The Troubles' – but by that point Liverpool's Irish Catholic community had lost much of its earlier Irishness and was muted regarding the Northern Ireland conflict. That anti-Irish racism had not vanished was evident as late as 2012, when three Irish marches were subject to 'threats, attacks and intimidation by Far Right groups and members of the loyalist/ Orange community'.[194] Had Irish Catholics paraded in Liverpool during the years of 'The Troubles' in Northern Ireland, major anti-Irish and sectarian street clashes could have occurred to a much greater extent. It is thus questionable whether street clashes and public disturbances are a sound indicator of whether racism 'replaced' sectarianism.

---

[190] Connolly, et al., 1992: 88, citing Rex, 1970.
[191] *Cairde na hÉireann Liverpool*, 'Under Pressure', 10.
[192] Jones, 1977: 50, cited by Law, 1981: 22.
[193] Jones, 1977: 50.
[194] *Cairde na hÉireann Liverpool*, 'Under Pressure', 9.

As Michelle Chambers remarked:

I have heard this theory that sectarianism in Liverpool was replaced by racism ... but I don't know if that is really true. I think the violence between Catholics and Protestants still continued even when the black community came to Liverpool. I think maybe it was another enemy for people to focus on but I think the old ones still continued.[195]

This point is supported by Neil Dulin: 'I think the focus sort of changed in the fifties and sixties, when you had other groups who were beginning to arrive in the city. I wouldn't say that the whole focus went then though. There were still real [sectarian] tensions in the fifties and sixties'.[196] John Pugh MP argues that 'racism was always there but it became more prominent as sectarianism declined'.[197] Councillor Anna Rothery expanded upon this perspective:

[Racism] was always there. It was constant ... In the forties and fifties you'd have quite blatantly on windows, 'No Blacks, Irish or Dogs'. I think what happened in terms of the Irish is that they were very much assimilated into the community here in Liverpool through the education system and through the curriculum. This is the colonialist way. They want everybody to be integrated into what they perceive to be the best way forward, and arguably they were more successful with the Irish community because they could work through the churches and through the religion. It was more difficult with the black community because, historically, the black community doesn't buy into religion so much ... they tend to stand alone.[198]

Conclusion: Racism as a Supplanter of Sectarianism?

There is a general consensus of opinion that racism is neither a new factor in Liverpool, nor that it displaced sectarianism. Rather, the two have co-existed. It is acknowledged however, that racism became more apparent in the twentieth century than sectarianism and that anti-black racism increased in salience relative to long prominent anti-Catholic sentiment, which itself was historically associated with anti-Irish racism, from which it could not be fully disentangled.

[195] Michelle Chambers, 7 April 2013.
[196] Neil Dulin, 14 March 2013.
[197] John Pugh, 22 March 2013.
[198] Cllr Anna Rothery, 19 February 2013.

However, rather than a growth of racism causing a decline of sectarianism or a decline in sectarianism causing a growth in racism, the suggestion is that the two phenomena simply coincided with each other, with the causal relationship being minimal. A causal relationship is apparent insofar as, while the Liverpool Irish anglicised, the black community and Chinese community became more visibly set apart than Catholics. However, this is not to say that racism towards the black community grew to the same extent as had racism towards the Irish, but rather that anti-black racism became more apparent as the Liverpool Irish had assimilated. Anti-Irish racism is still present in Liverpool, but, owing to a reduced presence on the streets of Liverpool from the 1970s until the mid-1990s, it is not as obvious. Problems with Irish parades in the city in 1996 and again in the twenty-first century indicated that old anti-Irish sentiments had not been entirely eradicated. Clashes at Irish marches were associated much more with anti-Irish racism and opposition to Irish republicanism than with Protestant hostility to Catholics. Opponents of such Irish parades were more Loyalist and political (and to critics, virulently racist) than they were Orange or religious, although individual members of the Order were present.

It is pointed out by the Irish community that they are often at the forefront of anti-racist marches in the city.[199] Likewise, the Orange Institution would refute the allegation of racism by pointing out that some members of Orange Lodges in the city are black. This point is made by the Grand Master of Liverpool, Billy Owens, 'We were parading through Toxteth, and some republican sympathisers began telling people in the area that we were from the National Front, but we had 30 or 40 black members in our lodges who explained the real position to them'.[200]

Newer aliens are still emerging. A shift from an anti-Catholic to an anti-Islamic focus is acknowledged by officials in the Orange Institution. Keith Allcock, an official of Bootle Province, commented, 'I am a firm believer that both religions [Protestant and Catholic] will end up having to get together to combat Muslims, because [Muslims] are the up and coming faith, overrunning everybody'.[201] Dave Hughes, an official from the Liverpool Orange Institution stated:

[199] *Cairde na hÉireann Liverpool*, 'Under Pressure'.

[200] Billy Owens (2012), cited by D. McSweeney, 'Liverpool's Orange Lodges and the Parading Season', *Guardian*, 21 June 2012. Available at: www.guardian.co.uk/uk/the-northerner/2012/jun/21/liverpool-northernireland.

[201] Keith Allcock, 12 March 2013.

It's a pity that some of the schools don't adopt the same attitude towards the 'Orange' kids as they do towards the Muslim kids within the school. I make no apologies for saying that because we have the same rights religiously as anybody else. We wouldn't stop anybody else having their religious rights.[202]

A shift in the direction of anti-Islamic hostility coincides with a shift of the populace of Liverpool. In 2001, prior to the 'terror attacks' of 9/11, blacks, Chinese, and Irish were the largest minority groups in Liverpool. By the 2011 census, the Asian community, the majority from Pakistan, India, Bangladesh (with some 'other Asian' countries, excluding China, who have their own data trend) had become Liverpool's largest minority group.[203]

It appears then that any immigrant community entering Liverpool has been subject to hostility. This chapter has demonstrated that racism was always an issue, although one often overshadowed by religious antipathy. Therefore, racism directed towards Liverpool's black and Chinese communities did not simply emerge as a by-product of better relations between Catholics and Protestants in the city, rather, it simply carried on existing and became more noticeable as sectarianism waned.

For many people in Liverpool, specifically the younger generations, religious division is not something which has occurred, to any great extent, in their living memory. They may, however, be aware of Irish ancestry in their family. Although this is not always the case, what is the case is that the Irish have been accepted into the Liverpool mainstream to a far greater extent than has the Liverpool black community. The latter has been viewed by many as recently arrived 'aliens', owing to a particular narrative which suggests that Liverpool's black community journeyed to Liverpool as a result of post-war immigration from the Commonwealth. Although this chapter has proven this to be a falsehood, 'it is important to remember that, in looking at the views of indigenous populations concerning immigrants, it is not so much the truth that matters but what people think is the truth'.[204] Therefore, for many people on Merseyside, the view of Liverpool's black community as 'aliens' or 'outsiders' has allowed the persistence of racism.

---

[202] Dave Hughes, 24 January 2013.
[203] Office for National Statistics, Neighbourhood Statistics, Area: Liverpool.
[204] Neal, 1991: 165.

8

The Emergence of a Common Identity: The Integration of the Irish and the Harmony of 'Merseybeat'

Throughout much of the nineteenth and the first half of the twentieth centuries there were two prevailing identities in Liverpool: Irish Catholic and Lancastrian Protestant. As this book has discussed, this era was characterised by antipathy and often physical confrontation between these sects. By the mid-twentieth century, however, these clashes had become increasingly ritualised. This chapter will argue that it was not simply a case of an Irish assimilation into a dominant host community which led to a decline of sectarianism. Rather, it was the dual assimilation of both identities into the newly emerging and dominant local character of 'Scouse' which had the most profound effect of subjugating sectarian vehemence. In addition, as the century progressed, many people (Catholic and Protestant) had begun to look beyond religion towards other forms of fulfilment.

The Influence of the Irish and the Shaping of the Scouse Identity

In 1892, John Denvir wrote that 'It is not without some justification that some consider [Liverpool] the Irish capital of England'.[1] After all, the 1891 census showed that 47,000 of the Liverpool population of 518,000 was Irish born (9 per cent), whilst the 1901 census of neighbouring Bootle indicated that 5,800 of the town's population of 58,000 were Irish born (10 per cent).[2]

---

[1] Denvir, 1892, cited by Kelly, 2003: 3.

[2] Kennedy, 2005: 846.

Such has been the influence of the Irish on the development of Merseyside's distinctiveness that Liverpool has also 'frequently been dubbed the "real capital" [of Ireland]'.[3] In 2013, the *Guardian* claimed that '75% of Liverpool's population has some Irish ancestry'.[4]

The *Irish Independent* noted, in an article on footballer Wayne Rooney's Irish heritage, 'Even today, when only 10% of the population of England is Catholic, 60% of Croxteth's children are baptised Catholic'.[5] Importantly, the majority of Catholics in Liverpool are likely to have some Irish heritage as a result of nineteenth-century famine emigration which reshaped the demography of the city. The same article, which made reference to the high ratio of Roman Catholic schools in the area, stated,

> This is an Irish part of town. All the older people, like Patricia Fitzsimons – Wayne Rooney's granny – were moved here in the slum clearances … They [referring to Croxteth residents] are Irish, Catholic, Evertonians and proud of it. Even before Wayne Rooney exploded onto the scene, Patricia Fitzsimons was famous locally for being born on March 17 – thus Patricia … If you want to see the influence that the Irish have had on England, Croxteth is a good place to start. 'Could Wayne have played for Ireland?' I ventured … 'Nah,' replied Patricia, 'He's English on the outside' … 'but Irish on the inside'.[6]

Whether 'Irish on the inside' or not, Wayne Rooney would still naturally opt to play for England. Because individuals are Catholic it does not mean that they are Irish or even feel in any way Irish. Indeed, it was the Church's policy in Liverpool to 'incorporate [through] "denationalising" Irishness, while maintaining Catholicism'.[7] The Anglicisation of Irish descendants has been an important factor in the reduction of sectarian animosity.

Liverpool-born Michael Kelly talked of experiencing a connection to Ireland through music:

> Although growing up in Liverpool, I learned almost nothing of the Liverpool Irish during my school days. From an early age I was exposed to a kind of music that told stories of a mythical land across the Irish

---

[3] D. McSweeney, 'The Irish are Coming Back to Liverpool', *Guardian*, 1 December 2011. Available at: www.theguardian.com/uk/the-northerner/2011/dec/01/liverpool-ireland.

[4] Ibid.

[5] 'Rooney is part of a generation Irish "on the inside"'. *Irish Independent*, 1 October 2006.

[6] Ibid.

[7] Kennedy and Kennedy, 2007: 903.

Sea ... There were people who spoke with a dialect that sounded like
my [Irish] grandparents and, without knowing it then, its essence was an
unseen umbilical cord.[8]

The kind of music to which Kelly refers was most likely Irish folk. The
famous *Z Cars* theme, known to many Liverpudlians as the anthem of
Everton FC, is derived from the Liverpool 'sea shanty' *Johnny Tod*, a
derivative of Irish folk. The Irish folk ballad: *The Fields of Athenry* has been
adopted by Liverpool FC supporters as *The Fields of Anfield Road*. *The
Leaving of Liverpool* and *I Wish I Were Back in Liverpool* are other notable
examples of songs of this genre which are centred upon the port and are
often performed by Irish folk bands such as The Dubliners. Scotland
Road-born Peter McGovern's *In My Liverpool Home* adopted this style.
Many Irish rebel songs (which share characteristics with a proportion
of Orange songs) also encapsulate elements of Irish folk and became
popular in Liverpool before the onset of 'skiffle' and 'rock and roll' in the
mid-twentieth century.[9]

Liverpool-born Séafra Ó Cearbhail, a member of *Cairde na hÉireann
Liverpool*, makes reference to the influence of Irish music (as well as other
Irish traits) on the development of Liverpool's unique character and culture.
He suggests that far from being the badge of distinction it once was, Irishness
became integrated as a feature of Liverpool's 'personality':

Liverpool is the most Catholic city in England because it [had] the greatest
Irish settlement ... Irish settlement in Liverpool was so profound and so
substantial in its effect on the social make-up and culture of the city that
Scouseness is Irishness in its Liverpool form. Irishness defined so many
aspects of this city, from accent, to radical politics, to popular music, to
poetry, to drama, to the whole thing. In a way, the success of Irishness
in Liverpool and its cultural growth meant that those fierce [sectarian]
lines became less obviously displayed, except for the Loyal [Orange]
Order, who probably felt uncomfortable with the level of Scouseness and
Irishness and Catholicism being so closely intertwined.[10]

Some of 'England's most English of rebels were actually second-generation
Irish, [including] John Lennon, whose grandfather came from Dublin

---

[8] Kelly, 2003: vi.
[9] See McManus, 1994.
[10] Séafra Ó Cearbhail, 14 March 2013.

and who explored this aspect of his lineage extensively in the mid-1970s'.[11] Yet alongside their distinctiveness, the second- and third-generation Irish began a process of national, religious, and cultural assimilation and bonding with the non-Irish and non-Catholic population which gradually 'removed cultural and social distinctions'.[12] Greg Quiery considers this point:

> How do you become a fully-fledged citizen? It might be that in Liverpool there was a way to become an equal person in local society. It was to become a Scouser ... It was to do with your attachment to the place and probably your attachment to a football team as well. You would then be 'in the club', as it were, and people who would be excluded from the club would not be subscribing to that, but you didn't get excluded from the club because of your religion. There are such a huge variety of people in Liverpool from all sorts of backgrounds that being a Scouser became a factor of acceptance.[13]

Belchem, Devaney, and Lane highlight some of the claimed distinctions of the local identity. Tony Lane describes the unique character of Liverpool's 'defiant and ready-witted people: Liverpudlians will talk confidently and unselfconsciously on equal terms with others regardless of their status; it shows, too, in their cheerful readiness to mock and puncture pretension'.[14] Professor John Belchem also refers to 'the "scouse" blend of truculent defiance, collective solidarity, scallywaggery and fatalist humour which sets Liverpool and its inhabitants apart',[15] whilst Devaney states, 'There is something about the city something intangible that comes from the guts of the city, from the bloodlines at its core and that is personified in those anarchic, revolutionary, "bolshie" individuals who categorically refuse to accept the status quo'.[16] It is suggested that some of Liverpool's renowned 'exceptionalism' (in contrast to dominant English character-istics) are a result of Liverpool's Irish heritage, although this is not to discount the input of other cultures, nor the resilience developed by the city's inhabitants amid economic woes.

---

[11] 'Rooney is part of a generation Irish "on the inside"'. *Irish Independent*, 1 October 2006.
[12] Papworth, 1981: 138.
[13] Greg Quiery, 25 March 2013.
[14] Lane, 1987: 14.
[15] Belchem, 2000a: 33.
[16] Devaney, 2011: 180.

Despite the influence of the Irish (and Irish Catholicism) on Liverpool, many began to reject (or forget) this aspect of their heritage as the twentieth century progressed.[17] As Lawlor comments, 'many people have chosen to discard their Irishness and their Catholicism and it tended to be both, rather than one or the other'.[18] Although loyalty to Ireland was, particularly in the late nineteenth and early twentieth centuries, a central facet of identity in 'Irish wards' such as Scotland and Vauxhall, demonstrated in the consistent election of Irish Nationalist councillors in Liverpool from 1875 until 1922,[19] after the establishment of the Irish Free State political identification was shifting towards support for the Labour Party. By the mid-twentieth century, although emigrants were still arriving in the port from Ireland,[20] the trend was very much downward and the directly Irish sense of the city declined.

It is noted that Irish immigration to the city has marginally increased in recent years,[21] but the numbers are tiny compared to earlier periods. A sense of Irishness nonetheless persisted. Born in 1966, Win Lawlor, a social worker for the Irish community in Liverpool, explained how, despite being born in the area, she was still brought up to celebrate Irish heritage:

> My dad was from County Meath, Ireland, and my mum's family was Louth. My mum was born in Rock Ferry [Wirral, Merseyside] and so was I, but I was part of the Irish community right from the beginning. I started Irish dancing at three. My mum and dad both spoke Irish. My dad taught us our prayers in Gaelic … I was brought up an Irish Catholic. We had the rosary every night. We had the priest round on a Friday. We never ate meat on a Friday and we always upheld every holy day of obligation. You were always in Mass.[22]

From this type of experience, a significant number of those born in Liverpool would still describe themselves as 'Liverpool Irish'; an identity fostered by some local associations. For example, *Irish Community Care Merseyside* stress that 'those born in England of Irish descent are very much part of the [Irish] scene'.[23]

---

[17] Today only 1.5 per cent of Liverpool's inhabitants identify as 'white Irish'.

[18] Win Lawlor, 21 February 2013.

[19] See O'Connell, 1971.

[20] McSweeney, 'The Irish are Coming Back to Liverpool', *Guardian*, 1 December 2011.

[21] Ibid.

[22] Win Lawlor, 21 February 2013.

[23] McSweeney, 'The Irish are Coming Back to Liverpool', *Guardian*, 1 December 2011.

Perhaps the most obvious legacy of Irish immigration can be seen, or rather heard, in the city's accent. It has been claimed that 'nowhere in Britain is more closely associated with a form of language than Liverpool'.[24] Although some debate has traditionally surrounded the origin of the local Liverpool brogue,[25] there is general consensus that it has been substantially influenced by the Irish tongue.[26] Clare Devaney wrote of the accent:

> Much maligned, celebrated, imitated and satirised, the Scouse accent, as one might expect, defies clear historical or etymological definition but is generally thought to have arrived on the boat from Ireland in the nineteenth century and to have taken hold in the social melting pot of the docks ... [It is] used both to establish a common identity and to assert a clear difference (principally from 'woolybacks', Lancastrians and Mancunians).[27]

The 'Scouse' accent evolved from a variety of influences in addition to Irish.[28] As such, it would be no more correct to state that the 'Scouse accent' has exclusively Irish origins any more than it would be to suggest that its origins lay mainly in the twentieth century.[29] As Crowley notes, 'not only were there literary representations of the Liverpool speech from the eighteenth century on, but there was also a long-standing sense that the language of Liverpool was distinctive'.[30] Even so, the prominence of Gaelic and 'Irish English' in the port is evident in Liverpool's dialect.[31]

In his 1973 doctoral thesis on the urban dialect of Scouse, the linguist Gerald Knowles contended that, 'the distinctive inflection of Scouse was a consequence of the influx of famine Irish in the middle of [the nineteenth] century'.[32] The accent is a product of 'the influx of Irish and Welsh into the

[24] Crowley, 2012: synopsis.
[25] For an account of this, see ibid.: 15–38 (chapter 2).
[26] Ibid., chapters 3 and 4.
[27] Devaney, 2011: 174.
[28] Ibid., 8.
[29] Crowley, 2012: xii ('Preface').
[30] Ibid., 106–7.
[31] Both the terms 'accent' and 'dialect' are deliberately used as there is ongoing debate as to what constitutes either description and, once more, what description, under the current disputed definitions, applies most soundly to the Liverpool brogue.
[32] P. Atkinson, 'Scouse: The Accent that Defined an Era'. *Times Higher Education*, 29 June 2007. Available at: www.timeshighereducation.co.uk/209515.article.

city [and] the mixing of these different accents and dialects'.[33] Although 'the origins of the Liverpool accent have been traced back to the 1750s',[34] there is truth in the claim that 'the accent [began to] develop its distinctive tones [more than] a century later when [over] half a million Irish men and women flooded into Liverpool between 1840 and 1850'.[35] Although it is contested whether, prior to the 'Great Hunger' (other than perhaps those in the affluent separated suburbs of Everton and areas of south Liverpool), residents of the port 'spoke in much the same way as the rest of Lancashire',[36] it is evident that 'successive waves of Irish immigrants changed the linguistic situation in Liverpool'.[37]

To support the claim of Irish influence on Liverpool's modern-day persona it is necessary briefly to explain its development. The term 'Scouse' itself, first and foremost, derives from the cheap sailor's dish of Lobscouse, the name of which most likely originated from the Norwegian stew of meat and vegetables called Lapskaus.[38] Crowley found that as early as 1797 scouse was being served in the Liverpool poorhouse,[39] although at this time the word 'Scouser' was not yet coined to refer to a resident of the port. The slang abbreviation for a 'Liverpolitan', at this time, was a 'Dicky Sam'.[40] This term was post-dated by the term 'W[h]acker', owing to the regular tendency for residents of the town to start or finish sentences with the word[s] 'w[h] ack/ w[h]acker'.[41] Birtill contends that the term W[h]acker, which emerged in the nineteenth century, was almost certainly due to the Irish and (more likely) the influence of the Gaelic language in the city:

People from the city were termed 'wackers' by outsiders because of their habit of referring to each other by the Irish word 'mhac' (pronounced

---

[33] P. Coslett, 'The Origins of Scouse'. BBC (30 April 2008). Available at: www.bbc.co.uk/ liverpool/content/articles/2005/01/11/voices_liverpoolaccent_feature.shtml.

[34] A. Powell, 'Is Cleaner Air Killing the Scouse Accent'. *Mail online* (2013) Available at: www.dailymail.co.uk/health/article-25752/Is-cleaner-air-killing-Scouse-accent.html.

[35] Ibid.

[36] Knowles, 1974: 17.

[37] Crowley, 2012, 19.

[38] L. Jay, 'Lapskaus'. My Little Norway (website) (27 November 2008). Available at: http://mylittlenorway.com/2008/11/lapskaus/.

[39] Crowley, 2012: xiii ('Preface').

[40] The origin of this term is contested. See ibid., 150–5.

[41] Lane, 1966: 114, 'A neutral form of address used by one Scouser to another, as in "whur's yer goin, wack?" Other phrase descriptions include 'A'right wack' or 'Aagho wacker' ['How goes it partner?'].

'wack', it is the word for son – mac – with lenition, which is used when addressing someone). Strictly speaking, the vocative case 'a mhac' should be used, but both appear in colloquial speech, sometimes together, as in: 'A mhac! A mhac ó!'[42]

In the 1950s, 'W[h]acker' was still a common slang term for a Liverpool resident,[43] although as the twentieth century progressed the phrase 'W[h]ack' was used less. Eventually the term was replaced, one commentator observing:

A term of address for a Liverpudlian is wack (or wacker), as in 'A'right wack?' but I must admit that I have heard this word more often in comedy sketches than on the streets of Liverpool. Another term of address, which I can recall hearing on many occasions, is 'laa', always accompanied by 'eh', as in 'Eh laa', which usually prefaces a question of some sort.[44]

The former Labour MP for Liverpool Walton, Peter Kilfoyle, also observed that 'Language is changing. When I was younger, I never heard anyone say "Eh Laa!" It was "Wack!"'[45] Indeed, another observer argues:

A language has been lost in my lifetime. I think it was TV that did it. Most of the words that were particular to Liverpool have gone, to be replaced instead by a national language, if not an international (from films) language. Only the accent remains.[46]

Increasingly, language was no longer determined by local phonological influences. Combined with the steady decline of Irish immigration, this may account for the abstraction of 'Irish' phraseology from the Liverpool dialect. Naturally, as the prevalence of phrases such as 'w[h]ack' decreased, the term 'w[h]acker' was devoid of applicability in relation to the city's inhabitants. The term 'Scouser', however, was increasingly utilised.

Unwin recalls, of the early twentieth century, 'There was a large room in St Martin's Hall, off Scotland Road, which was one of the cheapest eating places in the city. "Scouse Alley" they called it, and hundreds of plates of

---

[42] Birtill, 2013: 63.

[43] Crowley, 2012: 53.

[44] The Virtual Linguist (website), 'Scousers and Dicky Sams' (9 October 2008). Available at: http://virtuallinguist.typepad.com/the_virtual_linguist/2008/10/scousers-and-dicky-sams.html.

[45] Peter Kilfoyle, 23 January 2012.

[46] Walsh, 2011: 41.

steaming hot scouse were served every day at a penny a time'.[47] As such, scouse became known as the local Liverpool stew and 'provided for the city's members of the armed forces (NCOs and men) the term "Scousers" – [this] term, described as 'hardly ever used as a mark of affection', became common.[48] In August 1966, John Kerr wrote to the *Liverpool Echo* stating, 'When I was a boy the term Scouser was an insult used by non-Liverpudlians to describe people whose standard of living was so low they were reputed to exist on a diet of blind scouse – 'taters and water'.[49] It is typical of the city's defiant attitude that its residents would come to embrace the term 'Scouser' as their own. In this effort, pioneers of the 'Scouse Industry', such as Frank Shaw[50] and others, would come to mould the term to take on (internally at least), a positive slant.

Combined with the soaring popularity of Liverpool in the 1960s, many acts and entertainers benefited significantly on account of their home city and unique accent, with its 'melancholic, Irish-inflected oral traditions'.[51] Faced with such potential profits by highlighting local connections, 'the professional Scouser'[52] was born, boosted by the celebrated accents of the Beatles and the Mersey poets,[53] 'the Scouse inflection contributed to their distinctive image. It associated them with a particular location, and stories of the "Liverpool sound" and the "sound of Scouse" dominated the British media'.[54] The same article also asserted that, 'The distinctiveness of the Scouse accent is largely the result of immigration, particularly from the Celtic lands surrounding Liverpool's "quasi-inland" sea'.[55]

In 1950, Henri O'Hanri wrote an article in the *Liverpool Echo* entitled, 'It's the Irish in us!', in which he describes how 'the Gaelic Irish spelling and pronunciation of many words ... which are definitely Irish are in common use in Liverpool'. Examples included 'gob' for 'mouth' (from the Gaelic

---

[47] Unwin, 1983: 61–2.

[48] Crowley, 2012: 53, citing Farrell.

[49] Ibid., 61, citing Kerr.

[50] Ibid., Specifically chapter 4: 'Frank Shaw and the Founding of the "Scouse Industry"'.

[51] Williams, 2011: 129.

[52] Cllr Mike Murphy described how Liverpool's popularity at the time provided a platform for the personal profit of a group of individuals who benefited because of their accent and their home city of Liverpool.

[53] Devaney, 2011.

[54] Atkinson, 'Scouse: The Accent that Defined an Era'.

[55] Ibid.

'gob' – 'snout, beak, bill').[56] Tony Birtill expands the example: 'In Irish: "An gob atá air!", which literally means, "the beak on him!", is heard to this day in Liverpool as: "the gob on him!" The work also outlines the potential Gaelic origins of slang words and phrases still used today in Liverpool such as 'cac', 'slapper', 'ta rah', and 'smashin'.[57] Birtill's study, which also contends that 'the Irish language was widely spoken in Liverpool throughout the nineteenth century, and before', outlines that,

> the overwhelming majority of Irish migrants coming into Liverpool were mother-tongue (or first language) Irish speakers and English was their second language … a large proportion of these Irish were monoglot Irish speakers, many were bilingual and probably only a minority were monoglot English speakers … Another factor, frequently overlooked, is that the type of English spoken by these Irish migrants in itself constituted a linguistic difference: it was Hiberno-English, which consists of mainly English vocabulary, interspersed with Gaelic words and often using Irish syntax.[58]

Even sceptics have conceded that 'some phonetic effect of Irish Gaelic on the local speech cannot be excluded' and that 'the local form "owed much to the Irish … way of speaking English"'.[59] Nonetheless, Shaw suggests that 'very few of the Irish emigrants to Liverpool could speak the [Gaelic] language',[60] while Belchem writes of 'the overwhelming majority of [Irish] immigrants being English-speaking'.[61]

Such suggestions are refuted by the studies of Birtill and Papworth.[62] Crowley argues that 'there is in fact no research to show that [such] claim[s] [of overwhelming English-speaking] are accurate (although they have often been repeated); given the profile of many of the emigrants – rural and therefore poor – it seems likely that some of them must have spoken Irish [Gaelic]'.[63] Charters comments that, 'in 1847, 116,000 Irish refugees

---

[56] Crowley, 2012: 47, citing Henri O'Hanri's article in Liverpool Echo 'It's the Irish in us!', December 13 1950.

[57] Birtill, 2013: 13, 63.

[58] Ibid.

[59] Crowley, 2012: 48, citing D.W.F.H, 'Gaelic Words', *Liverpool Echo*, 3 January 1951 and Shaw 'Way of Speech', *Liverpool Echo*, 9 January 1951.

[60] Crowley, 2012: 60: n. 35.

[61] Belchem, 2007: 10.

[62] Birtill, 2013; Papworth, 1981.

[63] Crowley, 2012: 48.

arrived ... mostly from the Gaelic-speaking west'.[64] Birtill notes that 'the census figures of 1851 show 80% of the population in many areas of the west of Ireland, where many of the famine refugees to Liverpool originated, were still Irish speaking'.[65] Neal concurs, stating that Irish refugees were, 'mostly from the Gaelic speaking area of the West: Roscommon, Mayo, Galway and Sligo. They were rural people'.[66] Papworth, citing Witty, also states that, 'more Irish [Gaelic] was spoken in Liverpool than in Dublin'. Witty believed that, 'the children of Irish parents seldom prefer to converse in Irish, though many understand it'.[67] Denvir, also cited by Papworth, stated, 'nearly all in Crosbie Street [Liverpool] were from the west of Ireland, and, amongst them there was scarcely anything but Irish spoken'. Additionally, 'Denvir mentioned that his Aunt could speak several different Gaelic dialects'.[68] Born in Liverpool, in 1930, Tommy Walsh comments, 'My father was a native Irish speaker, who would have spoken little or no English until he came to England. He thought in Irish and prayed in Irish'.[69]

Such evidence, therefore, suggests that it is more than likely that Irish was once widely spoken in Liverpool with a Gaelic influence to the city's language. Shaw asserted that descriptions of 'Dublinees' ... 'might well be describing Liverpoolese' and that 'much of our [Liverpool's] speech ... came from Ireland'.[70] He was also not alone in noting the impact of Dublin phraseology on Liverpool. Neal believed that the Liverpool plural 'youse' was a product of the Dublin tongue,[71] and in his autobiography James Phelan, an Irish novelist, commented, '[I] felt myself in Dublin as soon as I heard the people speak'.[72]

It is important to acknowledge that the Irish were never the only arrivals in Liverpool. Indeed, 'whole areas belonged to the Welsh', who were, it has been argued, 'an ethnic community, because of their commitment to Welsh institutions and Welsh language [while] the Scots were held together by no

---

[64] Charters, 2003: 44.

[65] Birtill, 2013: 64.

[66] Ibid., citing Frank Neal, The Great Hunger Commemoration Service, St Anthony's, 3 October 1997.

[67] Papworth, 1981: 182, citing Witty.

[68] Ibid., citing Denvir.

[69] Walsh, 2011: 23.

[70] Shaw, 'Do You Want to Speak Scouse?', Liverpool Echo, 3 March 1955, cited by Crowley, 2012: 49.

[71] Frank Neal, 12 February 2010.

[72] Crowley, 2012: 46., citing Phelan, 1948: 201.

common language'.[73] However, as T. Oakes Hirst, 'a reputable linguist', observed in 1951, 'children of Irish parentage "retain some Anglo-Irish accent (or brogue)", which formed a contrast with the practice of children of Welsh parents and those of "other nationalities", whose speech forms "merge into one common type"'.[74] Even William Gladstone, who resided in the north end, 'where the majority [were] either Irish or of Irish decent',[75] did not escape the influence of Liverpool's dialect on his speech.[76]

Yet the Irish, despite their cultural and linguistic differences, did not live in isolation. As Pooley notes:

> A common experience of poverty must have created some bonds between the Irish and other low-income families from different cultural backgrounds. Although evidence of institutionalized and individual discrimination against the Irish is common, the experience of being Irish in Liverpool was certainly not one of total social and cultural isolation … for a proportion of Irish migrants the experience of living in Liverpool was one of integration rather than segregation.[77]

Despite sectarian tensions, association between Irish Catholics and English Protestants became routine in many workplaces. Such intermixing inevitably led to a crossover of local customs and speech patterns which ushered in the onset of a communal dialect. With the provision of factory work in the twentieth century such relations increased. By this time, the distinctiveness of 'Liverpool Irish' was lessening as Protestants and Catholics were progressively defining themselves as Liverpudlian rather than pursuing division on denominational or national lines.

Aided by the Catholic Church's attempts at 'deemphasising, any overarching (and unifying) Irish identity among the Liverpool Irish',[78] 'towards the end of the 19th century there was … a weakening of "cultural coherence and national identity" among the immigrant Irish community in Liverpool … This was a trend accelerated by a growing sense of identification

---

[73] Smith, 1986: 172, citing Pooley, 1977: 371.

[74] Crowley, 2012: 48, citing T. Oakes Hirst. 'Liverpool Speech: Some Local Pronunciations', *Liverpool Daily Post*, 29 January 1951.

[75] Birtill, 2013: 63, citing Scott and Hamilton Hay, 1907.

[76] Crowley, 2012: 29, 49, citing Picton, 1888: 211 and H.R. Shaw, 'Liverpool Accent', *Liverpool Daily Post*, 4 August 1950.

[77] Pooley, 1989: 75.

[78] Kennedy and Kennedy, 2007: 904.

among the Liverpool Irish with their host society'.[79] Nonetheless, as late as the 1950s, 'there were three Gaelic League branches and numerous parish céilís running weekly in Liverpool'.[80] Additionally, 'Sinn Féin, the Ancient Order of Hibernians, Irish Self-Determination League and Anti-Partition of Ireland League were all active and they, like the Gaelic League, had primarily Liverpool-born people as their members'.[81] The proportion of people identifying as 'Irish' in Liverpool has reduced considerably; just 1.4 per cent of Liverpool's population (still 0.5 per cent higher than the English and Welsh average)[82] and many Liverpudlians (with Irish heritage) would naturally feel more 'English'/'British' than (if at all) 'Irish'.

Tommy Walsh comments on the diverging attitude of Liverpudlians with Irish heritage: 'In my experience, Irish people born in Liverpool are either "more Irish than the Irish" or they simply aren't interested. There's also a smaller group who appear to resent having an Irish name and who are extremely anti-Irish'.[83] Yet, Irish heritage is still celebrated in the city. The existence of groups such as *Cairde na hÉireann Liverpool* and *Irish Community Care Merseyside*, as well as the annual celebration of the *Liverpool Irish Festival*, are testament to this. The legacy of Irish immigration has also been evident in the formation of the King's Liverpool Regiment, 8th (Irish) Battalion (now dissolved),[84] the Catholic Metropolitan Cathedral, Liverpool's twinning with Dublin, and the Institute of Irish Studies (the lattermost funded by the Irish Republic).

The Roots of a Common 'Scouse' Identity

Rogan Taylor speculates that the roots of 'Scousedom' lay in the mid- to late nineteenth century. After the arrival of famine Irish, the experience of 'collective suffering' began to breed (willingly or unwillingly) an attitude, transmuted through times of hardship, which spanned the religious divide:

---

[79] Ibid., 911.

[80] Walsh, 2011: 49. The Gaelic League (or Conradh na Gaeilge) is a non-governmental organisation for the promotion of the Irish language, while a céilí is a traditional Gaelic social gathering, which usually involves playing Gaelic, folk music, and dancing.

[81] Walsh, 2011: 52.

[82] Liverpool City Council (website), '2011 Census: Ethnicity in Liverpool'. Available at: http://liverpool.gov.uk/media/9899/ethnicity-and-migration.pdf.

[83] Walsh, 2011: 18–19.

[84] See Fitzsimons, 2004.

Scousers knew they were living in a tough town, but what I was never taught at school was how hard times were in the mid-nineteenth century. The stamp of Scousedom was made then. In five months, one and a half times the population of the city arrived in Liverpool. In those circumstances, what happens is anybody who has got two pennies to rub together, a bit of health, and a bit of luck gets out of there. What are you left with – the old, the young, the sick, and those with no pennies to rub together – what were famously called 'the dregs'. The city's foundation is based on 'the dregs' of that great exodus. The forging of the city in hardship has produced an incredibly powerful form of identity – which is most strongly fashioned in shared pain.[85]

This is a significant observation. It was through times of collective turmoil and frustration that populations grew so close. As David Charters writes, 'Scotland Road ... was built on the spirit of its people'[86] Jim Fitzsimons alludes to this:

The grandparents and parents of the young Merseyside Irish had flocked to Liverpool away from the hard times in Ireland ... The Irish way of life eventually became a big factor in the character of these families and mainly stayed that way in the struggle to exist during the acute poverty of the times. Irish immigrants had paid their way in this adopted country by their labour, almost all of it in heavy manual work. As the years passed many of them progressed into leaders of the community, being respected and welcomed by other citizens of this area.[87]

These struggles also applied to the Protestant residents of Everton, St Domingo, and Netherfield Road.[88] Although communities were divided from each other, both geographically and on religious lines, to some extent, a similarity of outlook must have been developing (even while these communities continued viewing each other as their antithesis). Solidarity continued to develop in the twentieth century, fuelled by two world wars, the 1930s depression, and post-war economic decline.

A distinction that has developed between the city and the rest of the country centred upon common 'Scouse' identity, reflected in modern 'Scouse, Not English' banners seen at football games. In 1950, an essay

---

[85] Dr Rogan Taylor, 27 November 2013.
[86] Charters, 2003: 46.
[87] Fitzsimons, 2004: 7.
[88] See Rodgers, 2010.

in the *Daily Post* recorded 'the irritation felt by Liverpudlians when BBC producers represent the local speech form as "Lancashire"'.[89] In 1999, the former Chair of Merseyside Police Authority, Margaret Simey, claimed that 'the magic of Liverpool is that it isn't England. We are global and we have learned to tolerate and respect each other's traditions'.[90] Likewise, Journalist Paul Morley suggests, 'Liverpool is not part of England ... it is an outpost of defiance and determination reluctantly connected to the English mainland'.[91] As Neal noted, 'the Irish presence has permanently affected the character of Liverpool, principally in the prominence of Catholicism but also in such things as the accent and attitudes of its people. Liverpool is in Lancashire but not of Lancashire'.[92] It is suggested that, as a result of influences from Ireland and elsewhere, Merseyside, culturally, is perhaps the most un-English of England's counties.

The Rise of Non-Sectarian Culture: The Advent of Merseybeat

In 1966, when John Lennon reputedly stated, 'We're more popular than Jesus', it was in the USA, not Liverpool, that the statement caused most controversy. As Mike O'Brian points out, 'It shows how much things had changed. If such as statement had been made 10 to 15 years earlier he'd have been run out of Liverpool by both the Catholics and the Protestants'.[93] In explaining the comment, Lennon later claimed that the statement was 'in relation to England ... we meant more to kids than Jesus or religion at that time'.[94] As a journalist at the same press conference pointed out, it was not just in Liverpool that 'children are repeating, "I like the Beatles more than Jesus"'.[95] The 1960s was an era of social, political, and cultural change.

---

[89] *Liverpool Daily Post*, 9 August 1950: 'About that Liverpool Accent (or Dialect)', cited by Crowley, 2012: 50.

[90] Museum of Liverpool, 2012: 86, citing Margaret Simey; Yo!Liverpool (website), 'Liverpool Quotes'. Available at: www.yoliverpool.com/forum/showthread.php?330-Liverpool-Quotes.

[91] Museum of Liverpool, 2012: 88, citing Paul Morley.

[92] Neal, 2006: 72.

[93] Mike O'Brian, 12 November 2012.

[94] 'The Beatles [More] Popular than Jesus'. Available at: www.youtube.com/watch?v=kZ6NL3iNNMs.

[95] Ibid.

People's perceptions were quickly being diverted away from the rigidities of biblical doctrine. As George Harrison noted, 'Christianity is declining and everybody knows about that'.[96] The Beatles became internationally recognised and their popularity brought renewed interest in their home city. For Liverpool, The Beatles, in turn, became an ingredient in the city's newly emerging identity.

In addition to football, the Merseybeat[97] phenomenon helped make the city internationally renowned in an arena separate from trade and shipbuilding, with the added effect of taking emphasis away from religion. The advent of The Beatles had a profound impact on the global music scene, and other local acts such as The Searchers and Gerry and the Pacemakers added to the enthralment. Liverpool had a reasonable claim to be 'the music capital of the world'[98] and Liverpool's youth found expression through making or enjoying music rather than subscribing to seemingly dated sectarian tunes. Merseybeat formed part of a broader cultural expression, embracing music, language, and sport. Previously, the 'Twelfth' and St Patrick's Day were welcome distractions from the tedium of slum living. As Clive Barker suggests, 'In 1956 ... Liverpool was still getting out of post-war doldrums, and entertainment was hard to come by'.[99] A decade later this was anything but the case.

In the early 1960s, Alun Owen, screenwriter of *A Hard Day's Night* (The Beatles' debut feature film), suggested that 'the multiracial population of the city "evolved an accent for themselves", borrowed from their Irish and Welsh grandfathers in response to the "problem of identity"'.[100] Although, as Crowley's work explains, from at least the mid-eighteenth century, there had been 'a link between the city and a form of language', by the 1960s, 'a linguistic identity was born'.[101] He comments that:

> In the aftermath of the Second World War ... (a war that wreaked consid-
> erable damage on the city), there was a renewed focus on language in
> Liverpool ... a precursor to the appearance of 'Scouse' – a category that

---

[96] 'George with Bigger than Jesus' (29 August 2007). Available at: www.youtube.com/watch?v=jPZVJcyHX6s&list=RDkZ6NL3iNNMs.

[97] The *Merseybeat* was the name of a local music magazine, a Liverpool band, and a more generic label for music from Liverpool in the 1960s era.

[98] Michael Murphy, 8 April 2013.

[99] Clive Barker, 1999, cited by Mulhearn, 2007a: 83.

[100] P. Atkinson, 'Scouse: The Accent that Defined an Era'.

[101] Crowley, 2012: 107.

appears to be linguistic and yet that bears (and has always borne) a great deal of cultural, social and indeed political resonance.[102]

The 'renewed focus' on Liverpool's 'language' was connected to the rise of The Beatles. Liverpool became 'a major attraction [and] many of the top recording labels vied with each other to sign up other groups and artists from the overwhelming array of talent that the Mersey sound had to offer'.[103] It has been suggested that the 'colonizing of the English pop music charts by the Mersey beat groups in 1963, and their later success in the international market [had a] considerable effect … on identity'.[104] The 'new sound emerging from the city was both indicative of and representative of the nation adapting to the modernity of an emerging "pop" culture'.[105] Steve Rotheram MP makes reference to this, as well as the growing cohesion of the port's inhabitants:

> Through The Beatles and the Merseybeat era … with the accent being an easy identifier, when you went abroad you became a 'Scouser'. It didn't matter whether you were Catholic, Protestant, or anything else; because people just wanted a piece of you. It was a badge of honour! It opened lots of doors for people, certainly for a Scouse lad with ladies who weren't from the area. They loved the Scouse accent. It was a cultural identity.[106]

Reverend John Williams agrees that, 'The Merseybeat made a huge contribution to unity!'[107] Woolley emphasises that the success of Liverpool's bands symbolised much more than the music they produced:

> Merseybeat was not so much about individual brilliance, although that was there in plenty, but about a generation of ordinary kids just picking up a guitar and a set of drums and getting together to make music, in an explosion of talent which put Liverpool, and the groups which emerged from it, at the centre of the world stage.[108]

The variety of prospective entertainment was such that the different elements of popular culture often overlapped. One of the founders of the

---

[102] Ibid.
[103] Woolley, 2008: 6. Also, see Du Noyer, 2002.
[104] P. Atkinson, 'Scouse: The Accent that Defined an Era'.
[105] Ibid.
[106] Steve Rotheram, 4 January 2013.
[107] John Williams, 17 November 2010.
[108] Woolley, 2008: 6.

'Mersey Scene', Adrian Henri, formed a band which managed to merge poetry and rock music: two prominent forms of entertainment in Liverpool. Litherland-born poet, Roger McGough, explained the connection between music and poetry at this time: 'The kids didn't see this poetry with a capital P – they understood it as modern entertainment, as part of the pop-movement'.[109] Councillor Rothery comments on the changing attitudes which were emerging in the 1960s:

> The music sort of fed back meaningful change and also it was about the era. It was the sixties. People were less hung up on what the issues were and more liberal in their perceptions and ideas. I think there was a natural challenge of those preconceived ideas that came before and a natural breaking down of barriers.[110]

Music was part of a changing culture in Liverpool. With so many emerging distractions people were less likely to get involved in sectarian disputes. As Reverend John Williams states, 'football, music, and the arts helped bring us out of the valley of darkness. They created unity. All these wonderful things happened in the sixties. It was a great time of liberation. People said, "So what if I go into a Catholic church! What is the point in maintaining this façade?"'[111] Williams added that the prominence of 'radical' and 'experimental' performing arts venues, such as the Unity Theatre on Hope Street, provided 'another outlet which allowed people to find a common bond'.[112] Additionally, television was a further dynamic which was disrupting the traditional monopoly of religious influences via pulpits. The 'continuing vitality of the Mersey pop music scene'[113] was coupled with,

> The decisive development that saw Liverpool appear as the focus of a variety of programmes that were not only crucial in the enregisterment of Scouse, but also central to the formation of popular culture itself on British television ... From the early 1960s a number of TV series that were located in Liverpool brought aspects of the city's culture to a national audience.[114]

---

[109] Mekons (website), 'The Liverpool Scene'. Available at: www.mekons.de/home/liver.htm.
[110] Anna Rothery, 19 February 2013.
[111] John Williams, 17 November 2010.
[112] Ibid.
[113] Crowley, 2012: 110.
[114] Ibid., 109.

Amongst such programmes were *Z Cars* (1962–78) and *The Liver Birds* (1969–78). Later shows included *The Wackers* (1975), *Boys from the Blackstuff* (1982), *Brookside* (1982–2003), and *Bread* (1986–91), amongst others. Topically, *The Wackers*, focused on a family who were 'half Protestant, half Catholic, half Liverpool football club supporters, half Everton supporters'.[115] The show attempted to draw 'humour from difference',[116] an approach which, although highlighting Liverpool's particular religious rivalry, may also have abridged religious tensions in reducing them to the butt of jokes. Other shows had a discernibly political undercurrent depicting the harsh realities of working-class Liverpool. Alan Bleasdale's BAFTA Award-winning drama series, *Boys from the Blackstuff*, 'was a powerful depiction of the despair of unemployment'[117] in depression-scarred 1980s Britain with a clear message articulated by Julie Walters' character *Angie*: 'Why don't you fight back, you b*****d? Fight back!'[118]

Concurrently, Liverpool's political make-up became much more decisively Labour and far less sectarian. John Williams remarks that, 'the 1960s swept away some of the aged conservatism ... not least in the new youthful "Beat city" of Liverpool, then "a fertile cradle of exceptional creativity and initiative"'.[119] As Alan Bleasdale (through the medium of his character *Snowy Malone*) comments, 'It was easy being a Socialist in the sixties, even in the seventies. It was fashionable then'.[120] Peter Kilfoyle, former MP for Liverpool Walton (a traditionally Tory seat until 1964), argues that such political realignment was a product of a general alteration of the city's outlook in the 1960s:

> Liverpool was a great place to be in the sixties. I could go from job to job. After Vatican II came in all these recommendations changed things ... I mean simple things where a women going into church would be expected to have something on her head ... were changed. The sixties was a time of

---

[115] A. Hayward (16 February 2014) 'Ken Jones Obituary' [*The Wackers*]. Available at: www.theguardian.com/tv-and-radio/2014/feb/16/ken-jones.

[116] TV.com (website), 'The Wackers: Show Summary'. Available at: www.tv.com/shows/the-wackers/.

[117] P. Coslett, 'Boys from the Blackstuff'. BBC (11 November 2007). Available at: www.bbc.co.uk/liverpool/content/articles/2007/10/09/boys_from_the_blackstuff_feature.shtml.

[118] Ibid.

[119] Williams, 2011: 127, citing Alan Edge, 2010.

[120] BBC television, *Boys from the Blackstuff*. Episode 1, 'Jobs for the Boys' (1980).

great flux and it affected every type of attitude: religious attitudes, sexual attitudes, moral attitudes, everything.[121]

Culturally, as well as politically, Liverpool was in flux in the 1960s and increasingly people's attention diverted from matters pertaining to religion. Just as many in the city began to take on a more socialist perspective, many were also embracing a Lennonist (as well as a Leninist) ideology. Lyrics like 'All you need is love' and 'Imagine there's no heaven' usurped long-standing sectarian dogmatism. In another sense music also had an effect in removing people from an exclusively religious mindset. As Rotheram suggests, 'I think music had a huge influence in helping to break up that religious divide. All of a sudden it didn't matter about your religion. It became, "can you play?" or "can you sing?"'[122]

Music and sport were not the only areas where Merseyside set the tone. The city became renowned for its entertainers and stand-up comedians. Belchem comments, 'a succession of Liverpool-born comedians … acquired national celebrity for their humour … This comic effloresce appears as a defining moment for Scouse, an early instance of economic decline and cultural assertion'.[123] It is claimed that 'humour kept spirits high against all manner of exploitation'.[124] Arthur Askey famously commented, 'You've got to be a comic to live in Liverpool'.[125] Another 'well-known humourist's explanation of the success of so many comedians [was that], "If you live in Liverpool you must either laugh yourself sick [or] burst into tears"'.[126]

In addition to the success of its comics, the city was also becoming famous for producing a number of playwrights, poets, and artists. In 1964, Liverpool's famous Everyman Theatre was opened on Hope Street as Arthur Dooley, Roger McGough, and Adrian Henri formed what became known as 'the Liverpool Scene'. George Orr claims the city for a time developed 'a better identity than any city, apart from London, which was always the fashion capital'.[127]

Poetry, comedy, music, television, left-wing politics, and football were all contingents shaping the character of Liverpool at the time and, as

---

[121] Peer Kilfoyle, 23 January 2012.

[122] Steve Rotheram, 4 January 2013.

[123] Belchem, 2000: 50.

[124] Dudgeon, 2012: 100.

[125] Cited by Belchem, 2000: 50; Dudgeon, 2012: 100.

[126] Lane, 1966: 4 ('Foreword').

[127] George Orr, 7 November 2013.

Bishop Tom Williams suggests, 'there was also an element of common sense ... people started avoiding situations that would lead to [religious] confrontation'.[128] Mike O'Brian echoes Williams' comments, 'When they opened the [Catholic] Metropolitan Cathedral [in 1967] they brought police in from all over the country because they were expecting murder. I'll always remember the story, some fella [policeman] was in from Manchester and he said "I wish somebody would wave an Orange flag so we'd have something to do!" People had learned sense by then'.[129]

Andy Burnham MP says of the sixties:

> Liverpool was a fairly prosperous city. It was giving everybody a job and with The Beatles and everything it was slightly ahead with a new way of thinking. Everyone was doing all right so nobody had a reason to be scapegoating anybody. Everybody was having a good time and forgetting it. Liverpool saw itself as different ... The Lancastrian Protestants and Irish Catholics were beginning to merge. Liverpool developed its own identity.[130]

As Neal notes, 'new types of entertainment channelled people into other activities and in other directions'.[131] With the relative affluence of the 1960s and the opportunities this provided, people were diverted from sectarianism and religion more generally. Later, as the century progressed, the political alternatives people were adopting meant that, amid the city's dramatic economic fall, the focus had moved onto 'a bigger enemy' than neighbours of a different religious persuasion.

Lawlor says the creation of a distinctive Scouse identity allowed 'people to unite whereas [religious] differences would have kept people separated ... you have got to find the similarities'.[132] The collective accent, label, and experiences, be they good or bad, helped people see their likenesses. Merseysiders developed a commonality which eclipsed denominational distinctions. The rise of The Beatles had helped bring attention to the city and engender common pride amongst its inhabitants. As Brenda O'Brian puts it, 'People realised there was more to life!'[133]

---

[128] Tom Williams, 23 March 2010.

[129] Mike O'Brian, 12 November 2012.

[130] Andy Burnham, 28 March 2013.

[131] Frank Neal, 12 February 2010.

[132] Win Lawlor, 21 February 2013.

[133] Brenda O'Brian, 12 November 2012.

It is not denied that, for many people, religion was still an important aspect of their identity. Ian Henderson claims that, 'even as late as the sixties, if a polling station was in a Catholic church, Protestants wouldn't vote in it'.[134] Nonetheless, for many people priorities were shifting away from religion and they began embracing a city-wide collective identity, which transcended religious division. The unique atmosphere of the 'all-embracing sixties'[135] was a crucial ingredient in the formation of the inimitable character of the city. It was the relative prosperity and cultural contributions of the 1960s which facilitated a common pride in the city, one which would be strengthened in the harsher economic climate which soon followed. This pride helped displace lingering sectarian hostilities and focus the attentions of the city's residents upon other supposed 'enemies' than those within. Hostility to the Conservatives (especially Margaret Thatcher), Westminster, and even other cities (notably Manchester) compounded the sense of unified 'Scouse' identity as internal religious rivalries passed largely into memory.

Andy Burnham MP makes this point, while suggesting that Liverpool's 'common identity' displaced lingering sectarian tensions:

> Somewhere along the line Liverpool developed a common identity. Somewhere Scouse identity almost became asserted as anti-English. The rise of that sentiment spells absolutely the end of sectarianism. At that point, people were defining themselves against the rest of England and not against each other internally. I think events like Hillsborough massively contributed to that. The feeling that the whole city was being done down by a London establishment: a political establishment, a media establishment, a police and legal establishment; that cemented a feeling that gave a death-knell to any sectarianism. On the whole, [sectarianism] is now a memory rather than anything else.[136]

This chapter has highlighted how the Scouse identity played an important role in uniting Liverpool residents. Amid cultural and sporting success, the 'Scouse industry' began to come to prominence around the 1960s. This did much to broaden outlooks away from matters pertaining to religion. The Scouse identity was coming to fruition with a certain arrogance. The city had reason to feel proud and this pride was important.

---

[134] Ian Henderson, 21 December 2012. Polling stations were not actually located within churches, but in part of a complex belonging to the Catholic Church.

[135] Peter Kilfoyle, 23 January 2012.

[136] Ibid.

Economic revival was partial and temporary in the 1960s and the city, in terms of financial clout, was far removed from two centuries earlier when 'considered the European capital of trade'.[137] Although the 1960s can be said to have been a 'golden era' for the city, in the early 1980s, Margaret Thatcher's Conservative Government was appearing to 'neglect Liverpool – to rot'.[138] As Jane Merrick, Political Editor for the *Independent*, highlights: the experience was further setting Liverpool apart. 'At the time, it did feel as if we were being cut adrift from the rest of the country. More than that, it was like we were living in another country'.[139] The distinctiveness of Liverpool, via the forging of common identities (after much division) amid economic decline, had led to the claim that it is,

> Unlike any other British city ... Liverpudlians have developed an attitude, one forged through diversity and change, opportunity and adversity. Liverpudlians see themselves as different, and independent, with a fair degree of scepticism towards authority. Indeed, Liverpudlians are seen by others as different, as a 'breed apart'. Liverpool may once have been a Lancashire city, but it had stopped being that by the middle of the 19th century. It is the least 'English' of all English cities, and has more in common with Dublin, Belfast and Glasgow than Manchester.[140]

Some aspects of that claim may be contested, as large-scale immigration and scepticism towards (Westminster) authority are apparent in other northern cities. Nonetheless, few would challenge the overall perception of Liverpool's distinctiveness. Of the variety of influences which helped construct the unique Scouse identity, some of the most prominent were Irish, more than in other English municipalities which experienced significant Irish immigration, such as Manchester and Birmingham.

One objection, perhaps expectedly, comes from the Grand Master of England's Orange Institution, who believed the emergence of the Scouse identity to have been a 'social change' rather than 'because of the Irish'.[141] Although Bather has a point that such a cultural shift encompassed many

---

[137] Museum of Liverpool, 2012: 14.

[138] J. Merrick, 'The "Socialist Firebrand" Derek Hatton Screwed Liverpool Just as Much as Margaret Thatcher Did'. *Independent* (16 April 2013). Available at: www.independent.co.uk/voices/comment/the-socialist-firebrand-derek-hatton-screwed-liverpool-just-as-much-as-margaret-thatcher-did-8575030.html.

[139] Ibid.

[140] Museum of Liverpool, 2012: 64.

[141] Ron Bather, 15 March 2010.

more elements than simply being a unilateral transposition from Ireland, even the organisation which he heads, although having many of its own unique customs and traditions, has inherited much from Ireland. If *an Gorta Mór* had not created huge Irish immigration into the port, it is unlikely that Liverpool Orangeism would have thrived as it did. Whilst the term 'Scouser' was originally externally imposed (often in a derogatory sense), it became embraced by the city itself, which forged an identity surrounding a dialect and a culture which set it apart from the rest of England. This 'common Scouse identity'[142] developed a distinction which eclipsed past sectarian frictions. Its characteristics comprised of loyalty, camaraderie, inimitability, humour, humility (as well as arrogance), assertiveness, defiance and solidarity – a way of collectively standing together against adversity. Even Liverpudlians who resent some of the dominant aspects of the Liverpool culture celebrate the identity of Scouse.

The constituent parts of this identity were not simply derived from the glory days of the sixties. 'The city is what it is because the people are what they are'[143] and it has been through much turmoil that Liverpool's exceptionality has evolved. Mullins comments on the stigma attached to being a Liverpudlian and the trait of self-protection,

> I live on the Wirral now, and every now and again you'll get, 'Hey, you haven't got your visa yet.' Sometimes you hear negative, derogatory comments. Now, personally, I don't know if all Scousers are, but I'm very defensive about Liverpool ... I think most Scousers are defensive. We need to be!'[144]

A poll of 4,000 people across Britain recently indicated that, based on their accent alone, even today, many people believe Scousers to be the most 'unintelligent' and 'untrustworthy' people in the UK.[145] Much of this may be owed to a general trend of negative publicity about the city from the national media.

In the 1980s, Liverpool, then controlled by the Militant council, was labelled as 'rebellious' and 'anarchic', and Liverpool fans who attended the

---

[142] John Williams, 17 November 2010.

[143] Paraphrasing a comment made by Williams, 2011: 137.

[144] Alf Mullins, 14 May 2012.

[145] V. Woollaston, 'Scousers have the "least intelligent and least trustworthy" accent ...'. *Daily Mail* (26 September 2013). Available at: www.dailymail.co.uk/sciencetech/article-2433201/Scousers-intelligent-trustworthy-accent--Devonians-friendliest.html.

FA Cup semi-final at Hillsborough in 1989, at which ninety-six people died and 766 were injured, were painted as the main culprits for the disaster, being described as 'ticketless thugs' who initiated 'a crush' and staged 'drunken attacks on the police'.[146] Frost and North describe how:

> The long-awaited inquiry into the Hillsborough disaster finally reported that the police and media had conspired to denigrate Scousers as drunken thugs who stole from the dead, to cover up their own failings. A nation saw that a city and its residents had been systematically maligned as, at best, over emotional and romantic, at worst, work shy scroungers that claim 'it's never our fault' and who have become residents of a 'self-pity city'.[147]

In 2004, Boris Johnson was made to apologise to the city, whose inhabitants, he alleged, 'wallow' in their 'victim status'. He also contended that, 'the city made a scapegoat of police in the wake of the Hillsborough disaster, refusing to acknowledge the part played by drunken fans at the back of the crowd who mindlessly tried to fight their way into the ground'.[148] The London Mayor would later cause controversy by claiming that The Beatles owed their success to London rather than Liverpool, for which Liverpool Mayor Joe Anderson demanded another apology,[149] yet, as an article in *Private Eye* stated, 'if everyone who offends Liverpool had to go on a penitential pilgrimage, half of Fleet Street would be on the next train to Lime Street'.[150]

In 1997, the *Observer* wrote of Liverpool's 'no-holds-barred self-pity dressed as grief, self-congratulatory sentimentalism, an affirmation of itself through the appropriation of cosmetic Celtism'.[151] The recognition of Liverpool's connection with Ireland is noteworthy, although so is the article's repetition of the phraseology describing Liverpool as a 'Self-Pity City' – the

[146] 'Hillsborough Football Disaster' (website). Available at: www.contrast.org/hillsborough/history/media.shtm.
[147] Frost and North, 2013: 3.
[148] '"Sorry" Johnson Sent to Liverpool'. BBC (16 October 2004). Available at: http://news.bbc.co.uk/1/hi/uk_politics/3749548.stm.
[149] P. Guy, 'Mayor of Liverpool Joe Anderson Demands Apology from Boris Johnson over Beatles Comments'. *Liverpool Echo* (3 January 2014). Available at: www.liverpoolecho.co.uk/news/liverpool-news/mayor-liverpool-joe-anderson-demands-6464928.
[150] www.superscouse.co.uk (website), 'Hackwatch: Beyond the Whinge', citing *Private Eye*, No 1118. Available at: www.superscouse.co.uk.
[151] Ibid., citing the *Observer*, 5 October 1997.

headline of an article in *The Times* after the murder of James Bulger in 1993 (a two-year-old boy who was abducted, tortured, and murdered by two ten-year-old boys). The article 'denounced the city as a "paranoia theme park" with a "self-pitying and incipiently barbaric culture"'.[152] Nine days earlier, another article for the newspaper had dubbed Liverpool: 'The mob, as self-pitying as it is self-righteous'.[153] The *Guardian* also made allegations of 'the self-pity issuing from Liverpool if anyone suggests that idle, violent city is, well, an idle, violent city'.[154] This was broadly typical of the journalistic comment published in relation to Liverpool at the time. As Paddy Shennan recalls,

> Within a few short days of James Bulger's murder the city of Liverpool was placed firmly in the dock – and there wasn't going to be a fair trial. It was February 1993, less than four years after Kelvin MacKenzie had defamed us and dragged our name through the mud [in relation to the Hillsborough disaster] – and there were still people queuing up looking for an excuse to put the boot in and inject the poison ... 'The city with a murder on its conscience' was a headline in *The Times*. Above it was the question 'as James Bulger was led to his death, what were the people of Liverpool doing?' Walter Ellis, the author of this shameful piece of non-journalism, wrote: 'Liverpool lives on emotion; fears and hatreds bubble constantly below the surface'.[155]

In 2001, pejorative comments were still being directed towards the city in relation to the tragic death of James Bulger. Charlotte Raven wrote in the *Guardian*:

> Scousers' propensity to linger over every misfortune until another comes to replace it makes them uniquely suited to the demands of the Bulger mourning marathon ... While other cities might have faltered and found something else to distract them, Liverpool's talent for nursing resentments ensured that it would feel, eight years on, just as enraged about Bulger's murder as it was the first moment it heard ... Liverpudlians refuse to let

[152] Ibid., citing the *Sunday Times*, 28 February 1993.

[153] Ibid., citing *The Times*, 19 February 1993.

[154] Ibid., citing the *Guardian*, 24 May 1993.

[155] P. Shennon, 'James Bulger Remembered: How Liverpool Came under Attack from the National Press After James's Murder'. *Liverpool Echo* (14 February 2014). Available at: www.liverpoolecho.co.uk/news/liverpool-news/james-bulger-remembered-how-liverpool-3322401.

anything go ... as long as there's still a drop of righteous indignation to be squeezed.[156]

Undoubtedly, the repetition of such provocative allegations has had an effect both on external perspectives of the city and on the establishment of an internally defensive demeanour. As Taylor comments, 'It's where the hammer falls again, and again, and again – It's almost like beating a horseshoe to make it tough. It drives this collectivism'.[157]

On Merseyside, the glory years of the sixties contrasted starkly with the gloom of the eighties. The unemployment figure had risen from 5 per cent in the mid-1960s to 20 per cent by 1981. Between 1979 and 1984, Liverpool lost nearly half of its manufacturing base, a staggering 40,000 jobs.[158] Although many left the city in search of work, on 7 June 1985, the *Liverpool Echo* reported that 'Almost 32,000 Merseyside youngsters were chasing just 112 careers'.[159] In such circumstances, defending one's religion was not at the forefront of many people's priorities. Under the leadership of Sheppard and Worlock, the hierarchies of the Catholic and Protestant Churches in Liverpool were working in unison to alleviate hardship.[160] In addition, the Irish could no longer, plausibly, be blamed for the city's adverse economic conditions, responsibility being directed squarely at Margaret Thatcher's neo-liberal capitalist strategies.[161] The Prime Minister appeared to blame the people of Liverpool for their own misfortune, telling Knowsley MP, Robert Kilroy Silk, 'The problem with your constituents is that they don't start up their own businesses. They've got no entrepreneurial spirit. They've got no get-up-and-go'.[162] Negative publicity over the Toxteth riots, Liverpool's Militant City Council, and the Heysel and Hillsborough disasters painted a bleak picture of the city which helped form a wedge between Liverpool and the rest of the country, and arguably contrasted with the global image of the city ... Arabella McIntyre-Brown describes this contrast:

---

[156] www.superscouse.co.uk (website), 'Hackwatch: Beyond the Whinge', citing the *Guardian*, 26 June 2000.

[157] Rogan Taylor, 27 November 2013.

[158] Figures cited by Frost and North, 2013: 8, 17.

[159] Ibid., citing *Liverpool Echo*, 7 June 1985.

[160] See Shepard and Worlock, 1988. Catholic Bishop Tom Williams and Protestant Revd John Williams also attest to this having been the case.

[161] Frost and North, 2013: 14–17.

[162] Ibid., 16–17, citing Kilroy-Silk, 1986: 45.

In Britain [the image of Liverpool] is fully formed as a depressed northern city populated by work-shy, bolshie trouble makers, comedians and criminals ... Everyone knows the docks are dead, the city is a hideous blot, Scousers are stupid and aggressive ... outside Britain, you say you come from Liverpool and peoples' faces light up with big smiles. It's almost certainly going to be one of two things that people associate with Liverpool: football or music.[163]

Notably, what was absent was any reference to a sectarian divide. The city's degeneration was taking precedence over any religious tension which, at any rate, was being displaced. In many people's minds (although the Churches' hierarchies may have been making some positive noises), God did not seem to be helping matters.

Conclusion

Although there were (and indeed still are), those in the city who would prefer to distance themselves from the term, by the end of the twentieth century, the description of 'Scouse' had become accepted by the majority of the Liverpool populace. From the dish and the accent, with its Irish influences, 'Scouse' would develop 'its status as the specific mode of cultural identity that often stands metonymically for the city of Liverpool and all its inhabitants'.[164] In considering how things currently stand, Irish community worker, Win Lawlor, comments,

Within any community you have broad-spectrum views and it's usually a minority that have extreme views. Within that category are both Irish and Orange views. Then you have those who will live and let live and also those who have family members on 'the other side', if anybody even thinks about 'the other side' any more.[165]

Few in Liverpool now think of 'the other side' in terms of a religious separation. In contrast, 'the other side' is often used to refer to those supporters of a rival football team. The connotations of 'them' and 'us' have shifted. Today, such terminology is most often used to differentiate between

---

[163] Arabella McIntyre-Brown, cited by Devaney, 2011: 174.
[164] Crowley, 2012: xv ('Preface').
[165] Win Lawlor, 21 February 2013.

Everton and Liverpool supporters, and, even then, for the majority, this statement is said in jest.[166] Solidarity has emerged in Liverpool which was not present when sectarianism was at its height. As such, such discordant terminology, which may once have been utilised to remark on division between the city's Irish Catholic and Lancastrian Protestant communities, began to be coined more frequently to highlight distinctions between the working class and the establishment, although such phraseology also refers to Liverpool set against the rest of the country.

Shared cultures with global reach, particularly in terms of music and the arts, did much to forge a common city identity to displace inter-communal sectarianism. A key aspect of this new unity was sporting success for the city's main football teams – neither religiously aligned – which prospered as the city failed economically.

[166] It is also often overshadowed by the terms 'we' or 'our' describing Scousers' collectivism.

9

Everton and Liverpool Football Clubs: New Gods

Previous chapters have demonstrated that both Orangeism and Catholicism are no longer as important as they once were to the Merseyside populace. Amid the decline in religious affiliation and sectarianism, Liverpool's two football clubs, Everton FC and Liverpool FC, have become the dominant repositories of identification. The pre-eminence of football does not, of course, *automatically* diminish sectarianism. In Glasgow, the presence of Celtic and Rangers has arguably consolidated Catholic versus Protestant and Scottish–Irish versus Scottish–British hostilities.[1] Indeed, it has been claimed that 'sectarian abuse and violence can manifest itself in a very visible and prominent way within Scottish football'.[2] In Liverpool, however, the football clubs are not associated with a particular side of the divide and the growth in their popularity divided the city on non-sectarian lines.[3] This chapter assesses the extent to which football in Liverpool constitutes the new godless religion. It begins, however, by assessing whether Liverpool *could* have gone the way of Glasgow in possessing two clubs with antagonistic support bases reinforcing an existing sectarian divide.

---

[1] See Advisory Group on Tackling Sectarianism in Scotland, 'Independent Advice'.

[2] The Scottish Executive (2006) 'Calling Full Time on Sectarianism'. Edinburgh: The Scottish Executive.

[3] Tom Williams, 23 March 2010.

The 'Green' of Goodison and 'Orange' of Anfield: Reality or Rhetoric?

There is a conviction in some quarters that, like in Glasgow, where 'Rangers and Celtic supporters drew/ [draw] upon their respective Protestant and Catholic allegiances to give a sharper edge to their rivalry',[4] the same is at least partially true for Liverpool. It has been traditionally claimed that Everton FC is 'the Catholic team' of Merseyside, whereas Liverpool FC is 'the Protestant team'. From a historical perspective, the proposition has a potential plausibility. Sectarianism was rife during the formative years of Liverpool's professional football clubs and the split of Everton FC resulted in drastically different make-ups of both the boardroom and shareholdings of the two clubs.

Everton FC and Liverpool FC were never religiously exclusive in terms of players or respective support bases. Nonetheless, sectarian bias has been alleged. Unlike Glasgow's Old Firm, associated with Catholic Irish identity (Celtic) or Protestant British Unionism (Rangers) (once seen as 'the establishment'),[5] Merseyside's divisions were never clear cut. Nonetheless, as Peter Day highlights (although he disputes whether it was ever the case), there was 'the belief that supporters and players of the two Liverpool football clubs were divided on sectarian lines with Liverpool being the Protestant team and Everton the Catholic'.[6] In 1996, an *Observer* article stated that Liverpool football clubs had 'shed sectarianism'.[7] As late as 2010, J.P. Dudgeon's study of Liverpool stated, 'Football is a religion. Everton is the Catholic team, Liverpool the Protestant, although it's nothing like as big a deal in a political or religious sense as Celtic and Rangers in Glasgow'.[8] Dudgeon provides no evidence of either team's professed religious partiality and is seemingly restating a regularly cited fallacy. Even more bemusing was Geoffrey Wheatcroft's 2004 assertion in the *Guardian*, that 'an echo of sectarian divisions can still be heard in football, so try not to confuse the two teams … Liverpool are the Catholic team … Everton are the Protestant team'.[9] The paper made the following correction two days later:

---

[4] Gallagher, 1987: 99.

[5] Walker, 2001: 48.

[6] Day, 2011: 112.

[7] Ibid., citing the *Observer*, 26 May 1996.

[8] Dudgeon, 2010: 153–4.

[9] G. Wheatcroft, 'Scouse for Cripes!: A Guide to Liverpool for the Truly Penitent'.

Several readers wrote in to point out that it was Liverpool who were traditionally the Protestant team and Everton the Catholic, and not the other way round, as we stated in this article. Many Liverpudlians insist that these affiliations now exist only as a memory and that sectarianism is repudiated in the city.[10]

It is noted that the paper did not rescind the claim of the football teams' religious connections, only that they had got it 'the other way round'.

Though it is necessary to point out that neither Dudgeon nor Wheatcroft are from Liverpool, and this might explain their misunderstanding, the belief of 'Catholic Everton' and 'Protestant Liverpool' (or at least that this was once the case) is still found within the city. Mike O'Brian, a Protestant and Evertonian, stated, 'People have separated football from religion, though they used to say that before every Everton game they used to have a priest in blessing the ball and that all spare kits went to St Francis Xavier's [Catholic] school'.[11] Likewise, Alf Mullins, another Protestant and Evertonian, recalled, 'People would say "Why are you supporting them?" They never then said, "They're bloody Catholics", but I knew what they meant. Everton did have Irish players, but you can't put a label of Catholicism on a club based on that'.[12]

Nonetheless, such labels were attached. David Kennedy has cited this point being made by Liverpool celebrities such as Cilla Black, who, in 2002, commented, 'In Liverpool, even in the two-ups and two-downs, most Protestants were Conservative and most Catholics were Labour, just as Everton was the Catholic team and Liverpool the "Proddy-Dog" one'.[13] The same year, football sociologist John Williams wrote, 'People "dressed" their houses to advertise Cup Final footballing allegiances, though my Mum would never allow my brother's Evertonian blue to go up in case neighbours or passers-by mistakenly took us for Catholics'.[14] Liverpool-born Tommy Smith, a Roman Catholic, stated that 'Catholics were traditionally Everton

Guardian (22 October 2004). Available at: www.theguardian.com/politics/2004/oct/20/conservatives.media1.

[10] Ibid.

[11] Mike O'Brian, 12 November 2012.

[12] Alf Mullins, 14 May 2012.

[13] *Liverpool Echo*, 17 December 2002, cited by Kennedy, 'Red and Blue and Orange and Green?' Everton Season 2009–10. Available at: www.toffeeweb.com/season/09-10/comment/fan/RedBlueGreenOrange.pdf.

[14] Williams, 2002: 10, cited ibid.

supporters and players, Liverpool were the Protestant team. [A friend] honestly thought that being a Catholic I wouldn't be happy at Anfield'.[15] Yet, Smith was a boyhood Red.[16] He went on to play for Liverpool, making 638 appearances between 1962 and 1978. He also captained the team and won many honours with them. Bishop Tom Williams also recalls allegations of religious partiality in Merseyside football. Although, like many others, he refutes them:

> You still get people who think that Everton is the Catholic team and Liverpool is a Protestant team, which isn't true. Everton and Liverpool football clubs were both founded by a Methodist church. Everton were not a Catholic club and Liverpool were not Orange Lodge. Of the three main people at Everton (Mahon, Cuff, and Baxter) two were Methodist and one was Catholic. Liverpool's first team, the old Macs, may have been mostly Orange Lodge, but they were never promoted as an 'Orange Lodge team'.[17]

The linkage of religious and football affiliations is also recalled by politicians from the city. Steve Rotheram MP said of the link between football and religion on Merseyside: 'it was [in existence], but it's not [anymore] … it was still there in the early sixties, but by the time I can remember (the late sixties early seventies), I never felt it was there. Today, there are as many Catholics who go to worship at Anfield as there are Protestants who worship at Goodison'.[18] Andy Burham MP recalls the Everton/Celtic and Liverpool/Rangers connection, which, as others also evoke, was often demonstrated in the donning of 'ski-hats' in blue–green (Everton–Celtic/Catholic) or red–blue (Liverpool–Rangers/Protestant), common for a time in the 1980s, although red–green hats (Liverpool–Celtic) were also prominent. He added,

> My children go to Catholic schools and so often teachers and head teachers are Evertonians within Catholic schools, I promise you, but it's melting away. People even say the opposite: 'Rangers and Everton have a connection and so do Liverpool and Celtic'. It has kind of gone

---

[15] Smith and Stuckey, 1980: 1, cited ibid.
[16] Liverpool FC (website), 'Tommy Smith: Profile'. Available at: www.liverpoolfc.com/history/past-players/tommy-smith.
[17] Bishop Tom Williams, 23 March 2010.
[18] Steve Rotheram, 4 January 2013.

with the mists of time, though I've never met a priest who supported Liverpool.[19]

Peter Kilfoyle MP (1991–2010) recalls, 'I used to get it in Parliament: "Oh yeah, you're an Evertonian – the Catholics." I'd say, "No, my uncle Willy was Catholic. He was an avid Liverpudlian. He'd die for Liverpool!" … I have never seen the football clubs as being identified with one [religion] or the other'.[20] However, Nadine Dorries MP recalled, 'in the fifties and sixties Everton were Catholic and Liverpool were Protestant … My Catholic family in Liverpool are all mad Everton supporters. I think it is still there to a degree. I don't think it's gone completely. I think there are still stronger, residual Catholic elements who are Everton supporters than Liverpool supporters'.[21] John Pugh MP gives a different interpretation of the situation:

> There was a loose belief that Catholics supported Everton and Protestants supported Liverpool, but I think people who follow football sat very loose on those sorts of issues. I grew up knowing some people are Evertonian, some people are Liverpudlians, but I didn't take that back to their religion. I never took it as 'Oh, he's an Evertonian, he must be a Catholic'. We talked about it, but it was never anything like, at any stage, the Celtic/ Rangers thing. There was nothing ever fundamental at Everton or Liverpool games except the football itself.[22]

George Orr, a member of the *Everton Heritage Society*, who was born and brought up in Liverpool, comments,

> Personally, all my family are from Northern Ireland and are all Protestant, not Orange Lodge, just normal Protestants. I was never told 'You can't watch Everton because they're a Catholic club'. There was nothing like that at all. They knew the southern Ireland connection in the 1950s, that's where the myth came from. Peter Farrell, Eglington, all these came over from the south of Ireland, maybe five or six players who were the backbone of the Everton team. You've got a lot of priests and nuns who would come along and watch the game. It was well known. They were in the stands and they could be seen, but it never got down to the schools or

[19] Andy Burnham, 28 March 2013.
[20] Peter Kilfoyle, 23 January 2012.
[21] Nadine Dorries, 13 March 2013.
[22] John Pugh, 23 March 2013.

the workplaces. It was not like Glasgow, where you can't watch Rangers if you're a Catholic and the other way round. Here, you support who you like.[23]

As David Kennedy notes, whether correct or not, 'a sectarian division between Everton and Liverpool football clubs is, for some, an irrefutable part of local football culture … For most, however, sectarian affiliation is more urban myth than reality: a tribal impulse amongst some fans to shore up and sharpen their identity by suggesting a deeper meaning to support for the two clubs'.[24] While 'orthodox opinion lies with the latter viewpoint',[25] the local understanding of the allegation has traditionally been that Everton was Catholic and Liverpool was Protestant.

One objector to Geoffrey Wheatcroft's *Guardian* article, Mark Hoskisson, 'an ex-Catholic but forever an Evertonian', did give credence to the alleged connection between football and sectarianism, offering an explanation for Everton's purported Catholic connection:

> [Although] the sectarian divide between the teams no longer exists except as a memory … the origins of Everton's Catholic support lie in the late 19th century when Dr Baxter, a prominent Catholic doctor and a leading light in the Catholic community, joined the Everton board. He brought with him the thousands of Irish Catholic families from the Scotland Road area who duly became Everton supporters, despite Everton's origins as a Methodist team (the old St Domingo's) … The Catholic dimension was maintained in various ways at Everton, not least in the 1950s when the core of the Everton team hailed from the Republic of Ireland.[26]

In contrast, two other letters in response to the *Guardian* article did not concede that sectarianism had ever been a factor of Merseyside football. Paul Tollet insisted that the claim of Everton and Liverpool's religious allegiances is an 'uncorroborated statement … Merseyside derbies have been famously trouble free due to the fact that there are no common divides between the

---

[23] George Orr, 7 November 2013.

[24] Kennedy, 2011: 552.

[25] Ibid.

[26] Kenrick, M. 'Catholic or Protestant? Is There any Truth to the Assertion that Supporting Everton is Related to One's Religious Background or Up-Bringing? [referencing a published letter in response to Geoffrey Wheatcroft's *Guardian* article, by Mark Hoskisson, 20 October 2004]. ToffeeWeb. Available at: www.toffeeweb.com/fans/beingblue/religion.asp.

two clubs, not geographic, social [or] religious. There isn't even a division by family with hardened Evertonian families having Reds amongst them and vice versa'.[27] Steve Rooney made similar comments:

> My own predominantly Catholic family has always been split between Red and Blue. Likewise, there are plenty of big Protestant families who are similarly divided in their support for the two clubs. One of the reasons that Everton and Liverpool have, mercifully, been able to maintain a relatively healthy, and for the most part friendly, rivalry is precisely because – unlike Glasgow – our footballing allegiances are in no way rooted in divisive sectarian religious differences.[28]

What is certainly true is that both teams can trace their roots back to the same Protestant chapel. St Domingo Football Club was formed from a Methodist Church in 1878. A year later, following better players from other congregations joining, the club changed its name to Everton FC (although the club was never based in Everton many of its players were from the locality, a predominantly Protestant area). The club was soon attracting attention from the Liverpool populace (Catholic and Protestant). As David and Peter Kennedy suggest, Everton FC was 'a cultural institution that enjoyed prestige and widespread support among all sections of Liverpool society'.[29]

Before the start of the 1881/2 season, Everton appointed their first club president, John Houlding (an Orangeman), who secured their residence at Anfield. Everton grew in strength and their standing led them to become one of the twelve founding members of the football league in 1888. Walvin argues that, 'by the 1890s the city had become the football centre of England, with Everton winning the league by 1891',[30] appealing to all segments of the local populace.

In addition to his Orange affiliations, John Houlding, a local businessman (brewer), was Chairman of the Everton Conservative Association, a Conservative councillor from 1884 and Alderman in 1895. Although 'his money and enterprise were largely responsible for the rise of Everton as one of the country's premier teams',[31] Houlding's 'ambition began to drive a

---

[27] P. Tollet, Letter to Geoffrey Wheatcroft, 20 October 2004, ibid.
[28] S. Rooney, Letter to Geoffrey Wheatcroft, 20 October 2004, ibid.
[29] Kennedy and Kennedy, 2007: 905.
[30] Walvin, 1994: 88.
[31] Ibid.

wedge between himself and the [Everton FC] committee'.[32] As Everton's distinction increased he began to charge higher rents and higher interest on loans, prompting a rift. The rupture was also based on both the club's 'governance structure' and a 'moral and political split over drink',[33] but was not 'sectarian-derived'.[34]

Following the split, Everton moved to Mere Green Field, which became Goodison Park. John Houlding subsequently attempted to reform the club on his own terms, but was overruled by the Football Association.[35] Houlding opted to rename his team, substituting 'Everton' for 'Liverpool'. The club also originally played in blue and white. As an Orangeman, it makes little sense that Houlding would attempt to adopt the name and colour of a team which was associated with Catholicism. Moreover, Everton's celebrations, to mark the move to Goodison Park, included a concert by a military band,[36] suggesting that any latent Irish nationalist sympathies were not significant enough to dispel association with British armed forces. As Kennedy and Collins observe:

> One important political aspect that was notable by its absence from the dispute was sectarianism between Catholics and Protestants ... Despite the high-profile bitterness of the dispute, the question of Catholicism was not a defining issue in the football crisis – indeed, a split within Protestant ranks over the drinks issue was to be the decisive one ... [Importantly], amongst the ruling committee members of Everton FC there was just one Catholic (J.C. Baxter), the rest were Protestants.[37]

David Kennedy notes that, in relation to Bootle FC, Everton FC, Liverpool FC, and Liverpool Caledonians FC (four of the most prominent Merseyside teams in 1892), 'directors from Church of England background were predominant'[38] and that 'the shared Presbyterianism of many of the clubs' major figures could be argued to have been a unifying force'.[39] Nonetheless, Everton FC and Liverpool FC adopted two different approaches to governance structures, which reflected a political divide:

[32] Lupson, 2006: 66.
[33] Kennedy and Collins, 2006: 778.
[34] Ibid., 770–1.
[35] Lupson, 2006: 66.
[36] Ibid., 67.
[37] Kennedy and Collins, 2006: 76, 771.
[38] Kennedy, 2005: 849.
[39] Kennedy and Kennedy, 2007: 897.

The political differences between Houlding and Mahon were broadly reflected among leading members at this time. On the Conservative side were Houlding, Simon Jude and Edwin Berry; the Liberals, led by George Mahon, included Dr James Clement Baxter, William Claydon and Will Cuff.[40]

As John Williams writes, 'Everton had a more democratic structure, and the Goodison club was more amenable to supporter input'.[41] In 1902, 'the ten serving directors of Everton FC owned only 7 per cent of its shares. At Liverpool FC ... the eight serving directors owned 56 per cent of the club shares'.[42] Necessarily, this contrast had an effect in terms of the influence of those running the clubs and 'there were differences between the club boardrooms with respect to religious background. For example, the Liverpool FC directors were almost exclusively Church of England, whereas there was a much more diverse variation of religious backgrounds amongst the directors of Everton FC'.[43] Paul Wharton, Chairman of Everton Heritage, suggests:

> If you looked at anybody as being 'the religious team', then you'd have to say Liverpool was that. John Houlding and John McKenna were both Orangemen and they set up Liverpool when we came to Goodison. [At Everton] the St Domingo influence lasted until 1949 when Cuff died. He was the last Domingon. As far as I'm concerned, Everton have been open to all religions and all creeds.[44]

From its formation, Liverpool FC was dominated by Protestants – even if this did not extend to the terraces – and it has been asserted that 'the amount of people involved in the ownership and control of Liverpool who were also key figures in the WMCA (the vanguard of anti-Catholic politics) is quite remarkable'.[45] In addition to Houlding, other influential figures in Liverpool's formation such as John McKenna (an Irish Protestant), Edwin Berry, and Benjamin Bailey all had links with the WMCA and the Orange Order.[46] Likewise, in its embryonic period, many players for Liverpool FC

[40] Corbett, 2012: 367.
[41] Williams, 2011: 125.
[42] Kennedy and Collins, 2006: 778.
[43] Kennedy, 2005: 849.
[44] Paul Wharton, 7 November 2013.
[45] Kennedy, 2011: 556.
[46] Ibid.

were Scottish Presbyterians. As James Walvin explains, 'Houlding with a pitch and no team ... turned to Scotland for a totally new team, forming, in 1892, Liverpool FC (known, for obvious reasons, as the "team of Macs")'.[47] Under Houlding, Liverpool FC did have a predominantly Protestant edifice, but this situation began to change after 1902:

> At Liverpool FC, the 'Houlding' period – does seem to be defined by a pronounced Tory Party–Masonic Protestant profile. In the context of sectarian tensions in Liverpool society at this juncture, this does lend some weight to the often-made claims concerning the historical sectarian division between Everton and Liverpool football clubs. However, after Houlding's death in 1902, and the restructuring of the club – including a vast growth in share ownership – any obstacle that may have been placed in the path of Catholics achieving a position as director of the club seems to have been removed. Three Catholics – John Joseph Hill, Thomas Crampton, and William Harvey Webb – joined the Liverpool board in the years following the shake-up.[48]

If Houlding was the most obvious connection between Orangeism and Liverpool FC, perhaps Dr James Clement Baxter, a director, later Chairman, and a prominent Liberal Catholic, who financed much of the building of Goodison Park, was the most identifiable link between Everton and Irish Catholicism.[49] In contrast to Liverpool FC's Protestant constituents, 'frequent press reports of directors James Clement Baxter and Alfred Wade attending Irish Nationalist League meetings would have underlined for the public a sense of the general sectarian tone of the men inhabiting the Everton boardroom'.[50] Another Everton director, William Witford, was also described as 'an ardent home-ruler'.[51] Although George Mahon was a 'staunch Methodist and organist at St Domingo parish church',[52] he was also an advocate of Irish Home Rule.[53] Although born in Liverpool, he was 'brought up and educated in Ireland'.[54]

[47] Walvin, 1994: 89.
[48] Kennedy and Kennedy, 2007: 906–7.
[49] Corbett, 2012: 38.
[50] Kennedy, 'Red and Blue and Orange and Green?' Everton Season 2009–10. Available at: www.toffeeweb.com/season/09-10/comment/fan/RedBlueGreenOrange.pdf.
[51] Kennedy, 2011: 554.
[52] Corbett, 2012: 367.
[53] Kennedy, 2011: 555.
[54] Corbett, 2012: 367.

Everton's Catholic label of repute and Liverpool's Protestant label derived from this juncture of each club's histories. At the end of the nineteenth century, regardless of their religion, Everton directors were Liberal and as such were advocates of Irish Home Rule, while Liverpool's Board were mainly Protestant Conservatives. Nonetheless, as Kennedy argues, such a 'demonstrable difference in terms of attitude to religious [and political] affairs between the clubs at boardroom level' did not 'translate into the clubs operating along sectarian lines'.[55] Instead:

> All available evidence points toward a non-partisan approach to community relations by the clubs, with neither Everton nor Liverpool predominantly favouring one particular religious denomination over another ... More typical of Everton and Liverpool's community support, however, was their aiding of secular causes, such as alms-giving to local hospitals ... They also appear to have taken an interest in alleviating the hardship of the local labour force in periods of economic downturn.[56]

In 1909, the final of the Catholic Charity Cup, between St Bridget's YMS (Young Men's Society) and St Francis de Sales, was held at Goodison Park, 'gathering over one thousand spectators'.[57] The same year, the Catholic School Cup final, between St James's and St Alban's, was held at Anfield, also attracting a 'large gathering'.[58] If it had been true that Liverpool FC was a 'Protestant club', surely it would not have hosted such an event, let alone in 1909, when religious tensions were so high in Liverpool.

The issue of whether or not Liverpool FC was 'Orange' is contested within the ranks of the Orange Institution itself. Grand Master Ron Bather believes that, 'primarily, Liverpool was a very Protestant football club, as virtually all the initial team that played for Liverpool were all Scottish Presbyterian religion',[59] although he acknowledges that, as the twentieth century progressed, this became less apparent. Lodge Master and Liverpool fan Dave Hughes suggests that, 'The Orange connection between the Orange Institution and Liverpool Football Club was very, very firm at one time'.[60] On the other hand, when Billy Tritton, a Bootle Orangeman who

---

[55] Kennedy, 2011: 557.
[56] Ibid., 560.
[57] *Liverpool Catholic Herald*, 8 May 1909.
[58] Ibid.
[59] Ron Bather, 15 March 2010.
[60] Dave Hughes, 24 January 2013.

has been in the Institution since 1932 (also a Liverpool FC fan), was asked, 'Would everybody in the lodge in your day have been a Liverpool fan?' he responded, 'Oh no! There was a lot of Evertonians and there still are in the lodge today. Alex Stevenson, who played for Everton, was in the Institution as well'.[61]

Alex Stevenson was an international who played for Everton from 1934 to 1949 and Bootle from 1949 to 1950. He attained seventeen caps for Northern Ireland, in addition to seven playing for Éire. Everton had bought him from Rangers. Corbett claims that 'no Irish Catholic has played for Rangers since Stevenson's departure'.[62] Yet the *Scotsman* states that 'Alex Stevenson, despite sharing the religious persuasion of the then vast majority of the club's support, attracted much grief from those [Rangers] fans when turning out for them as an Irishman in the 1930s'.[63] This suggests that Stevenson was a Protestant. Certainly, it would have been odd for an Irish Catholic to have played for Rangers at this time. Additionally, both the *Scotsman* and the *Daily Record* claim that it was not until 2013 that Rangers signed their first Irish Catholic player in Jon Daly.[64] In seeking to clarify Stevenson's religion, contact was made with his nephew, Paul Stevenson Wade, who responded, 'Yes, Alex was my uncle, and brother of my late mother, Mable. He was born and raised in the north Dublin City areas of East Wall/ North Strand/ Fairview. He was baptised into the Church of Ireland/ Protestant religion'.[65] Therefore, Tritton's recollection of Alex Stevenson's presence in a Bootle lodge is a credible proposition.

Billy Tritton also directly disputed the suggestion of religious partiality in Merseyside football, arguing, 'There's as many Roman Catholics as there are

[61] Billy Tritton, 12 March 2013.

[62] Corbett, 2012: 543, Little evidence has been found supporting the suggesting that Alex Stevenson was Catholic. In contrast, web resources repeatedly claim that he was, in fact, an Irish Protestant. It may have been the case that Corbett is basing Stevenson's alleged 'Catholicism' on his commitment to the Republic of Ireland, whom he subsequently managed after leaving Bootle. He was born in Dublin, though gained caps for the Protestant dominated northern team.

[63] A. Smith, 'John Daly Could be Rangers' First Irish Catholic Player'. *Scotsman* (29 March 2013). Available at: www.scotsman.com/sport/football/latest/john-daly-could-be-rangers-first-irish-catholic-player-1-2865146.

[64] Ibid.; H. Keevins 'Dundee United Star Jon Daly: I'd Have No Problem Becoming First Irish Catholic to Play for Rangers'. *Daily Record* (29 March 2013). Available at: www.dailyrecord.co.uk/sport/football/football-news/dundee-united-star-jon-daly-1791101.

[65] Email correspondence with Paul Stevenson Wade, 14 January 2014.

Protestants watching both of the teams. It's not like Celtic and Rangers'.[66] Doris Bennett, a former lodge member and Evertonian, recalled how many in the Institution were Evertonians: 'Years ago, mainly Catholics played for Everton and mainly Protestants played for Liverpool. That's what it was, but you only have to look at where Everton is situated to disprove it. St Luke's [situated in the corner of Goodison Park], is a Church of England church'.[67]

Importantly, the leadership of both Liverpool and Bootle Orange Institution are also split in terms of their individual football affiliation. Keith Allcock, Chief Steward of Bootle Province, comments, 'There is not one team that represent just one religion. In Glasgow, it stands out a lot. They've got a team for each of them, but in Liverpool it hasn't been like that. I'm only a Liverpudlian because I lived close to Anfield'.[68] Tommy Buckley, Grand Master of Bootle, added, 'I'm an Evertonian because my mate Billy took me to the Everton matches. My eldest son is a Liverpudlian, my middle son is an Evertonian, and my youngest son is a Liverpudlian. It's nothing to do with religion. It's just the fact it's their team'.[69] The Grand Master of England, Ron Bather, is a Liverpool fan, while Grand Master of Liverpool, Billy Owens, is an Everton fan. As noted, Bather emphasised that support for both clubs was 'mixed', while stating that the teams were 'perceived to be' religiously partisan.[70] Owens, commenting on Everton's alleged Catholic disposition, said, 'I never considered that it was a Catholic team or a Protestant team'.[71]

Original research supports the suggestion of 'mixed' support for the Merseyside clubs, by the membership of the Orange Institution. Of a surveyed 215 members, 27.2 per cent stated that they were Evertonians, while 42.1 per cent stated they were Liverpudlians. Some 21.7 per cent of the selections were made for Rangers (many ticked two boxes, coupling their support for a Merseyside team with the Glasgow club). A further 9 per cent stated that they supported a different or no team.[72] Despite the Orange Order's schism in terms of football affiliation, Bather contends that, 'When I used to follow Liverpool in the sixties and seventies, every home game, you would have the [Orange] flutes playing on the Kop [terrace]'.[73]

[66] Billy Tritton, 12 March 2013.
[67] Doris Bennett, 5 March 2013.
[68] Keith Allcock, 12 March 2013.
[69] Tom Buckley, 12 March 2013.
[70] Ron Bather, 15 March 2010.
[71] Billy Owens, 15 March 2010.
[72] See Appendix 4.1, Section C results.
[73] Ron Bather, 15 March 2010.

Yet, other Liverpool attendees interviewed, such as Steve Rotherham MP, Cliff Whittingham, and Ian Woods, had no such recollection. Whittingham recalled a Kop chant which indicated the religious mix:

> I remember distinctly around 1984–6, fashion and football go hand in hand (well, in Liverpool they do). The fashion, at the time, was to have another club's colours half and half with your club and you either chose Rangers or Celtic, and every week on the Kop, without fail, the shout would go up: 'Rangers!–Celtic!–Rangers!–Celtic!' I was always siding with Rangers, just by default, being Protestant. Whether it was just in my imagination or because I was shouting it, 'Rangers' always did seem louder. When I asked about this I was told that Liverpool were supposedly the Protestant club, as opposed to Everton who were the Catholic club.[74]

When Rotheram was asked about hearing 'flutes in the Kop end', he responded:

> Never, no, though there did used to be a chant in the seventies-eighties of 'Celtic–Rangers'. In other words, the Catholic half of the Kop and the Protestant half would divide, and one would shout 'Celtic' and the other would shout 'Rangers', but I haven't heard that for decades now. We also used to sell scarves, half Liverpool-half-Celtic and half Liverpool-half-Rangers.[75]

This chant extended to Everton FC. Andy Burnham MP has similar recollections from Goodison: 'In my youth, people used to chant "Rangers–Celtic" at games'.[76]

The former Everton manager, Howard Kendall, recalls Everton–Celtic hats even when signing in the 1960s.[77] Considering Everton's tendency to sign players from Éire, this is unsurprising. Councillor Mike Murphy recalls 'seeing a lot of priests at Goodison'.[78] Despite a sizeable Irish contingent consistently following both teams, Everton 'established a frequent supply line in Irish talent, a connection so rich as to be described as an Éireann tradition'.[79]

---

[74] Clifford Whittingham, 10 January 2014.

[75] Steve Rotheram, 4 January 2013.

[76] Andy Burnham, 28 March 2013.

[77] Howard Kendall, 17 November 2010.

[78] Michael Murphy, 8 April 2013.

[79] Kennedy, 'Red and Blue and Orange and Green?' Everton Season 2009–10. Available at: www.toffeeweb.com/season/09-10/comment/fan/RedBlueGreenOrange.pdf.

In contrast, it was claimed that 'Ireland was a virtually untapped market for Liverpool FC until the end of the twentieth century [while], the impact of Scottish players and managerial staff is arguably unequalled at Anfield'.[80] Some believe diverging scouting patterns to be the raison d'être for the teams' supposed ethno-religious connections. Bishop Tom Williams claims, 'the reason people think that every priest in Liverpool is an Evertonian is because in the fifties Tommy Eglington and most of the other players were Irish. Billy Bingham though was a Northern Ireland Protestant [Everton player 1961–3, Everton manager 1973–7].[81] Joe Benton MP directly links Everton's Irish contingent with its 'Catholic' label:

> One of the reasons Everton got the Catholic tag is that we had three or four Irish clubs that we got players from. Other clubs did too … They were good hunting grounds. I think because there were so many Irishmen in the side at one particular time Everton got that tag – Farrell, Eglington, Cummins, O'Neill – At one time there were six or seven Irish internationals in the Everton team … but it would be totally wrong to make a comparison between Everton and Liverpool and Celtic and Rangers.[82]

Nonetheless, Corbett writes that 'Everton possessed so many Irish players in the mid-1950s that there was a contemporaneous joke that twenty minutes could pass without a Protestant touching the ball'.[83] Tommy Eglington himself emphasised Everton's connection with Éire in recalling his playing days: 'Back in the fifties, Everton was the team in Ireland. We had a number of Irish players then and the boats would be full of fans coming over every Friday night to watch us'.[84] Everton's tendency to recruit from Ireland was long-standing. This, coupled with the Home Rule sympathies of some of its original board members, may explain the alleged predisposition of the *Liverpool Catholic Herald* to publish comment on Everton and Everton Reserve fixtures ahead of Liverpool fixtures.[85]

[80]   Ibid.

[81]   Tom Williams, 23 March 2010, Notably, Bingham attended the same primary school as Ian Paisley Junior.

[82]   Joe Benton, 18 May 2012.

[83]   Corbett, 2012: 283.

[84]   Ibid., 162, citing Tommy Eglington.

[85]   Cited by Billy Smith, who has done a significant proportion of archival research in various Liverpool newspapers: author of 'The Blue Correspondence', Discussion in St Luke's Church, Goodison Road, 1 February 2014.

David Kennedy adds that connections with 'Dundalk and Dublin teams Shamrock Rovers and Shelbourne', which reaped a 'harvest of Irish talent', were supplemented by 'the employment of former Manchester United captain and Irish international John Carey as manager in 1958 [which] gave the team a distinctive "Hibernian" flavour'. This contrasted with 'some talk of a less welcoming attitude towards Irish-born players at Liverpool', who scarcely signed an Irish player until their recruitments of a 'host of Irish internationals in the 1980s',[86] which, ironically, resulted in Everton's 'popularity in Ireland being taken over by Liverpool'.[87] Since their inception, Liverpool have had 'a staggering 149 Scots-born players who went on to play first-team football' compared with only twenty-eight first team players from Ireland.[88] Nonetheless, Liverpool has always employed Roman Catholic playing staff and enjoyed support from Liverpool's Catholic population. Liverpool's Scottish signings were not exclusively Protestant, the arrival of the devout Catholic Matt Busby in the 1930s providing one such example. Liverpool also readily recruited players from local Catholic backgrounds, including players such as Gerry Byrne, who attracted the club's attention whilst playing for the Liverpool Catholic Schoolboys team.[89] Everton similarly recruited Scottish players of different religions.

Further evidence dismissing the teams' supposed ethno-religious affiliations is offered by former Everton FC player and manager, Howard Kendall, who could 'not recall any religious talk, between players or staff [as] concentration was entirely on being together and winning the football match'.[90] When questioned about Liverpool's Protestant label and Everton's Catholic label, Kendall replied, 'the only thing I can say is that it was never on my mind when Everton came in for me. I'm Church of England. It was never mentioned. I was never asked questions about it. Harry Catterick, the manager who signed me, never asked a religious question'.[91] These contrast with the Glasgow experience of Liverpool-born Alan Stubbs, a Celtic player between 1996 and 2001, who claims of his time at the club: 'Being Church of England ... It could have been a problem had it got out. It was all quite hush hush ... The club wanted that all kept quiet – the line was that I didn't really

---

[86] Kennedy, 2011: 558.

[87] Corbett, 2011: 283.

[88] Kennedy, 2011: 559.

[89] Ibid.

[90] Howard Kendall, 17 November 2010.

[91] Ibid.

go to church ... and the press officer would dead bat any other question about religion away'.[92] Howard Kendall also commented on the absence of sectarian consideration in scouting patterns at Everton: 'When you go and sign a player, you don't ask questions about religion or anything, you only ask, "can he play?" You'd delve into a player's character. You'd see if he had a reputation of him being a problem to his former club, but you wouldn't delve into his religion'.[93]

Ironically, given the Protestant label once (largely erroneously) applied to Liverpool, the current situation is that, as Peter Kilfoyle suggests, 'today Liverpool would say they have a special relationship with Celtic'.[94] Burnham also makes this point, 'Football fashions do change a bit. Liverpool played Celtic a lot and we bought Duncan Ferguson and a few other players from Rangers'.[95] Orr agrees that 'Liverpool, at this time, are more associated with Celtic'.[96] This is a connection which aggravates some Orangemen, such as Dave Hughes, who stress the affiliation between Liverpool FC and Northern Ireland Protestants. Hughes claims, 'the LFC and Celtic connection comes from "You'll Never Walk Alone". Both teams use it'.[97] Everton FC also shares the 'Grand Old Team' anthem with Celtic. Hughes adds that 'Northern Ireland Protestants generally support Liverpool and Northern Ireland Catholics generally support Manchester United',[98] which intuitively rings true but is lacking empirical confirmation. Lynn Hughes agrees: 'On a Saturday, the Derry Club is full of lads from lodges coming over for the Liverpool match'.[99] A similar claim (which substituted Manchester United for Everton), was made by Belfast-born Billy Smylie, who suggested, 'In the seventies and eighties mostly Rangers fans followed Liverpool and I think it came from Loyalists from Belfast coming to watch Liverpool. At Everton, there were a lot of Republican fans. You used to get a lot of Ulster flags flown at Anfield'.[100]

Yet, even if we were to take as a given that this was once the case (and it is unlikely that things have ever been so clear cut), evidence suggests that both

[92] Stubbs, 2013: 103.
[93] Howard Kendall, 17 November 2010.
[94] Peter Kilfoyle, 23 January 2012.
[95] Andy Burnham, 28 March 2013.
[96] George Orr, 7 November 2013.
[97] Dave Hughes, 10 March 2013.
[98] Ibid.
[99] Lynn Hughes, 10 March 2013.
[100] William John Smylie, 18 January 2014.

Everton and Liverpool enjoy support from the entirety of the island of Ireland, both clubs having numerous supporters' associations in both the Republic of Ireland and Northern Ireland.[101] In addition, Dave Hughes concedes that, 'both Everton and Liverpool are supported by the membership of the Orange Institution'.[102] He also contrasted the Liverpool situation with Edinburgh (Hearts over Hibs), Glasgow (Rangers over Celtic), and Northern Ireland (Linfield over long-defunct Belfast Celtic), where members of the Orange Order would overwhelmingly favour one club over the other. Moreover, Cliff Whittingham does not agree that Celtic's association with Liverpool FC is purely down to the shared association of 'You'll never walk alone'. He highlights the offer of friendship by Celtic in 1989:

> The first thing that happened after Hillsborough, on the football pitch, was that Glasgow Celtic was the first club to offer their hand of friendship as regards playing: a friendly match in Glasgow. That day made me think, 'I'll never have a bad word to say about Celtic'. Celtic made us so welcome that day. They looked after everyone. They had consideration. It's worthy of note, that day there was no away section. The whole of Celtic's ground was like, 'Come in and we'll look after you'. Now considering that we were known as the Protestant club and the Rangers bias – Rangers scarves probably outsold Celtic two to one – when we went to Celtic that day there wasn't an ounce of trouble.[103]

The few authors who have studied Liverpool and Everton in recent decades reject religious partiality. George Orr insisted he 'can't see anything at all now that would make Everton or Liverpool a Protestant or Catholic club'.[104] Likewise, football historian Peter Lupson commented, 'People say Everton and Liverpool were biased to one faith or the other, but, in reality, they just never were. Both clubs signed Catholics and both clubs signed Protestants. They also enjoyed a very healthy relationship with each other'.[105] Greg Quiery, a Northern Ireland-born Catholic, and a researcher on the Liverpool Irish, distinguishes between the role of football in Liverpool

---

[101] See Everton FC (website), 'Supporters' Clubs Directory'. Available at: www.evertonfc.com/tickets/regional-branches-directory.html; Liverpool FC (website), 'LFC Official Supporters Clubs'. Available at: www.liverpoolfc.com/fans/lfc-official-supporters-clubs.

[102] Dave Hughes, 10 March 2013.

[103] Cliff Whittingham, 10 January 2014.

[104] George Orr, 7 November 2013.

[105] Discussion with Peter Lupson (author of *Thank God for Football* and *Across the Park*), in St Luke's Church, Goodison Road, 1 February 2014.

and Glasgow: 'In Glasgow, the whole football culture there is a continuing driving force for sectarianism. It might well be an engine which keeps the conflict going, [whereas] I've never found any evidence of sectarianism in Liverpool football or even a particular ethnic group, within Liverpool, supporting either team'.[106]

As such, David Kennedy argues, that the stark political parallels between the clubs in their early histories mean that 'claims of a religious schism cannot simply be dismissed as the product of a tendency among some supporters to look for convenient binary opposites'.[107] Nonetheless, he highlights the absence of discriminatory policies in recruitment patterns to attain that 'there is no compelling argument to sustain the case that football on Merseyside followed the path taken in Glasgow or Belfast',[108] insisting that 'the claim of religious differences has little or no meaning in defining the relationship of the modern-day Everton and Liverpool football clubs'.[109] As Tommy Buckley, Grand Master of Bootle's Orange Institution, puts it, 'It's nothing to do with religion. It's football'.[110] Given this, football in Liverpool held the potential to unite, rather than polarise, the population in love of a common pastime.

The Role of Football in Dispelling Sectarianism

As early as 1932, Liverpool's Lord Mayor observed that Liverpool and Everton football clubs had done more 'to cement good fellowship ... than anything said or done in the last 25 years'.[111] Given the raw sectarianism still evident in the inter-war years, the Mayor's comment was significant. It highlighted the potential of football to unite people in the city, reducing animosities to those of the benign, merely sporting, variety. This section examines the extent to which shared passions for football and strong support for Liverpool or Everton began to displace the local populace's obsessions with religious affiliations. Put simply, did 'red or blue' replace 'orange or green' as primary badges of identification?

---

[106]   Greg Quiery, 25 March 2013.

[107]   Kennedy, 2011: 560.

[108]   Ibid.

[109]   Kennedy, 2011: 552.

[110]   Tommy Buckley, 12 March 2013.

[111]   Kennedy, 2011: 561, citing Lord Mayor Cross, *Liverpool Echo*, 5 January 1932.

It would require considerable change to supplant a city's culture based upon religious rivalry. As Greg Quiery notes,

> Once Orangeism becomes a deeply embedded part of working class culture, passed down from grandfather to father from father to son, coupled with all the music, mythology, ceremonies, and festivals that go with it, it's very hard to break down. It's something which goes right through people's culture. Similarly, on the Catholic side, the Catholic parish structure was an all-embracing culture, which catered for your every need.[112]

So what could break down such sturdy identities? What helped displace the music, mythology, ceremonies, and festivals? Maria O'Reilly is one of many in Liverpool who believe, 'for a lot of people, football is the new religion'.[113] Steve Higginson argues, 'Football has always been a religion. Identity with the football teams has got greater as religion has declined'.[114]

Reverend John Williams agrees that football became 'a great inspiration' and a distraction away from poverty and ethno-religious identity: 'People had nothing, so they needed something. They needed a purpose. Football became the new purpose'.[115] In place of ethnic and religious distinctions, Everton and Liverpool helped to 'bolster weakly felt local identity – to act as community totems'.[116] Noting that 'there were many efforts made to get rid of sectarianism' by diversion into sporting pursuits, Bishop Tom Williams attests, 'We have football to support local communities, to support local kids, to give the ideal that you represent your school, your town, or your local colours'.[117] Had Everton and Liverpool been formed along competing ethno-religious lines then things could have been much different, but support for either team was not conditioned by such affinity. As such, football culture would come to displace sectarian culture.

The leading football clubs took prominence over local sporting alternatives. Despite their existence, neither Gaelic sports, nor Irish Catholic football teams, were promoted in Liverpool by either the Catholic Church, Nationalist politicians, or a sizeable enough proportion of the Catholic

---

[112] Greg Quiery, 25 March 2013.
[113] Maria O'Reilly, 15 March 2013.
[114] Steve Higginson, 11 February 2013.
[115] John Williams, 17 November 2010.
[116] Kennedy, 2011: 566.
[117] Tom Williams, 23 March 2010.

community to challenge the emerging dominance of Everton and Liverpool FC.[118] The Catholic community did not become directly associated with a particular sporting outlet and as such sectarianism would not have a sporting outlet in the city. This contrasted with the situation in Glasgow and Belfast.

It could have been that religious affiliations and sport divided the city. In 1885, 'some 25 of the 112 clubs playing in the city had connections with religious organisations'.[119] Yet despite the 'spate of Irish teams' that emerged in the 1880s and 1890s, such as Bootle Celtic, Bootle Hibernians, Liverpool Hibernians, Celtic Swifts, Celtic Rovers, and 5th Irish ('The Irishmen'), these clubs had 'a relatively short lived an inauspicious history [and] none could claim to have been embraced by the local Irish community in a manner that some Irish clubs in Scotland and Northern Ireland have been'.[120] Séafra Ó Cearbhail argues that the reason sectarianism 'didn't develop to the extent it has in Belfast or Glasgow is probably around the football teams. Liverpool and Everton have a mixture of fans of all or no [religious] persuasions. There is no particular sport or football team for people to gather their [section-alised] loyalties around'.[121]

In Liverpool, 'the Irish Catholic community did not sustain an independent form of football representation'.[122] Instead, despite the existence of smaller teams representing their own ethno-national characteristics, they went to watch either Everton or Liverpool. From its infancy, football had an unparalleled appeal in the city. The first Merseyside Derby between Everton and Liverpool took place on 13 October 1894 and 'was watched by a new record league attendance of 44,000 – including the Lord Mayor of Liverpool'.[123]

The Liverpool Review also noted that Scotland Road was 'congested' by 'an apparently endless procession' on route to Goodison.[124] Everton and Liverpool were two of the best teams in England and attracted support from across the city. Thus, 'football appears to have provided a bridgehead between the Liverpool Irish and the host community',[125] a situation assisted by friendly relations between the two clubs. As Lupson claims,

[118] Kennedy and Kennedy, 2007: 903.
[119] Lupson, 2006: 59.
[120] Kennedy and Kennedy, 2007: 898.
[121] Séafra Ó Cearbhail, 14 March 2013.
[122] Kennedy and Kennedy, 2007: 894, 895.
[123] Johnson, 2010: 32.
[124] Mulhearn, 2007b: 69–70, citing the *Liverpool Review*, 14 October 1894.
[125] Kennedy and Kennedy, 2007: 895.

Some have suggested that the passion of their support has sectarian roots, Everton allegedly being Catholic and Liverpool the Protestant one. But this is quite wrong. In fact, far from being divided by sectarian or any other kind of social or political loyalties, the two clubs share a common heritage and enjoyed a degree of harmony and understanding unmatched between clubs in other major UK cities.[126]

With Anfield and Goodison Park sitting in close proximity, fidelity to either team was not dictated by geographic location, nor on religious grounds. Family allegiances played a part, though it was certainly not (and still is not) uncommon for families to be split and as such 'there is no comparison with Celtic and Rangers'.[127]

This mixed affiliation within families was an important reason in the solidarity which helped transcend sectarian division. Whereas areas were once segregated based on religion, the same has never been true for football affiliation. Families, friendships, schools, and neighbourhoods have always been mixed Blue and Red. Support for either team provided a social escape from the constraints of religious affinity and diminished the importance of sectarian badges.

It is acknowledged that school football rivalry was not entirely bereft of religious tensions. Alf Mullins, who attended a Church of England school in Garston, comments, 'when our school had football competitions it seemed to be that little bit keener when we were playing St Francis [Catholic school]'.[128] Joe Benton MP, who attended a Catholic school in Bootle, also confesses this point, while insinuating that ultimately the sport brought people closer:

> Lurking in the background was always 'well that's a Protestant school' or 'they're a Catholic school', but later on when we'd all left school we used to come across the same faces that you'd played football against as kids and good comradeship built up. In a way the [denominational school system] was divisive, but we were taught (and I know it happened in non-Catholic schools too) that you had to have respect for everyone.[129]

Bishop Tom Williams insists that school football was a uniting rather than a dividing factor in Liverpool:

[126] Lupson, 2008: 7.
[127] Joe Benton, 18 May 2012.
[128] Alf Mullins, 14 May 2012.
[129] Joe Benton, 18 May 2012.

School football teams were important. I remember, when I was a kid, I think it was in 1958, St Anthony's were playing St Sylvester's (the two biggest parishes in Liverpool) in a schoolboy football match – Under 15s. It was the final of the Echo Cup. It was played at Anfield and 13,000 people watched the match. It wasn't 'Catholic' football. It was school football. They'd quite happily have been supported by their Church of England mates. They had their own leagues and their own systems. That maintained a kind of identity, but I firmly believe that's why football thrived in Liverpool, because of school football teams.[130]

By the mid-twentieth century, football rivalry was surmounting sectarian hostility. The Merseyside Derby overshadowed both St Patrick's Day and the Twelfth of July celebrations. In 1948, Goodison Park recorded its highest attendance in a match between Everton and Liverpool, with 78,299 supporters present.[131] 'Orange Day' could attract up to 30,000 people, but this number went into decline. Football was emerging as a uniting factor in the city, eclipsing religious difference, even if religious identification remained. Andy Burnham MP offers anecdotal support:

My mum and dad were a mixed marriage ... My dad was notionally Protestant but not church going and my mum was Catholic and very church going. My mum was an Evertonian and dad was an Evertonian. The first time he went to my mum's house to meet all her family he was very worried. He didn't know whether he'd be accepted. My mum's brother opened the door and his first words were, 'Roy, we'd rather have a Protestant Evertonian than a Catholic Liverpudlian. You're very welcome here'. That was 1964 and tells you something about the mind-set of that era. My uncle's quote to my dad sort of says it all. People were aware of their religious identity but actually weren't that bothered about it.[132]

Football began to assume the status of a surrogate for God-fearing religion. Orr makes this point:

All my family were from Northern Ireland. I used to have to go to church twice on a Sunday. Constant it was. On a Sunday you couldn't put the telly on. You couldn't play records. You couldn't do anything. It was a

---

[130] Tom Williams, 23 March 2010.
[131] The Stadium Guide (website), 'Goodison Park: History and Description'. Available at: www.stadiumguide.com/goodison/.
[132] Andy Burnham, 28 March 2013.

really strict Protestant family. Football just took you away from all of
that. It was your own time, your own space. You loved that club. I still
do now. I'm not ashamed to say it. When I say I love Everton, I really do
love Everton … it's more than football. It's a way of life. It is a religion![133]

The idea of football being 'the faith' of Merseyside is often articulated. John
Pugh MP stated that, 'Football is the religion of Liverpool'.[134] Pugh is not
alone in this assertion. Councillor Mike Murphy believes that, 'people
transferred their allegiance. Without a doubt, football has become a new
religion for a lot of people'.[135] Tony Birtill also comments, 'so many things
seem more important than sectarianism. For a lot of people, football is more
important than religion'.[136] Additionally, Clare Devaney writes,

> Liverpool finds its security and sanctuary in its icons, shared beliefs
> and identity as a collective … while the influence of Church may well
> be less pronounced for many of the new generation, ask about the other
> communal mass of creed, worship and unwavering faith – football – and
> you will be hard pressed to find a neutral answer to the eternal question:
> 'Red or Blue?'[137]

The language surrounding football is an important factor in relation to its
assertion as a 'religion'. Ian Woods states, 'Football possibly did displace
religion. Evertonians probably say the same sort of things as us: "Anfield
is our church. Liverpool is our belief." For Evertonians, Goodison is their
church and Everton is their belief'.[138] Commentaries upon football matches,
such as 'keeping the faith', denote this to be the case. Some supporters have
described Everton as their 'gracious team',[139] while others have referred to
Anfield as the 'Home of the Gods'.[140] Football sociologist John Williams
referred to football chants by Liverpudlians as 'hymns to their football

[133] George Orr, 7 November 2013.
[134] John Pugh, 23 March 2013.
[135] Michael Murphy, 8 April 2013.
[136] Tony Birtill, 29 September 2012.
[137] Devaney,2011: 173–4.
[138] Ian Woods, 12 November 2013.
[139] 'Liverpool Scene Batpoem'. (23 March 2009). Available at: www.youtube.com/watch?v=m0GUbAImHuw.
[140] Trip Adviser (website), 'Home of the "Gods": Review of Anfield Stadium'. Available at: www.tripadvisor.co.uk/ShowUserReviews-g186337-d999329-r180170267-Anfield_Stadium-Liverpool_Merseyside_England.html.

heroes',[141] while Everton's former manager, David Moyes, was known by some as the 'Moyesiah', after helping the club to transform its footballing fortunes. Until recently, the club also had inscribed on a section of the Upper Gwlady's Street, the words, 'In Moyes we trust'. Such statements could be seen by some to be a 'worship of false idols', although many supporters simply would not care. There is something tangible about football that is not necessarily present in religion. As football fanatic Stephen Maloney puts it, 'In God we can trust. In Everton we believe!'[142]

Andy Burnham MP also commented on the swap over of footballing phraseology with religious terminology:

> People are exposed to religious imagery and have been in their youth. Liverpool is a more religiously conscious city than most, I would say. When I was in church, when I was younger, people would use [football] match analogy. My granddad would say 'there's a good gate in here today'. There was language of the two, the language of the match and the language of Mass. I often found they were interchangeable.[143]

Burnham does not, however, agree that football has become a 'new religion'. Despite his regular attendance at Everton games, he states, 'I wouldn't put it like that, personally. I'd say it's become an expression of their identity ... to call yourself a Catholic would be a weird thing to do these days. Football is a kind of soft, easy form of a social marker'.[144]

Unsurprisingly, the idea of football as a 'new religion', does not sit too easily with Catholic Bishop Tom Williams. Unlike the former Shadow Home Secretary, however, the high-ranking clergyman does not entirely refute the suggestion:

> The idea that football has replaced religion is a half-truth. They can go together. Football has the element of religion in it, in terms of fervour and support and going to support 'your side', and people talk about having 'the faith', but football has borrowed that terminology. For some people it's replaced it. Some people are more fervent about their football team than they are about their faith, but for many, they have borrowed the language and the ritual. There is a ritual. You wear your colours, it's your flag, you

---

[141] Williams, 2011: 130.

[142] Regularly cited by Stephen Maloney, chief organiser for the 'Walnut Blues' Everton supporters association.

[143] Andy Burnham, 28 March 2013.

[144] Ibid.

say, 'that's my religion', but I think that borrows the language. It doesn't just replace it. I joke, I say, 'to be a good Catholic, you've got to be an Evertonian, because we understand what sufferings about.[145]

Nonetheless, as Orr points out, 'For many fans, they haven't got a religion apart from football'.[146] Whittingham too, makes this point, 'to many people football is all they've got ... It has become a form of religion to them ... Liverpool FC is always there. You can get annoyed, you've lost today, but the belief and the hope is always there that you're going to do better next week'.[147] In such circumstances, with few appealing alternatives, and when it seems that there isn't too much on the horizon, football provides hope. Certainly, for many people, this was the case in the 1980s. Although the sport has the ability to enrich quality of living, football isn't solely an alternative to a mundane existence. For many, football has become almost an essential part of their essence. In Liverpool, when some people die it has been known for their coffins to be draped with an Everton or Liverpool flag. Others have had their urns buried or ashes scattered at Goodison Park or Anfield.[148] If somebody is killed in a traffic accident, the colours of their respective denomination – red or blue – are the colours of tributes left for them at the site of the event. Each year, both clubs host christenings, weddings, and funeral receptions at their stadiums.[149]

As the twentieth century progressed, with each footballing accolade achieved by the clubs, football became increasingly synonymous with the city and its inhabitants, a success story amid wider economic failure. Religion was becoming an afterthought to football among the citizenry. Former Protestant Party leader, Roy Hughes, agreed that the colours of the city had changed. He states, 'People need something. They're looking for an identity or a badge. It's amazing that twenty-two men kicking a ball around a pitch can conjure up so much passion. Football keeps a lot of people off the

---

[145] Tom Williams, 23 March 2010.

[146] George Orr, 7 November 2013.

[147] Cliff Whittingham, 10 January 2014.

[148] D. Ward, 'Goodison Park to End Fan Burials'. *Guardian* (16 June 2004). Available at: www.theguardian.com/uk/2004/jun/16/football.davidward.

[149] Everton FC (website), 'Hospitality & Events'. Available at: http://www.evertonfc.com/content/hospitality; Liverpool FC (website). Available at: http://web.archive.org/web/20140328125355/http://www.liverpoolfc.com/corporate/conferences-events/celebrations-and-events.

streets, as [Orange] lodges did'.[150] The Evertonian journalist Neil Roberts claims his footballing allegiance 'forges my identity more than anything else'.[151] One of the reasons churches set up sporting bodies was 'to counter the threat of apostasy among young parishioners'.[152] Ironically, for many people in Liverpool today, football is their only 'religion'. Although the local footballing rivalry can induce intense passions, resentments between fans or clubs have never been as pernicious as had been religious sectarianism. For most of the clubs' histories, there was a 'camaraderie of the terraces',[153] where Reds and Blues would sit together, which represented how many people were 'proud to be part of the Merseyside football family'.[154] 'It was friendly banter'.[155] Cliff Whittingham, a Liverpool fan, recalls how Evertonians and Liverpudlians would sit together at derby games:

> I've watched the derby in every single area of Goodison Park. I've been in every section and I can honestly never, ever remember seeing any problems. You'd get a bit of banter, a bit of effing and blinding here and there, but never anything serious. In the Lower Gwladys Street, Liverpool always had a section right behind the goal on the derby day. It felt about 300 people, but it might have been maybe 150–200, and Everton always had a section on the Kop when we played at Anfield. Everton were always just to the side of the goal, Main Stand side.[156]

Amidst the football-related violence of the 1970s and 1980s, a narrative developed of how Everton and Liverpool fans were willing to 'stand together' (most particularly against Manchester United supporters), with the city showing 'a solidarity which seems to transcend everything'.[157] Referring to the 1984 League Cup final replay, at Maine Road, Tom Williams remarked of the togetherness which was distinct in the Merseyside football rivalry at the time:

> When we played Liverpool, at Man City's ground, in the League Cup, I remember we went on the coaches all together. The Manchester police

---

[150] Roy Hughes, 13 November 2012.
[151] Roberts, 2011: 13.
[152] Kennedy and Kennedy, 2007: 897.
[153] Scraton, 1999: 55.
[154] Roberts, 2011: 79.
[155] Ian Woods, 12 November 2013.
[156] Cliff Whittingham, 10 January 2014.
[157] Andy Burnham, 28 March 2013.

couldn't cope with Reds and Blues being on the same coach. It just didn't enter their heads. They couldn't comprehend it. They were saying, 'Blues over there and Reds over there.' People were saying, 'Hey, that's my son', 'Hey, that's my brother', or 'that's our kid'. That's when we sang 'Merseyside'. We were both equal, we were both at the same level and that rivalry was very healthy.[158]

Whittingham adds, 'I think the first time "Merseyside" was chanted was 1984 in the Milk Cup. Those chants were still there in 1986, and the final in 1989 after Hillsborough. In 1986, at Wembley, in the centre of the programme, there were no separate team photos. They [the players] were all together, one red, one blue, next to each other'.[159] This also reflected strong inter-club relationships. Liverpool has completed more direct transfers with Everton than any other club.[160]

In the Premier League era, the Merseyside derby has increased in hostility. Transfers between the clubs prompted supporter acrimony. Former Everton and Rangers Captain, David Weir, recalls the atmosphere when England international, Nick Barmby (whom Bishop Tom Williams referred to as 'Judas'), joined Liverpool in 2000: 'Crossing the park to play for "them" was not quite Rangers–Celtic, but not far away'.[161] Abel Xavier was the last player to switch between the clubs, in 2002. Since then no transfer between the local rivals has taken place. As Everton defender, Leighton Baines (ironically a boyhood Liverpudlian), commented in 2011: 'It's Liverpool or Everton – you don't do both'.[162] 'Banter' began to be taken less generously by a generation of Evertonians. In retaliation to jibes about their lack of form and silverware, some Blues blamed Liverpool fan involvement in the 1985 Heysel Stadium disaster, which prompted British clubs to be banned from European competitions at a time when Everton arguably had the best team in Europe.

Howard Kendall, Everton's manager at the time, believes that, in the long term, Heysel resulted in changing attitudes between Everton and Liverpool fans:

[158] Tom Williams, 23 March 2010.
[159] Cliff Whittingham, 10 January 2014.
[160] LFC Stats Blog (website), 'Switching Sides "Crossing the Park"'. Available at: www.darryljon.dsl.pipex.com/liverpoolevertonswitchingsides.html.
[161] Weir, 2011: 125.
[162] A. Hunter, 'It's Liverpool or Everton: You Don't Do Both, Says Leighton Baines'. *Guardian* (30 September 2011). Available at: www.theguardian.com/football/2011/sep/30/leighton-baines-everton.

I think the European ban had a lot to do with it, because Liverpool where involved in that tragedy and we'd just had success in Europe and it meant we were unable to compete in Europe's top competition. We'd won the Cup Winners Cup and we felt we had a good chance in the European Cup as well ... It was humour years ago and bitterness has crept in and I honestly think that it was related to that tragedy.[163]

After the Heysel Stadium tragedy, 'Liverpool as a city was labelled as feral, Neanderthal and barbaric'.[164] Yet any antipathy from Evertonians was not as obvious as it could have been, as the city tended to unite over its perceived maltreatment by government and amid negative perceptions from outsiders. As Burnham highlights, 'In the 1986 final at Wembley everybody sang "Merseyside". In that era there was always a sense of a bigger enemy and it was Maggie [Thatcher]. It was London. It was the sense that there was anti-Liverpool feeling around. People ... even though they had their own differences internally, were focusing on the bigger issues'.[165]

This situation helps paint a picture of an entirely different relationship between the football 'sects' in Liverpool to the religious sects which pre-dated them. Even with such a contentious event as Heysel acting as a 'legitimate' excuse for resentment between the fan sets, Liverpudlians and Evertonians stuck together. The city's response to the Hillsborough disaster, in 1989, was another example of the solidarity that had emerged on Merseyside, which had completely transcended religious differences.

In relation to both Heysel and Hillsborough, as Walvin writes, 'the media instantly made the association between a decaying industrial maritime city – the flagship of urban decay – and the alleged violence and indiscipline of their football fans. The press portrait was of fans, from Britain's most blighted city, running out of control'.[166] Some of the most slanderous claims came from the *Sun* newspaper, under the duplicitous headline *'The Truth'* – a headline which Kelvin MacKenzie, the paper's editor, it later emerged, wanted to read 'You Scum'. The subheadings of this front page 'report' stated: 'Some fans picked pockets of victims; Some fans urinated on the brave cops; Some fans beat up PC giving kiss of life'. Such allegations were fallacies based on 'police or Police Federation sources'.[167]

---

[163] Howard Kendall, 17 November 2010.
[164] Frost and North, 2013: 104.
[165] Andy Burnham, 28 March 2013.
[166] Walvin, 1994: 188.
[167] Scraton, 1999: 115.

Clare Devaney also wrote of how the city 'collectively recoiled' at such 'misrepresentation, slur and slander, battening down the hatches to protect its own'.[168] The *Sun* told the nation that much blame for the disaster was attributable to Liverpool fans. Evertonians and Liverpudlians knew differently and a boycott of the tabloid began, with copies of the *Sun* burnt publicly and a refusal to purchase still evident today. Such a response was a part of a collective demonstration of solidarity. As Ian Woods states, 'in the eighties, people picked on our city and we stuck together especially in relation to the Tory Government and Hillsborough'.[169] Woods, a Hillsborough attendee on that day, talked of the united front shown by the people of Liverpool:

> The next day in Liverpool the mood was very sombre. I actually went up to Anfield. I put flowers on the pitch the next day … there were thousands there. That was everyone's church, Catholic or Protestant, that's where people went to pray to God or reflect on whatever else went through your mind silently. I saw a lot of people praying there. It affected Everton as much as Liverpool. It wasn't a football thing then. It was a city thing. It was a family thing. It was Merseyside united again.[170]

'Collective mourning had begun'.[171] Rogan Taylor, when asked, 'Do you think Hillsborough had an effect in uniting the city?', replied, 'I think the city was already united. I think what it provided was a stage on which the city's core unity, based on collective suffering, as I would describe it, once again showed itself'.[172]

Unity in grief was to be accompanied by unity in bitterness. David Hendrich summaries the response:

> The city of Liverpool was brought to its knees that day due to the loss of life and the subsequent cover-up and smear campaign that followed. The city begged its government for help and its government turned their back and looked away. Such was the level of that cover-up that it is only now, 23 years later, that the truth has finally come out. When Thatcher and her cohorts turned their back on Liverpool, the people of the city came together in a show of defiance the likes of which had never before

---

[168] Devaney, 2011: 174.

[169] Ian Woods, 12 November 2013.

[170] Ibid.

[171] Taylor, Ward, and Newburn, 1995: 178.

[172] Rogan Taylor, 27 November 2013.

been witnessed in the United Kingdom. A city smeared became a city united.[173]

In September 2012, a report exonerating Liverpool fans of blame for the Hillsborough disaster was published, which stated explicitly that 'multiple factors were responsible for the deaths of the 96 victims of the Hillsborough tragedy and that the fans were not the cause of the disaster'.[174] Evertonians displayed solidarity with Liverpool fans at a number of subsequent fixtures, emphasising the unity of purpose on the issue of justice for the victims' families.

A commonality developed which has pushed sectarian tensions to the periphery. As Andy Burnham again comments:

> Liverpool is religiously divided, politically divided, and football divided, but Liverpool doesn't let the divides get in the way. There is more solidarity against a common enemy: the London media, Thatcher, the establishment. That is what the Hillsborough story is – the red and blue, all political colours, everybody in the end fought on Hillsborough together and that's why it succeeded.[175]

Each week, 30,000 to 40,000 fans attend Goodison Park or Anfield collectively to worship their teams. Attendance at the city's two cathedrals, even when combined, does not compare with attendance at the football stadiums, and if attendance at individual churches were to be taken into account the figures would still be eclipsed by the proportion of teams who play Sunday football and whose families go to watch. On Merseyside, football is a more obvious part of culture than religious denomination. In fact, for many, football is their religion and their team is their denomination. Although some residents may still drink in an Orange club or a Catholic Parochial club, it is football, not theology, which dominates conversation. Kendall appositely states that 'Everton and Liverpool are

[173] D. Hendrich, '5 Reasons the Liverpool vs. Everton Rivalry Comes with Mutual Respect' (22 October 2012) *Bleacher Report.* Available at: http://bleacherreport.com/articles/1380929–5-reasons-the-liverpool-vs-everton-rivalry-comes-with-mutual-respect/page/6.

[174] 'Hillsborough: The Report of the Hillsborough Independent Panel, 12 September 2012. London: The Stationery Office, p.1, The report also highlighted 'a series of obstacles in the search for justice', including 'an unprecedented process of review and alteration' of police statements.

[175] Interview, Andy Burnham, 28 March 2013.

two families',[176] the biggest on Merseyside. They live in relative harmony (certainly when compared to the past fractures between the 'Green' and the 'Orange'). One anecdote from conducting this research was telling in revealing the relative strengths of Orange/Green versus Red/Blue affiliations. Interviewing in an Orange club in north Liverpool, the author revealed that half of his family are Catholic, to which the bar server (a lifelong member of the Orange Order), responded reassuringly, 'This may be an Orange club, but we're very welcoming towards Catholics'. However, having revealed that I was an Evertonian, the same server flippantly replied, 'You're a Blue? You're in the wrong pub!'[177]

Officials in Bootle's Orange Institution give examples of members' footballing priorities conflicting with religious ceremonies. Tommy Buckley, Grand Master of Bootle Province, commented,

> We had to alter our reformation celebrations last year because a derby match was on. The bands were saying, 'We won't be there because half our band goes [to] the football match' ... They'll come to meetings and say, 'Sorry I've got to go [early], Everton are on', or 'Liverpool are on'. There are loads like that ... We've done our parade list for this coming year and there's always one parade where you'll get, 'I can't come out. The derby match is on.' Football is taking precedence over it.[178]

There is some truth in the suggestion that, on Merseyside, football seems to have eclipsed much else, not merely religion but also politics. In December 2013, Professor Jon Tonge made this point in a *Daily Post* article, when commenting on the paltry turnout in a Liverpool Riverside by-election:

> The winning candidate generously described the mass abstentions as 'a respectable turnout in the circumstances'. She excused the triumph of the apathetic on the grounds that 'it's December, it's dark and it's wet and it's cold'. It will be all of those things the next time Everton or Liverpool play at home. That won't stop tens of thousands of people rolling up – or heading to the pub to watch 11 men kick a ball of wind into a net. Fair enough, we all love football, but is it really so much more important than democracy?[179]

[176] Howard Kendall, 17 November 2010.
[177] Conversation with Lynn Hughes, December 2012.
[178] Tom Buckley, 12 March 2013.
[179] *Liverpool Daily Post*, 12 December 2013.

Tonge's observation is apposite. Increasingly, and in line with the national trend, many Merseysiders are becoming uninterested in municipal contests – 'They're all the same', being a frequent retort to electoral canvassers of all political parties. Everton and Liverpool, however, have retained their distinction. Many Liverpudlians, Blue and Red, while losing interest in both religion and politics, have reserved their focus for their football teams, many often mimicking a phrase of a footballing icon (for half the city, at least), in Bill Shankly: 'Football's not a matter of life and death. It's more important than that'.[180]

In practice, however, as tragedies like Hillsborough have portrayed, on Merseyside, football allegiance takes a back seat to issues which are, in reality, much more important. As Ian Woods puts it, 'Liverpool is a part of me ... You have your family, your friends, and you have Liverpool Football Club'.[181] He did, however, set out priorities, 'You love it, but not in the same way as you love your family. If you lose a match you get over it, but if you lose a member of your family I don't think you ever quite get over that'.[182] Paul Coslett may be right in stating that 'Football is in many ways the heartbeat of Liverpool',[183] but, as the renowned football academic, Dr Rogan Taylor, puts it,

> In the end, football doesn't fucking matter and that's what's so beautiful about it. It's apparently so unbelievably important, but it doesn't matter one jot. I don't think anything else manages to combine the seriousness and the utter irrelevance. It's a bunch of overpaid tarts running round on a pitch for fuck sake!'[184]

Conclusion

Walker contends that, in Glasgow, 'Rangers and Celtic loyalties are the most visible example of "Orange and Green" allegiances which feed off the situation in nearby Northern Ireland'.[185] Had Liverpool's two football teams been split on similarly stark ethno-national and ethno-religious lines, a

---

[180] Cited by Murphy, 2005: 29.
[181] Ian Woods, 12 November 2013.
[182] Ibid.
[183] P. Coslett, 'The Origins of Scouse'. BBC (30 April 2008).
[184] Rogan Taylor, 27 November 2013.
[185] Walker, 2012: 377.

similar situation to Glasgow might have been possible. In contrast, despite some historic suggestion that Everton was 'Catholic' and Liverpool was 'Protestant', neither club has held any significant denominational affinity (notwithstanding that both clubs are ultimately products of the same Methodist Chapel). One factor which aided the success of Everton and Liverpool (and their ability to maintain neutrality, rather than potentially seeking the promotion of a denominationally partisan fan base), was that no noteworthy effort was made by either Irish Nationalist or Catholic organisations within the city to promote a rival ethno-religiously based football team, a point explained by Kennedy and Kennedy:

> Given the Catholic Church's endeavours in Liverpool to ensure that the Irishness of its congregation was minimalized both culturally and politically it seems reasonable to suggest that encouragement to set up and/or support ethno-religious sporting organisations capable of mobilising ethnic, or even nationalist, sentiments would have run counter to its strategy, [whilst] … the Liverpool Irish political community appears to have had no interest in forming or supporting the development of an Irish alternative to the professional football clubs of the host community, as nationalists had done elsewhere.[186]

There were 'no obvious examples of hostility' to the presence of Irish Catholic clubs on the local football scene', with the reason they failed to become organisations attracting mass support being 'difficulty … attracting the financial and moral support of the Liverpool Irish community itself'.[187]

Everton and Liverpool became overwhelmingly the two dominant teams in the area, both attracting support from the city's Catholic and Protestant populations. With no prominent Irish or Catholic teams to rival the host clubs, both clubs became repositories for the affection of the city's residents and became identified with Liverpool (the city) causes. That both clubs attracted support further afield did not hinder cross-sectarian appeals. Although Everton were the first English club to have a supporters' association set up in Ireland, Liverpool developed a very sizeable following of Irish supporters.

As the twentieth century progressed, the success of Everton and Liverpool heralded adoration and veneration from the city's populace, a love and admiration which, as this chapter has argued, eventually displaced

---

[186] Kennedy and Kennedy, 2007: 904.
[187] Ibid., 909–10.

ethno-religious identifications and ultimately sectarian antipathy. Although Bishop Tom Williams talked about this collectivism, he also drew comparisons of a transferred sectarian undercurrent: 'When you get that sort of hatred [in football], when banter becomes hatred, that's when tribalism is at its worst. It's like sectarianism, when you hate the other side simply for who they are'.[188] Kilfoyle has also pointed out the tendency for 'hostility reminiscent of the Orange and the Green'[189] to be displayed in recent times between some football fans on Merseyside. Nonetheless, as this chapter has portrayed, historically, such resentment has been uncharacteristic in terms of local footballing rivalry, in which banter has been a much more prevalent ingredient to relations in the 'friendly derby', than genuine abhorrence. Although, in the Premier League era, relations between the clubs' supporters did sour, recent memorials of the Hillsborough disaster have reinvigorated some collectivism, which, historically, has typified the Merseyside Derby, a derby which, this chapter has argued, has almost no resemblance to the animosity often displayed during 'Old Firm' encounters.

Glasgow and Liverpool are cities with much in common, both major destinations for the famine Irish in the nineteenth century. Both cities 'inherited' a sectarian situation comparable in some respects to that of Belfast. Sectarian dimensions were propped up by situations distinct to either city. Belfast has endured long-standing political and sectarian problems. In Glasgow, rivalry between the respective followers of the city's main soccer teams, Rangers and Celtic, allowed sectarianism an outlet via the principal sport and most successful soccer teams in Scotland.[190] As the reputation of Rangers 'as a bulwark of Protestant and Unionist ascendancy is well established',[191] so 'Irishness' is also asserted to be "the primary identity" of Celtic'.[192] Walker contends that, in recent years, 'Catholic community solidarity in relation to Celtic [has been] reinforced, [while] old grievances are given expression through support for the [Glasgow] club[s]'.[193]

This does not apply to fans on Merseyside. Issues of Catholic identity or Irish Republican politics, or Loyalism and Protestantism are insignificant to the vast majority of Liverpool and Everton supporters. Cultural, religious,

---

[188] Tom Williams, 23 March 2010.
[189] Peter Kilfoyle, 23 January 2012.
[190] Gallagher, 1987: 99.
[191] Kennedy, 2011: 557.
[192] Walker, 2001: 48, citing Bradley.
[193] Walker, 2001: 50.

and political assimilation has occurred in the city and the repudiation of sectarian associations by its main clubs has been an important part of bridge-building and the dilution of older animosities.

While Celtic and Rangers can be said to have provided forums for sectarian displays, despite strong attempts at rebuttal by both clubs, Everton and Liverpool aided the displacement of sectarian affiliation by emerging as (predominantly) secular alternatives. Many in Liverpool have become spiritually indifferent and often a person's only 'religion' is their football team. Ostentatious religious symbols of denominational affiliation have markedly declined, generally limited to an annual display of orange bunting abounding Everton Brow in north Liverpool around the 'Twelfth' celebrations and some displays of Irish tricolours in historically Irish areas on 17 March. In contrast, denotations of football allegiance are increasingly displayed in houses, offices, cars, even in terms of the names of children (where once many Liverpool names had religious connotations, such as William, Lily, Mary, or Patrick, today many christen their children with the names of their footballing icons).[194] To 'wear your colours' no longer means displaying a green shamrock or an orange lily, but instead refers to clothing signifying football attachment. As such, it is argued that the colours of the city have, quite literally, changed from green and orange to red and blue.

[194] The author has recently had it revealed to him that his father attempted to name him Graeme, after Graeme Sharp, who played for Everton. A common female name in Liverpool is Mia, standing for 'made in Anfield'. In addition, recently a friend named his son Leighton, after Everton left-back Leighton Baines.

Conclusion

This research has challenged the conventional premise on the degeneration of sectarianism on Merseyside. The generally accepted proposition, expressed in the admittedly limited existing literature and commentary, that post-war slum clearance simply 'bulldozed away' the religious 'ghettos', ridding the city of sectarianism, was considered to be too simple an explanation for the corrosion of a social, religious, economic, xenophobic, tribal, and traditional dispute that had raged for nearly two centuries. This is not to say that the council's rehousing programme did not play its part. It did, and this study has never deviated from that point, whilst urging the consideration of variables to be less parsimonious. As Roy Hughes puts it, 'Scotland Road and Netherfield Road [major sites of sectarianism] both arrived in Kirkby [along with many other areas of transfer]. Neighbours now, for the first time, were of another religion. People would meet in the street or at work and a Catholic and Protestant would fall in love. Resultantly, people said, "so and so has married a Catholic, keep the Orange songs down a bit"'.[1] Moreover, in breaking up the old 'Orange strongholds', the Protestant Party could no longer rely on a micro-majority of supporters to keep them in office. It is probable, however, that this powerbase would not have survived regardless of rehousing.

The 'new aliens' hypothesis has also been examined in depth. It is true that as Liverpool sectarianism went into remission, racism directed against Liverpool's black and Chinese communities became more obvious. Racism had been a factor in Liverpool arguably longer than had sectarianism. Liverpool's black and Chinese communities had never reached that point where 'assimilation means that the migrant community is absorbed totally into the host population, to the point in which it's indistinguishable'.[2]

---

[1] Roy Hughes, 13 November 2012.
[2] Frank Neal, 12 February 2010.

Liverpool's black and Chinese communities could not 'assimilate' as easily as the Irish, through a combination of physical characteristics, poverty, and even greater territorial isolation (in central and south Liverpool) than that originally encountered by the immigrant Irish. Thus 'Scouseness' for a long time did not envelop the black and Chinese communities as comprehensively as it could for those of Irish descent. White Protestants and Catholics, in their new localities such as Kirkby and Skelmersdale, began to become a homogeneous body of white 'Scousers', their denomination mattering much less without physical boundary lines, such as Great Homer Street, and with diminishing cultural and social differences relating to their territorial origins.

In terms of the reduction of sectarianism, the Roman Catholic Church, whilst segregationist in its approach to education and perpetuating divisions in that respect, also played a significant role. The Church had done its best to 'de-Irishise' its congregations, and this was coupled with a declining proportion of Irish entering Liverpool, yet the Irish culture and language by the mid-twentieth century had already infected Liverpudlians of all creeds. A commonality of accent and custom was transcending previous sectarian divisions. Liverpudlians were becoming distinct, the Wars had thawed inter-communal rivalry given the common foe and by 1964 the politics of the city changed, as people voted according to class rather than religion. Labour, under the Braddocks, had begun its movement toward secularism over Catholicism, and though the party is still seen as 'Catholic' to this day by some Protestants in the city, many other Protestants, now influenced by television and reaping the benefits of the newly formed welfare state, changed their outlook. Conservatism lost its pull, as did Orangeism.

While the Orange Institution was still strong in the 1960s, with the death of figures like George Wise and Conservative 'boss' Archibald Salvidge, the Order's political influence had waned considerably. People had 'begun getting their political education from trade unions, rather than the Orange Order'.[3] The lack of flamboyant rhetoric by Protestant orators was an important factor. Longbottom's death in 1962 signalled an end to that chapter of Liverpool's history, prompting the removal of anti-Catholic demagoguery and its replacement by benign tolerance, as a prelude to integration. Sectarian skirmishes still took place on 'Orange Day' and

[3] Mike O'Brian, 12 November 2012.

St Patrick's Day, but became confined to these occasions. Maria O'Reilly recollects having her Catholic crucifix ripped off her neck in the fifties by an Orangeman,[4] while Brenda O'Brian recalls a Catholic on Linacre Road, 'getting a bucket of ice water as the lodges went past' and 'drowning a child' in the Orange procession.[5] Susanne Loughlin notes how 'violence would happen on the way back [from Southport] when they'd all been drinking all day ... I remember nasty violent things ... you'd see somebody bleeding'.[6] Doris Bennett remembers that, as late as the 1970s, 'there were quite often fights. A bandsman of ours got quite badly attacked. My niece was once King Billy and a man ran over and put a knife to her neck'.[7] Clearly, problems did not vanish overnight and fears of past disorders were highlighted in 1971 when a headbutt on an orange ribbon seller, on London Road, Liverpool, prompted the judge to deem that the event 'could have started a riot'.[8] This may have been an overstatement; no sectarian riot had taken place in the city since the first decade of the twentieth century, the Liverpool Corporation Act, 1912 imposing strict limitations on public processions. Inter-marriage did much to thaw division. Of course, the increasing incidence of mixed marriages might be seen as a *consequence* of improved relations, rather than a cause. However, the evidence from interviewees is that mixed marriages increased as part of a determination to throw off restrictive religiously sectarian shackles which had dominated Liverpool life. From the liberating 1960s onwards, people were no longer prepared to accept Church-influenced 'selection' of their life partners. Previously, the pressure for single religion partnerships was considerable, as Councillor Jimmy Mahon recalls from the early 1950s:

I was about sixteen and met a young lady. Now we never mentioned religion or anything like that. We were going out for about four or five months and there were possibilities that there could have been a wedding at the end of it. My mother happened to find out that she was Orange Lodge. Well I've never seen a change in a woman so much. She transformed from a sweet, mild mannered lady and went round to the house and told her mother, in no uncertain terms, that she couldn't go out

[4] Maria O'Reilly, 15 March 2013.
[5] Brenda O'Brian, 12 November 2012.
[6] Susanne Loughlin, 13 February 2013.
[7] Doris Bennett, 5 March 2013.
[8] *Liverpool Echo*, 17 July 1971.

with me anymore. That was the law then. Her mother said the same thing
because she was Orange: 'You can't go near a Catholic'.[9]

Such strife over mixed marriage lasted until at least the mid-sixties, as
Loughlin recalls,

> I went out with a lad whose parents were staunch Orange Lodge and if
> they'd have known he was going out with me, a Catholic, they'd have
> hung, drawn, and quartered him; he'd probably have been battered within
> an inch of his life, and I was not allowed up his path [for that reason]. All
> his mates couldn't believe he was going out with a Catholic, so we didn't
> stay together. He wasn't a bad bloke, but if his parents had known he was
> going out with a Catholic there'd have been hell to pay. That was in the
> sixties, maybe 1965–6.[10]

Indeed, various interviews revealed how families at one time had 'split up', or
how members had been 'ostracised' because they 'married out'. Nowadays, it
is almost unheard of for families to break up over religion.[11]

As such, when the Grand Master of Bootle, Tom Buckley, was asked why
the Orange Institution on Merseyside had declined at a faster rate than in
Glasgow or Belfast, he replied, 'It could be because you have got a lot of mixed
marriages here. Unfortunately, our rules state that if you start cohabitating
with a Catholic then you have to leave the Institution'.[12] Bennett agrees with
this perspective: 'The main cause of the decline of Orangeism was mixed
marriages. People got sick of being told what they could and could not do'.[13]
Mixed marriages weakened the once-powerful Orange Order in Canada to
the point where the organisation simply relaxed the prohibition, in order not
to antagonise. This did not arrest decline there, however, and the Order's
strictures on Merseyside, whilst maintained, appear increasingly nominal or
redundant.

---

[9] Jimmy Mahon, 24 April 2012.

[10] Susanne Loughlin, 13 February 2013.

[11] Doris Bennett, Lynn and Dave Hughes, Mike and Brenda O'Brian, Tom Williams, et al.
made such points.

[12] Tom Buckley, 12 March 2013, Neil Dulin (14 March 2013) echoed this point:
'One issue that has undermined [the Orange Order] is the issue of inter-marriage.
They've got to maintain that bloodline, in a sense. Once your sons and daughters start
marrying Catholics and your grandchildren are Catholics it becomes very difficult be an
Orangeman'.

[13] Doris Bennett, 5 March 2013.

As has been pointed out, mixed marriage was but one reason for the decline of the Orange Institution amid a wider derailment of Liverpool sectarianism. General apathy, population decline, diminished family size, and internal splits within the organisation also played their part, whilst a loss of religious observance and loss of interest by younger people were seen as the most important factors. Indeed, Loughlin claims, 'There's not as much hype about it now, because kids have a lot more given to them. We've become richer, so, with the invention of computers, a man on a horse and a parade is nothing, whereas to us that was fascinating. Kids today aren't in the least bit interested'.[14] This perspective is in line with Neal's proposition that a key reason for the decline of sectarianism was 'relative affluence'.[15]

The onset of secularism and the resigned acceptance that there are 'a lot of people who just don't believe in religion anymore',[16] is also important. Census figures indicate that in Liverpool's erstwhile sectarian strongholds Christian affiliation remains extensive. However, religious practice is much rarer and once-tribal denominational affiliation far less relevant. As Keith Allcock states, 'Christianity as a whole in this country is declining ... You'd be surprised at how many people in the [Orange] Institution don't know what the Reformation was'.[17] Buckley adds, 'We've got a big church here at the front of the building. We own it and only six people from the Bootle Province attend it. It should be part of an Orangeman's obligation. The qualifications of an Orangemen say they will "regularly attend public worship"'.[18] Additionally, less veneration is being afforded to religious leaders of both denominations:

> If the priest said you couldn't do it, then you couldn't do it and that was it. A lot of people were more scared of the priest than they were the police, because he ruled the roost. The vicars were the same. Whatever the man of the church said was right; people sincerely believed that. Football has taken the place of religion and John Lennon didn't help either. He said he was more important than God. That was the sixties. That did change something in people's minds. They thought 'well the great John Lennon said it, so there must be something in it'.[19]

---

[14] Susanne Loughlin, 13 February 2013.
[15] Frank Neal, 12 February 2010.
[16] Doris Bennett, 5 March 2013.
[17] Keith Allcock, 12 March 2013.
[18] Tom Buckley, 12 March 2013.
[19] Doris Bennett, 5 March 2013.

While football devotion and 'Beatlemania escapism' became prominent in the sixties, religion was slowly eclipsed. For the (many) continuing believers, Worlock and Sheppard's ecumenical 'better together' philosophy helped set an example. Furthermore, as journalist Will Hutton puts it, 'In England and Wales most people understand how to reconcile faith and reason, which does not necessarily mean regular worship inside a church. That does not mean they do not honour faith but they no longer want to fight'.[20] Many 'got fed up with all the bitterness'.[21]

This work has also stressed that the development of a common Scouse identity displaced traditional religious affiliations. The emergence of a common identity came slowly. In the 1960s, the Catholic community was still attempting to assert its (increasingly confident) identity with the building of a Cathedral (designed by a Protestant), which opened in 1967. This era coincided with the gradual 'sloughing off of the more unpleasant aspects of the past and an anticipation of a future in which the prejudices and bitterness between Catholic and Protestant were forgotten'.[22] The Anglican Cathedral (designed by a Catholic) was finally completed in 1978. The cathedrals are located less than half a mile away from each other and joined by Hope Street. Both Cathedrals would eventually be embraced wholeheartedly by Liverpudlians, the Catholic building labelled as 'Paddy's wigwam' in (mainly) affectionate jest.

As Belchem puts it, 'Scouse is a recently invented tradition, a cultural response to the city's decline'.[23] The two cultures, English Protestant and Irish Catholic, became one within the same city. People began to look past the constraints of low living standards and take solace in the intrinsic worth of the city. The development of shared customs and a unique brogue (which transgressed denominations) extended this commonality to their neighbours regardless of their creed. The accent, which both Netherfield and 'Scottie Roaders' shared, gave the communities a common bond. The song *In My Liverpool Home* became 'an emotional anthem for generations of Merseysiders',[24] an expression of commonality as the old religious

---

[20] *Observer*, 15 July 2007.

[21] Doris Bennett, 5 March 2013.

[22] Tulloch, 2008: 135.

[23] Ibid., 33.

[24] 'Farewell to "Home" Legend. Peter McGovern, Composer of One of Liverpool's Most Famous Songs, has Died at the Age of 78' (4 April 2006) *Crewe Chronicle*. Available at: www.crewechronicle.co.uk/news/local-news/farewell-to-home-legend-5642277.

animosities waned. The following verse, added later by The Spinners, highlights how attitudes in Liverpool had changed:

> 'What's your religion?' a fella once said.
> So I climbed in me wellies and I kung-fu'd his head!
> 'Don't be angry', he cried, 'I'm not starting a nark.'
> 'Do you worship at Anfield or Goodison Park?'[25]

Music was an extremely important component of this new Scouse identity. The bands of the Merseybeat promoted 1960s Liverpool under a common badge. The success of The Beatles had shot the city to international stardom, and bands like Gerry and the Pacemakers and The Searchers added to the sense of a city with its own distinctive culture, not one split by old religious feuds. The city delivered fifty-six songs to the number one spot in the UK singles' chart over the next four decades, with twenty-three of these number one slots being won in the 1960s alone.[26] At this time, people born in Liverpool began to become very proud of their roots. Regardless of Irish or Lancastrian decent, they were now Scouse or Liverpudlian. The success of the city's music scene, however, was not the only cause for excitement. Liverpool's melodious prestige was rivalled only by its footballing attainment.

Football displaced the sectarianism which Bohstedt claims had previously been a 'substitute opiate'.[27] As the success of Everton FC and Liverpool FC soared, so did their city-wide support base. It did not matter whether you were 'Green or Orange', so long as you were 'Blue or Red'. Fans watched their teams surpass themselves in terms of silverware, as they became two of the most successful clubs in English football. Moreover, the rivalry between Everton and Liverpool was one of the most affectionate in the game. The Merseyside derby quickly became known in footballing circles as 'the friendly derby'. Merseyside became a county in its own right on 1 April 1974, and during the 1989 FA Cup Final at Wembley (played just five weeks after the Hillsborough disaster) fans from both teams chanted the name of their famous county in unison. This expression of solidarity is indicative of the common bond shared by the community of Liverpool at this time.

---

[25] The Spinners, track 24, 'In My Liverpool Home', 'Maggie May, The Best of The Spinners', released 1978.

[26] The Beatles, 17, Gerry and the Pacemakers, 3, The Searchers, 3: number 1 singles recorded and released by Liverpool-born artists between 1960 and 1969.

[27] Bohstedt, 1992: 200.

The cross-community sense of comradeship was spreading. McMullen contends that: 'if you met someone abroad and they mentioned they were from Scottie Road or Netherfield Road, you embraced them because we had this togetherness ... There was a real camaraderie about the old Scottie Road and the surrounding area'.[28] Slum clearance played a part in establishing the new Scouse identity. Both the communities of Netherfield and Scotland Road were threatened by the bulldozers and shared a mutual adversary in the Liverpool Corporation Housing Committee. Moreover, with the decline of the docks 'eroding life in the district',[29] it was more important than ever to establish some degree of working-class solidarity. As Belchem puts it, 'Liverpool could not afford internal divisions'.[30]

Prior to the mid-twentieth century, two separate identities had existed in Liverpool, both regarding the other as 'the enemy'. It was only when a new joint identity emerged that hostility really began to subside. As the inhabitants of the city relocated, the city slumped in economic fortune and a social class paradigm displaced the existing ethno-religious framework. Despite the city's downturn, the city's two football teams became key repositories of loyalty and red and blue began to eclipse green and orange, amid broader societal processes of secularism, even if the outright repudiation of religion was less marked in Liverpool.

Nonetheless, even in twenty-first-century Liverpool, the legacy of the green and orange divide is still evident. Phrases like, 'dirty, black, protestant liar'[31] survive to this day, though they are now said more in jest than with any real ferocity or ill feeling. In October 2011, a sizeable (1,500 strong) procession took place in Liverpool to commemorate the thirtieth anniversary of the republican hunger strikes, organised by *Cairde na hÉireann*.[32] Later that day, Liverpool's faction of the 32 County Sovereignty Movement (allegedly linked to the Real IRA) launched their own (much smaller) parade in the city. These rallies, coupled with the small loyalist counter demonstrations

[28]   Rodgers, 2010: 112–13, citing an interview with Kevin McMullen.

[29]   Ibid., 111.

[30]   John Belchem, 25 March 2010.

[31]   Lane, 1966 (*Lern yerself Scouse*, vol. 2, *The ABZ of Scouse*) 'deals with The North End and Bootle Scouse'. This is still a used idiom in Bootle and north Liverpool. The expression had nothing to do with race. It was used as a derogatory way of describing the personal hygiene and ethical integrity of Protestants and Orangemen.

[32]   The rallies were organised by the Liverpool Irish Patriots Band, *Caidre na hÉireann Liverpool* and the *James Larkin Republican Flute Band*.

that took place,[33] indicated that Liverpool remained a city in which Irish constitutional issues continued to provoke at least some political interest.

During 2012, three 'Irish' marches were targeted by far-right and Loyalist groups.[34] Over a century after major rioting between the Protestant British and Catholic Irish had disfigured Liverpool, sectarian issues (although the label of sectarian is contentious) continued to figure. In July 2013, a front-page headline article in the *Liverpool Echo* carried a message from Liverpool's elected Mayor, Joe Anderson, which 'urged the city's Irish-related marchers to calm down or face restrictions'.[35]

The contentious parades of the early twenty-first century were different, however, from the Catholic versus Protestant battles of old. Orange marches were no longer attacked by Catholics. Republican marchers eschewed religious affiliations and were met with chants of 'No Surrender to the IRA', which had replaced cries of 'No Popery'. Although Liverpool loyalists dominated the protests against republican parades, these tensions were anti-Irish and, in particular, anti-Irish republican, rather than anti-Catholic. This point was made by Séafra Ó Cearbhail, of *Cairde na hÉireann Liverpool*:

> We're not the Green Lodge, we're not Green Orangemen. We're Irish Republicans. The founding father of Irish Republicanism was Wolfe Tone [a Protestant]. Religion is never the issue for us. We're republicans. We're socialists. People's personal faith doesn't come into it. We're not a Catholic party. We're not a Catholic band. We're not a Catholic movement. Inter-marriage and inter-cultural celebration is neither a threat, nor a challenge to us, we'd embrace it.[36]

Nonetheless, even if the religious element is removed, it can be said that, unlike other English cities, Liverpool remained exceptional in playing host to contentious Irish questions over 150 years after the waves of Irish immigration. Yet, this was not a return to the 'bad old' sectarian days which engendered widespread community sentiment, but more an outworking of residual Irish issues which did not excite many beyond a relatively small, if 'hard core', segment of the Liverpool populace.

[33] A small Loyalist counter demonstration took place in Derby Square in protest to the 'James Larkin' rally. This seemingly unplanned protest was dealt with by Merseyside Police before any trouble could emerge.
[34] See *Cairde na hÉireann Liverpool*, 'Under Pressure'.
[35] *Liverpool Echo*, 15 July 2013.
[36] Séafra Ó Cearbhail, 14 March 2013.

In 1996, Tony Birtill, in the one article which comes close to explaining sectarian decline in Liverpool, declared:

> Numerous forces led to this change: a general decline in interest in religion as a political issue, shared experiences of all sections of the community during World War II, slum clearances and rehousing, all helped to increase working-class unity and advance the cause of labour. Soccer, a divisive force in Scotland, helped bring people together in Liverpool, with Everton FC and Liverpool FC enjoying support from both Catholics and Protestants.[37]

This research has found that all these point have pertinence, but, in closing, it is argued that the most important factors were a change in attitudes towards theology, coupled with the development of a common identity, the new 'religion' of which became football. Most people on Merseyside still identify as 'Christian', but with an attitude that 'Christians worship the same God, who (if one exists) would certainly not pick and choose between Protestants and Catholics'.[38] As early as 1971, Midwinter wrote that, 'in the heartland of the Orange and Papist feud, football became the secular religion of Liverpool'.[39] Only a tiny minority still somehow try and identify Everton FC as 'Catholic' and Liverpool FC as 'Protestant'. As Loughlin puts it,

> I was born in 1948 and I have never, ever seen either team as being partial to either denomination. To me, you're either an Evertonian or a Liverpudlian. I never saw it as a Catholic or Protestant thing. I mean, we've got a mixed family. We've got some who are Evertonians and some who are Liverpudlians, but we're all Catholics. It was just who you chose to support.[40]

This, in some ways, says it all. Today, on Merseyside, a 'mixed' family means Blue and Red, not Orange and Green. Sectarianism remains a significant memory for older generations in Liverpool, its consignment to history part of a complex, multi-faceted process of shifting identity, class politics, housing policy, and secularism, the interplay of which has banished the divisions which for so long prevailed.

---

[37] *Irish Post*, 27 January 1996.
[38] *Observer*, 15 July 2007.
[39] Midwinter, 1971: 133.
[40] Susanne Loughlin, 13 February 2013.

Recording 'lived experience' of sectarianism in Liverpool has proven an important method of understanding what it was and why it declined. As time passes and people sadly pass away, these collective memories are lost. While archival records are important resources, they are no parallel to actually hearing somebody talk about 'what things were like', 'how things have changed', and 'why they have changed'. Although recollections are open to the reproach of being subjective, unreliable, and even, on occasion, of being fallacious, testimonies are still useful as a way of determining the 'truth' of a matter. In a similar fashion, social researchers can use collective memories, interpretations, and perspectives to see if a theory fits. Not once has an interviewee said, 'X is the reason, and X alone!' There was always a multitude of perspectives, which often corresponded with and sometimes differed from the views of others, but from the plethora of perspectives a good deal of consensus emerged.

Almost two centuries have passed since Liverpool's first sectarian riot in 1819, and the port has changed unrecognisably. Socially, politically, demographically, structurally, and culturally the city is transformed. Notably, today the Irish Catholic emigrants are no longer the outcast minority, and, arguably, neither are Liverpool's black and Chinese communities, certainly not to the extent they once were. However, south Liverpool, in particular, has a rapidly emerging Arab population, which is only likely to increase owing to a need to assist refugees from the Middle East. Once more the UK is dealing with a refugee crisis it is partly responsible in creating. Moreover, Liverpool (like elsewhere in the UK) has to deal with the issue of racism. Where the term 'Paddy' was once used disparagingly, the term 'Paki' took its place, and, likewise, while anti-Popery has declined to a footnote, Islamophobia has risen significantly. Elements of the British media are reporting on Muslims in a similar fashion to the way they once reported the Irish,[41] claiming, for example, that '1 in 5 British Muslims sympathise with Jihadis'.[42] That article 'drew record number of complaints' and is alleged to have been designed 'to incite racial or religious tensions'.[43] In the face of such propaganda, it could be claimed that Liverpool (a city which is still, in terms of religious identification, the most Christian in England) could be facing a different kind of

---

[41] See Hickman, 2012.

[42] The S*n, 23 November 2015.

[43] M. Smith, 'Pollster Behind "1 in 5 Muslims Have Sympathy with ISIS" Claim Condemns How the Sun Presented Survey'. Mirror (24 November 2015). Available at: www.mirror. co.uk/news/uk-news/pollster-behind-1-5-muslims-6891687.

racial and religious conflict. Today, however, Liverpool is not the main port of call for refugees. Culturally, it is distinct and its contemporary character developed largely as a result of Irish assimilation. Liverpool, as a city, has learned that it can embrace immigrants of different religions and be stronger as a consequence.

Select Bibliography

The works listed here include books, articles, studies, reports, and interviews referred to in this volume. However, the bibliography excludes films, public talks, and online resources. The aforementioned, and any other omitted resources, can be found in the book's footnotes.

Books and Chapters

Aughton, P. (2008) *Liverpool: A People's History*, 3rd edn. Lancaster: Carnegie Publishing Ltd.

Belchem, J. (2000a) 'The Liverpool-Irish Enclave', in D.M. MacRaild (ed.), *The Great Famine and Beyond: Irish Migrants in Britain in the Nineteenth and Twentieth Centuries*. Dublin: Irish Academic Press.

—— (2000b) *Merseypride*. Liverpool: Liverpool University Press.

—— (2006) *Liverpool 800: Culture, Character and History*. Liverpool: Liverpool University Press.

—— (2007) *Irish, Catholic and Scouse: The History of the Liverpool-Irish, 1800–1939*. Liverpool: Liverpool University Press.

Belchem, J., and B. Biggs (eds) (2011) *Liverpool City of Radicals*. Liverpool: Liverpool University Press.

Belchem, J., and D. MacRaild (2006) 'Cosmopolitan Liverpool', in J. Belchem (ed.), *Liverpool 800: Culture, Character and History*. Liverpool: Liverpool University Press.

Birtill, T. (2013) *A Hidden History: Irish in Liverpool*. Liverpool: Liverpool Authors.

Blair, C. (2008) *Speaking for Myself: The Autobiography*. London: Little, Brown.

Bohstedt, J. (1992) 'More than One Working Class: Protestant and Catholic Riots in Edwardian Liverpool', in J. Belchem (ed.), *Popular Politics, Riot and Labour: Essays in Liverpool History, 1790–1940*. Liverpool: Liverpool University Press.

Boyce, F. (1999) 'From Victorian "Little Ireland" to Heritage Trail: Catholicism, Community and Change in Liverpool's Docklands', in R. Swift and S. Gilley (eds), *The Irish in Victorian Britain: The Local Dimension*. Dublin: Four Courts Press.

Brewer, J.D., and G.I. Higgins (1998) *Anti-Catholicism in Northern Ireland, 1600–1998: The Mote and the Beam*. Basingstoke: Macmillan.

Briggs, A. (1956) *Friends of the People: The Centenary History of Lewis's*. London: B.T. Batsford Ltd.

Bruce, S. (1989) *God Save Ulster: The Religion and Politics of Pailseyism*. Oxford: Oxford University Press.

Bruce, S., R. Glendinning, I. Paterson, and M. Rosie (2004) *Sectarianism in Scotland*. Edinburgh: Edinburgh University Press.

Burke, T. (1910) *A Catholic History of Liverpool*. Liverpool: Tingling.

Charters, D. (2003) *Liverpool: The World in One City*. Liverpool: Bluecoat.

Connolly, M., K. Roberts, G. Ben-Tovim, and P. Torkington (1992) *Black Youth in Liverpool*. Culemborg: Giordano Bruno.

Cooke, T. (1987) *Scotland Road: 'The Old Neighbourhood'*. Birkenhead: Birkenhead Press.

—— (1999) *The Pubs of Scottie Road*. Liverpool: The Bluecoat Press.

Corbett, J. (2012) *The Everton Encyclopedia*. London: deCoubertin.

Costello, R. (2001) *Black Liverpool: The Early History of Britain's Oldest Black Community, 1730–1918*. Liverpool: Picton Press.

Cowper, A. (1948) *A Backward Glance on Merseyside*. Birkenhead: Willmer Bros. & Co. Ltd.

Crawford, E.M. (1997) 'Migrant Maladies: Unseen Lethal Baggage', in E.M. Crawford (ed.), *The Hungry Stream: Essays on Emigration and Famine*. Belfast: The Centre for Emigration Studies.

Crowley, T. (2012) *Scouse: A Social and Cultural History*. Liverpool: Liverpool University Press.

Davies, S. (1996) *Liverpool Labour: Social and Political Influences on the Development of the Labour Party in Liverpool, 1900–1939*. Keele: Keele University Press.

Davis, G. (1991) *The Irish in Britain, 1815–1914*. Dublin: Gill and Macmillan.

Day, P. (2008) 'Pride Before A Fall? Orangeism in Liverpool since 1945', in M. Busteed, F. Neal, and J. Tonge (eds), *Irish Protestant Identities*. Manchester: Manchester University Press, 273–88.

Denvir, J. (1892) *The Irish in Britain: From the Earliest Times to the Fall and Death of Parnell*. London: Kegan Paul, Trench, Trübner.

Devaney, C. (2011) 'Scouse and the City: Radicalism and Identity in Contemporary Liverpool', in J. Belchem and B. Biggs (eds), *Liverpool City of Radicals*. Liverpool: Liverpool University Press.

Devine, T.M. (ed.) (2000) *Scotland's Shame? Bigotry and Sectarianism in Modern Scotland*. Edinburgh: Mainstream.

Du Noyer, P. (2002) *Liverpool: Wondrous Place. From the Cavern to the Capital of Culture*. London. Virgin Books.

Dudgeon, J.P. (2010) *Our Liverpool: Memories of Life in Disappearing Britain*. London: Headline Review.

Elliott, J. (2006) *Once Upon a Time in Liverpool*. Flintshire: MiddleView.

Ellis, A.T. (2004) *God Has Not Changed: The Assembled Thoughts of Alice Thomas Ellis*. London: Continuum.

Ferriter, D. (2004) *The Transformation of Ireland, 1900–2000*. London: Profile Books.

Fitzpatrick, D. (1989) 'A Curious Middle Place: The Irish in Britain, 1871–1921', in R. Swift and S. Gilley (eds), *The Irish in Britain, 1815–1939*. London: Pinter.

Fitzsimons, J. (2004) *A Personal History of the 8th Irish Battalion: The King's Liverpool Regiment*. Liverpool: Starfish Multimedia.

Ford, A. (2012) 'Living Together, Living Apart: Sectarianism in Early Modern Ireland', in A. Ford and J. John McCafferty (eds), *The Origins of Sectarianism in Early Modern Ireland*. Cambridge: Cambridge University Press.

Fraser, T.G (ed.) (2000) *The Irish Parading Tradition: Following the Drum*. London: Palgrave Macmillan.

Frost, D. (2008) 'The Maligned, the Despised and the Ostracised: Working-Class White Women, Inter-Racial Relationships and Colonial Ideologies in Nineteenth- and Twentieth-Century Liverpool', in S. Haggerty, A. Webster, and N.J. White (eds), *The Empire in One City?* Manchester: Manchester University Press.

Frost, D., and P. North (2013) *Militant Liverpool: A City on the Edge*. Liverpool: Liverpool University Press.

Frost, D., and R. Phillips (2011) *Liverpool '81: Remembering the Riots*. Liverpool University Press, Liverpool.

Furnival, J., and A. Knowles (1998) *Archbishop Derek Worlock, His Personal Journey*. London: Geoffrey Chapman.

Gallagher, T. (1987) *Glasgow: The Uneasy Peace. Religious Tension in Modern Scotland, 1819–1914*. Manchester: Manchester University Press.

Gascoigne, P., and H. Davies (2004) *Gazza: My Story*. London: Headline.

Gifford, T., W. Brown, and R. Bundley (1989) *Loosen the Shackles: First Report of the Liverpool 8 Inquiry into Race Relations in Liverpool*. London: Karia Press.

Gilley, S. (2000) 'Roman Catholicism and the Irish in England', in D.M. MacRaild (ed.), *The Great Famine and Beyond: Irish Migrants in Britain in the Nineteenth and Twentieth Centuries*. Dublin: Irish Academic Press.

Gilmour, R. (1999) *Dead Ground: Infiltrating the IRA*. London: Warner.

Gray, T. (1972) *The Orange Order*. London: The Bodley Head.

Hall, J.F. (1939) *The Dock Road*. Liverpool: Book Clearance Centre.

Helmond, M.V., and D. Palmer (1991) *Staying Power: Black Presence in Liverpool*. Liverpool: National Museums & Galleries on Merseyside.

Henderson, R.F. (1967) *Pastor George Wise, Founder of the Protestant Reformer's Memorial Church*, Liverpool. n.p.

—— (1978) *Seventy-Five Years of Protestant Witness*. s.n.

Herson, J (1989) 'Irish Migration and Settlement in Victorian England: A Small-Town Perspective', in R. Swift and S. Gilley (eds), *The Irish in Britain, 1815–1939*. London: Pinter.

—— (2008) '"Stirring Spectacles of Cosmopolitan Animation": Liverpool as a Diasporic City, 1825–1913', in S. Haggerty, A. Webster, and N.J. White (eds), *The Empire in One City?* Manchester: Manchester University Press.

Hocking, S. (1879) *Her Benny*. Liverpool: Bluecoat.

Houston C., and W.J. Smyth (1981) *The Sash Canada Wore: A Historical Geography of the Orange Order in Canada*. Toronto: University of Toronto Press.

Jarman, N. (2012) *Defining Sectarianism and Sectarian Hate Crime*. Belfast: ICR.

Johnson, S. (2010) *Everton: The Complete Official Record*. London: deCoubertin Books.

Kanya-Forstner, M. (2000) 'Defining Womanhood: Irish Women and the Catholic Church in Victorian Liverpool', in D.M. MacRaild (ed.), *The Great Famine and Beyond: Irish Migrants in Britain in the Nineteenth and Twentieth Centuries*. Dublin: Irish Academic Press.

Kelly, B. (2006) *For What It's Worth: My Liverpool Childhood*. Stroud: Sutton Publishing.

Kelly, M. (2003) *Liverpool, the Irish Connection: The Story of Some Notable Irish People Who Helped in its Creation*. Formby: Michael Kelly.

Kerrigan, J.P. (2009) *A Bowl of Scouse: The Forgotten People and Hidden Events Beneath the Surface of Liverpool's History*. Birkenhead: Countyvise.

Kilroy-Silk, R. (1986) *Hard Labour: The Political Diary of Robert Kilroy-Silk*. London: Chatto & Windus.

Kinealy, C. (1994) *This Great Calamity: The Irish Famine, 1845–52*. Dublin: Gill & Macmillan.

King, C. (1965) *The Orange and the Green*. London: Macdonald.

Lamb, C.L., and E. Smallpage (1935) *The Story of Liverpool*. Liverpool: Daily Post Printers.

Lambert, S. (2001) *Irish Women in Lancashire, 1922–1960*. Lancaster: Centre for North West Regional Studies.

Lane, L. (1966) *Lern yerself Scouse*, vol. 2, *The ABZ of Scouse*. Liverpool: Scouse Press.

Lane, T. (1987) *Liverpool Gateway of Empire*. London: Lawrence & Wishart.

Law, I. (1981) *A History of Race and Racism in Liverpool, 1660–1950*. Liverpool: Merseyside Community Relations Council.

Liechty, J., and C. Clegg (2001) *Moving Beyond Sectarianism: Religion, Conflict, and Reconciliation in Northern Ireland*. Dublin: Columba Press.

Liverpool Black Caucus (1986) *The Racial Politics of Militant in Liverpool: The Black Community's Struggle for Participation in Local Politics, 1980–1986*. Liverpool: University of Liverpool and The Runnymede Trust.

Longley, C. (2000) *The Worlock Archive*. London: Geoffrey Chapman.

Lupson, P. (2006) *Thank God for Football!* London: Azure.

—— (2008) *Everton FC & Liverpool FC: Across the Park, Common Ground*. Liverpool: Trinity Mirror Sports Media.

Lynn, I.L. (1982) *The Chinese Community in Liverpool: Their Unmet Needs with Respect to Education, Social Welfare and Housing*. Liverpool: Merseyside Area Profile Group.

Lunn, K. (2008) 'Reconsidering "Britishness": The Construction and Significance of National Identity in Twentieth-Century Britain', in B. Jenkins and S.A. Sofos (1996) *Nation and Identity in Contemporary Europe*. London: Routledge.

McAuley, J.W., J. Tonge, and A. Mycock (2011) *Loyal to the Core: Orangeism and Britishness in Northern Ireland*. Dublin: Irish Academic Press.

Macilwee, M. (2008) *Tearaways: More Gangs of Liverpool, 1890–1970*. Wrea Green: Milo Books.

MacKay, D. (1990) *Flight from Famine: The Coming of the Irish to Canada*. Toronto: McClelland & Stewart.

McManus, K. (1994) *Ceilis, Jigs and Ballads: Irish Music in Liverpool*. Liverpool: The Institute of Popular Music, University of Liverpool.

MacRaild, D.M. (1999) *Irish Migrants in Modern Britain, 1750–1922*. London: Macmillan Press.

—— (2005) *Faith, Fraternity and Fighting: The Orange and Irish Migrants in Northern England, c.1850–1920*, Liverpool: Liverpool University Press.

Maddocks, G. (1991) *Liverpool Pals: A History of the 17th, 18th, 19th and 20th (Service) Battalions, The King's (Liverpool Regiment) 1914–1919*. London: Leo Cooper.

Melville, H. (1969) [1849] *Redburn: His First Voyage*. Evanston, IL: Northwestern University Press.

Members of the Merseyside Socialist Research Group (1992) *Genuinely Seeking Work: Mass Unemployment on Merseyside in the 1930s*. Birkenhead: Liver Press.

Midwinter, E. (1971) *Old Liverpool*. Devon: David and Charles Ltd.

Morris, R.J. (ed.) (1986) *Class, Power and Social Structure in British Nineteenth-Century Towns*. Leicester: Leicester University Press.

Muir, R. (1906) *William Roscoe: An Inaugural Lecture. Liverpool*: Liverpool University Press.

—— (1907) *A History of Liverpool*. Liverpool: Liverpool University Press.

Mulhearn, D. (2007a) *Mersey Minis*, vol. 1, *Landing*. Liverpool: Capsica.

—— (2007b) *Mersey Minis*, vol. 5, *Leaving*. Liverpool: Capsica.

Murphy, A. (1995) *From the Empire to the Rialto*. Birkenhead: Liver Press.

—— (2005) *'It's not your leg son …': The Book of Shankly*. Bath: Naked Guides Limited.

Museum of Liverpool (2012) *Liverpool the Story of a City*. Liverpool: Liverpool University Press.

Neal, F. (1988) *Sectarian Violence: The Liverpool Experience, 1819–1914*. Liverpool: Newsham Press.

—— (1997) 'Black '47: Liverpool and the Irish Famine', in E.M. Crawford (ed.), *The Hungry Stream: Essays on Emigration and Famine*. Belfast: The Centre for Emigration Studies.

O'Brien, M. (2011) 'Liverpool 1911 and its Era: Foundational Myth or Authentic Tradition?', in J. Belchem and B. Biggs (eds), *Liverpool City of Radicals*. Liverpool: Liverpool University Press.

O'Connor, F. (2013) *Liverpool: It All Came Tumbling Down, Updated Edition*. Birkenhead: Countyvise.

O'Mara, P. (1933) *The Autobiography of a Liverpool [Irish] Slummy*. Liverpool: Bluecoat.

O'Neill, M. (2010) *St Anthony's, Scotland Road, Liverpool: A Parish History, 1804–2004*. Leominster: Gracewing.

Perrett, B. (1990) *Liverpool: A City at War*. London: Robert Hale.

Pooley, C. (1989) 'Segregation or Integration? The Residential Experience of the Irish in mid-Victorian Britain', in R. Swift and S. Gilley (eds), *The Irish in Britain, 1815–1939*. London: Pinter.

Power, M. (ed.) (2011) *Building Peace in Northern Ireland*. Liverpool: Liverpool University Press.

Putnam R. (2000) *Bowling Alone: The Collapse and Revival of American Community*. New York: Simon & Schuster.

Rees, D.B. (2011) *A Portrait of Battling Bessie: Life and Work of Bessie Braddock, a Liverpool MP*. Nottingham: Leen Editions.

Rex, J. (1970) *Race Relations in Sociological Theory*. London: Weidenfeld & Nicolson.

Roberts, N. (2011) *Blues and Beatles*. Durrington: Pitch Publishing.

Rodgers, K. (2010) *The Lost Tribe of Everton & Scottie Road*. Liverpool: Trinity Mirror Media.

Rogers, N. (1998) *Crowds, Culture and Politics in Georgian Britain*. Oxford: Clarendon Press.

Rooney, B. (1987) *Racism and Resistance to Change: A Study of the Black Social Workers Project, Liverpool Social Services Department, 1975–1985*. Liverpool: Merseyside Area Profile Group.

Rosie, M. (2004) *The Sectarian Myth in Scotland of Bitter Memory and Bigotry*. Basingstoke: Palgrave Macmillan.

Salvidge, S. (1934) *Salvidge of Liverpool: Behind the Political Scene, 1890–1928*. London: Hodder & Stoughton.

Scraton, P. (1999) *Hillsborough: The Truth*. Edinburgh: Mainstream.

Scott, D., and J. Hamilton Hay (1907) *Liverpool*. London: Adam & Charles Black.

Sharples, J. (2004) *The Pevsner Architectural Guide to Liverpool*. London: Yale University Press.

Shaw, F. (1971) *My Liverpool*. Wirral: Gallery Press.

Sheppard, D. (2002) *Steps Along Hope Street*. London: Hodder & Stoughton.

Sheppard, D., and D. Worlock (1988) *Better Together*. London: Hodder & Stoughton.

Sibbett, R.M. (1915) *Orangeism in Ireland and Throughout the Empire*. London: Henderson and Co.

Simmonds, C. (2000) *Nobody in Particular*. London: Bantam Books.

Smith, J. (1986) 'Class, Skill and Sectarianism in Glasgow and Liverpool, 1880–1914', in R.J. Morris (ed.), *Class, Power and Social Structure in British Nineteenth-Century Towns*. Leicester: Leicester University Press.

Smith, T., and D. Stuckey (1980) *I Did It the Hard Way*. London: A. Barker.

Smyth, M., and R. Moore (1996) 'Researching Sectarianism', in M. Smyth and R. Moore (eds), *Three Conference Papers on Aspects of Segregation and Sectarian Division*. Derry Londonderry: Templegrove Action Research.

Stark, W. (1967) *The Sociology of Religion*, vol. 2, *Sectarian Religion*. London: Routledge & Kegan Paul.

Steele, M. (2008) 'Transmitting Ideas of Empire: Representations and Celebrations in Liverpool, 1886–1953', in S. Haggerty, A. Webster, and N.J. White (eds), *The Empire in One City?* Manchester: Manchester University Press.

Stubbs, A. (2013) *How Football Saved My Life*. London: Simon & Schuster.

Sugden, J.P., and A. Bairner (1993) *Sport, Sectarianism and Society in a Divided Ireland*. Leicester: Leicester University Press.

Swift R., and S. Gilley (eds) (1989) *The Irish in Britain, 1815–1939*. London: Pinter.

Taafe, P., and Mulhearn, T. (1988) *Liverpool: A City that Dared to Fight*. London: Fortress Books.

Taylor, K. (2011) 'From the Ground Up: Radical Liverpool Now', in J. Belchem and B. Biggs (eds), *Liverpool City of Radicals*. Liverpool: Liverpool University Press.

Taylor, R., A. Ward, and T. Newburn (1995) *The Day of the Hillsborough Disaster*. Liverpool: Liverpool University Press.

Torkington, N.P.K. (1983) *The Racial Politics of Health: A Liverpool Profile*. Liverpool: Merseyside Area Profile Group.

Tulloch, A.R. (2008) *The Story of Liverpool*. Stroud: The History Press.

Tyndale Harries, W. (1946) *Landmarks in Liverpool History*. Liverpool: Philip Son & Nephew.

Unwin, F. (1983) *Reflections on The Mersey: Memoirs of the Twenties and Thirties*. Neston: Gallery Press.

—— (1986) *Mersey Memories*. Neston: Gallery Press.

Waller, P.J. (1981) *Democracy and Sectarianism: A Political and Social History of Liverpool, 1868–1939*. Liverpool: Liverpool University Press.

Walsh, T. (2011) *Being Irish in Liverpool*. Liverpool: St Michael's Irish Centre.

Walvin, J. (1994) *The People's Game: The History of Football Revisited*. Edinburgh: Mainstream.

—— (2011) 'The Liverpool Way', in J. Belchem and B. Biggs (eds), *Liverpool City of Radicals*. Liverpool: Liverpool University Press.

Weir, D. (2011) *Extra Time: My Autobiography*. London: Hodder & Stoughton.

Williams, B. (2010) *The Northern Ireland Peace Process and the International Context*. Dartford: Pneuma Springs.

Williams, J. (2002) *Into the Red: Liverpool FC and the Changing Face of English Football*. London: Mainstream Publishing.

Wong, M.L. (1989) *Chinese Liverpudlians: A History of the Chinese Community in Liverpool*. Birkenhead: Liver Press.

Woods, J. (1995) *Peace in My Time?! One Scouser's War*. Preston: Palatine Books.

Woolley, E. (2008) *The Golden Years of Merseybeat*. Liverpool: Bluecoat.

Journal Articles

Birtill, T. (1988) 'Liverpool Mystery? (Loyalist) Hardliners Linked with Mersey Collection Con'. *Labour and Ireland*, 22 (October 1988).

Buck, J. (2011) 'The Role of *Ne Temere* in the Decline of an Irish Custom

Regarding the Religious Affiliation of the Children of Mixed Marriages'. *Australasian Journal of Irish Studies*, 11: 28–43.

Clarke, C. (2007) 'Race, Place and Space: Liverpool's Local-Born Blacks'. *Antipode: A Radical Journal of Geography*, 39(2): 367–9.

Damer, S. (1989) 'A Tale of Two Cities: Sectarianism in Glasgow and Liverpool'. *International Journal of Urban and Regional Research*, 13(3): 515–18.

Evans, B. (2012) 'Fear and Loathing in Liverpool: The IRA's 1939 Bombing Campaign on Merseyside'. *Transactions of the Lancashire and Cheshire Historical Society*, 161: 25–46.

Herbert, M. (2010) 'Rioting between the Orange Order and the Irish in Manchester', *Manchester's Radical History* (website). Available at: http://radicalmanchester.wordpress.com/2010/03/31/rioting-between-the-orange-order-and-the-irish-in-manchester/.

Hickman, M. J., L. Thomas, H.C. Nickels, and S. Silvestri (2012). 'Social Cohesion and the Notion of "Suspect Communities": A Study of the Experiences and Impacts of Being "Suspect" for Irish Communities and Muslim Communities in Britain'. *Critical Studies on Terrorism*, 5(1): 89–106.

Jackson, D. (2003) '"Friends of the Union", Liverpool, Ulster, and Home Rule, 1910–1914', *Transactions of the Historic Society of Lancashire and Cheshire*, 152: 101–32.

Jenkins, G. (2010) 'Nationalism and Sectarian Violence in Liverpool and Belfast, 1880s–1920s'. *International Labor and Working-Class History*, 78: 164–80.

Kennedy, D. (2005) 'Class, Ethnicity and Civic Governance: A Social Profile of Football Club Directors on Merseyside in the Late Nineteenth Century'. *International Journal of the History of Sport*, 22(5): 840–66.

—— (2011) 'Special Issue: The Split: A Social and Political History of Everton and Liverpool Football Clubs, 1878–1914'. *Soccer and Society*, 12(4): 471–567.

Kennedy, D., and M. Collins (2006) 'Community Politics in Liverpool and the Governance of Professional Football in the Late Nineteenth Century'. *Historical Journal*, 49(3): 761–88.

Kennedy, D., and P. Kennedy (2007) 'Ambiguity, Complexity and Convergence: The Evolution of Liverpool's Irish Football Clubs'. *International Journal of the History of Sport*, 24(7): 894–920.

MacRaild, D.M. (2002–3) 'Wherever Orange is Worn: Orangeism and Irish Migration in the 19th and Early 20th Centuries'. *Canadian Journal of Irish Studies*, 28(2) and 29(1): 98–116.

MacRaild, D.M., and J. MacPherson (2006) 'Sisters of the Brotherhood: Female Orangeism on Tyneside in the Late Nineteenth and Early Twentieth Centuries'. *Irish Historical Studies*, 35(137): 40–60.

McVeigh, R. (1990) 'The Undertheorisation of Sectarianism'. *Canadian Journal of Irish Studies*, 16(2): 119–22.

McVeigh, R., and B. Rolston (2007), 'From Good Friday to Good Relations: Sectarianism, Racism and the Northern Ireland State', *Race and Class*, 48(4): 1–23.

Margalit, A. (2008) 'Sectarianism'. *Dissent*, 55(1): 37–46.

Murshed, S.M. (2010) 'On the Salience of Identity in Civilizational and Sectarian Conflict', *Peace Economics, Peace Science and Public Policy*, 16(2): 1–20.

Neal, F. (1990–1) 'Manchester Origins of the English Orange Order'. *Manchester Region History Review*, 4(2): 12–24.

—— (1991) 'A Criminal Profile of the Liverpool Irish'. *Transactions of the Historic Society of Lancashire and Cheshire*, 40: 161–200.

Picton, J.A. (1888) 'Does Mr Gladstone Speak with a Provincial Accent?'. Notes & Queries, 7th series, 6: 210–11.

Power, Maria (2014) 'In Pursuit of the Common Good: Derek Worlock and David Sheppard, and the Ecumenical Response to the 1981 Toxteth Riots'. *Crucible: The Christian Journal of Social Ethics*: 26–33.

Smith, J. (1984) 'Labour Tradition in Glasgow and Liverpool'. *History Workshop Journal*, 17: 32–56.

Walker, G. (2001) 'Identity Questions in Contemporary Scotland: Faith, Football and Future Prospects'. *Contemporary British History*, 15(1): 41–60.

—— (2012) 'Scotland's Sectarianism Problem: Irish Answers?' *Political Quarterly*, 83(2): 374–83.

Booklets, Magazines, and Pamphlets

Finch, J. (1986) 'Statistics of Vauxhall Ward, Liverpool: The Condition of the Working Class in Liverpool in 1842'. Liverpool: Taulouse Press.

Henderson, R.F. (1978) 'Seventy-Five Years of Protestant Witness'. Liverpool: s.n.

Rodgers, E. (1881) 'Revolution of 1688, and History of the Orange Association of England and Ireland'. Belfast: W&G Baird.

Stanford, P. (2004) 'Two Tribes Who Became One City', *The Tablet*, 10 January 2004.

Dissertations and Theses

Bullough, O. (1990) '"Remember the Boyne": Liverpool Orange Processions, 1919–1939'. MA University of Warwick.

Day, P. (2011) 'The Orange Order in Liverpool since 1945'. M.Phil., University of Liverpool.

Ingram, P. (1987) 'Sectarianism in the North West of England, with Special Reference to the Class Relationship in the City of Liverpool, 1846–1914'. PhD, Lancashire Polytechnic.

Knowles, G. (1974) 'Scouse: The Urban Dialect of Liverpool'. PhD, University of Leeds.

Papworth, J.D. (1981) 'The Irish in Liverpool, 1835–71: Segregation and Dispersal'. PhD, University of Liverpool.

O'Connell, B. (1971) 'The Irish Nationalist Party in Liverpool, 1873–1922'. MA, University of Liverpool.

Roberts, K.D. (2015) 'The Rise and Fall of Liverpool Sectarianism: An Investigation into the Decline of Sectarian Antagonism on Merseyside'. PhD, University of Liverpool.

Reports

Ashton, A. (1910) 'The Liverpool Religious Riots: The Commissioner's Report'. London: Home Office.

Glifford, T., W. Brown, and R. Bundley (1989) 'Loosen the Shackles: First Report of the Liverpool 8 Inquiry into Race Relations in Liverpool'. London: Karia Press.

'Hillsborough: The Report of the Hillsborough Independent Panel', 12 September 2012. London: The Stationery Office. Available at: http://hillsborough.independent.gov.uk/repository/report/HIP_report.pdf.

McVeigh, R., 'Sectarianism in Northern Ireland: Towards a Definition in Law'. Belfast: Equality Coalition, April 2014. Available at: www.niassembly.gov.uk/globalassets/documents/ofmdfm/inquiries/building-a-united-community/written-submissions/equality-coalition.pdf.

Northern Ireland Office (2002) 'Race Crime and Sectarian Crime Legislation in Northern Ireland: A Summary Paper'. Belfast: Northern Ireland Office. Available at: http://cain.ulst.ac.uk/issues/sectarian/docs/nio1102b.pdf.

The Scottish Executive (2006) 'Calling Full Time on Sectarianism'. Edinburgh: The Scottish Executive.

Recorded Interviews

Keith Allcock (12 March 2013)
Ron Bather HDGM (15 March 2010)
Professor John Belchem (25 February 2010)
Doris Bennett (5 March 2013)
Joe Benton (18 May 2012)
Tony Birtill (29 October 2012)
Tom Buckley (12 March 2013)
Rt Hon Andy Burnham MP (28 March 2013)
Reginald Chadwick (9 August 2013)
Michelle Chambers (7 April 2013)
Nadine Dorries MP (13 March 2013)
Neil Dulin (14 March 2013)
Yvonne Susan Fearnehough (23 January 2013)
Billy Hayes (2nd February 2013)
Ian Henderson (21 December 2012)
Steve Higginson (11 February 2013)
Jean Hartrick Hill (26 October 2012)
Dave Hughes (24 January 2013/10 March 2013)
Lynn Hughes (10 March 2013)
Roy Hughes (13 November 2012)
Howard Kendall (17 November 2010)
Peter Kilfoyle (23 January 2012)
Win Lawlor (21 February 2013)
Susanne Loughlin (13 February 2013)
Cllr James 'Jimmy' Mahon (24 April 2012)
Alf Mullins (14 May 2012)
Cllr Michael Murphy (8 April 2013)
Professor Frank Neal (12 February 2010)
Brenda O'Brian (12 November 2012)
Mike O'Brian (12 November 2012)
Séafra Ó Cearbhail (14 March 2013)
Maria O'Reilly (15 March 2013)
George Orr (7 November 2013)
Billy Owens HDGM (15 March 2010)
Helen Owen (27 March 2013)
Dr John Pugh MP (22nd March 2013)
Greg Quiery (25 March 2013)
Steve Rotheram MP (4 January 2013)

Cllr Anna Rothery (19 February 2013)
William 'Billy' John Smylie (18 January 2014)
William 'Billy' John Tritton (12 March 2013)
Paul Wharton (7 November 2013)
Clifford Whittingham (10 January 2014)
Reverend John Williams MBE (17 November 2010)
Bishop Thomas Anthony Williams (23 March 2010)
Ian Woods (12 November 2013)

Appendices

Appendices 1.1–1.2   Tables portraying the proportion of faith schools in cities/local authorities, per capita of population and in relation to the overall number of schools/colleges (Primary, Secondary, 16–18, Special, and Academies) in that locality

Appendices 2.1–2.2   Orange lodge numbers in Liverpool and Bootle Province

Appendix 3   Twelfth of July Orange parade – newspaper attendance estimates

Appendix 4.1–4.6   Results of Orange Order Questionnaire

Appendix 1.1
'Faith School' Analysis: Cities and Local Authorities in England

City/Local Authority	Number of schools/ colleges	Number of 'faith schools'	Percentage of 'faith schools' to number of schools/ colleges	Population	Number of faith schools per capita of population
Birmingham	535	107	20.0%	1,073,000	0.0099
Leeds	298	68	22.8%	751,500	0.0090
Sheffield	216	34	15.7%	552,700	0.0061
Manchester	224	68	30.4%	503,100	0.0135
Liverpool	185	73	39.5%	466,400	0.0156
Bristol	172	27	15.7%	428,200	0.0063
Croydon (London)*	154	23	14.9%	363,400	0.0063
Barnet (London)*	164	42	25.6%	356,400	0.0117
Ealing (London)*	112	13	11.6%	338,400	0.0038
Newcastle-upon-Tyne	105	24	22.9%	280,200	0.0085

* Biggest three London boroughs, in terms of population, according to the 2011 census.
Sources: www.education.gov.uk/schools/performance/; http://data.london.gov.uk/
datastorefiles/documents/2011-census-first-results.pdf; www.ons.gov.uk/ons/taxonomy/
index.html?nscl=Population; www.theguardian.com/uk/datablog/2012/jul/16/2011-
census-results-data (last accessed 25 April 2014).

Appendix 1.2
'Faith School' Analysis: Merseyside and Liverpool City Regions

Region	Number of schools/ colleges	Number of 'faith schools'	Percentage of 'faith schools' to number of schools/ colleges	Population	Number of faith schools per capita of population
Liverpool	185	73	39.5%	466,400	0.0156
Wirral	135	35	25.9%	319,000	0.0109
Sefton	110	49	44.5%	273,800	0.0178
St Helens	71	33	46.5%	175,300	0.0188
Knowsley	68	32	47.1%	145,900	0.0219
Halton	77	23	29.9%	125,800	0.0182
Merseyside total	646	245	37.9%	1,506,200	0.0162

Sources: www.education.gov.uk/schools/performance/; http://data.london.gov.uk/ datastorefiles/documents/2011-census-first-results.pdf; www.ons.gov.uk/ons/taxonomy/ index.html?nscl=Population; www.theguardian.com/uk/datablog/2012/jul/16/2011-census-results-data (last accessed 25 April 2014).

Appendix 2.1
Number of Orange Lodges in Liverpool Province

Year	Number of lodges	Source
1815	1	Neal, 1988: 40
1830	3	Neal, 1988: 40
1835	13	Neal, 1988: 70
1845	25	Neal, 1988: 71
1885	78	Neal, 1988: 185
1909	156	*Liverpool Weekly Mercury*, 17 July 1909
1915	197	MacRaild, 2002–3: 103
1951	187	Day, 2011: 98
1959	178	Orange Order: Bootle Province
1962	165	Day, 2011: 98
1974	177	Day, 2011: 98
		23 new lodges owing to the addition of two new districts in Speke and Kirkby
2013	91	Orange Order: Bootle Province

Appendix 2.2
Number of Orange Lodges in Bootle Province

Year	Number of lodges	Source
1959	32	Orange Order: Bootle Province
2013	14	Orange Order: Bootle Province

Appendix 3.1
Twelfth of July Orange Parade – Newspaper Attendance Estimates

Year of parade	Parade location	1st Newspaper's attendance estimate	2nd Newspaper's attendance estimate	Highest estimate
1819	Liverpool	[M] 90#		90
1820	Liverpool	[M] 90#		90
1842	Liverpool	[H] 2,000#		2,000
1844	Kidderminster	[C] 20,000#		20,000
1845	Newton le Willows	[S] 2,000#		2,000
1850	Liverpool	[T] 200		200
1851	Liverpool	[M] 2,000 – 3,000#		3,000
1854		[CH] 1,300 – 1,400#		1,400
1859		[H] 20,000#		20,000
1860	West Derby	[M] 300–400		400
1870	Dingle	[P] 16,000 [6,000 participants, 10,000 supporters]	[C] 9,000 [3,000 participants, 6,000 supporters]	16,000
1876	Knowsley	[MA] 7,000 – 8,000 Orangemen and 60,000–80,000 'supporters'#		88,000
1880	Hale Park	[P] 150,000	[C] 'at least 100,000'	150,000
1885	Hooton Park	[P] 8,000		8,000
1886	Zoological Gardens	[P] 5,000		5,000
1890	Halton Castle	[P] 'not more than 3,000'		3,000
1900	Buckley	[P] 3,000	[M] 3,000	3,000
1905	Wirral Park	[P] 10,000		10,000
1909	Pemberton	[M] 12,500		12,500
1910	Southport	[P&M] 15,000	[E] 5,000	15,000
1912	Bebington	[F] 15,000~		15,000
1920	Barnston	[E] 6,000–7,000	[P] 6,000*	7,000

Year of parade	Parade location	1st Newspaper's attendance estimate	2nd Newspaper's attendance estimate	Highest estimate
1921	New Brighton	[E] 12,000–14,000*		14,000
1922	Knowsley Park	[P] 10,000*		10,000
1923	New Brighton	[P] 12,000*		12,000
1924	Knowsley Park	[P] 16,000*		16,000
1925	New Brighton	[P] 7,000*		7,000
1926	Upholland	[P] 12,000–13,000*		13,000
1927	Knowsley Park	[P] 10,000*		10,000
1928	Upholland	[P] 10,000*		10,000
1929	New Brighton & Southport	[P] 20,000*	[V] 'Several Thousand'	20,000
1930	Southport	[E] 10,000	[P] 10,000*	10,000
1931	Southport	[P] 30,000*		30,000
1932	Southport	[P] 10,000*		10,000
1934	Southport	[P] 20,000*		20,000
1935	New Brighton	[P] 10,000*		10,000
1936	New Brighton	[P] 10,000*		10,000
1937	New Brighton	[P] 12,000*		12,000
1938	Southport	[P] 10,000*		10,000
1939	Southport	[E] 'Several Thousand'	[V] 'Several Thousand'	'Several Thousand' [Not presented numerically]
1940	N/A	[E] 'No Procession'		N/A
1949	Southport	[V] 20,000		20,000
1950	Southport	[V] 20,000	[E] 17,000	20,000
1951	Southport	[E] 20,000		20,000
1955	Southport	[P] 30,000		30,000
1960	Southport	[V] 10,000	[E] 30,000	30,000
1965	Southport	[P] 10,000		10,000
1970	Southport	[V] 12,000		12,000
1971	Southport	[E] 10,000		10,000
1975	Southport	[P] 20,000		20,000
1980	Southport	[V] 20,000 [11,000 from Merseyside]	[E] 20,000	20,000

Year of parade	Parade location	1st Newspaper's attendance estimate	2nd Newspaper's attendance estimate	Highest estimate
1985	Southport	[P] 20,000		20,000
1990	Southport	[E] 5,000	[P] 5,000	5,000
1994	Southport	[E] 2,000–2,500		2,500
1998	Southport	[E] 5,000		5,000
1999	Southport	[E] 5,000–6,000		6,000
2000	Southport	[E] 'Hundreds'	[P] 'Hundreds'	'Hundreds' [Presented numerically as 1,000]
2010	Southport	[V] 3,000	[E] 4,000	4,000
2011	Southport	[E] 'Huge Crowds'	[V] 'Thousands'	'Thousands' [not presented numerically]
2012	Southport	[E] 3,000	[V] 3,000	3,000
2013	Southport	[E] 5,000–6,000	[V] 5,000–6,000	6,000

Key
* Figure and source cited by Bullough, 1990
# Figure and source cited by Neal, 1988
~ Figure and source cited by Smith, 1984

Newspaper Key
C = *Daily Courier*
CH = *Liverpool Chronicle*
E = *Liverpool Echo*
F = *Liverpool Forward*
H = *Liverpool Herald*
M = *Liverpool Mercury*
MA = *Liverpool Mail*
P = *Liverpool Daily Post*
P & M = *Liverpool Post and Mercury*
S = *Liverpool Standard*
T = *Liverpool Times*
V = *Southport Visiter*

Appendix 4.1
Results of Orange Order Questionnaire (All Ages)

Age of respondents (215 respondents)	
25 or below	35
26–49	79
50 or above	81
No age provided	20

Results of Orange Institution Questionnaire: All Ages

'Section A' results: 'Why has Orangeism declined in Liverpool?'

All 1st and 2nd preferences (492 selections)*	
Loss of interest by younger members	22.8%
Factional splits	14.8%
Slum clearance (1960s)	14.4%
Reduction in family size and population decline	11.2%
General apathy	13.4%
Relative decline in religious observance	23.4%

* The instructions of the questionnaire were seldom observed, hence a larger ratio of preferences than sum of sample. Calculations come to more than 430, as many respondents gave more than one '1st' or '2nd' choice. All choices are represented.

Only clear 1st preferences (159 selections)*	
Loss of interest by younger members	29.6%
Factional splits	12.6%
Slum clearance (1960s)	15.1%
Reduction in family size and population decline	6.2%
General apathy	11.3%
Relative decline in religious observance	25.2%

* Calculations come to less than 215 as questionnaires which indicated more than one '1st' preference were discounted. This was also the case for any questionnaire which did not provide a 'clear 1st preference'.

'Section B' results: 'Please rank in order the most important aspects of your identity'

All 1st and 2nd preferences (464 selections)	
Protestant	35.8%
Scouse/Liverpudlian	19.2%
English	23.0%
British	19.0%
European	3.0%

Only clear 1st preferences (161 selections)	
Protestant	59.0%
Scouse/Liverpudlian	17.4%
English	12.4%
British	8.1%
European	3.1%

'Section C' results: 'What football team do you support/feel most affiliated to?'

(235 selections)	
Everton FC	27.2%
Liverpool FC	42.1%
Rangers FC	21.7%
Other	2.6%
None	6.4%

Appendix 4.2
Results of Orange Institution Questionnaire (25 or below)

'Section A' results: 'Why has Orangeism declined in Liverpool?'

All 1st and 2nd preferences (76 selections)	
Loss of interest by younger members	22.4%
Factional splits	10.5%
Slum clearance (1960s)	11.8%
Reduction in family size and population decline	15.8%
General apathy	14.5%
Relative decline in religious observance	25.0%

Only clear 1st preferences (28 selections)	
Loss of interest by younger members	28.6%
Factional splits	17.9%
Slum clearance (1960s)	7.0%
Reduction in family size and population decline	0.0%
General apathy	17.9%
Relative decline in religious observance	28.6%

'Section B' results: 'Please rank in order the most important aspects of your identity'

All 1st and 2nd preferences (67 selections)		Only clear 1st preferences (32 selections)	
Protestant	32.8%	Protestant	43.7%
Scouse/Liverpudlian	22.4%	Scouse/Liverpudlian	25.0%
English	26.9%	English	21.9%
British	17.9%	British	9.4%
European	0.0%	European	0.0%

'Section C' results: 'What football team do you support/feel most affiliated to?'

(36 selections)	
Everton FC	36.1%
Liverpool FC	50.0%
Rangers FC	8.3%
Other	2.8%
None	2.8%

Appendix 4.3
Results of Orange Institution Questionnaire: 26–49

'Section A' results: 'Why has Orangeism declined in Liverpool?'

All 1st and 2nd preferences (177 selections)	
Loss of interest by younger members	28.3%
Factional splits	10.7%
Slum clearance (1960s)	9.6%
Reduction in family size and population decline	9.0%
General apathy	13.0%
Relative decline in religious observance	29.4%

Only clear 1st preferences (63 selections)	
Loss of interest by younger members	47.6%
Factional splits	9.5%
Slum clearance (1960s)	1.6%
Reduction in family size and population decline	1.6%
General apathy	7.9%
Relative decline in religious observance	31.7%

'Section B' results: 'Please rank in order the most important aspects of your identity'

All 1st and 2nd preferences (166 selections)		Only clear 1st preferences (66 selections)	
Protestant	34.9%	Protestant	53.0%
Scouse/Liverpudlian	23.5%	Scouse/Liverpudlian	22.7%
English	22.9%	English	9.1%
British	15.7%	British	10.6%
European	3.0%	European	4.5%

'Section C' results: 'What football team do you support/feel most affiliated to?'

(86 selections)	
Everton FC	30.2%
Liverpool FC	40.7%
Rangers FC	20.9%
Other	3.5%
None	4.7%

Appendix 4.4
Results of Orange Institution Questionnaire: 50 plus

'Section A' results: 'Why has Orangeism declined in Liverpool?'

All 1st and 2nd preferences (191 selections)	
Loss of interest by younger members	17.8%
Factional splits	19.4%
Slum clearance (1960s)	20.9%
Reduction in family size and population decline	11.5%
General apathy	11.5%
Relative decline in religious observance	18.8%

Only clear 1st preferences (56 selections)	
Loss of interest by younger members	14.5%
Factional splits	12.5%
Slum clearance (1960s)	32.1%
Reduction in family size and population decline	7.1%
General apathy	12.5%
Relative decline in religious observance	21.4%

'Section B' results: 'Please rank in order the most important aspects of your identity'

All 1st and 2nd preferences (185 selections)		Only clear 1st preferences (53 selections)	
Protestant	39.5%	Protestant	71.7%
Scouse/Liverpudlian	15.7%	Scouse/Liverpudlian	7.5%
English	21.6%	English	11.3%
British	20.5%	British	5.7%
European	2.7%	European	3.8%

'Section C' results: 'What football team do you support/feel most affiliated to?'

(89 selections)	
Everton FC	21.3%
Liverpool FC	39.3%
Rangers FC	29.2%
Other	2.2%
None	7.9%

Appendix 4.5
Results of Orange Institution Questionnaire: No age provided

'Section A' results: 'Why has Orangeism declined in Liverpool?'

All 1st and 2nd preferences (48 selections)	
Loss of interest by younger members	22.9%
Factional splits	18.8%
Slum clearance (1960s)	10.4%
Reduction in family size and population decline	10.4%
General apathy	20.8%
Relative decline in religious observance	16.7%

Only clear 1st preferences (7 selections)	
Loss of interest by younger members	14.3%
Factional splits	28.6%
Slum clearance (1960s)	42.9%
Reduction in family size and population decline	0.0%
General apathy	14.3%
Relative decline in religious observance	0.0%

'Section B' results: 'Please rank in order the most important aspects of your identity'

All 1st and 2nd preferences (46 selections)		Only clear 1st preferences (10 selections)	
Protestant	28.3%	Protestant	80.0%
Scouse/Liverpudlian	13.0%	Scouse/Liverpudlian	10.0%
English	23.9%	English	10.0%
British	26.1%	British	0.0%
European	8.7%	European	0.0%

'Section C' results: 'What football team do you support/feel most affiliated to?'

(24 selections)	
Everton FC	25.0%
Liverpool FC	45.8%
Rangers FC	16.7%
Other	0.0%
None	12.5%

Appendix 4.6
'Other' comments in 'Section A' on the decline
of Orangeism

Age of respondent	Location/District of respondent	Respondent's comment
17	Southport	'The violence which can be caused puts others off participating'
24	Bootle	'Lack of understanding about its history'
28	Fazakerly	'Younger people need to show more interest'
31	Anfield	'The running of the Orange Order. The divides that are put in place by the higher authority'
40		'Break-up of the Orange Order due to split in 80s between the Orange Order and the Independent Order'
41	South [Liverpool]	'Marriage into other religions'
44		'Too many leaders looking after their own interests'
49	Croxteth	'Mixed marriage'
50		'Pressure from the rest of society'
51	Bootle	'Schools teach too much about foreign religions'
53	Walton	'The younger people don't want to get involved anymore. Back in the 70s and 80s you automatically went into the Order from babies because of your own family'
59	Anfield	'Society has changed, making things like the Orange Order, Unions etc less important'
60	Everton	'Older generation dying off'
61	Bootle	'Underestimated the feelings of younger members (20–30 year olds)'

Index